A perspective on the Signs of Al-Quran

Through the prism of the heart

—In the backdrop of the age of information and the age of disinformation; The age of reason and the age of disregard; The age of science and the age of sound-bites; The age of disbelief and the age of fanaticism; The age of connectivity and the age of disconnection; The age of satiation and the age of emptiness; The age of mega-cities and the age of loneliness—The age on the brink.

Visit www.booksurge.com to order additional copies
Comments to the author may be emailed at Saeed325@gmail.com

Table of Contents

V

Acknowledgements

This work is based on personal reflections from the perspective of a grateful believer in his spiritual infancy. This work cannot possibly be, and is not any more than an earnest attempt to make an approach towards the Signs (Ayah) and symbolism of the Quran.

Today's Muslim, (defined by social or political belonging), beset by anarchy, intolerance and assault, both from within and outside, finds his or her self in the vortex of despair. Civilizations will rise and fall. This is a historical fact. The geographical arc of North African, Middle-Eastern and South-Asian nations, the crescent of political Islam, is negotiating the abyss of its fall. This is a matter of political dynamics and is not the matter of this book. It merits a separate focus. Spirituality depends upon nothing else but personal sincerity. In adversity it discovers its worth and wings. The spirit will not be confined to a border or a condition. It is transcendental. The environment bears signs and these signs offer learning and tests of faith. It is said; in the same vein that one's enemy is one's teacher and that pain can become the pivot of change. Adversity distills and purifies faith, as pain forces self-inquiry and introspection. When the desolation of a charred forest is at its peak, the dormant seed is stirred by the silent call of renewal and the ashes on the forest-floor will yield to its pristine stalk.

The soul is the collective and competing consciousness of the body and the spirit. The body finds the environment real. The spirit finds it a manifestation of another Reality. The body senses and reacts to its environment while the spirit ponders its signs. The Quran is an Arabic recital so its sound is integral to its form. Its verses are called "signs" and like all signs they are to be meditated upon. The sound and signs of the Arabic Quran, which appeal to the heart and not just the mind, are lost to any literal translation.

Yet, with my very limited understanding of Arabic I had to rely heavily on English translations of the Arabic Quran. To add some breadth to the narrow scope of any one literal translation, I referenced multiple translations. So that the mind could be led by the heart, I studied the English texts in the backdrop of a recorded Arabic recitation.

Some of the English texts, I used often, are listed below. The list includes some other works which are not translations of the Quran, but are rich in their meditative content:

The Glorious Qur'an Translation by Mohammed Marmaduke Pickthall
The Qur'an A new translation by Thomas Cleary 2004
The Holy Quran English Translation by Abdullah Yusuf Ali
Approaching the Quran by Michael Sells
The Heart of the Quran by Lex Hixon
The Message of the Quran Translated and Explained by Muhammad Asad.
Muhammad, his life based on the earliest sources by Martin Lings
A return to the Spirit by Martin Lings
Muhammad: A biography of the Prophet by Karen Armstrong
The life of Muhammad by Muhammad Husayn Haykal. Translated from the 8th edition by Ismail, Ragi A. al Faruqi

I would be remiss if I did not mention a few websites that have been tremendously helpful. These sites have brought the Quranic text, recital and interpretations from multiple sources to the desktop and PDA. The sites I used the most frequently are "Islamicity.com/QuranSearch/", "QuranExplorer.Com" and "QuranPDA.com".

I am also indebted to Usama Cannon, the charismatic youth leader at the Taleef Collective; Tahir Anwar, the youthful Imam at the San Jose Mosque; Dr Behnam Sadeghi, PhD, Assistant Professor, Department of Religious Studies at Stanford University; Michael Wolfe, the prolific author and filmmaker; Dr David Dahl, PhD, a caring healer; and my closest friends, Masood Alavi and Zainul Abedin, who are no longer of this world, amongst many others who have taken the time and effort to review and improve upon my work. I must also thank my Silicon-Valley fellows John Reinhardt and Hafiz Khan. Hafiz's proficiency in Arabic has been a great resource. The Arabic inserts in this book are his idea and labor. The encouragement of my wife Bhoomija and daughters, Aila and Ayesha, my son-in-law Kapil, my siblings and their families made this effort a labor of love. My wife reminds me, fairly, of the deficit between my 'talking the talk' and 'walking the walk'. May my 'walk' *now* be better than the brazen laxity of lost-yesterdays. I seek forgiveness and mercy because I dread the fairness of justice.

Yet, this is first, a work of faith—Faith, because I bring no other credentials. Faith, because I bear witness that there is no god but God and Muhammad (may peace be upon him) is the last messenger of God.

Personally, I have also found encouragement and drawn inspiration from the prayer and invitation of the Prophet (peace be upon him) in his last sermon {*Khutbah*}, "All those who listen to me shall pass on my words to others and those to others again; and may the last ones understand my words better than those who listen to me directly". "O God", he concluded in the same sermon "be my Witness that I have conveyed Your Message to your people." The Divine Message is The Arabic Al Quran.

To those who may approach this book from another faith, let me say in the inimitable words of the thirteenth century, Sufi-poet, Maulana Jalaluddin Rumi, "This (Al Quran) is a symbol of God's knowledge, all knowledge belonging to God, not this only. After all, in the time of Moses and Jesus the Quran existed. God's speech existed, but it was not in Arabic."[1]

God is both personal and universal. The personal God is an intimate God and no two intimate relationships are alike. The same God is universal too so that all human beings are equal and equally special. The heart is that place within us which is both intrinsically personal and universal—our inner core with the capacity to hold the universe, the sanctum with infinite doors. It is that organ of faith that expands with inclusion. It grows when it is tolerant and is richer by giving. God's speech in Arabic is aimed at the heart.

This book is merely one perspective from the moving train of life. I invite you to start this book from any chapter and exit as you will. The order of the chapters is accidental. My hope is that this work, despite all its short-comings and unintended errors, will serve the purpose of opening a door of entry to the Arabic Quran— the "last cycle" of Divine Revelation.

1 *Discourses of Rumi* By Arthur John Arberry

Prologue

First and foremost

It is customary in Islamic practice that the Divine messengers be mentioned with respect and reverence. Texts written by Muslims customarily attach the abbreviation 'PBUH', meaning "may peace be upon him" every time any Divine Prophet's name is mentioned. Prophets as God's chosen are first and foremost amongst God's creatures in rank and proximity to God. To know and respect the proper place and rank of anything and everything is part of spiritual conscientiousness. By offering our respects and our prayer of peace for God's own emissaries we are imploring God to unlock the doors to our own guidance. Praise belongs only to God and blessings belong to those who have earned proximity to Divine Glory and Majesty. We gain no worth except by discernment. We can gain no peace except by first wishing it for the deserving. We also acknowledge that those who have lived in full alignment to the Divine Will never 'die'. These, the purest of the human spirits are the 'truly successful', bestowed and blessed with Divine peace. May God accept that every reference to a Prophet in this manuscript is preceded and followed by an imploration of peace upon the Prophet. May we thus join the Chorus of Truth.

سُبْحَٰنَ رَبِّكَ رَبِّ ٱلْعِزَّةِ عَمَّا يَصِفُونَ ۝ وَسَلَٰمٌ عَلَى ٱلْمُرْسَلِينَ ۝ وَٱلْحَمْدُ لِلَّهِ رَبِّ ٱلْعَٰلَمِينَ ۝

Limitless in His Glory is thy Sustainer,
The Lord of almightiness,
[exalted] above anything that men may devise by way of definition!
And peace be upon all His message bearers.
And all praise is due to God alone,
The Sustainer of the worlds[2]

---

2 Al Quran 37:180-182. As interpreted by Muhammad Asad

The struggle of the soul

This book is about spirituality from the Islamic view-point. It is not about religion. Spirituality and religion are inseparable but they are not synonymous. Spirituality is an extra dimension of religion. This dimension is the path to God anchored in the earnest orthodoxy of religious practice. The orthodoxy of a religion is the rich soil that nurtures the tree of spirituality. Under the shade of this tree is the repose of life. The tree itself manifests the consciousness of the soul. Frithjof Schuon, the Sufi Scholar of the 20th century and an advocate for the "transcendent unity of religions", lays out, in his inimitable precision, the struggle facing the soul: .

> What are the great troubles of the soul? A false life, a false death, a false activity, a false rest.
> A false life: passion which engenders suffering;
> A false death: egoism which hardens the heart and separates it from God and His mercy;
> A false activity: dissipation, which casts the soul into an insatiable vortex and makes it forget God, who is Peace;
> A false rest or a false passivity: the weakness and laziness which deliver up the soul without resistance to the countless solicitations of the world.[3]

Islamic Spirituality, as we shall see is about Sincerity {*Ikhlas*} –Sincerity of thought, sincerity of purpose and sincerity of action. Sincerity eases the struggle that Frithjof Schuon defines.

All Sincere Paths lead to God

There are many Holy Scriptures as there are many Holy messengers. It follows therefore that the spiritual highway has many lanes. To quibble with this, from within the perspective of any one religion is to be sanctimonious rather than spiritual. Within this sanctimony lies the danger of constricting the 'heart' and thereby missing the Truth. Yes, within religions there are human innovations and resultant "half- truths" and sadly some of these innovations were for the benefit of those who invented them. Yet the word of God is discernible as it is living and immutable, be it as "Divine Word-made-flesh"[4] in the case of Jesus Christ or "Divine Word-made-Book"[5] in the case of the *last* prophet, Muhammad. The last Word-made-Book is the Holy Quran. The Quran does not refute or deny other messengers with a Divine mission; instead it claims and represents culmination and finality to the essential message of all prophets, starting with Adam. 'Last' *implies* a 'first' and 'prior'; the Quran is clear and explicit about the spiritual unity of their missions. The multiplicity of religions, notwithstanding man's propensity

---

3 Spiritual Perspectives and Human Facts, by Frithjof Schuon,. A new translation by P.N.Townsend
4 Phraseology borrowed from Martin Lings
5 Phraseology borrowed from Martin Lings

to err, is not man's error. It is God's Will and is repeatedly stated:

وَلِكُلِّ أُمَّةٍ رَّسُولٌ

For every community there is a messenger[6]

And

لِكُلٍّ جَعَلْنَا مِنكُمْ شِرْعَةً وَمِنْهَاجًا ۚ وَلَوْ شَاءَ ٱللَّهُ لَجَعَلَكُمْ أُمَّةً وَاحِدَةً

*For each of you We have appointed a law and traced out a path and if God had
so willed, He would have made you one community*[7].

True, that the verses preceding this last verse (quoted above) point to a
measure of erosion of prior revelations (given the disputes amongst their
respective followers), yet there lingers in these messages an essential core, as
would be implied by the statement "confirming the truth of whatever truth there
still remains of earlier revelations":

وَأَنزَلْنَا إِلَيْكَ ٱلْكِتَبَ بِٱلْحَقِّ مُصَدِّقًا لِّمَا بَيْنَ يَدَيْهِ مِنَ ٱلْكِتَبِ وَمُهَيْمِنًا عَلَيْهِ
فَٱحْكُم بَيْنَهُم بِمَا أَنزَلَ ٱللَّهُ ۖ وَلَا تَتَّبِعْ أَهْوَآءَهُمْ عَمَّا جَآءَكَ مِنَ ٱلْحَقِّ

*And unto thee [O Prophet] have We vouchsafed this Divine Writ, setting forth
the truth confirming the truth of whatever there still remains of earlier
revelations and determining what is true therein.
Judge, then, between the followers of earlier revelations in accordance with what
God has bestowed from upon high and do not follow their errant views,
forsaking the truth that has come unto thee*[8]

The prophet Muhammad and therefore his followers are commanded to remain
anchored in the certainty of the final message and be fully immersed in its Truth.
To be immersed is to be no place else.

In another verse, as if to discourage fruitless debate and thereby possibly
impugn other messengers (a danger for the novice believer), the Quran states
that not all the names of all the messengers were disclosed to the prophet; the
"holier than thou" attitude constricts the heart, and handicaps the spiritual quest.

وَلَقَدْ أَرْسَلْنَا رُسُلًا مِّن قَبْلِكَ مِنْهُم مَّن قَصَصْنَا عَلَيْكَ وَمِنْهُم مَّن لَّمْ نَقْصُصْ عَلَيْكَ

*We have sent messengers before you. About some We have told you,
and about some We have not told you* [9]

---

6 Al Quran 10:47
7 Al Quran 5:48
8 Al Quran 5:48 as interpreted by Muhammad Asad
9 Al Quran 40:78

إِنَّ ٱلَّذِينَ ءَامَنُواْ وَٱلَّذِينَ هَادُواْ وَٱلصَّٰبِئُونَ وَٱلنَّصَٰرَىٰ مَنْ ءَامَنَ بِٱللَّهِ وَٱلْيَوْمِ ٱلْأَخِرِ
وَعَمِلَ صَٰلِحًا فَلَا خَوْفٌ عَلَيْهِمْ وَلَا هُمْ يَحْزَنُونَ ۝

And verily, the faithful, and the Jews and the Sabians and the Christians —
Whoever believe in God and the last Day and act piously, no fear shall come
upon them nor shall they grieve [10]

Worthy of note also in the preceding surah is the non-definitive classification "Sabians". Though there are some scholars with the view that the Sabians are a group from amongst the Jews, there are others without a definite opinion. If one were to follow the latter view, the Quran is telling us that there are others beyond the followers of the three monotheistic religions who shall find God's Peace. Even if the Sabians can be identified, it is quite clear that the test of God-consciousness is to be left with God. The spiritual spark resides in the innermost niche of the heart disqualifying us from questioning another person's spiritual quest. The spiritual-center and the spiritual struggle are within. One's earnest conscientiousness must therefore turn its focus within one's own "Straight and Sincere Path".

Sincerity focuses inwards. Outwardly it manifests tolerance

It is a historical fact that each successive monotheistic religion has been more tolerant of its chronological predecessor. The opposite has not been true. Succeeding religions have held within their beliefs the doctrine of 'continuity of prophets'. Tolerance has been precious little the other way around. Judaism has considered Christianity an errant religion as has Christianity considered Islam. Many if not most of those who believe that Moses parted the Red Sea to save his people, doubt the virgin-birth of Jesus. And many if not most of those who believe in the blessed virgin Mary doubt the Quran as God's direct Word and the prophecy of Muhammad. The renewal embodied by Jesus was considered detraction by the day's 'religious establishment', like wise the renewal embodied by the Quran has met its own resistance. Intolerance of faith is a potential pitfall for any 'religious establishment'. The equivalent and likely pitfall for the soul seeking renewal is a relapse, certainly not intolerance. Intolerance is a flaw of the heart likely to attach itself to the mighty, seeking to block any change, rather than to those who want to escape from under the might. The renewer merely seeks to protect and preserve the renewed Message. The establishment and other powers that be, will label such conscientiousness, 'exclusivism.' The 'religious establishment' of our times, is fond of citing, as evidence of Quranic intolerance and exclusivism, a verse that exhorts the believers to stay anchored in the message of the Quran:

---

10 Al Quran 5:69

يَـٰٓأَيُّهَا ٱلَّذِينَ ءَامَنُواْ لَا تَتَّخِذُواْ ٱلۡيَهُودَ وَٱلنَّصَـٰرَىٰٓ أَوۡلِيَآءَ

O you, who have renewed your faith, do not take the Jews and the Christians as your allies and patrons {awliyaa} [11]

It helps the cause of these dissenters that some poor renderings have translated *awliyaa* to 'friends'. It cannot be so. The Quran allows the marriage of a Muslim to a Jew or a Christian. How could it then prohibit friendship? Far from forbidding friendship with the Jews and the Christians, the Quran is merely reinforcing the message of reliance on God Alone. God and not some other pre-existing human authority is the '*Wali* (singular of *Awliyaa)*.

وَكَفَىٰ بِٱللَّهِ وَلِيًّا وَكَفَىٰ بِٱللَّهِ نَصِيرًا

Sufficient is God as a patron and protector {Wali}
Sufficient is God as a Helper [12]

Or take it from Joseph; there can be no better authority than this young man, who was once a little child abandoned in a dark and dank well by his own brothers. Witness Joseph's gratefulness to his *Wali* upon being finally reunited with his parents, at the end of his long and arduous ordeal:

۞ رَبِّ قَدۡ ءَاتَيۡتَنِى مِنَ ٱلۡمُلۡكِ وَعَلَّمۡتَنِى مِن تَأۡوِيلِ ٱلۡأَحَادِيثِۚ فَاطِرَ ٱلسَّمَـٰوَٰتِ وَٱلۡأَرۡضِ أَنتَ وَلِيِّۦ فِى ٱلدُّنۡيَا وَٱلۡأَخِرَةِۖ تَوَفَّنِى مُسۡلِمًا وَأَلۡحِقۡنِى بِٱلصَّـٰلِحِينَ ﴿١٠١﴾

"O my Sustainer! You have indeed bestowed on me some aspect of power, and taught me some aspects of interpretation of dreams; Creator of the heavens and the earth, You are my Protector { Wali'} in this world and in the Hereafter, Let my return (in death) be of a soul in submission and join me with the righteous." [13]

Having said so, it must be clearly understood by the believer and the nonbeliever (who cares to understand) that the Quran reminds the Muslim that God and His Prophet take precedence over any other relationship, including the relationships of blood. Many muslims, including Noah and Abraham and Lot had to endure the pain of leaving a loved-one behind in the way of God. A Muslim after all places God, his Message and the Messenger at the very center of his core. They who 'fight the believers for their beliefs and expel them from their homes or support their expulsion' are to be avoided:

---

11 Al Quran 5:51
12 Al Quran 4:45
13 Al Quran 12:101

$$لَّا تَجِدُ قَوْمًا يُؤْمِنُونَ بِٱللَّهِ وَٱلْيَوْمِ ٱلْأَخِرِ يُوَآدُّونَ مَنْ حَآدَّ ٱللَّهَ وَرَسُولَهُ وَلَوْ كَانُوٓا$$

$$ءَابَآءَهُمْ أَوْ أَبْنَآءَهُمْ أَوْ إِخْوَٰنَهُمْ أَوْ عَشِيرَتَهُمْ أُوْلَٰٓئِكَ كَتَبَ فِى قُلُوبِهِمُ ٱلْإِيمَٰنَ وَأَيَّدَهُم$$

$$بِرُوحٍ مِّنْهُ وَيُدْخِلُهُمْ جَنَّٰتٍ تَجْرِى مِن تَحْتِهَا ٱلْأَنْهَٰرُ خَٰلِدِينَ فِيهَا رَضِىَ ٱللَّهُ عَنْهُمْ وَرَضُوا$$

$$عَنْهُ أُوْلَٰٓئِكَ حِزْبُ ٱللَّهِ أَلَآ إِنَّ حِزْبَ ٱللَّهِ هُمُ ٱلْمُفْلِحُونَ ﴿٢٢﴾$$

Thou will not find folk who believe in God and the Last Day loving those who oppose God and His messenger: even though they be their fathers, or their sons or their brothers, or their clan. As for such, He has written faith upon their hearts and has strengthened them with a Spirit from Him, and He will bring them into Gardens underneath which rivers flow, therein to abide forever. God is well pleased with them, and they are well pleased with Him. They are God's party. Surely! is it not God's party who are the successful? [14]

This too is a test of faith. Abraham sums up the pain of a dutiful and submitted heart when he leaves his father:

$$إِلَّا قَوْلَ إِبْرَٰهِيمَ لِأَبِيهِ لَأَسْتَغْفِرَنَّ لَكَ وَمَآ أَمْلِكُ لَكَ مِنَ ٱللَّهِ مِن شَىْءٍ$$

Except that Abraham said to his father: "Certainly I shall ask forgiveness for thee but I have no power to do aught for thee against God." [15]

Robert Frager, Ph.D, relates an incisive incident related to his spiritual guide, Sheikh Muzaffar, who was once invited to perform Islamic Prayers in a Paris Cathedral. After having performed the prayers the Sheikh turned down a request for a reciprocal gesture. "Absolutely Not", was the Sheikh's response. Explaining further to his hosts who must have been rather befuddled, no doubt, he said: "I have a right to pray in your cathedral because I love Jesus. But you cannot pray in our mosque because you do not love Muhammad". [16]

Islam honors the prophetic chain. Islam also respects those whose practice differs from theirs. In Medina when around sixty delegates of the Najran-Christians were visiting the Prophet in the Mosque of Medina, the guests were allowed to pray in the Mosque, not withstanding the fact that they faced East during their services. Through providential design, as the last of the major messages, Islam has a natural disposition for religious tolerance. The followers of Islam must zealously guard this Divine gift. It is a gift not to be merely acknowledged. It must be conscientiously honored. God is *Al Muqaddim*, the One who determines the sequence and precedence of objects and events and

---

14 Al Quran 58:22
15 Al Quran 60:4
16 Heart, Self and Soul, Robert Frager, Ph.D, pg 14, Theosophical Publishing House 2006

beings. Jesus renewed and realigned the message of Moses and his predecessors. Muhammad renewed and realigned the message of Jesus and Jesus' predecessors. A 'muslim' (and the Muslim)[17] cannot but honor each and every prophet in the prophetic caravan. The Truth is that each new cycle of revelation is meant to open new doors. Spiritual doors do not close, they lead to new vistas. Sincerity is an unfolding quest. To love Muhammad is to love Jesus and Moses too. Rumi reminds us all:

There are those who accept the law of Moses and not the grace and love of Jesus,
Like the Jewish King who killed Christians.
This is not right. Moses is inside the soul of Jesus as Jesus is in the soul of Moses.
One era belonged to one; then it was the other's turn, but they are one being[18]

Sincere approach to the Quran

The Quran is meant to be guidance for those who are spiritually hungry and sincere, the "*muttaqeen*", and who are open to Faith, believing in "*ghaib*" (the reality beyond human grasp and therefore embraceable only by the "heart"), who beseech their Lord, share their wealth with others and apart from believing in the Quran, believe as well in other Divine revelations bestowed before the Quran itself.

Says the Quran in attestation of the messenger who bore it, and those who were his close companions:

$$ءَامَنَ ٱلرَّسُولُ بِمَآ أُنزِلَ إِلَيْهِ مِن رَّبِّهِۦ وَٱلْمُؤْمِنُونَ كُلٌّ ءَامَنَ بِٱللَّهِ وَمَلَـٰٓئِكَتِهِۦ وَكُتُبِهِۦ وَرُسُلِهِۦ$$

$$لَا نُفَرِّقُ بَيْنَ أَحَدٍ مِّن رُّسُلِهِۦ$$

The messenger believes in what has been revealed to him from
His Lord, and (so do) the believers; they all believe in God and
His angels and His books and His messengers; [And they say:]
"We make no difference between any of His messengers"[19]

For the believer the Arabic Quran is the purest form of Holy Scripture. It is the un-altered word of God. In the word of God is Certainty, Truth, Grace and the immutability of a living message, ripe with relevance to a person's time and condition. It bears a message that is adaptable across the diversity of culture as it is across the chasm of time:

---

17 I use 'muslim' with a lower-case 'm' to refer to the spiritual muslim, anyone who submits to God. I use 'Muslim' with upper-case 'M' to refer to the social-muslim who declares by way of the *Kalima* to be a 'Muslim'
18 *The Soul of Rumi* by Coleman Barks. Published by Harper Collins 2002
19 Al Quran 2:285

كَلِمَةً طَيِّبَةً كَشَجَرَةٍ طَيِّبَةٍ أَصْلُهَا ثَابِتٌ وَفَرْعُهَا فِى ٱلسَّمَآءِ ۝ تُؤْتِىٓ أُكُلَهَا كُلَّ حِينٍ بِإِذْنِ رَبِّهَا

A good word is as a good tree
Its root is firm; its branches are in Heaven.
It gives forth its fruit at all times, by the permission of its Lord. [20]

The believers also hold that just as Muhammad validated the prophethood of his predecessors, (many of them being mentioned in the Quran itself), his predecessors made a corollary testament of those who would in turn follow them. Divine guidance is based on spiritual continuity through a preordained brotherhood between the prophets. The prophets are committed to this brotherhood:

وَإِذْ أَخَذَ ٱللَّهُ مِيثَـٰقَ ٱلنَّبِيِّـۧنَ لَمَآ ءَاتَيْتُكُم مِّن كِتَـٰبٍ وَحِكْمَةٍ ثُمَّ جَآءَكُمْ رَسُولٌ مُّصَدِّقٌ لِّمَا مَعَكُمْ لَتُؤْمِنُنَّ بِهِۦ وَلَتَنصُرُنَّهُۥ قَالَ ءَأَقْرَرْتُمْ وَأَخَذْتُمْ عَلَىٰ ذَٰلِكُمْ إِصْرِى قَالُوٓا۟ أَقْرَرْنَا قَالَ فَٱشْهَدُوا۟ وَأَنَا۠ مَعَكُم مِّنَ ٱلشَّـٰهِدِينَ ۝

And, Lo, God accepted, through the prophets, this solemn pledge [from the
followers of earlier revelation]: "If, after all the revelation and the wisdom
which I have vouchsafed unto you, there comes to you an apostle confirming the
truth already in your possession, you must believe in him and succor him".
"Do you" - said He - "acknowledge and accept My bond on this condition?"
They answered: "We do acknowledge it."
Said He: "Then bear witness [thereto], and I shall be your witness. [21]

Martin Lings, an enlightened Islamic Sufi, who rested in Islam after his spiritual journey within and into Catholicism, Buddhism and Hinduism, cites the following text in St. John, XVI, 12-15 as Christ's prophesy of Prophet Muhammad:

I have yet many things to say unto you, but ye cannot bear them now. Howbeit when he, the Spirit of truth, is come, he shall guide you into all the truth: for he shall not speak from himself; but what things so ever he shall hear, these shall he speak: and he shall declare unto you the things that are to come.

The Quran is the last Word of God, revealed to the last prophet. For those who quibble with this belief must contend with the historical absence of another book or credible prophet since the advent of Islam. Indeed speaking to those who doubt the Quran, the Quran itself lays open the challenge to produce an equivalent book.

---

20 Al Quran 14:24-25
21 Al Quran 3:81. Interpreted by Muhammad Asad in "The Message of the Quran"

قُل لَّئِنِ ٱجۡتَمَعَتِ ٱلۡإِنسُ وَٱلۡجِنُّ عَلَىٰٓ أَن يَأۡتُواْ بِمِثۡلِ هَـٰذَا ٱلۡقُرۡءَانِ
لَا يَأۡتُونَ بِمِثۡلِهِۦ وَلَوۡ كَانَ بَعۡضُهُمۡ لِبَعۡضٍ ظَهِيرًا

Say: "Verily, though mankind and the jinn should assemble to produce the like of this Qur'an, they could not produce the like thereof though they were helpers one of another".[22]

The equivalency to the Quran does not mean another book equivalent in words or verses or chapters, or rhythm or grammar. It must meet the equivalency of beauty, inspiration, living relevance, and a million other intangibles. It must make grown men break down and cry, make violent men drop their swords, make young and old women want to cover their heads and to kiss it, and it must make you want to wash your hand and rinse your soul before you touch it. The equivalent book must transform hearts and change the world as the Quran did, is doing, and will continue to do. The equivalent book must be miraculously committed to the heart of its unlettered reciter and it must inspire other words and books and deeds until the seven seas, and then some more, if they were ink, could bear no more. The *Mathnavi* of Rumi, the world's best known inspired book by the best known ancient-poet of the modern world, is inspired by the Quran. It is called by some as the Persian Quran. But make no mistake; the Quran is not of it. The *Mathnavi is of the Quran.* The Quran inspired the *Mathnavi.* The *Mathnavi* cannot inspire a Quran-equivalent. Rumi would be the first one to say that. The Truth of the Quranic verse about the inimitability of the Quran could be better understood by the non-Muslim western mind if the challenge was made to produce the like of Prophet Jesus: "If all mankind and *Jinn* should attempt they could not produce the like of Jesus". This should bring home another point unique to the Quran. If Jesus were amongst us today, he, Jesus, would be the prime if not singular source of spiritual renewal for his followers. Today, in his stead, is the church and the clergy. It cannot but be a poor substitute. The Quran, on the other hand, is amongst us today and to a Muslim it is the prime and supreme source of spiritual renewal. It does not warrant, nor does it allow for a substitution.

The Quran is a living companion of the sincere

The Quran has both an exoteric and esoteric content. Says the Quran of itself:

---

22 Al Quran 17:88

هُوَ ٱلَّذِىٓ أَنزَلَ عَلَيْكَ ٱلْكِتَـٰبَ مِنْهُ ءَايَـٰتٌ مُّحْكَمَـٰتٌ هُنَّ أُمُّ ٱلْكِتَـٰبِ

وَأُخَرُ مُتَشَـٰبِهَـٰتٌ ۖ فَأَمَّا ٱلَّذِينَ فِى قُلُوبِهِمْ زَيْغٌ فَيَتَّبِعُونَ مَا تَشَـٰبَهَ مِنْهُ

ٱبْتِغَآءَ ٱلْفِتْنَةِ وَٱبْتِغَآءَ تَأْوِيلِهِۦ ۗ وَمَا يَعْلَمُ تَأْوِيلَهُۥٓ إِلَّا ٱللَّهُ

*He it is who has bestowed upon thee from on high this Divine Writ, containing
messages that are clear in and by themselves and these are the essence of the
Divine Writ- as well as others that are allegorical.*
*Now those whose hearts are given to swerving from the truth go after that part
of the Divine Writ which has been expressed in allegory, seeking out [what is
bound to create] confusion and seeking [to arrive at] its final meaning [in an
arbitrary manner]; But none save God knows its final meaning.*[23]

The exoteric content holds plain and unambiguous guidance. This guidance
establishes the principles of ethics and conduct. There are five basic principles,
often called the five pillars of the conduct of Faith: Testament of Faith in One
God and the Seal of his prophets, Muhammad, Daily prayers and prostrations,
fasting, sharing of wealth, and based on affordability, a once-in-a life-time
pilgrimage to the *Kaabah*. The sincere believer, trying to live within the matrix of
the "clear message", will find in the esoteric content an invitation to reflection
and contemplation. Contemplation is the food of the spirit. It changes the person
from the inside out. For those who embrace the Quran in its totality, anchored in
its "unambiguous guidance", the contemplative ground is fertile as it is limitless,
because *"But none save God knows its final meaning."* These verses of the
Quran are *not without* meaning. It is quite the opposite. These verses have a
depth and richness of meaning. The meaning is limited by the capacity and
sincerity of the seeker and therefore has a personal and indigenous
characteristic. It cannot and must not be boxed into a dogma.

وَإِن مِّن شَىْءٍ إِلَّا عِندَنَا خَزَآئِنُهُۥ وَمَا نُنَزِّلُهُۥٓ إِلَّا بِقَدَرٍ مَّعْلُومٍ

*And whatever there is, its storehouses are with Us;
And We only distribute it in allotted measures*[24]

The Quran is a spiritual kaleidoscope both in its Arabic form and its meaning.
The form and content of the imagery is anchored in and compounded by the
richness of the Arabic language. The fabric or building blocks of the Arabic
language are its 'root' words. Almost every word is derived from a list of root-
words; each root-word consisting of three (rarely 4) consonants. A root word
may spawn many words with meanings of varying and even opposite shades.
Contemporary, 'spoken', languages morph with the force of cultural changes.

---

23 Quran Al-Imran 3:7-8. Interpreted by Muhammad Asad in "The Message of the Quran"
24 Al Quran 15:21, translation taken from *The Qur'an , A biography*, by Bruce Lawrence

The Quranic Arabic is not a 'spoken' language and it retains (by virtue of word-association via root-words) it's classical (or pristine) 'mind-set'. Words associated via a single root can often be suggestive of a theme or thematic connectivity. For example the root-word *'wjd* is common to *'wujood*, meaning 'existence' *'wajada*, meaning 'to find' and *"wujd"* meaning 'means or ability'. It is difficult to resist the suggestion (offered by this word-association), that 'finding' and 'knowing' and 'being' are connected. And that 'finding' one's self is to 'come into being' and 'becoming empowered'! See what these co-rooted words suggest to you: *'Sidq* (meaning truth), *'Sadaqa* (meaning that which is given in God's name, 'charity' if you will), *'Sadiq* (the one who is truthful and lives by the truth) and *'Mutasadiq* (one who gives).

The contemplative quality of the Arabic Quran becomes the source of its universal appeal and cultural neutrality. The Moroccan, the Turk, the Persian, the Chinese, the Indonesian Muslim or the Western Sufi will anchor their contemplative endeavors in the Arabic of the Quran. It is here that the composite radiance of infinite colors is stored. Each will take his or her "allotted measure".

As an example of the Quran's kaleidoscopic imagery, consider life's beating heart and the pulsating quality inherent in all levels of the universe as expounded in the sound vision of Surah *An Naziat* (That which rises). In this mystical Surah is depicted the pulsating interplay and interdependence between motion and time; mass and gravity, creating, shaping and sustaining life as we know it. Some interpreters of the Quran accord this to be an allusion to the pulsating rhythm that sustains the expansions of the constellations. Others interpret it as the angels at work fulfilling His bidding. Quite often the *Ayahs* (verses) of the Quran will invoke the *Ayahs* (signs) of Nature, giving us the license and invitation to reflect.

An Naziat is interpreted variously, yet inclusively, by Assad, Pickthall, Yousuf Ali and M. H. Shakir as follows:

وَٱلنَّزِعَتِ غَرْقًا ۝ وَٱلنَّشِطَٰتِ نَشْطًا ۝ وَٱلسَّٰبِحَٰتِ سَبْحًا ۝ فَٱلسَّٰبِقَٰتِ سَبْقًا ۝
فَٱلْمُدَبِّرَٰتِ أَمْرًا ۝

Consider those [stars] that rise up only to set
And move [in their orbits] with steady motion
And float [through space] with floating serene
And yet overtake [one another] with swift overtaking
And thus they fulfill the [Creator's] behest[25]
.....

---

25 Al Quran 79:1-5 as interpreted by Muhammad Asad

By the (angels) who tear out (the souls of the wicked) with violence;
By those who gently draw out (the souls of the blessed);
And by those who glide along (on errands of mercy),
Then press forward as in a race,
Then arrange to do (the Commands of their Lord), [26]
... ...
By those who drag forth to destruction,
By the meteors rushing,
By the lone stars floating,
By the angels hastening,
And those who govern the event, [27]
... .
I swear by the angels, who violently pull out the souls of the wicked,
And by those who gently draw out the souls of the blessed,
And by those who float in space,
Then those who are foremost going ahead,
Then those who regulate the affair. [28]

Standing by the shore, the Surah would apply to the mesmerizing beat of the restless sea. The incessant rise and fall of the waves, dissipating into the floating foam, one yielding to the other, breathing and sustaining life between each rise and fall. Not random, not wanton but intricately regulated and severally essential.

By those that rise to then crumble
And move in harmony
And float with serenity
And supersede unrelentingly
And so fulfill the Creator's bidding [29]

At a more personal level it evokes the living heart-beat of life. More meaningfully, therefore, the surah encompasses images of incessant and tireless creation at all levels, weaving the personal and cosmic into one grand scheme. There is a common theme and rhythm in the heart-beats of nature. In these rhythms are means and signs of expansion and contraction, inhalation and exhalation, life and death, creation and rebirth. All interconnected and interdependent, controlled by a single cosmic scheme. The microcosm mirrors the complexities and magnitude of the macrocosm.

---

26 Al Quran 79:1-5 as interpreted by Yusuf Ali
27 Al Quran 79:1-5 as interpreted by Picktall
28 Al Quran 79:1-5 as interpreted by Shakir
29 Al Quran 79:1-4

The symbolism of the Quran is entrenched in the Arabic language itself. It follows therefore, that the experience of the Quran is incomplete without its Arabic recitation. The rapturous rhythms of Arabic recitation aim straight at the heart, where its meaning takes root. Each verse (*ayah* in Arabic, meaning "sign") is laden with a "sound vision"[30], transforming the message into a living message. Just as the sky and the earth, the setting and rising of the sun and the changing of the seasons are signs (*ayahs*) of the Compassionate Creator, so are the verses (*ayahs*) of the Quran.

The Quran is not just a 'book'. The book is merely one form of it.

After years of study, I can only tell you this that I do not have the words to 'define' or 'describe' the Quran. To approach the Quran is like approaching a light source. The light reveals everything, other than itself. Likewise the Quran's seeker becomes its subject. Rumi does not want you to call it just a book when he says, "Now with fifty grams of ink one can transcribe the whole Quran. This is a symbol of God's knowledge, all knowledge belonging to God not this only. After all in the time of Moses and Jesus the Quran existed. God's speech existed, but it was not in Arabic."[31]

The Quran existed before it became a bound book. It is therefore not a book. It is more like a *sea of signs.* These signs are formless visuals for the inner eye and soothing resonance for inner hearing. They draw us out of ourselves into a mystical vastness, obscuring selfhood and its boundaries of form and time. Like the Nature-lover who is drawn ever deeper into the obscurity of wilderness, the seeker of the Quran is drawn into the immanence of Wholeness. All signs manifest the Unity of Divine Will, Divine Purpose and Divine Mercy; beyond space, beyond time and beyond dogma. The edicts of the Quran, by their sanction or forbiddance are meant to change our actions. The signs of the Quran are meant to change our thoughts.

The *Arabic* Quran was revealed in stages as *needed* by the Prophet's mission. Through the Prophet it has become a *revelation upon us* (7:3). It is in this context, perhaps, that Rumi urges us to start *needing* and *wanting* God. The Arabic Quran would then become for us a *meaningful* revelation (instead of being merely a venerated book). And what are the *meaningful* aspects of these revelations? We will let the Arabic Quran speak for itself:

A wondrous mystical recital {*Quran an Aajaban*} (72:1); full of parables (17:89); bearing for mankind guidance (2:185), learning (12:2) wisdom, healing {*Quran al hakeem*} (36:2) and mercy (17:82). It reveals itself to the reciter in stages (17:106), but has been made easy to remember (54:17, 54:22, 54:32 and 54:40). Above

---

30 Approaching the Quran by Michael Sells
31 *Discourses of Rumi* By Arthur John Arberry

all it is a clear path to God (36:69)—An Open Book {*Quran in Mobeen*} (15:1), free from discrepancy (4:82), bearing solace for the sincere believers; (17:9), admonition (17:41) (38:1) for the disbelievers. Inimitable (17:88), glorious {*Quran un Majeed*} (85:21, 50:1) and bountiful {*Quran un kareem*} (56:77); bearing immensity {*Quran al Azeem*} (15:87) and revealing an ever increasing depth to the discerning seeker. (41:3)

The Quran speaks to the many within one soul

There are terms used by the Quran to make a distinction between humans based on the state of their heart or the level of their spiritual consciousness. Terms such as *"Zalimeen"*, *"Kafireen"*, *"Muslimeen"*, *"Momineen"* have no similar English synonyms and neither should they. The rich symbolism of these terms can only conform to the receptacle of understanding. The form and color of a liquid conforms to the form and color of the vessel. A translated equivalent not only limits the symbolism but is also molded in the shape of the vessel. The term *Zalimeen* for example is used in the story of Adam

وَيَٰٓـَٔادَمُ ٱسْكُنْ أَنتَ وَزَوْجُكَ ٱلْجَنَّةَ فَكُلَا مِنْ حَيْثُ شِئْتُمَا

وَلَا تَقْرَبَا هَٰذِهِ ٱلشَّجَرَةَ فَتَكُونَا مِنَ ٱلظَّٰلِمِينَ

O Adam dwell thou and thy wife in the garden and eat both of you,
whatever you may wish,
but do not approach this tree, lest you become Zalimeen[32]

Zalimeen has been variously translated as "wrong doers", "transgressors" and "unjust" by Yousuf Ali, Pickthall, and M. H. Shakir respectively. Neither of these words truly captures the breadth of the symbolism here. The root word for *Zalimeen* is *Zulm*. The latter implies putting something in other than its proper place, to be in darkness, lacking vision and clarity, thereby engendering the propensity to transgress, be unjust and do wrong. Eating the forbidden fruit would lead to a transformation of consciousness, mirroring the transplantation from Paradise. Adam and Eve would enter the state of *Zulm*, separated from their proper place with God in Paradise, disengaged from the Truth, and entangled in the illusory. It is a state where the new "self" is disconnected from the only "Self". The illusion of the self masks the true Self.

Similarly *Kafireen* has been translated as "Atheists", "Disbelievers", "Unbelievers", "Deniers of Truth" and rarely (and thankfully only rarely by Muslim scholars) as "infidels". The early Quranic surah delivers a message to the prophet's early

---

32 Al Quran 7:19

tormenters:

$$\text{قُلْ يَـٰٓأَيُّهَا ٱلْكَـٰفِرُونَ ۝ لَآ أَعْبُدُ مَا تَعْبُدُونَ ۝ وَلَآ أَنتُمْ عَـٰبِدُونَ مَآ أَعْبُدُ ۝ وَلَآ}$$

$$\text{أَنَا۠ عَابِدٌ مَّا عَبَدتُّمْ ۝ وَلَآ أَنتُمْ عَـٰبِدُونَ مَآ أَعْبُدُ ۝ لَكُمْ دِينُكُمْ وَلِىَ دِينِ ۝}$$

Say: O you who disbelieve {Kafiroon}
I do not serve {la abidu} that which is master over you
Nor do you serve that who is Master over me {Ma abud}
I will not worship that which you worship
Neither will you worship that Who I worship
Unto you, your way and unto me my way[33]

A prophet conveys a Divine message and speaks to all. On his lips the surah has a proclamatory value. The follower on the other hand must internalize the message as it speaks to the reader's self. The residual experience from the recitation of the surah is one of affirmation of one's own faith as opposed to the obsession with another's divergence. The call of the "*Mabud*" (the Master, the One who is served, the One who is worthy of all the devotion, the One who draws adulation) has been heard by the "*abd*" (an adoring slave, one who serves, one who is devoted, one who adulates). The *abd* is purposefully committed to follow the way (*Deen*) shown by the *Mabud*. It has a hymnic quality for a purposeful lover, putting all distraction aside, undertaking the journey to his or her Master, if not yet Beloved.

Kafir is a person in the state of *Kufr*. To be in *Kufr* is to be misaligned with God. Nominally, it is to be outside His message, un-heedful of final accountability. Yes, the state becomes deeper with callousness, doubt, rejection and hostility, but even a 'Muslim' can and is likely to find his or her self in the un-heedful state. To hoard wealth, to be dishonest, unjust or unkind—any of these conditions—reflect misalignment with God and His revelations, and expose the person's un-heedfulness of final accountability. A person is not defined by a label but by the person's own state of a consciousness and conscientiousness. The state of *Kufr* is known to God as it is a state *known* to the *Kafir*. There is therefore, from the perspective of the non-prophet, no purpose served as there is no grace in looking for *kufr* outside of one's self. It has been attributed to Umar, son of Khattab, the second caliph of Medina, and a companion of the prophet that every verse revealing the torment awaiting the *Kafir* has a relevance to the disobedient 'Muslim'.

An uninspired translation of this Surah risks rendering the Surah to be about the Atheist instead of being about the reader and his *Mabud*. This Surah as any other

---

33 Al Quran 109:1-6

Surah must be directed inwards. When contemplating the Quran the Muslim must direct the message (*both the promise of deliverance* and *the admonition*) *inwards*, not withstanding its relevance to some-one else.

There are similar considerations associated with the terms *Muslimeen* (typically substituted as 'muslims') and *Momineen* (typically substituted as the 'believers' or the 'faithful'). The term 'muslim', derived from root verb "*aslama*", meaning 'he surrendered himself', has a spiritual as well as a social connotation. From the spiritual perspective *any one* and everyone who surrenders to God, is a *muslim* ('muslim' with a lower-case 'm'). *All* prophets are in this fold. This is the Quran's declaration. The spiritual patriarch Abraham is amongst the best of muslims. This too is the Quran's declaration. From the social perspective a Muslim ('Muslim' with a capital 'M') is one who professes belief in God, the Quran, and therefore the prophethood of Muhammad and all preceding prophets. It is a personal declaration made in the form of the *Kalima*, admitting the individual to the local or at-large community {*umma*}. The declaration however does not by itself amount to surrender {to God}. Surrender to God is an attained and demonstrated state achieved by a growing inner consciousness and a persistent outward scrupulousness. The action and the preceding intent determine the state. The *state* defines the person. The Quran speaks to the states of doubt (*kufr*), ignorance (*zulm*), surrender (*islam*) and faith (*Emaan*). These are states people find themselves in. More significantly though, these are states *within* the searching heart. The searching heart must confront itself through a personal and persistent introspection until it is conditioned to test and align every thought towards surrender. This is the process by which the heart burnishes faith and itself. The heart is faith. The Quran is not the standard by which we must judge others; judgment is Divine. The Quran is the inspiration by which we must move and lift ourselves. It is directed to the heart that recites it, calling the many *within it* (and of course each one of us) to the Abode of True Peace and Unity.

The Quran yields to the sincere

There are also other terms with some measure of mystery attached to them. One such term in the Quran is "*Jinn*". *Jinns* and humans are almost always paired together in the Quran. It is therefore inferred that *Jinns*, like humans, are agents of free-will. Taking the last chapter of the Quran as an example, one finds the diversity of interpretation. Thomas Cleary in *The Qur'an A new translation* uses the word "demonic" in translation. Muhammad Asad in *The Message of the Quran* uses the phrase "invisible forces". Fittingly, Abdullah Yusuf Ali and Dr. Mohsin, retain the word *Jinn* in their interpretations. One can and must reasonably ask, if it is really possible to grasp the color of every knot and strand of the Divine tapestry? The Quran speaks of eternity and the message is given to all generations this side of eternity. Must we not make allowances for the limitation of our current knowledge? Must we also not accept providential intent? Not only is there no loss in the quality or integrity of the message that the Quran bears without an explicit understanding of the term *Jinn,* the resultant malleability places an effective demand for greater reflection. The malleability itself makes allowances for the limits of our current knowledge and the non-obsolescence of the message.

As an example of the transcendence of the Divine Signs, consider God's claim of Universal Dominion: Lord of East and West (26:28 & 73:9) {*Rabb al Mashriq wal Maghrib*}, Lord of the two Easts and Lord of the two Wests (55:17) {*Rabb al Mashriqayn wa Rabb al Maghribayn*} and Lord of all [infinite] Easts and all [infinite] Wests (70:40) {*Rabb al Mashariq wal Magharib*}. The Quran speaks, as it does here, to every quantum of consciousness. From the perspective of an Arab trader bound to a trading caravan, fourteen centuries ago, a pair of Easts and many Easts conveyed an immeasurable Dominion, both worldly and heavenly; on many planes both real and mystical. Two Easts and two Wests found a new meaning when man discovered that the world was spherical and there indeed were two routes to the East, the first heading directly East and the second heading *West*? Today, the infinite Easts and infinite Wests take a new meaning as we discover in awe, a newer perspective; of a tiny, spinning ball we call Earth, revolving around the gaseous and liquid magma of a constant fire, we call the Sun, dwarfed in a moving galaxy, we call the Milky Way, amongst a billion other galaxies, in an ever expanding Universe! Today we can appreciate not just the immensity but the intricacy of Divine Design. Is it not an aspect of Divine Mercy that in the 'relativity of space' we can still assign and rely upon definitive co-ordinates? The 'reliable illusion' of our definitive global positioning in a moving universe is an aspect of Divine bounty. It is by design too that the Quran transcends any single context. Divine Signs have a living meaning. The Dominion of God extends to the limits of our *current* consciousness *and beyond*.

Any translation of the Quran is a reflection, conditioned by the changing perspective of its translator. The Quran is meant to be recited, contemplated, and used as guidance in the *approach* to God—a process without end, but a process that is transformational and regenerative. The Quran's interpretation and translation are therefore neither ever static nor ever complete. What is anchored and complete is its *form.* In his prologue to Muhammad Asad's *"Message of the Quran",* Hasan Gai Eaton writes:

"It is axiomatic from the Islamic perspective that the Quran cannot be translated, because the *form* of God's revelation, that is the Arabic itself, is not merely incidental to its meaning but essential to it. The Arabic of the Quran does not, however limit the Quran to one "literal" interpretation, but by the virtue of the power of its vocabulary allows for a depth of meaning that would be lost in any translation. A rendering into another language, therefore, is not and never can be the Quran as such, but merely an interpretation of it"

This should not serve as discouragement to one uninitiated in Arabic, in fact quite the contrary. Firstly the majority of the Muslim world can only recite Arabic and their understanding of Arabic is limited. There are many who cannot read but listen to it several times a day. Secondly, the Quran can be approached in stages, very small stages. Many Muslims will initiate their approach to the Quran with two chapters. The first chapter, *Surah Fatiha* (literally the opening), is in fact the opening window to the Quran and is the essence of the spiritual pursuit. The second of the two chapters is *Surah Ikhlas* (Chapter of Sincerity) which is the essence of Reality itself, the goal of the spiritual pursuit. With an eye on posterity perhaps, and the sure knowledge that Islam would move beyond the borders of Arabia, the Prophet is documented to have said that Surah *Ikhlas* was equivalent to a third of the Quran. This chapter with four short verses can be memorized in minutes and by itself is enough to sustain a believer for a life-time! Thirdly, the fraternity of interpreters, their perspectives, and interpretations are vast, rich and growing. Fourthly and most importantly is the promise made in the Quran itself:

$$\text{وَلَقَدْ يَسَّرْنَا ٱلْقُرْءَانَ لِلذِّكْرِ فَهَلْ مِن مُّدَّكِرٍ}$$

"We have made the Quran easy to comprehend and remember[34]"

And this too has been foresworn, witnessed by all elements of creation, big and small, high and low; categorically and unconditionally: "Disallowed and therefore impossible is the non-delivery of recompense to the sincere and persevering heart".[35]

---

34 Al Quran 54:17 54:22 54:32 54:40
35 Al Quran 95

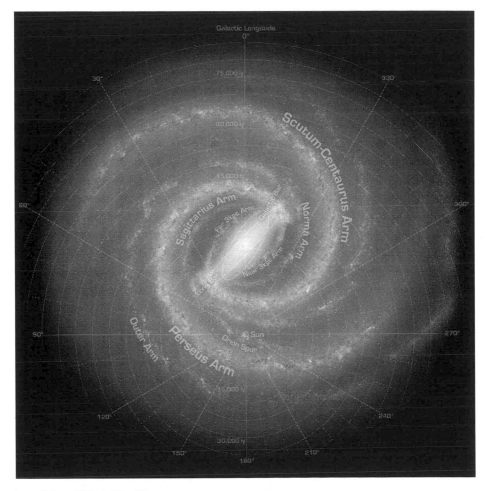

A rendition of The Milky Way

[How large is the Universe? The correct answer is that we will never know. Each second the observable Universe expands by a 196,000 miles in all directions. We simply do not know how much of the Universe is 'hidden' from us. Contemporary scientific wisdom puts our home galaxy, at 100,000 light years across with hundreds of billions of stars. The Universe has hundreds of billions of other galaxies. Our own solar system is not at the centre of our galaxy, much less at the center of the Universe.

If our entire Solar System were scaled down to the size of a quarter, the Sun at the center, would be a sub-microscopic particle, and the nine orbiting planets orbiting the sun along the circumference of the coin would be sub-sub-microscopic. The Milky Way would then be the size of China! Even at this scale we cannot fathom the size of the 'observable' Universe.]

Reflection

"Islam is mostly a matter of the heart.
It has no priesthood, no effective hierarchy.
Every person faces God alone" [36].

The heart is the seat of 'knowing'

An inquisitive mind with an open heart reaffirms its belief with each passing day that the more one learns; the more one learns that there is more to know than what one knew there was to know. Then there is the vast unknown beyond the certain portals of birth and death. The enigma of our bodily existence starts at birth. Life begins ostensibly without personal choice and without worldly knowledge. The worldly knowledge of our time and place of our birth is passed on to us. We accept these markers without any personal corroboration. We begin to know about ourselves through others and only through the death of others do we 'know' of the certainty of our own impending death. The knowledge of one's own mortality is a conviction. 'Personal' death defies proof or validation in this realm. One's own death is not a 'fact' of the body. It is the transcendental 'fact' of the unknown. It's 'certainty' therefore underscores the bounds of our knowledge in this realm. Death is the end of 'free-will', for those who consider themselves the agents of their actions. It is the continuation of 'pre-destination' for those who choose to view life as such. Death, nevertheless, goads us to look beyond into the unknown and unseen.

We will acquire a vast body of scientific knowledge, yet the bulk of what we will know is tacit knowledge. This form of knowing manifests itself as a feeling, a sense, a perception, an intuition or just a hunch. It is a highly personal kind of knowledge that defines us as individuals. We use tacit knowledge to recognize the face of a friend or a relative. We use tacit knowledge (in conjunction with "instinctual knowledge, if you will) to discern whether there is an expression of love or hate, happiness or despair, peace or anger, in someone's eyes.

However we cannot fully explain this process of discernment. We can only "see it in their eyes". Our individual awareness, limited as it is, far exceeds our ability to communicate in words. Tacit knowledge cannot be fully articulated, or distilled, yet it shapes us as human beings. It cannot be taught in a formal textual process, although it gets conveyed every day, subliminally and subconsciously between parent and child, master and disciple and in a spiritual sense between the heart and the mind. This knowledge stems from and resides within the growing reservoir of a very personal inner-intellect.

An informed mind is a humble mind that must make room for this other inner-intellect. The art of reflection is the art of seeing through the heart. The Quran invites those who are willing to recognize the limits of human perception and therefore open to "seeing through the heart".

ذَٰلِكَ ٱلۡكِتَٰبُ لَا رَيۡبَ ۛ فِيهِ ۛ هُدًى لِّلۡمُتَّقِينَ ۞ ٱلَّذِينَ يُؤۡمِنُونَ بِٱلۡغَيۡبِ وَيُقِيمُونَ ٱلصَّلَوٰةَ وَمِمَّا رَزَقۡنَٰهُمۡ يُنفِقُونَ ۞ وَٱلَّذِينَ يُؤۡمِنُونَ بِمَآ أُنزِلَ إِلَيۡكَ وَمَآ أُنزِلَ مِن قَبۡلِكَ وَبِٱلۡأَخِرَةِ هُمۡ يُوقِنُونَ

This is the Book without doubt.
With guidance for those who seek spiritual Ascension.
And believe in {ghaib} (the unfathomable reality of afterlife)
And are steadfast in prayer.
And give in alms from what God has given them
And believe in what has been revealed to you (Muhammad)
And what has been revealed to (other prophets) before you
And who have certain faith in the Hereafter[37]

The great mystic poet of the thirteenth century Jalaluddin Rumi "locates knowledge in the heart rather than in the imagination or intellect. Even with all its vulnerabilities and weaknesses the heart cannot lie; for all of its alleged powers, the intellect cannot but lie".[38]

Spirituality is internal. Religion tends to be external

Spirituality is the quest for a "Meaning" that will not fail. The "Meaning" must be lived when found and grows when it is lived. From the Islamic perspective; I would call this Meaning, *Deen*. Many others will call it religion. *Deen*, in turn calls this Meaning "God"—One, Alone, Absolute". There are *many* paths to God, within and outside of (organized) religion, conditional, of course, upon the yearning to *seek* the One Absolute God.

---

37 Al Quran- 2:1-4
38 *Rumi on the Prophets and Revelation* by John Renard

إِنَّ ٱلَّذِينَ ءَامَنُواْ وَٱلَّذِينَ هَادُواْ وَٱلنَّصَـٰرَىٰ وَٱلصَّـٰبِـِينَ مَنْ ءَامَنَ بِٱللَّهِ وَٱلْيَوْمِ ٱلْأَخِرِ
وَعَمِلَ صَـٰلِحًا فَلَهُمْ أَجْرُهُمْ عِندَ رَبِّهِمْ وَلَا خَوْفٌ عَلَيْهِمْ وَلَا هُمْ يَحْزَنُونَ ۝

Those amongst the believers and the Jews, and the
Christians and the Sabians, who have faith in God and the end of time and
strive to do good and to be just have their reward secure with their Lord.
Without fear and dejection shall they be.[39]

The Quran categorically refutes the concept of the "chosen people (of a religion)" advanced by Jews and Christians of their time. The necessary and sufficient determinants of salvation are human intentions and actions. God the grateful Master never ignores what is earnestly submitted to Him. It is also true, and not lost upon the discerning heart, that earnestness has failed its test if submission is to any other but God.

وَقَالُواْ لَن يَدْخُلَ ٱلْجَنَّةَ إِلَّا مَن كَانَ هُودًا أَوْ نَصَـٰرَىٰ ۗ تِلْكَ أَمَانِيُّهُمْ ۗ قُلْ هَاتُواْ بُرْهَـٰنَكُمْ
إِن كُنتُمْ صَـٰدِقِينَ ۝ بَلَىٰ مَنْ أَسْلَمَ وَجْهَهُۥ لِلَّهِ وَهُوَ مُحْسِنٌ فَلَهُۥٓ أَجْرُهُۥ عِندَ رَبِّهِۦ وَلَا
خَوْفٌ عَلَيْهِمْ وَلَا هُمْ يَحْزَنُونَ ۝

And they claim, "None shall enter Paradise unless he be a "Jew "or a "Christian"
A wishful belief!
Say "Produce your evidence if you are truthful."
Without a doubt, any one who willfully surrenders to God
And acts with the grace of goodness
Will have his reward with his Lord
All such need have no fear nor will they be grievous[40]

Love and spirituality ("or '*Deen*' when it encompasses striving for harmony with the Absolute Source), are matters of the heart, encompassing knowledge that is tacit, and as such there can be no compulsion or coercion in this process.

لَآ إِكْرَاهَ فِى ٱلدِّينِ ۖ قَد تَّبَيَّنَ ٱلرُّشْدُ مِنَ ٱلْغَىِّ

"Deen takes root without coercion".
"The truth (as willing seekers will discern) stands clear of error" [41]

Deen **is not dogma**

Submission to God does not imply the abandonment of reason or the election of

---

39 Al Quran 2:62
40 Al Quran 2:111-112
41 Al Quran 2:256

reclusion. Contrary to popular belief, reason (science, if you will) does not stand in the way of God. While today's science of reason immerses itself into the imponderables of Heisenberg's Uncertainty Principle, and Quantum Physics, blurring the distinction between mass and energy or particle and wave, science has been and will always be an evolving discipline. With each discovery, valiant and far-reaching as it is, the mystery deepens and the domain expands. Besides matter there is 'dark matter', matter that is invisible and unaffected by light, matter which manifests itself by its gravitational field but is itself hidden and elusive. Besides the gravitational energy that we know of, there exists also its opposite that science calls 'dark energy'. Our universe is infinite in infinite ways; infinite in its expanse, equally infinite in its smallness and infinite in its mystery; diverse but harmonious; unpredictable but reliable; relative in time and space but real, in perpetual motion yet static, fleeting yet with a "here" and "now." Science and personal spirituality have no conflict and not only can they coexist but are complementary. The contemplation of the cosmos is a humbling experience. Humility places the mind and heart at the threshold of the spiritual door. Isaac Newton, the famous physicist recognized the limitations of his scientific inquiry when he wrote: "this most beautiful system of the sun, planets and comets could only proceed from the counsel and dominion of an intelligent and powerful Being"[42].

The earth is not at the center of the universe and man's perch on earth is a poor vantage point. The scientist and the spiritual heart must both infer from and contemplate upon manifested signs. Science neither can nor will it ever 'uncover' God. Science neither can nor will it ever prove or disprove God. God by definition is that or who we cannot comprehend. The Big Bang theory does not explain the cosmos, it exposes the puzzle. The Big Bang is that arbitrary starting-point in time and space that mercifully precludes us from having to contemplate the 'nothingness' before the bang and the 'nothingness' before the 'nothingness'. Like the maddening conundrum of the chicken and the egg as to which came first, the cosmos presents its own conundrums. The Quran speaks of genesis with the perfect balance of faith and plausibility, pleasing to the heart and acceptable to the mind:

ثُمَّ ٱسْتَوَىٰٓ إِلَى ٱلسَّمَآءِ وَهِىَ دُخَانٌ فَقَالَ لَهَا وَلِلْأَرْضِ ٱئْتِيَا طَوْعًا أَوْ كَرْهًا قَالَتَآ أَتَيْنَا طَآئِعِينَ

And He [it is who] applied His design to the skies, which were [yet but] smoke;
and He [it is who] said to them and to the earth,
"Come [into being], both of you, willingly or unwillingly!"
To which both responded, "We do come in obedience." [43]

---

42 *A History of God*, Karen Armstrong Ballantine Books 1993 pg 304
43 Al Quran 41:11 as interpreted by Muhammad Asad

There are those who look for scientific prophesies in the Quran, to 'prove' that it is the word of God'. For example, a commonly cited verse is deemed by some to be an allusion to a big-bang type event:

أَوَلَمْ يَرَ ٱلَّذِينَ كَفَرُوٓاْ أَنَّ ٱلسَّمَٰوَٰتِ وَٱلْأَرْضَ كَانَتَا رَتْقًا فَفَتَقْنَٰهُمَا ۖ وَجَعَلْنَا مِنَ ٱلْمَآءِ كُلَّ شَىْءٍ حَىٍّ ۖ أَفَلَا يُؤْمِنُونَ ۝

Have not those who disbelieve known that the heavens and the earth were of one piece,
Then We parted them, and we made every living thing of water?
Will they not then believe? [44]

The Quran by its very non-dogmatic concept of God and its allegorical style is impregnable to 'scientific assault'. And while such 'proofs' may work for some and while religious edicts must withstand the test of earnest rationality, I am with Rumi when he says that "divers have no need for shoes" and that "One comes to God through being bewildered". It diminishes faith to bolster belief by scientific corroboration.

It is 'organized religion', which divides the community into clergy and laity (experts and novices) that feels threatened by science. It is certainly not the belief in God that science threatens. Science collides with myths and dogmas and some of the myths shattered by science have threatened 'organized clergy'. "Anti-heresy squads" and witch-hunts are the defensive tools of an entrenched clergy, which further fortifies itself by the rigidness of its dogmas. Christ, the man of faith was a threat to the Pharisees much as Galileo, the man of science, was to the Church. Dogmas are human constructs—the territorial demarcations of belief, by those who consider belief to be their territory. Newton who was irked by the Christian dogma of 'The Trinity' was no less a man of faith when he qualified the "Powerful Being" as "He is eternal and infinite, omnipotent and omniscient; that is His duration reaches from eternity to eternity; His presence from infinity to infinity; He governs all things and knows all things that are or can be done" [45] [46].

True faith is always personal at its core. The purpose of "organizing" in religion must not be to organize or define the interaction between man and God. It must be to organize and facilitate human interaction, so that one soul may inspire and elevate another. It cannot be said any better than what the Prophet himself said: "The faithful are mirrors for the faithful".

---

44 Al Quran 21:30 as interpreted by Pickthall
45 *A History of God*, Karen Armstrong Ballantine Books 1993 pg 304
46 Newtons description of God reminds me of the Throne Verse. I cannot resist noting that Karen Armstrong mentions in her book that Newton was in communication with Edward Pococke, the Arabic professor at Oxford!

Dogma and doctrine is not the same thing. A dogma takes birth from a rigid interpretation of doctrine thereby robbing the doctrine of its spiritual breadth and depth. Consider two verses of the Quran that allude to space and time:

$$ٱلَّذِى خَلَقَ سَبْعَ سَمَٰوَٰتٍ طِبَاقًا$$

He created the seven Heavens, harmoniously ordered[47]

$$إِنَّ رَبَّكُمُ ٱللَّهُ ٱلَّذِى خَلَقَ ٱلسَّمَٰوَٰتِ وَٱلْأَرْضَ فِى سِتَّةِ أَيَّامٍ$$

Lo! Your Lord is Allah Who created the heavens and the earth in six Days [48]

Do the seven heavens refer to the seven bodies visible to the naked eye in the sky, the sun and the moon and the planets Mercury, Venus, Mars, Jupiter and Saturn? Or are there exactly seven levels of creation of which the very first includes us and all the other galaxies (and so all within the grasp of human knowledge), *or* does seven metaphorically imply *infinitude* (of Heavens)? Was the universe created in exactly one-hundred-and-forty-four hours, or are the days a celestial unit of time, or does six imply finitude of time? Or are there other meanings not contemplated here? All interpretations should be perfectly acceptable as a matter of 'belief'. A contemplative approach will be at peace with all interpretations and the offered variety is deemed inclusive as opposed to being contradictory. The diversity of interpretations is the very source of the richness and beauty of the belief. A dogmatic approach on the other hand would tend to cling to a single interpretation, to the exclusion of all others. A dogma takes root in a narrow interpretation, clipping the very wings of contemplation. The 'purity' of a Divine verse is not served by its narrow interpretation. It is actually preserved in its living essence. A contemplative approach to revelation seeks to embrace this essence, howsoever unreachable it may be. Somewhere along the path the contemplative heart becomes a participant in the mystery; freed from the distractions of the "why" and "how" of dogma.

More often than not dogmas and the myths woven around them are designed to protect and promote hierarchical religious establishments and their vested interests. The Quran warns against those who make religion needlessly complicated by fabricating religious edicts in the name of God:

$$فَمَنْ أَظْلَمُ مِمَّنِ ٱفْتَرَىٰ عَلَى ٱللَّهِ كَذِبًا لِّيُضِلَّ ٱلنَّاسَ بِغَيْرِ عِلْمٍ$$

Then who does more wrong than one who invents a lie against God, to lead mankind astray without knowledge? [49]

If anything, shattered myths enhance personal spirituality. The *Kalima*—a

Muslims testification of Oneness—in its very essence is a 'myth buster'. Everything, the *Kalima* declares, is created by a Single Creator. Everything is relative and transient, except the One–Absolute and Transcendental.

Reflection is an insight into possibilities

Reflection is not alien to science nor does it run contrary to the scientific spirit. A scientist's arsenal has room for both intellectual diligence and insightful reflection. The work of science uncovers the wonderment of nature and is in itself an *ayah*. Except for the intellectually passionate amongst us (this group would include the scientists), we are bridled with spiritual inertia. We find it too onerous to contemplate the very small or the very big and too disconcerting to bank upon the unverifiable. We are most comfortable when we are unchallenged. We find security in conformity.

To reflect is to break out of the personal and communal prison to see with the eye of the heart, hear the rich sounds of silence, touch the purity of our inspired core, smell the fragrance of universal harmony and taste the sweetness of peace. Feel good words, you think? Hardly! Jacob, who lost his eyes grieving his lost son, re-found sight by the scent from Joseph's shirt.

Through reflection the heart opens itself, unencumbered by the limitations and exactness of logic, to experience the immeasurable beauty and truth, summarily discarded by the naked eye yet manifested in the grand and small. The diamond is akin to coal. Sugar takes root from the bitterness of a fruit. The cast-away reed becomes a flute with a lover's breath. As Rumi says:

> How should the foam fly without the wave?
> How should the dust rise to the zenith without the wind?
> Since you have seen the dust, see the Wind;
> Since you have seen the foam, see the Ocean of Creative Energy.
> Come; see it, for insight is the only thing that avails.[50]

Reflection makes meaning out of knowledge. Knowledge as mere information is just that—mere information. A data-bank is a valueless resource if it does not expose an underlying co-relation. True knowledge must reveal some aspect of the truth. If knowledge as information is to be aware of what there is and what transpires, consider how little we will ever know and how far we have to go in the context of the following assertion in the Quran:

---

50 Translated by R.A. Nicholson. Rumi, Poet and Mystic P. 37

وَعِندَهُۥ مَفَاتِحُ ٱلْغَيْبِ لَا يَعْلَمُهَآ إِلَّا هُوَ ۚ وَيَعْلَمُ مَا فِى ٱلْبَرِّ وَٱلْبَحْرِ ۚ وَمَا تَسْقُطُ مِن وَرَقَةٍ

إِلَّا يَعْلَمُهَا وَلَا حَبَّةٍ فِى ظُلُمَٰتِ ٱلْأَرْضِ وَلَا رَطْبٍ وَلَا يَابِسٍ إِلَّا فِى كِتَٰبٍ مُّبِينٍ ۝

"And the keys of the unseen are with God who alone knows them.
And God Knows what is on the land and in the Sea
And not a leaf falls but God knows it
And there is not a single grain in the dark crevices of the earth,
And nothing green and nothing dry,
But is recorded with certainty"[51]

يَعْلَمُ مَا يَلِجُ فِى ٱلْأَرْضِ وَمَا يَخْرُجُ مِنْهَا وَمَا يَنزِلُ مِنَ ٱلسَّمَآءِ وَمَا يَعْرُجُ فِيهَا ۚ وَهُوَ ٱلرَّحِيمُ

ٱلْغَفُورُ ۝

"He knows that which goes down into the earth and that which comes out from
it, and that which descends from the heavens and that which ascends into it. He
is The Merciful, The Forgiving."[52]

These preceding verses speak to the totality of happening –A happening of not just things and forms but also of thoughts, wills and actions. A leaf, a tree, a crevice, the earth, the sea and the heavens are all part of one grand and immutable record. So is a smile, a tear, a wail, a prayer, a complaint or a call for help. All are recorded irrespective of their significance or consequence. The book of record would be incomplete if it missed the leaf that fell and the event of its falling. With God, Knowing, Willing and Creating are one and the same. Therefore nothing is for naught and no soul is without a purpose, much less without a Guardian!

وَمَا تَحْمِلُ مِنْ أُنثَىٰ وَلَا تَضَعُ إِلَّا بِعِلْمِهِۦ ۚ

"No female conceives or gives birth except with His Knowledge."[53]

No one and no condition is outside Divine knowledge and no one is ever truly abandoned:

وَمَن يَتَّقِ ٱللَّهَ يَجْعَل لَّهُۥ مَخْرَجًا ۝ وَيَرْزُقْهُ مِنْ حَيْثُ لَا يَحْتَسِبُ ۚ وَمَن يَتَوَكَّلْ عَلَى ٱللَّهِ فَهُوَ

حَسْبُهُۥٓ ۚ إِنَّ ٱللَّهَ بَٰلِغُ أَمْرِهِۦ ۚ قَدْ جَعَلَ ٱللَّهُ لِكُلِّ شَىْءٍ قَدْرًا ۝

And unto everyone who is conscious of God,

---

51 Al Quran 6:59
52 Al Quran 34:2
53 Al Quran 35:11

He [always] grants a way out [of unhappiness]
And provides for him in a manner beyond expectation;
And for everyone who places his trust in God,
He [alone] is enough.
Verily God always attains to His purpose:
Indeed, unto everything has God appointed its [term] and measure[54]

Islam—*Deen* or religion?

Submission to God (Islam) is not exactly a 'religion'. It is both less and more. It has been called a 'way of being'—'way' meaning 'path or journey' and 'being' meaning 'consciousnesses. God is present (and so worshipped) not just in the mosque. God is present (and so worshipped) when eating, working and sleeping. To classify Islam as an organized religion is to miss its essence. This would be the Judaeo- Christian centric view. It is classified as a religion by the necessity (often cultivated) to distinguish it from Judaism or Christianity, given that the latter are classified as organized religions. Islam attempts to break the "box" of religion. First, the 'fold of Islam' claims <u>all</u> prophets. Secondly, The Quran calls Islam a "*Deen*" as opposed to *Madhhab* (Arabic equivalent of 'religion', accurately translated as "Schools of law or thought" and literally meaning that which is "taken away"). *Madhhabs*, therefore refer to the interpretations ("take-aways") of *Deen*. It is noteworthy that *Madhhabs* correctly refer to the various schools of thought propounded by scholars of the Quran and Sunnah, like Abu Hanifa, Malik ibn Anas, Imam Shafi, Ibn Hanbal, Jafar al Sadiq, making *Deen* an order above *Madhhab*; the latter derives from the former. *Deen* is the essence and *Madhhab* is its derivative. If *Madhhab* is a river, *Deen* is its water! Not only does *Deen* transcend any *single* interpretation, it *cannot* possibly be *limited* to a single interpretation. *Deen* is mystical and *Madhhab* is an attempt to demystify it. *Deen* is rich poetry aimed at the heart. *Madhhab* is prose, aimed at the probing mind. *Deen* is commonly translated as the "way" or "path" {of life}, "obedience" and "submission". In the context of Islam, it is the way of life with God as the Sovereign, God at the center, God as the Source and God as the Goal. It is a path that starts from God and leads to God, and yet the path reveals itself only by God's Grace. It is a re-generative spiritual process in which compliance feeds faith and faith feeds insightfulness—A path on many planes of being and knowing, characterized by the 'willing' quality of the surrender to the Sovereign. The lowest plane of this path is the plane of 'Surrender in word' (testament). This is the plane of the Muslim {*Islam*}. The highest plane of this path is the 'Surrender of the self'. This is the plane of the muslim {*Ehsan*}. Between these planes is the journey of 'alignment' of the 'self' to the Divine; a journey with

---

54 Al Quran 65:2-3. The Message of the Quran, Translated and explained by Muhammad Asad

many planes of "Surrender in thought" {*Emaan*} to the Divine. The Divine being known by the attributes which It has assigned to Itself.

"*Deen*" shares its root word with "*dayn*", the latter meaning "debt". From this perspective too it suggests the nature of the relationship between man and God, moving towards a final reckoning with God—"*Yaumuddeen*", literally the day of *Deen*, richly the day of reckoning or the moment of the direct encounter with Truth.

The word Islam itself is derived from the root verb "*aslama*" translated "he surrendered himself (to God)" and its derivative "*muslim*" is translated as "one who surrenders". Other derivatives of the same root-word mean peace, harmony and reconciliation. "*Muslim*" has been used in the contexts preceding the time of Prophet Muhammad in passages dealing with earlier prophets and peoples. The first (chronological) use of the word is in Surah 68 verse 35 in the context of a parable that makes a distinction between people, who cognizant of God, live life conscientiously and those who pursue temporal gain, iniquitously. Muhammad Asad, who rested in Islam via Judaism, in his footnote 17 to Surah 78 reminds the reader of the non-denominational scope of these terms, stating that "it should be borne in mind that the 'institutionalized' use of the terms (muslim and Islam)—that is their exclusive application to the followers of Prophet Muhammad represents a definitely post-Quranic development and hence must be avoided in a translation of the Quran"[55] The spiritual muslim is not to be confused with the social or political muslim. Any one who has surrendered to God is a spiritual muslim. It is noteworthy too that the classification of the followers of Muhammad as 'Muhammadans' is a foreign construct. The term no doubt was invented to provide the 'muslim' equivalency to the term 'Christians'. Islam is the 'final cycle of revelation' amongst many cycles of revelation. All prophets are spiritual muslims. So are the Disciples of Jesus. The Quran relates the pledge of the Disciples to Jesus:

❖ فَلَمَّآ أَحَسَّ عِيسَىٰ مِنْهُمُ ٱلْكُفْرَ قَالَ مَنْ أَنصَارِىٓ إِلَى ٱللَّهِ قَالَ ٱلْحَوَارِيُّونَ نَحْنُ أَنصَارُ ٱللَّهِ ءَامَنَّا بِٱللَّهِ وَٱشْهَدْ بِأَنَّا مُسْلِمُونَ ۝

And when Jesus became aware of their refusal to acknowledge the truth, [he
asked: "Who will be my helpers in God's cause?"
The white-garbed ones replied:
"We shall be (thy) helpers (in the cause) of God.
We believe in God, and bear thou witness
that we have surrendered ourselves unto Him." {Washhad bi anna muslimun}[56]

---

55 The Message of the Quran, Translated and explained by Muhammad Asad, footnote 17 to verse 68, page
   1011-1012
56 Al Quran 3:52. As interpreted by Muhammad Asad.

Yes, in Islam there is a defined orthodoxy, and there are common practices and boundaries, fixed prayers, rituals and a vibrant concept of a fraternity, but a person's path to God is unmistakably direct and without intermediaries. The prayers and rituals, practices and boundaries are essential and indispensable aids to help stay and light the course. Yet, the connection to God is a matter of personal awareness alone. The state of a muslim's awareness is related to the level of his or her submission and is an ongoing process, never ending and never completed. The truth of an action is the underlying intent. Submission too is measured by intent, always known to God and truly known by God *alone*. Deen is the quest for the Master's assent. This quest is both outwardly inwards (an action purifying the heart) and inwardly outwards (a belief purifying an action), until the inwards and outwards have lost distinction. Outwardly inwards are those endeavors that bring us closer to God by our interaction with fellow creatures. Inwardly outwards are those precepts of faith that we cultivate and which then become the underlying motive of our actions. To be just, equitable, compassionate, kind, charitable, giving and modest must be both an intention and a manifested act. Our inner quest must and will affect our interaction with others. Truly "righteous deeds" therefore are inseparable from "sincere faith". Prayer and *Dhikr* are the innermost efforts to purify the heart, so that the heart may become the place of God, making room thereby for fellow creatures, until the heart desires no less for another than what it desires for itself. A person's stature or station of spiritual awareness is based solely on the conscientiousness of this quest. This again is known only to God and is not for the mortal to judge or dispute. Life is a journey with a purpose. Deen is the journey's light, its passage and its purpose. Any other purpose is simply the loss of time and opportunity:

وَٱلْعَصْرِ ۝ إِنَّ ٱلْإِنسَٰنَ لَفِى خُسْرٍ ۝ إِلَّا ٱلَّذِينَ ءَامَنُوا۟ وَعَمِلُوا۟ ٱلصَّٰلِحَٰتِ وَتَوَاصَوْا۟ بِٱلْحَقِّ وَتَوَاصَوْا۟ بِٱلصَّبْرِ ۝

As certain as a days waning,
Man faces decline and diminishment
Except he be of those in the pursuit of faith and righteous deeds,
And embraces truth, and embraces patience. [57]

The myopia of time

Our temporal existence is trapped in the illusion of space and time. We determine spatial co-ordinates by referencing the stars, because they are transfixed in the sky. Are they? No! The stars are *not* stationary. The stars too are moving! They *appear* stationary to us out of their sheer *distance* from us.

And what about the aspect of distance? How big is the Universe and how far can we 'see'? That depends upon where one is in time! Time, and not space, defines for us the physical boundaries of the universe. We only see the light that has traveled to us and light from outer distances has simply not had the time to reach us. Closer to us, lightning and thunder originate at the same place and the same moment in time, however we will experience the lightning first and the thunder later. What is a serial experience to us is a concurrent event. The stars we observe in the night sky may not even be there today and what we observe is their state eons ago; the past ushers itself into the present. Time itself is illusory or as science calls it, relative. In a spiritual sense the past, the present, and the future are not serial but the same moment in timelessness. We cannot fathom this concept and we are not designed to.

Our experience is designed to be serial; serial stimuli and serial responses; distinct causes triggering distinct effects. The effect always manifesting itself in due time, what we call the "response time". On a spiritual plane the just and pious action is rewarded the moment it is willed. The 'when' and 'how' and 'where' are a mystery to us. God (*Al Mujeeb*) never fails to respond to the sincere caller in a manner and time deemed most wise by Divine Wisdom {*Al Hakeem*}. A prayer is not a pill that provides relief as soon as it is popped. It is more like a seed. A seed must wait to germinate and the tree must wait to bear its fruit. Faith challenges us to be patient and hopeful, an effort that by itself is both genuinely liberating and intrinsically spiritual. Faith is to know with certainty that *just and earnest* prayers are always heard and *just and earnest* intentions and actions *always* find repose in the Truth and that Truth *shall* prevail {*Emaan*}. The measure of the fullness of time, relative to our serial experience, and the measure of the fulfillment contemplated in the Divine response, is fully and solely with God. It is not only outside the scope of our knowledge but beyond our capacity to measure, much less to expect. What better illustration of this than in the fulfillment of the prophecy of Jesus. The apparent triumph of his oppressors at the moment of his crucifixion was the illusion of its time. For ever it will be Jesus who, by the Divine Will, prevailed:

$$\text{وَمَكَرُواْ وَمَكَرَ ٱللَّهُ ۖ وَٱللَّهُ خَيْرُ ٱلْمَٰكِرِينَ}$$

And the unbelievers schemed (against) Jesus
But God brought their scheming to naught
For God is above all schemers[58]

The prison of dogma

Dogmatic views of God, Resurrection, Hell and Heaven lend themselves open to

---

58 Al Quran 3:54

notions of being illogical and irrational. However dogma is symptomatic of shallowness and not the concern of the spiritual seeker. The 'unknown' cannot be 'nailed' to a dogma. It is something that is first acknowledged and subsequently 'known' by differing degrees and levels, differentiated by the contemplative depth of the student. The Quran has repeated reminders of accountability, via the 'process' of resurrection and the 'stations' of Hell and Heaven, yet it does not give rigid definitions of these things. In chapter 101 verses 1-9, for example, the Quran describes 'resurrection' (*Al Qaria*). It starts with posing the question on behalf of the reader *"What is the Qaria? And what will illustrate to you the Qaria?"* It then answers the questions with similitudes. *"It will be the Day when humankind will be like moths swarming in confusion and the mountains will be like fluffs of wool".* Then follows the allusion to the station of Heaven, *"And whoever's (good deeds) will register in the balance will be happy and secure".* Followed by the allusion to the station of Hell *"And whoever's weight (of good deeds) does not register on the scale, will be engulfed in a spiraling loss. And what will illustrate to you this (loss)—Raging Fire".* These verses hold a message of unavoidable accountability, the weight of deeds over the material, the significance of free-will and the urgency of seizing the opportunity. The content and context are contemplative and entirely un-dogmatic.

In accenting the personal nature of the relationship between man and God, the Quran uses the Arabic word *Rabb* for God. This word *Rabb* captures, inclusively, the meaning of Creator, Sustainer, Nourisher, Cherisher, Guide, etc. The relationship with God is not static. His Face is every where, but He cannot be seen. He is *not* this and He is *not* that. One approaches Him and can never touch Him. A dogmatic concept of Him is a dead-end. He is more than we can possibly attribute to him. A belief that Jesus is the son of God is incongruent with the fundamental Muslim tenet that God "neither begets nor is begotten". Yet if adulation for God, or veneration of Jesus is the seed of the belief, it must flower to a belief that *all* humans are loved by God and all humans are therefore figuratively the children of God.

وَجِئْتُكُم بِـَايَةٍ مِّن رَّبِّكُمْ فَٱتَّقُواْ ٱللَّهَ وَأَطِيعُونِ ۝ إِنَّ ٱللَّهَ رَبِّى وَرَبُّكُمْ فَٱعْبُدُوهُ ۚ هَـٰذَا صِرَٰطٌ مُّسْتَقِيمٌ ۝

I [Jesus] come to you with a sign from your Sustainer,
So keep your duty to God and obey me.
It is God who is my Sustainer {Rabb} and your Sustainer {Rabb}.
So serve Him. This is a straight path' "[59]

---

59 Al Quran 3:50-51

It must not stop here either. We have it upside down when we say that God has the caring and loving attributes of a mother or a father. God's are the most beautiful attributes and from Him *flow* motherhood and fatherhood. All that is beautiful can be traced back to God and all that which is not, comes directly from the center of the free-willed self. A muslim-heart rejects dogma because dogma limits the heart's inherent inclination and capacity {*fitra*} to know God. The heart that has cleared the cobwebs of dogma is ready to receive God and God's Will. The presence of God in one heart is like in no other.

The thirteenth century, Sufi-poet, Maulana Jalaluddin Rumi's in his Mathnavi, ruminates, with poignant beauty, over the heart that longs to be filled. It is the heart of a shepherd, calling God and overheard by Moses:

> "O God lead me to you, so that I may become your slave.
> I will clean your sandals and comb your hair,
> and sew your clothes, and fetch you milk."

Moses, incensed by this blasphemous manner of prayer, shames the shepherd, "God is a Spirit and you defile Him by your ignorance!" Heartbroken, the shepherd rips his clothes and flees into the desert.

Moses was tuned to the shepherd's words not to his heart. Dogmas live in the mind and *not* the heart. In this life we are witnesses to the *actions* and *deeds* of our fellow human beings but have a poor insight into their *thoughts* and *motivations*. Moses would learn this lesson in the company of God's roving servant, Khidr. Moses had misjudged the shepherd and had done wrong by God, elaborates Rumi:

> Why have you driven my servant away from Me?
> I cherish not the form and the words, I cherish the inside and the state of the heart
> Because the heart is the substance and words are mere accidents.
> How long will you dwell on words and forms?
> A burning heart is what I want!

A common objection to the belief in One God and our Return to God revolves around the concept of Hell. Why would a merciful God have Hell? This objection only reflects the objector's failure to accept personal responsibility. It exposes an instinctive desire to be free of accountability. Accountability is the price to pay for free-will. This is by God's design. Hell and Heaven are essential pieces of this design. Hell is that destination (condition) which a soul consciously, proactively and consistently pursues and therefore brings upon itself. God does not wrong us, we wrong ourselves. Everyone is given the chance to repent and avoid the chastisement of Hell:

أَوَلَمْ نُعَمِّرْكُم مَّا يَتَذَكَّرُ فِيهِ مَن تَذَكَّرَ وَجَآءَكُمُ ٱلنَّذِيرُ

Did We not grant you a life long enough so that whoever was willing to reflect could reflect? And a warner came to you! [60]

Hell and Heaven are also stations of awareness. A misplaced belief that nurtures a false objective, perishable and illusory, will end in nothingness. Paradise is lost by callous disregard for truth and beauty (co-rooted with good). Hell and Heaven are of the soul's choosing. Hell exists so that God like a loving parent may warn (as He persistently does) against the consequences of wrong personal choices. Heaven exists so that God like a loving parent may re-offer us proximity to Himself in the house that we left upon our sojourn to earth. It is entirely in our jurisdiction, to heed the warning or mock the offer.

وَمَا ظَلَمْنَٰهُمْ وَلَٰكِن ظَلَمُوٓاْ أَنفُسَهُمْ فَمَآ أَغْنَتْ عَنْهُمْ ءَالِهَتُهُمُ ٱلَّتِى يَدْعُونَ مِن دُونِ ٱللَّهِ مِن شَىْءٍ لَّمَّا جَآءَ أَمْرُ رَبِّكَ وَمَا زَادُوهُمْ غَيْرَ تَتْبِيبٍ ۝

And We wronged them not, but they wronged themselves.
The gods that they called upon apart from God were of no use to them when the Command of your Sustainer came.
The gods increased them only in destruction. [61]

Submission to God is emancipation

Submission is a progressive state of being and as such is a journey. As a muslim's journey progresses, the meaning of the Quran itself changes shades from the literal to the mystical and deep. The Quran speaks to the person's spiritual condition and station. Believers will hold various levels of belief from the very literal to the very mystical. Both the literal and the mystical meanings have their function. The former, shakes the inertia and lights a spark, the latter, opens the Heavens. The first, removes the cobwebs of the heart, the second, fills it with love. The worship of God starts with the fear of death and the fear of God. It matures into the station of longing for God, where life represents separation from God and death bears re-union with Him. Fear is a necessary condition but it is the starting point of the process. God is to be feared for no other reason but for His holding us accountable for willful actions that are hurtful to His creation and to our fellow creatures. His fear must propel us to take stock of ourselves and to align ourselves with His Will, now! His Will is one of Truth, Love and Justice, for all. The essence of worship is love, and the hope of realizing Oneness. Fear of death and fear of hell become secondary and the fear of losing God in paradise becomes primary fear. Divine love and mercy is the sole

---

60 Al Quran 35:37
61 Al Quran 11:101

goal. Submission becomes immersion in Oneness. Substance displaces form. Says God to Moses in Rumi's Mathnavi:

> Kindle in your heart the flame of love,
> And burn up utterly thoughts and fine expressions...
> No need to turn to the Kaabah when one is in it,
> And the divers have no need of shoes[62]

Resurrection in Quranic terms, in the context of a single Reality, is a moot point. Death is a transformation of state (consciousness). The state of death has its similarities with the state of sleep. Sleep (God takes away the soul 6:60) relinquishes free-will and discards time, but it does not unlink itself from the knowledge and experience acquired by the awake body and the free-willed soul. Dreams replay this knowledge and experience outside the spatial and chronological constraints of matter and time, reshuffled and reapportioned though they may be. Death like sleep relinquishes free-will and expunges time. Like sleep, it cannot and will not unlink itself from the consciousness of the living soul (God will inform the soul of what it was doing 6:60).

وَهُوَ ٱلَّذِى يَتَوَفَّىٰكُم بِٱلَّيْلِ وَيَعْلَمُ مَا جَرَحْتُم بِٱلنَّهَارِ ثُمَّ يَبْعَثُكُمْ فِيهِ لِيُقْضَىٰ أَجَلٌ مُّسَمًّى ۖ ثُمَّ إِلَيْهِ مَرْجِعُكُمْ ثُمَّ يُنَبِّئُكُم بِمَا كُنتُمْ تَعْمَلُونَ ۞

He it is who takes your souls at night
And He knows what engages you by day,
Then He brings you back into wakefulness
So that the appointed term may reach its fullness,
Then to Him will you return
Then He will inform you of what you were doing [63]

From the perspective of life's journey, death represents a milestone just as the milestone of birth before it. Somewhere within these milestones human life acquires free-will and somewhere in the proximity of these milestones and outside of them, free-will is ceded to its Source. Everything starts from a single imperishable Source and will return to the same Source.

قَالُوٓاْ إِنَّا لِلَّهِ وَإِنَّآ إِلَيْهِ رَٰجِعُونَ ۞

Say: To God We belong, and to Him is our return[64]

God {*Al Baqi*} is the One transcendental Ground of Being:

---

62 *The Mathnavi Book* ii -7 by Maulana Jalalu-'d-din Muhammad Rumi. Abridged and Translated by E.H. Whinfield
63 Al Quran 6:60
64 Al Quran 2:156

كُلُّ مَنْ عَلَيْهَا فَانٍ ۝ وَيَبْقَىٰ وَجْهُ رَبِّكَ ذُو ٱلْجَلَٰلِ وَٱلْإِكْرَامِ ۝

All that is in (existence) is to perish, but forever will remain the Being of your Sustainer, Full of Majesty and Grace.[65]

Death is end of time, not being.

Time is the medium of learning. Past experience affords today's knowledge and guidance. It could be said therefore that a creature endowed with the capacity to understand the march of time also bears the capacity of free-will. Death is both the end of time and the end of free-will. Death ushers us into a new consciousness, unencumbered by the false ego of I, me and mine. Time is the chasm between us and what is truly Real. Death seals this chasm. Rumi cannot wait to be on the other side:

> If death is a man let him come close to me
> so I may clasp him tightly to my bosom.
> I will take from him a soul—pure and colorless.
> He will take from me a colored robe.
> No More! [66]

From the perspective of death, life is knowledge in the books of deeds. Materiality and time are life's grand illusions—illusions because what is Real cannot perish. What does not perish and is therefore Real (transcendental) are the thoughts, motivations, feelings, fears and aspirations of the free-willed soul. These are the defining attributes of a soul. The substance and the worth of life's journey are measured by the sincerity and the beauty of these transcendental attributes. Resurrection is the awakening to a new perspective, when 'substance' is other than material:

ٱلْقَارِعَةُ ۝ مَا ٱلْقَارِعَةُ ۝ وَمَآ أَدْرَىٰكَ مَا ٱلْقَارِعَةُ ۝ يَوْمَ يَكُونُ ٱلنَّاسُ كَٱلْفَرَاشِ ٱلْمَبْثُوثِ ۝ وَتَكُونُ ٱلْجِبَالُ كَٱلْعِهْنِ ٱلْمَنفُوشِ ۝ فَأَمَّا مَن ثَقُلَتْ مَوَٰزِينُهُ ۝ فَهُوَ فِى عِيشَةٍ رَّاضِيَةٍ ۝ وَأَمَّا مَنْ خَفَّتْ مَوَٰزِينُهُ ۝ فَأُمُّهُ هَاوِيَةٌ ۝

The Qaria (calamity, shattering)
What is the Qaria? And what will illustrate to you the Qaria?
It will be the Day when humankind will be like moths swarming in confusion
And the mountains will be like fluffs of wool
And whoever's (good deeds) will register in the balance
Will be happy and secure

---

65 Al Quran 55:27
66 Divan e Kabeer poem 1326

And whoever's weight (of good deeds) does not register on the scale
Will be engulfed in a spiraling loss
And what will illustrate to you this? Raging fire[67]

To die, like to dream, is to conquer time so as to bring the past and future into the present. The present anchors itself in the bliss of God's light (in the light of heaven) or in the burning agony of an undeveloped awareness (in the darknesses of Hell). Heaven and Hell are stations of consciousness and knowledge, not limited to or by the body and the material. They are defined of necessity in material and bodily terms, to make allowance for the limits of our experience and imagination, in the here and now of our worldly lives. The conscious spirit in heaven is in a state of sublime awareness. The physical plane is not lost to it. No possibilities are outside its knowledge. Nothing intrinsically good—the essence of beauty {Hasana}—is ever lost to it. Every kernel of goodness is both the kernel and its blossom. The spirit in heaven unlocks the mystery by becoming a part of it.

An undeveloped soul, trapped in the material realm cannot 'see' anything else. It has no knowledge of Reality. Heaven is a state of peace and light, with Reality laid bare. Hell is a place that the unconscious soul fashions for itself. Unable to discern Reality it is trapped in the illusion of the body, weighed down by the burden of its inflated ego. This unawakened soul cannot grasp the "Life-line of God" and it free falls into the vortex of emptiness. It lives the worst nightmare akin to that of a mother who has dropped her womb.

In Heaven, God's Countenance is the joyous light. In this light exists everything that is beautiful, because goodness is the beauty's essence. In Hell there is no discernment. In the darknesses of rebellious ignorance and callous disregard, light has the feel of fire. It becomes an 'unending' misery of a soul still trapped in the illusion of 'time'. The body that disregarded the spirit now becomes the fuel for the fire of its chastisement and purification.

In a sense Heaven and Hell, Body and Spirit, Light and Darkness are here and now as consciousness, as they are there and then outside of time. There is only one Light and there are as many darknesses as there are deeds and motivations misaligned with God. The distance from God, in ignorance of Reality and its Unity, bears the agony of hell.

Eternity is another plane of knowledge and being. It does not preclude other knowledge on other planes, such as our current plane. It folds the knowledge of our 'current' plane. This knowledge includes our thoughts, intentions, actions and other manifestations of our 'being' on earth. This knowledge is no longer anchored in the markers of time. It will be ours to savor or ours to regret but certainly not ours to disown or evade. The goodness in them will be magnified

67 Al Quran 101:3-9

and will become the living source of our bliss and the evil in them will be exacting, and the source of our torment. We can abate our torment *now*. This is the incessant call of the Quran. There is ready redemption through sincere repentance (or honest introspection, if you like).

Will there be mercy for those who denied human destiny and clung to their lusts and avarice? It is a matter only known to God. A merciful God He is and within His power it is to bring awareness to those who were wont to being heedless. While Paradise is a place of abode forever, His Mercy does not shut the doors of Hell for ever.

إِنَّ جَهَنَّمَ كَانَتْ مِرْصَادًا ۞ لِلطَّغِينَ مَآبًا ۞ لَّبِثِينَ فِيهَآ أَحْقَابًا ۞

[On that Day], verily, Hell will lie in wait for all those who deny the truth
a goal for all who are wont to transgress the bounds of what is right
In it shall they remain for a long time[68]

Only God in His complete wisdom knows the period of a 'long-time' in eternity. The burning anguish of Hell, repeatedly stated to a *living* soul, is itself a merciful reminder that the time for taking stock and making amends is not yet lost! Until death forecloses the opportunity to make amends (30:57), there is hope of forgiveness and mercy for the heart in awe of the Truth.

True blindness is of the heart

The Quran is a book of signs. The signs of the Quran speak only to the seeking heart. The heart cannot be coerced; it must want and it must be willing. An open-heart is a pre-requisite to undertaking a rewarding study of the Quran. It is the wakened heart that stirs the soul. The eye of the heart is the contemplative eye. Indeed for hearts reluctant or closed, blind to possibilities beyond the sensory sight, the Quran says:

بَلِ ٱدَّٰرَكَ عِلْمُهُمْ فِى ٱلْءَاخِرَةِ بَلْ هُمْ فِى شَكٍّ مِّنْهَا بَلْ هُم مِّنْهَا عَمُونَ ۞

Their Knowledge ends at the hereafter;
Rather, they are in doubt of it; Or rather they are blind to it[69]

God leads the willing heart to the peace of surrender:

فَمَن يُرِدِ ٱللَّهُ أَن يَهْدِيَهُۥ يَشْرَحْ صَدْرَهُۥ لِلْإِسْلَٰمِ

"So whoever God wishes to guide, God opens the heart to submission"[70]

---

68 Al Quran 78:21-23 as interpreted by Muhammad Asad
69 Al Quran 27:66
70 Al Quran 6:125

Faith replaces doubt, yet it does not enter through the door of mental reasoning or logic alone. It seeks the heart because it must reside in the heart. The mind seeks to breakdown mysteries into discrete components and acceptable causes and effects. It analyzes by disintegration. It must test and verify. It is therefore limited by what it knows, or by the extent of its knowledge base. There is no knowledge-base beyond death. The mind must therefore relegate spiritualism to the realm of metaphysics. It is relieved to give the realm a name that sounds "scientific", thereby hoping to one day unlock the mysteries of this realm. It must not submit so it relegates. The heart seeking to contemplate a mystery as a whole is willing and capable of accepting, embracing and submitting to the Unknown.

The Arabic Quran, the speech of God, is to be recited, heard, heeded and contemplated by the intellect of the heart. Beauty, peace and wisdom, these priceless intangibles, are received and valued by this spiritual core. The seeking soul shall be stirred and soothed, exhorted and shaken, broken and remade through this intimate discourse. The seeker shall return with a sharpened quest. The heart shall be scrubbed clean of strife and doubt; expanded in capacity and deeper in insight. Only those who are spiritually deaf, dumb and blind will not return (2:18). "Reading the Quran is like climbing a mountain. The higher one climbs, the further one can see."[71] A new insight leads to a new logic. Consider the logic of the shade and the sun:

$$\text{أَلَمْ تَرَ إِلَى رَبِّكَ كَيْفَ مَدَّ ٱلظِّلَّ وَلَوْ شَآءَ لَجَعَلَهُۥ سَاكِنًا ثُمَّ جَعَلْنَا ٱلشَّمْسَ عَلَيْهِ دَلِيلًا}$$

Don't you see how your Lord extends the shade?
Instead of making it stand still at will?
And we have made the sun its guide[72]

How wonderful to look at the shade as the gift of the sun! The very thing we seek refuge from, the hot sun, is itself the guide of the shade! Indeed where there is hardship there is ease! Such is the order and harmony of The Divine Creation!

Or to look at the sky, hoisted without pillars, not as something that is just there but a thing that reflects perfection:

$$\text{أَفَلَمْ يَنظُرُوٓاْ إِلَى ٱلسَّمَآءِ فَوْقَهُمْ كَيْفَ بَنَيْنَٰهَا وَزَيَّنَّٰهَا وَمَا لَهَا مِن فُرُوجٍ}$$

Do they not look at the sky above them?
How We have spread it and made it beautiful and free of all faults[73]

---

71 Yousuf Ali, *Translation and Commentary of the Holy Quran*
72 Al Quran 25:45, Thomas Cleary , *The Quran, A new translation.*
73 Al Quran 50:6

The honeycomb is not the hub of a chaotic swarm of bees. It is the nexus of the quintessential song and dance of devotion.

وَأَوْحَىٰ رَبُّكَ إِلَى ٱلنَّحْلِ أَنِ ٱتَّخِذِى مِنَ ٱلْجِبَالِ بُيُوتًا وَمِنَ ٱلشَّجَرِ وَمِمَّا يَعْرِشُونَ ۝

Your lord inspired the bee, saying:
Choose dwellings in the hills and in the trees and in trained vines;
Then from all of fruits partake
And traverse faithfully the vistas unfolded by your Sustainer[74]

The perfect form of the honeycomb is not an accident. It has been planned in microscopic detail, to deposit and enshrine the pristine amber and sweetness of honey.

How many of our Sustainer's gracious offerings do we callously disregard!

Insight and understanding do no die when the lights are turned off or when the skies are darkened by the thunderous clouds. They live and thrive in a seeking heart, standing sitting and lying down. Spiritual blindness is not the unfortunate loss of eye-sight; it is instead an insidious disease of the heart:

فَإِنَّهَا لَا تَعْمَى ٱلْأَبْصَرُ وَلَٰكِن تَعْمَى ٱلْقُلُوبُ ٱلَّتِى فِى ٱلصُّدُورِ ۝

For indeed it is not their eyes that grow blind, but it is the hearts, which are in their bosoms, that grow blind. [75]

---

74 Al Quran 16:68
75 Al Quran 22:46

A view of the sun from Baja California during an eclipse on July 11, 1991, with the moon sliding in front of the sun.
Photo Credit Credit: NASA

A Teachable Moment in the skies.

This is my Lord

At creation's dawn, confided Gabriel to man

Uninspired is the heart that is ruled by the mind.[76]

False assumptions negate sound logic

Logic and reason are great gifts to human-kind and are the guide-posts to our present journey. In our daily lives, we use logic and reason for self-validation, to guide our actions and to form the basis of our discourse with fellow human beings. But often, logical reasoning will lead to divergent conclusions. This is so because logic and reason rely on assumptions. These assumptions can often be un-examined or un-verifiable and may even be unfounded. The Greek-Mythology based its rationale on an intricate set of assumptions. If you assume that a god holds the sun in one hand and the moon in the other, then the changing of hands by a tiring god would result in an earthquake—sound logic, but questionable assumptions. A story, that I unfortunately cannot attribute to a source (because I read it many decades ago), reveals the significance of assumptions:

The owner of a tropical plantation was a typically tough and un-relenting task-master. Scores of slaves worked his fields and the owner drove them hard. Under his constant oversight the slaves worked like—well—slaves, without rest or reprieve. The owner's enterprise was just about optimal, working like it should, he thought, and it was time that he himself took a break. So one day, the owner had a brilliant idea. He summoned the slaves to his station, his proud remake of a prison watch-tower. After they had all gathered, he removed the false glass-eye which he

---

76 Translation of Allama Iqbal's Subhe Azal yay muj se kaha Jibrail ne, Jo aqal ka ghulam ho wo dil na kar kabool

always wore, placed it on the highest ledge on the station, and warned the slaves that in his absence from his station, (for an important mission no doubt), the glass-eye would continue to oversee their work. Then with the eye securely perched, the owner left and the slaves went back to work. By day's end when the owner came back to claim his eye, everything was like it always was. The slaves had delivered their daily toil and the owner was mightily pleased. Everyday, he would leave the glass-eye to watch over them, and come back at sun-down. No problems. And so it went on--- until one day, on an unusually early return to the fields he found the slaves taking a siesta. Angry and perplexed, he approached the eye on the ledge and there lay the explanation. Some-one had covered the eye with a hat!

Our rationality is colored by our assumptions and not by our genes. So it is that a conflict may often involve two rational sides, their stands and conclusions diametrically opposed. The conflict stands not from want of logic or reason. It stands because the starting assumptions between the sides are incompatible. Indeed one side's hero is the other's villain. One side's wrong is the other's right. If there is a single truth then right must always be right and the action of a hero must always be worthy. Logic and reason do not by themselves guarantee the truth. More consequential in the search for truth are our assumptions and their intrinsic validity. Just as external conflicts ensue from divergent view points, a person's internal conflicts may often be an affliction of confusing or ungrounded assumptions. Our assumptions can lead us closer to the truth as they can lead us further away from it.

The Pharaohs built magnificent pyramids to provide shelter and provisions for their afterlife. These gigantic edifices are a ringing testament to human prowess, ingenuity, engineering and organization. They provide proof-certain of a civilization, highly evolved both technologically and socially. The pyramids at one level are marvels of science and engineering. Yet at another level they are also a tragic testament to human mis-belief, nurtured by the chronic human propensity to innovate in matters related to human destiny and afterlife. The grandeur of the pyramids has survived the ravages of the shifting sands of time, but the innovative myths of the Pharaohs afterlife are brutally exposed. The wonder- status not withstanding, the assumptions on which the Pharaohs and their grand master-builders built the pyramids, stand negated.

Iconoclast

If there is one truth then it can only be reached with the negation of false assumptions. An examination of the essence versus the superfluous, tuning out the noise from the signal. The muslim starts his spiritual journey by the negation of all gods and the affirmation of The Absolute.

"There is no god but God"

This "*Kalima*" is the bedrock of belief and therein lies the spiritual and intellectual emancipation of the muslim heart and mind —A relief from dogmas and mis-beliefs. In its essence the *Kalima* is liberation from the personal prison of a spiritual quagmire. Nothing is rightfully worshipped except God. There is one Creator and everything else is God's creation {*Tawheed*}. We have a direct bond with the Creator and a common bond with all that God has created. Spiritual emancipation and temporal equality and fraternity are at the heart of the *Kalima*. The *Kalima* rejects dogma and embraces both the simplicity and profundity of Oneness.

And so it was with Abraham who found his Lord:

فَلَمَّا جَنَّ عَلَيْهِ ٱلَّيْلُ رَءَا كَوْكَبًا قَالَ هَٰذَا رَبِّى فَلَمَّآ أَفَلَ قَالَ لَآ أُحِبُّ ٱلْأَفِلِينَ ۝ فَلَمَّا رَءَا ٱلْقَمَرَ بَازِغًا قَالَ هَٰذَا رَبِّى فَلَمَّآ أَفَلَ قَالَ لَئِن لَّمْ يَهْدِنِى رَبِّى لَأَكُونَنَّ مِنَ ٱلْقَوْمِ ٱلضَّآلِّينَ ۝ فَلَمَّا رَءَا ٱلشَّمْسَ بَازِغَةً قَالَ هَٰذَا رَبِّى هَٰذَآ أَكْبَرُ فَلَمَّآ أَفَلَتْ قَالَ يَٰقَوْمِ إِنِّى بَرِىٓءٌ مِّمَّا تُشْرِكُونَ ۝ إِنِّى وَجَّهْتُ وَجْهِىَ لِلَّذِى فَطَرَ ٱلسَّمَٰوَٰتِ وَٱلْأَرْضَ حَنِيفًا وَمَآ أَنَا۠ مِنَ ٱلْمُشْرِكِينَ ۝

"When the night fell over him, he saw a star and he said, "This is my Lord."
But then when it set he said "I do not love what goes down".
Then when he saw the moon rising he said "This is my Lord." But when it set, he said, "if my Lord does not guide me I will be among the people who err." Then when he saw the rising sun, he said, "This is my Lord. This is the greatest." But when it set he said, "O my people I am innocent of your idolatry."
"I have turned my face to the One who created the heavens and the earth." [77]

A more profound meaning of the *Kalima*, espoused in the symbolism of Abraham turning his face towards God, is that *nothing* is transcendental and therefore *Real, except* God. Abraham's quest for God is the balance of *Fikr* and *Dhikr*. God is not what the mind can demystify. Anything *created* can be de-mystified, *not* the Creator. God is what the heart will accept after the mind has rejected everything that it can or ever will. "There is no God" is offered by the mind after it has quashed all fallacies. "But God" offers the heart because God is beyond the mind. The mind needs to find purposefulness in things around it. The heart needs God to find its *own* purpose.

---

77 Al Quran 6:76-79. Mohammad Asad. "*The message of the Quran*"

إِنَّ فِى خَلْقِ ٱلسَّمَـٰوَٰتِ وَٱلْأَرْضِ وَٱخْتِلَـٰفِ ٱلَّيْلِ وَٱلنَّهَارِ لَـٰيَـٰتٍ لِّأُوْلِى ٱلْأَلْبَـٰبِ ﴿١٩٠﴾ ٱلَّذِينَ يَذْكُرُونَ ٱللَّهَ قِيَـٰمًا وَقُعُودًا وَعَلَىٰ جُنُوبِهِمْ وَيَتَفَكَّرُونَ فِى خَلْقِ ٱلسَّمَـٰوَٰتِ وَٱلْأَرْضِ رَبَّنَا مَا خَلَقْتَ هَـٰذَا بَـٰطِلًا سُبْحَـٰنَكَ فَقِنَا عَذَابَ ٱلنَّارِ ﴿١٩١﴾

Surely in the creation of heavens and earth
And in the alternation of night and day,
Are signs for people of understanding;
Those who remember God while standing, sitting and reclining,
Contemplating and reflecting upon the creation of the heavens and the earth:
"Our Sustainer, You did not create this in vain! Glory to You!
Save us then from the torment of the fire" [78]

Abraham did not discover religion, neither did he discover God. He discovered his connection with God. The Supreme Creator, plainly manifested, to the discerning heart. The stars, the moon, the sun, the changing of night to day and day to night, these are plain signs (*Ayahs*) of the Supreme Creator and the Supreme Sustainer—they portend His mercy (30:50). So are the mountains and the plains, the cycles of spring and fall, sowing and harvesting, life and death. So are the seed and the soil, and the fig and the olive. So are the beasts of provision and the beasts of burden. These are a form of revelation, directed to all that are willing to "receive" it.

وَمِنْ ءَايَـٰتِهِ ٱلَّيْلُ وَٱلنَّهَارُ وَٱلشَّمْسُ وَٱلْقَمَرُ لَا تَسْجُدُوا۟ لِلشَّمْسِ وَلَا لِلْقَمَرِ وَٱسْجُدُوا۟ لِلَّهِ ٱلَّذِى خَلَقَهُنَّ إِن كُنتُمْ إِيَّاهُ تَعْبُدُونَ ﴿٣٧﴾

Among His Signs {Ayahs} are the Night and the Day,
And the Sun and the Moon.
Prostrate not to the sun and the moon, but Prostrate to God,
Who created them, if it is truly God that you worship. [79]

Abraham did not belong to a religion. He simply reasoned with his heart to realize that all creation flowed from God and therefore he belonged to God.

مَا كَانَ إِبْرَٰهِيمُ يَهُودِيًّا وَلَا نَصْرَانِيًّا وَلَـٰكِن كَانَ حَنِيفًا مُّسْلِمًا وَمَا كَانَ مِنَ ٱلْمُشْرِكِينَ ﴿٦٧﴾

Abraham was neither a "Jew" nor a "Christian" but one who turned away from
all that is false having surrendered himself to God
And he was not of those who ascribe divinity to aught beside Him [80]

Furthermore, submission is the natural order of the Universe. The sun and the

---

78 Al Quran 3:190-191
79 Al Quran 41:37
80 Al Quran 3:67

moon, the stars and the trees themselves are in perpetual servitude, doing what they are bidden to do; thus exemplifying their total submission. Man alone has the freedom of election. Man must elect submission and he will be tested in the election. In his election of submission, Abraham would nurture his awe, and then his friendship and there from his love and thereof his devotion to his Lord. This is the progression of spiritual "knowing" and spiritual longing.

The non displaceable passion—Purity

In its limited capacity and its serial mode of experience the human heart can make room for no more that a single loss, a single longing or a single passion at a time. It will move on in time finding or accepting a displacement. Abraham, as the prophets after him, Noah, Moses, Jesus, Muhammad, found this non-displaceable longing and passion for God's assent. The purity of their passion was sustained by the absolute unity of the Goal. The lives of God's messengers were lived by and for the purity of this passion. Says the Quran about the purity of this passion:

$$\text{ضَرَبَ ٱللَّهُ مَثَلًا رَّجُلًا فِيهِ شُرَكَآءُ مُتَشَٰكِسُونَ وَرَجُلًا سَلَمًا لِّرَجُلٍ هَلْ يَسْتَوِيَانِ مَثَلًا ٱلْحَمْدُ لِلَّهِ بَلْ أَكْثَرُهُمْ لَا يَعْلَمُونَ ۝}$$

God sets forth a parable:
A man who has for his master several partners, all of them at variance with one another, and a man depending wholly on one person:
Can these two be deemed equal as regards their condition?
[Nay,] all devotion is due to God [alone]: but most of them do not understand this[81]

Abraham would forsake his father and offer to forsake his son. Moses would forsake the riches of the Pharaoh's court, Jesus would forsake his life and Muhammad would forsake his home and heritage in the pursuit of God.

Abraham's submission was *not* an act of spiritual *conversion*. It was rather an act of spiritual reversion. As an iconoclast he swept aside the complex web of human innovations regarding god-hood, reverting instead to a Supreme Creator and the absolute. Abraham was before Moses and Jesus and Muhammad. Abraham was also amongst the "*muslimeen*". He was a *muslim* before there was religion.

Idol worship in its deeper sense is a worship of anything material or transitory. The obsessive pursuit of power, fame, pleasure and wealth is idol worship. The self, gorging in these pursuits becomes a monstrous idol itself. To 'worship an idol' is to cultivate delusion. The most deluding idol is perhaps the idol of self-

---

81 Al Quran 39:29

obsession. The soul which is part body and part spirit, the mix which makes us human, becomes spiritually deaf, spiritually blind and spiritually mute. Such a soul imperils its humanity. The 'seeker' and 'the sought' are inextricably mired in each other's weaknesses. (22:73)

What is material is confined to time and space, and materiality confines the seeker to the cage of his or her egocentric orbit. Spirituality by definition transcends space and time and self. It looks beyond what cannot be seen and touched but can only be 'known' by an inner sense. The material is a manifestation of the essence. Light is invisible until it strikes an object. We 'see' light when it is scattered by dust or gases and we 'see' its colors when it is refracted by a prism. Light manifests itself by the reflective or refractive qualities of other objects. We cannot feel light but we can feel it manifested when the living rise at dawn. We cannot hear light but it is manifested in the song of the lark. The obvious is a manifestation of the hidden. To be obsessed with the material or the obvious is to jeopardize the opportunity of contemplating the essential. To look beyond the material and the obvious is to look for the truth. Abraham's journey to surrender, started with his freeing himself of whatever was (and is) false. The sun and the moon are quintessential symbols of the material realm. Abraham saw them as manifestations with no independent stature of their own. He then turned inwards. His father, Azar, was his blood-line. But blood is of the body. The blood of the spirit is love. And above and alongside all love is the love of God. He then turned to whatever he owned. Surely, an able son, improbable in birth, is an infirm father's most needed, most wanted, and most prideful possession. Not so for Abraham. He offered his son to God, knowing that only God is the bestower {*Al Wahhaab*} and God only is the inheritor {*Al Warith*}; man truly does not own anything except what is bestowed by God.

Abraham chose the eternal over the temporal. "*La uhibbu 'l afilineen*". I love not things that set. This was the underlying belief that shaped Abraham's approach to life. He was giving because nothing was his to own. He was "tender-hearted"[82] because you cannot be otherwise when you are in love. He was patient and persevering because adversity causes the heart to expand; Un-afraid of death, because death was the door to the Truth and the lasting Union. This was the *Deen* of Abraham.

Abraham had moved beyond the illusory to the Real; from the material to the spiritual; from the personal self to the Divine Self. These are the terms of surrender as Jalaal al Din Rumi's nightingale learns:

> The nightingale says to the rosebush, "What is in your heart?
> Declare it this instant. No other is near; only you and I."
> The rosebush answers, "So long as you are with yourself, entertain not this ambition.

---

82 Al Quran 9:114

Make a special effort to transport the burden of selfhood out of this earthly abode."
The eye of the needle of passion is narrow;
know for a certainty that it will not admit any thread
when it perceives it to be of double strand.[83]

Pursuit of beauty—the journey without bounds

Deen is the pathway to unlocking life's hidden meaning and its transcendental nature. The pathway assigns to life a purpose and a direction. Along this pathway the purpose evolves into spiritual yearning. Away from God we are separated from our Source and the True Self:

$$فَإِذَا سَوَّيْتُهُۥ وَنَفَخْتُ فِيهِ مِن رُّوحِى فَقَعُوا۟ لَهُۥ سَٰجِدِينَ ۩$$

I have fashioned him (Adam) and breathed into him of My Spirit (Ruh)[84]

The Christian mystic of the fourteenth century, Meister Eckhart said "the Truth is native to us". The Quran adds timelessness to the Truth, having ingrained it into every soul, born, or waiting to be born:

$$وَإِذْ أَخَذَ رَبُّكَ مِنۢ بَنِىٓ ءَادَمَ مِن ظُهُورِهِمْ ذُرِّيَّتَهُمْ وَأَشْهَدَهُمْ عَلَىٰٓ أَنفُسِهِمْ أَلَسْتُ بِرَبِّكُمْ ۖ قَالُوا۟$$
$$بَلَىٰ ۛ شَهِدْنَآ ۛ أَن تَقُولُوا۟ يَوْمَ ٱلْقِيَٰمَةِ إِنَّا كُنَّا عَنْ هَٰذَا غَٰفِلِينَ ۩$$

And (remember) when thy Lord brought forth from the Children of Adam,
from their reins, their seed, and made them testify of themselves,
(Saying): Am I not your Lord?
They said: Yea, verily. We testify.
(That was) lest ye should say at the Day of Resurrection:
Lo! Of this we were unaware [85]

Spiritual yearning does not diminish living, it enhances it. It is fundamentally the pursuit of beauty. Beauty is not to be confused with glamour. Beauty is not skindeep. True Beauty is always unfolding, never static, and is therefore more a process than an object. The process itself purifies the heart nurturing sincerity and discernment, so that the heart in turn becomes the amplifying medium of beauty. God too amplifies beauty, calling an act contemplated in the quest of God's assent, as a 'beautiful loan'(*Qarde Hasana*) to God, to be returned by God with a manifold increase.

---

83 *Mystical Poems of Rumi 1*, First Selection, Poems 1-200. Translated by A.J.Arberry, pg 11-12
84 Al Quran 15:29
85 Al Quran 7:172. As interpreted by Pickthall. Referred to as the Covenant of 'Aalast' (Am I not)

مَن جَآءَ بِٱلْحَسَنَةِ فَلَهُۥ عَشْرُ أَمْثَالِهَا

Whoever brings a beauteous deed, he shall have ten-fold like it,[86]

The quality of existence depends on the quality of knowledge and it may be said that without knowledge there is no existence. Without discernment, knowledge remains untapped, leaving existence short of its potential. Spiritual yearning is the yearning for True Beauty which as the Quranic prayer teaches us is transcendental.

فَإِذَا قَضَيْتُم مَّنَسِكَكُمْ فَٱذْكُرُوا۟ ٱللَّهَ كَذِكْرِكُمْ ءَابَآءَكُمْ أَوْ أَشَدَّ ذِكْرًا ۗ فَمِنَ ٱلنَّاسِ مَن يَقُولُ رَبَّنَآ ءَاتِنَا فِى ٱلدُّنْيَا وَمَا لَهُۥ فِى ٱلْءَاخِرَةِ مِنْ خَلَٰقٍ ۝ وَمِنْهُم مَّن يَقُولُ رَبَّنَآ ءَاتِنَا فِى ٱلدُّنْيَا حَسَنَةً وَفِى ٱلْءَاخِرَةِ حَسَنَةً وَقِنَا عَذَابَ ٱلنَّارِ ۝

There are those amongst humans who pray
"O our Sustainer, grant to us in this worldly life"
And there is no portion for them at time's end.
Amongst them are those who pray
O, our Sustainer, grant us in this life beauty
And in the end of time beauty
And save us from the agony of fire[87]

Fire is the opposite of peace. Fire has the quality of rage and insatiability, the quintessential image of pride and self-worship. It has no control over itself. In its frenzy it devours indiscriminately. It feeds on the other to sustain itself. Peace has the quality of harmony in which the self cherishes the other. Harmony perfects itself in Unity and Universality. Fire on the other hand cannot exist in Unity and Universality because fire needs the other as fodder. The ashes that the fire leaves behind are pure and amorphous. They yield no fuel to the fire. Those who purify themselves by morphing into formless Unity are impervious to fire. Their souls are incandescent.

قُلْنَا يَٰنَارُ كُونِى بَرْدًا وَسَلَٰمًا عَلَىٰٓ إِبْرَٰهِيمَ ۝

And We said to the fire, cease and bear peace for Abraham[88]

It is the loving heart, soft and open, which receives the Truth of Unity. It is the cold heart, hard and closed that cannot embrace the Truth. The former embraces love with all its pain, the latter rejects love with all its rage. Abraham's father disowns his son for rejecting his gods.

---

86 Al Quran 6:160
87 Al Quran 2:200-201
88 Al Quran 21:69

قَالَ أَرَاغِبٌ أَنتَ عَنْ ءَالِهَتِى يَتَإِبْرَٰهِيمُ لَئِن لَّمْ تَنتَهِ لَأَرْجُمَنَّكَ وَٱهْجُرْنِى مَلِيًّا ۝ قَالَ سَلَٰمٌ عَلَيْكَ سَأَسْتَغْفِرُ لَكَ رَبِّىٓ إِنَّهُۥ كَانَ بِى حَفِيًّا ۝

He (Abraham's father said to Abraham) "Do you detest my gods? Abraham?
If you don't restrain yourself, I'll stone you.
Now leave me alone for a long time."
Abraham said 'Peace be upon you.
I will seek forgiveness for you from my Lord,
He is the Most Gracious (Hafiyyaa)[89]

Abraham embraces the pain that only love can bring and prays for his father:

رَبِّ ٱجْعَلْنِى مُقِيمَ ٱلصَّلَوٰةِ وَمِن ذُرِّيَّتِى رَبَّنَا وَتَقَبَّلْ دُعَآءِ ۝ رَبَّنَا ٱغْفِرْ لِى وَلِوَٰلِدَىَّ وَلِلْمُؤْمِنِينَ يَوْمَ يَقُومُ ٱلْحِسَابُ ۝

O my Lord! Bring upon me the conscientiousness of worship,
And among my offspring too, Our Lord!
And accept my prayer.
Our Lord! Shade us with your forgiveness; me, my parents,
And those who believe,
On the day to which is assigned Reckoning. [90]

The redemption of Adam

Who was Abraham? Providence chose to keep Abraham outside of history. He lives instead in human consciousness like Adam. Adam falls by his temptation to the fruit of the timeless tree. Abraham symbolizes the redemption of Adam, and he himself personifies a magnificent tree in the vast meadow of time, wise and old by its trunk, young and sensitive by its leaves. Steady, yielding, benevolent, patient, uncomplaining, anchored in the ground by its firm roots, free to dance with the winds by the willingness of its limbs. The subjects of history take the color of the historian's ink, the shape of his pen and the perspective of his station. Abraham is too rich and deep to need history's pages to save him from oblivion. He lives in all the major texts of scripture. The Quran mentions Abraham as *Haneef* (one in quest of the Absolute Truth and whose belief and worship are pure) and *Khaleel Allah* (God's intimate friend). Abraham finds voice in God's words:

---

89 Al Quran 19:46-47
90 Al Quran 14:40-41

إِنِّى وَجَّهْتُ وَجْهِىَ لِلَّذِى فَطَرَ ٱلسَّمَـٰوَٰتِ وَٱلْأَرْضَ حَنِيفًا ۖ وَمَآ أَنَا۠ مِنَ ٱلْمُشْرِكِينَ

For me [Abraham], I have aligned my being, wholly and truly, towards Him Who created the heavens and the earth, and never shall I be of those who adopt another object or being of worship[91]

And God does not wait for the Day of Judgment to declare Abraham's place in Heaven:

وَمَنْ أَحْسَنُ دِينًا مِّمَّنْ أَسْلَمَ وَجْهَهُۥ لِلَّهِ وَهُوَ مُحْسِنٌ وَٱتَّبَعَ مِلَّةَ إِبْرَٰهِيمَ حَنِيفًا ۗ وَٱتَّخَذَ ٱللَّهُ إِبْرَٰهِيمَ خَلِيلًا

Who can bear more beauty in his way than one who submits his whole being to God, spreads beauty and goodness, and joins the pathway of Abraham, the true and pure in Faith?
For God did take Abraham for a friend. [92]

Abraham is the spiritual man, the fundamental man, the beautiful man. Not by virtue of his learning, because he probably was not a very learned man; Not by virtue of his ambition, because he was not an ambitious man. He did not live in a gated or guarded house. A passing wayfarer could not miss him and food was always on offer, specially the occasional roasted calf. Every thing that he owned was probably always within sight and sound. Around him there was nothing out of place. Work and rest, need and offering mingled peaceably into each other. There were no 'dividing lines' between this and that or him and the other. He lived in an age where the day was measured by the sun and the months were reckoned by the moon. In a period when solitude in the depth of the night and the stillness of the stars, did not breed loneliness but a sense of a wider belonging, so wide that it left nothing outside. The cosmos was One.

Abraham represents the soul reposed in Unity. Anything outside of this Unity is illusory. The one who lives in Unity knows that nothing is outside of It. To love God, as God should be loved, is to love your fellow creatures. To love your fellow creatures as they should be loved is to love God. To know is to exist. To know the transcendental Truth is to exist transcendentally. To exist outside of the Truth is to be dispossessed, surrounded by emptiness, like a bird grounded in a boundless, open vacuum. There is no lift in the flapping wings, when the winds that give flight are lost to them.

---

91 Al Quran 6:79
92 Al Quran 4:125

Moon in orbit about the Earth taken by *Galileo* from a distance of about 6.2 million kilometers (3.9 million miles). The brightly colored Earth contrasts strongly with the moon, which reflects only about a third as much sunlight as Earth.
Photo Credit: NASA

The fact that we can place the moon and the earth precisely in their known orbits exposes the flawless movements of these bodies in their prescribed orbits. Doing what one is bidden to do is the essence of submission.

The Message

"All those who listen to me shall pass on my words to others and those to others again;
And may the last ones understand my words better than those who listen to me directly.

Be My Witness O God That I Have Conveyed Your Message to Your People." [93]

Revelation

The Quran is Holy Scripture. Not the first. But it is the last. The Quran, today in a tangible book form, started as and continues to be a recital in Arabic. The Quran was revealed to Prophet Muhammad by the Holy Spirit[94] (*Ruh ul Qudus*) or Gabriel, the Arch Angel, if you will. Muhammad received and recited the Quran in stages, during a period that stretched approximately twenty-three years, starting in Mecca in the year 610-CE . Muhammad was then 40 years old. The period of twenty-three years was an existential period for him. When the mounting danger to him from the Meccan establishment reached its mortal peak by the thirteenth year of his prophethood, he miraculously managed to break free of their dragnet to the safety of Medina. Ten years later, having prevailed in existential wars waged by his relentless enemies and having survived multiple assassination attempts, Muhammad the beloved leader of Medina would return to the acclaim of Mecca. The return to Mecca symbolizes the success of his mission, as it would not only coincide with the completion of the revelation but also with the wholehearted embrace of his message by the very people whose violent opposition forced him to leave his birth place. The pace and place of revelation was providentially measured. Providential Wisdom willed it so:

---

93 The last sermon of the Prophet
94 The same Holy Spirit that "strengthened" Jesus in his cradle. (2:87)

إِنَّا نَحْنُ نَزَّلْنَا عَلَيْكَ ٱلْقُرْءَانَ تَنزِيلًا ۝

It is We Who have sent down the Qur'an to thee by stages.[95]

The Quran is compiled into 114 chapters (*Surahs*). Each *Surah* is subdivided into verses. There are over 6500 verses in the Quran. Every day, 5 times a day a Muslim will recite, in Quranic Arabic, a Surah or some verses of it, several times.

The Quran is a meditative book. It takes root in the heart and unfolds in steps measured to the heart's strengthening. It cannot be rushed. This was true for its messenger and far truer for today's reciter.

وَقَالَ ٱلَّذِينَ كَفَرُوا لَوْلَا نُزِّلَ عَلَيْهِ ٱلْقُرْءَانُ جُمْلَةً وَٰحِدَةً ۚ كَذَٰلِكَ لِنُثَبِّتَ بِهِۦ فُؤَادَكَ ۖ وَرَتَّلْنَٰهُ تَرْتِيلًا ۝

And those who disbelieve say:
Why is the Qur'an not revealed unto him all at once?
(It is revealed) thus that We may strengthen thy heart therewith;
And We have arranged it in the right order.[96]

The depth of the message conforms to the capacity of the heart:

فَتَعَٰلَى ٱللَّهُ ٱلْمَلِكُ ٱلْحَقُّ ۗ وَلَا تَعْجَلْ بِٱلْقُرْءَانِ مِن قَبْلِ أَن يُقْضَىٰٓ إِلَيْكَ وَحْيُهُۥ ۖ وَقُل رَّبِّ زِدْنِي عِلْمًا ۝

High above all is God, the King, the Truth!
Be not in haste with the Qur'an before its revelation to thee is completed,
And say, "O my Lord! Advance me in knowledge[97]

The attributes associated to the Quran in the Quran itself are:

Glorious Quran {Quran un Majeed} (85:21, 50:1)
Bearer of wisdom and healing {Quran al hakeem} (36:2)
Mystical recital {Quran an Aajaban} (72:1)
Most venerated {Quran un kareem} (56:77)
Guidance for mankind (2:185)
Free from discrepancy (4:82)
Arabic Quran is the bearer of learning (12:2)
The Open Book {Quran in Mobeen} (15:1)
The Book of immensity {Quran al Azeem} (15:87)
Bearer of good news for the sincere believers (17:9)

95 Al Quran 76:23
96 Al Quran 25:32
97 Al Quran 20:114

Bearer of depth to the discerning (41:3)
A clear path to God (36:69)
Bearer of Admonition (17:41) (38:1)
Bearer of Healing and Mercy (17:82)
Inimitable (17:88)
Full of parables (17:89)
It reveals itself to the reciter in stages (17:106)
Made easy to remember (54:17,54:22,54:32,54:40)

Preservation

The Quran has remained fully intact and completely unaltered through the ages. From the Divine perspective this was pre-ordained:

$$إِنَّا نَحْنُ نَزَّلْنَا ٱلذِّكْرَ وَإِنَّا لَهُۥ لَحَٰفِظُونَ ۝$$

Without a doubt, We have, sent down the Remembrance;
And We indeed will guard it [98]

$$إِنَّ عَلَيْنَا جَمْعَهُۥ وَقُرْءَانَهُۥ ۝$$

It is for Us to collect it and to promulgate it (Quran) [99]

From our perspective, this may be credited to the tradition of memorizing the Quran and to its meticulous cataloging during the time of the prophet. The formal Muslim-prayer, *Salaat*, requires the Muslim to recite the Quran from memory. Five daily Salaats in numerous separate groups required memorization by many. During the prophet's lifetime, many Muslims had assumed the duty of committing the Quran to heart so that they could not only lead the prayers but also teach the Quran to others. Those who committed the Quran to memory were called *Huffaz*, literally "protectors". The tradition of memorizing has only grown over the ages. Today this number is literally in the hundreds of thousands. The *Hafiz* (singular of *Huffaz*, one who has committed the Quran to memory) is venerated amongst the Muslims as one of God's instruments for the Quran's preservation. A grand demonstration of the practice of the tradition of memorizing is made during the month of Ramadan (fasting), when during the course of nightly prayers (*Tarawih*) through the month, the *Hafiz* recites the complete Quran, exclusively from memory. The *Tarawih* serves as a formal recital of the complete Quran in almost every communal mosque in the world. The vibrancy of this practice is evident not just by the sheer number of mosques around the world where this form of prayer takes place but also by the rich

---

98 Al Quran 15:9
99 Al Quran 75:17

diversity of both the congregants and the *Huffaz* —young, mature and infirm, black and white, yellow and brown, rich and poor, standing shoulder to shoulder in aligned rows, all facing the Kaabah, drawing the Quran into their silent souls. The recital is straight from the heart of the *Hafiz*, where it has been committed since childhood by the Surah, the verse, the word, the letter and its intonation; a recital, interrupted only by unified prostrations and salutations of peace. Amongst the congregants immediately behind the Imam are backup *Huffaz* deeply tuned and synchronized, ever-vigilant against the slightest slip in the recital. Most will recite or listen with their eyes closed and the world blocked out. The recital is directed inwards and the heart is the listener.

The Quran is divinely protected {*lawhin mahfooz*}. This is the declaration that the Quran makes of itself (85:22). Every word is Divine and timeless. These words are primordial keys to unlock the doors of inner consciousness — A consciousness that must flow towards and into Universality and Unity. These words are light too, meant to drive away the many darknesses of a life centered on anything but the Truth. So that the book is not confused with the recited word, the physical book is called the *Mus'haf*. The veneration of the book itself, the *Mus'haf*, by its followers is incomparably unique. It is perhaps more comparable to the veneration of the image of Jesus by the Christians. Yet, it is the word _in_ the heart that is the Quran. It is to the heart that the recital speaks and it is in the heart where it has been and continues to be preserved.

Beginning and ending of revelations

The very first revelation (In the year 610 CE) took place in the Meccan cave of Hira in the Mountain of Light {*Jabl Noor*}. This revelation is now labeled verses 1-6 of Surah 96

بِسْمِ ٱللَّهِ ٱلرَّحْمَٰنِ ٱلرَّحِيمِ

ٱقْرَأْ بِٱسْمِ رَبِّكَ ٱلَّذِى خَلَقَ ۞ خَلَقَ ٱلْإِنسَٰنَ مِنْ عَلَقٍ ۞ ٱقْرَأْ وَرَبُّكَ ٱلْأَكْرَمُ ۞ ٱلَّذِى

عَلَّمَ بِٱلْقَلَمِ ۞ عَلَّمَ ٱلْإِنسَٰنَ مَا لَمْ يَعْلَمْ ۞

In the name of God, the Source of Mercy, the Compassionate and Merciful
Recite in the name of your Sustainer, He who created.
Created mankind from a clot
Recite for your Sustainer is the most Bountiful {Al Akram} Who taught by the pen.
Taught man what he did not know [100]

Amongst the closing revelations are the Chapter of Divine Help {*Surah An-Nasr*}

---

100 Al Quran 96:1-5

and the verse of the Divine Seal. The former was revealed during the last pilgrimage of the prophet at Mina. Tradition has it that the prophet understood that this revelation signified the approaching conclusion of his mission and therefore his life on earth. Immediately after this revelation the prophet delivered his "Farewell Sermon". *An-Nasr* declares that God's last message, timelessly enshrined in heaven, had taken hold on earth. The soul seeking the threshold of the gates of Divine Forgiveness and Mercy needs to journey no far than the depth's of its inner heart:

إِذَا جَآءَ نَصْرُ ٱللَّهِ وَٱلْفَتْحُ ۝ وَرَأَيْتَ ٱلنَّاسَ يَدْخُلُونَ فِى دِينِ ٱللَّهِ أَفْوَاجًا ۝ فَسَبِّحْ

بِحَمْدِ رَبِّكَ وَٱسْتَغْفِرْهُ إِنَّهُ كَانَ تَوَّابًا ۝

When with God's help comes the triumph
And you have seen masses entering the deen of God.
Immerse yourself in the praise of your Sustainer
(Take account) and seek His forgiveness
Mercifully Forgiving is He[101]

God assured Muhammad that he, who was gripped by fear upon the first revelation, was now victorious in his mission. In awe of the immensity of his mission and in tune with the eternal destiny of his message, he concluded the farewell sermon summing up his purpose in life and the prophecy of his message:

"All those who listen to me shall pass on my words to others and those to others again; and may the last ones understand my words better than those who listen to me directly. Be My Witness O God That I Have Conveyed Your Message To Your People." [102]

Muhammad joined his Master approximately three months after the Farewell Sermon.

The verse of the Divine Seal, received by the Prophet in the year 632 CE conveys the fulfillment of the Prophet's mission. The Quran had been enshrined on Earth. God, who in the very first revelation had declared to the Prophet that God is most Bountiful, had now delivered the Divine Bounty—the bounty of peace of a heart in submission—now and in the forever of Paradise:

ٱلْيَوْمَ أَكْمَلْتُ لَكُمْ دِينَكُمْ وَأَتْمَمْتُ عَلَيْكُمْ نِعْمَتِى وَرَضِيتُ لَكُمُ ٱلْإِسْلَـٰمَ دِينًا

"This day your deen reaches its fullness and the fulfillment of My favor to you
and I have approved for you the deen of Islam." [103]

---

101 Al Quran 110
102 The Farewell Sermon of the Prophet
103 Al Quran 5:3

The last verse[104] of the Arabic Quran, the conclusion of revelation to the Prophet, says it all. These parting words of God, left by the Prophet for us, convey both the stern-warning and the joyous-hope that is the Quran. We are to remember at all times that life is a test and a trust with a sure reckoning:

وَٱتَّقُوا۟ يَوْمًا تُرْجَعُونَ فِيهِ إِلَى ٱللَّهِ ثُمَّ تُوَفَّىٰ كُلُّ نَفْسٍ مَّا كَسَبَتْ وَهُمْ لَا يُظْلَمُونَ

Be conscious of the Day when you shall be brought back to God.
Then shall every soul be paid in full for what it has earned, and none shall be dealt with unjustly. [105]

Prophet Muhammad and the Quran are inseparable

The most meaningful miracle of Muhammad's prophethood is the miracle of the Quran. The complete delivery of which, in the face of overwhelming odds and adversity, took twenty three years of unwavering faith. He was himself frightened by his first revelation. He would be mocked for his message by the very people who regarded him as the most trustworthy amongst them. He would be severely persecuted by all but a few of his fellow citizens and clansmen. He would be forced to leave the city of his birth, to keep himself and his followers alive. He would be plotted and warred against in his new city. He would bury loved ones who had fallen in battle, and come close to falling in battle himself.

In all of this was the miraculous Hand of Providence. The message would be revealed to the Prophet in stages, so that he could purify and strengthen his heart. He was to live the message being revealed and both the message and his example were to outlive his time on earth—immortalized for posterity:

إِنَّا أَعْطَيْنَٰكَ ٱلْكَوْثَرَ ۝ فَصَلِّ لِرَبِّكَ وَٱنْحَرْ ۝ إِنَّ شَانِئَكَ هُوَ ٱلْأَبْتَرُ ۝

Indeed we have given you abundance and perpetuity {Kawthar}.
So stay steadfast in prayer and servitude to your Sustainer.
He who taunts and despises you, faces a dead end.[106]

God lives outside of time, so it may be said, as a matter of faith, that Muhammad was sent to live the Quran *and* that the Quran was meant to guide Muhammad. Muhammad exemplifies the Quran as does the Quran exemplify Muhammad. The Quran guided Prophet Muhammad in his mission and his mission was to deliver the Quran. Quranic revelations therefore have contextual backgrounds, but their message is *not* limited to these contexts. The deeper meaning of the revelation anchors itself in the present. The *Ayahs* of the Arabic Quran are a living message. The life of the prophet {*Sunnah*} is an illustration. He

---

104 Muhammad Asad cites the 'uncontested evidence' Ibn e Abbas
105 Al Quran 2:281
106 Al Quran 108

lived the Quran, in his steadfastness against adversity, perseverance against persecution, humility in triumph; with a heart that was always open to love, compassion and caring for any creature that came into his life. The Quran is very explicit:

$$مَّن يُطِعِ ٱلرَّسُولَ فَقَدْ أَطَاعَ ٱللَّهَ$$

Those who obey the messenger obey God[107]

Islam

What is the message of this last creed? This question was asked by the Negus (king) of Abyssinia of a group of Muslims seeking Asylum in the Christian kingdom of Abyssinia. The prophet's cousin, Jafar, son of Abu Talib spoke on behalf of these 80 Muslims—adults and some children fleeing the unbearable persecution by the Quraish of Mecca.

Martin Lings describes this exchange as follows:

> When they all assembled, the Negus spoke to them and said: "What is the religion wherein ye have become separate from your people, though ye have not entered my religion nor that of the folk that surround us?" And Jafar answered saying: "O King, we were a people steeped in ignorance, worshipping idols, eating unsacrificed carrion, committing abominations, and the strong would devour the weak. Thus we were, until God sent us a Messenger from out of our midst, one whose lineage we knew, and his veracity and his worthiness of trust and his integrity. He called us unto God, that we testify to His Oneness and worship Him and renounce what we and our fathers had worshipped in the way of stones and idols; and he commanded us to speak truly, to fulfill our promises, to respect the ties of kinship and the rights of our neighbors, and to refrain from crimes and from bloodshed. So we worship God alone, setting naught beside Him, counting as forbidden what He hath forbidden and as licit what He hath allowed."

Islam is a state of the sincere heart. It is an approach to God in this life and therefore a way to live. This 'way of life' would stand by the name given to it by God (Islam), and not by the name of Muhammad. God's guidance is primordial. Starting with Adam's displacement from paradise, God's revelations were received by a chain of prophets before Muhammad. He, Muhammad was the final seal and the final restorer. The Quran does not abrogate what came before it, although it does assert that previous messages have been deliberately tampered with, offering the simple proof that the Jews and Christians would have not had a divergence of views if this was not the case. The Quran makes no distinction between the preceding prophets; Divine revelation has taken different forms (such as the Divine Word becoming Flesh and the Divine Word

---

107 Al Quran 4:80

becoming Book) but its essence has not changed. The Divine Will, in all its manifestations, is One. Moses is not forgotten by Jesus and Jesus is not forgotten by Muhammad. There can be no 'abrogation'. Though there is a progression in the form and outward edicts of revelation. Progression is Providential:

$$ \text{مَا نَنسَخْ مِنْ ءَايَةٍ أَوْ نُنسِهَا نَأْتِ بِخَيْرٍ مِّنْهَا أَوْ مِثْلِهَا ۗ أَلَمْ تَعْلَمْ أَنَّ ٱللَّهَ عَلَىٰ كُلِّ شَىْءٍ قَدِيرٌ} $$

We do not abrogate any Sign
Or let it be forgotten
Unless We bring one containing betterment or with the same content
Do you not know that God measures out all things[108]

There is debate amongst scholars of the Quran as to whether the preceding verse was revealed in context to Quran itself or to the preceding revelation. The sheer forcefulness of this verse nevertheless makes its relevance transcend its context. All Divine Signs and Directives in all their manifestations represent the Oneness of Truth. Abrogation of Truth is not possible. A change to its approach is. Change itself is a manifestation of the *Qudarat* of God and its Wholeness. Likewise, forgetfulness of Truth is a condition of an impious heart. A change in the outwardly aspect of religious practice is merely a change in approach to the Truth and does not change the essential purpose of the practice. For example when the Muslims were directed to face the Kaabah, away from the far mosque in Jerusalem, though there was a change of direction, there was no change or doubt as to Who was being worshipped. The line of Prophets starting from Adam and ending with Muhammad has a united heritage. This continuity runs both ways and is evident to all earnest views. "Those to whom We gave the Scripture recognize the Quran as they recognize their sons (6:20)." The Prophet too is instructed to "follow the legacy of Abraham"[109] and is reminded that "truly you have a good example in Abraham".[110]

The heart is the seat of faith. The Quran, says as much ('God comes between a man and his heart' 8:23) and it therefore aims at the reader's heart. It seeks a willing heart because the discourse is intimate and personal. It conveys a warning with an un-abating sense of urgency as it conveys hope with a sense of affection. God allows and exhorts us to make amends. This is an aspect of His mercy. All amends must be made here and now. This is an aspect of His warning. Both messages are recurring and are delivered with clarity, consistency and certainty. It bears the Divine Word in Arabic, spiritually

---

108 Al Quran 2:106
109 Al Quran 16:124
110 Al Quran 60:4

congruent with the message of Abraham, Noah, Moses, Jesus and the many other thousands of messengers before Muhammad.

The Arabic Quran is non-translatable, as the language, its sounds and symbolism are inextricably woven together. For the believer the Quran is more than a book and the "translated" (more accurately "interpreted") study is supplementary to its recital. Although the basic meaning of the Quran is unmistakably plain, each verse is like a kaleidoscope. The message takes a new form, reveals a new dimension and instills a deeper harmony with each undertaking. Each verse takes on its own significance, unfolding new depths, richer messages and a growing realization, always drawing the Truth closer to the reciter. A process not dissimilar to the creative cycle at the fountain of Kafur in Paradise:

إِنَّ ٱلْأَبْرَارَ يَشْرَبُونَ مِن كَأْسٍ كَانَ مِزَاجُهَا كَافُورًا ۝ عَيْنًا يَشْرَبُ بِهَا عِبَادُ ٱللَّهِ يُفَجِّرُونَهَا تَفْجِيرًا ۝

Truly the righteous shall drink from a filled cup flavored with Kafur;
A fountain from which the slaves of God drink, making it flow with greater
abundance. [111]

The physical book of the Quran is compiled in an order that is different from the order of revelation. It is providentially so as the Divine message consistently "confronts time". Apart from the desire or goal of reading from the beginning to the end, the reader may directly access any Surah and start imbibing the clarity of its message and the depth of its beauty.

The two most recited chapters of the Quran

The two most recited Surahs of the Quran are the "*Surah Fatiha*" and "*Surah Ikhlas*". *Surah Fatiha* is the opening surah of the Quran (*Fatiha* literally is "The Opening"). This surah is like a compact between man and God — A compact drawn and offered by God to man in seven unmistakably plain verses. It is recited as a recurring preamble to almost all Muslim prayer on all occasions. Just during the course of the 5 daily prayers, this Surah may (some worshippers more than others) be recited as many as 44 times. Its significance is reinforced elsewhere in the Quran:

وَلَقَدْ ءَاتَيْنَاكَ سَبْعًا مِّنَ ٱلْمَثَانِي وَٱلْقُرْءَانَ ٱلْعَظِيمَ ۝

And We have bestowed upon you seven verses, oft-repeated and the Grand
Quran [112]

---

111 Al Quran 76:5-6
112 Al Quran 15:87.

The compact starts with the declaration of The Supreme Reality (stipulation of Fact if you will):

بِسْمِ اللَّهِ الرَّحْمَنِ الرَّحِيمِ ۝ الْحَمْدُ لِلَّهِ رَبِّ الْعَالَمِينَ ۝ الرَّحْمَنِ الرَّحِيمِ ۝ مَالِكِ يَوْمِ الدِّينِ ۝

In the name of God,
The benevolent, the Merciful,
Praise belongs to God, the Sustainer of all planes of existence,
The benevolent, The Merciful
Master of the Day of determination.

It is then followed with the declaration of personal and collective intent, man's part of the compact, addressed directly to God. We are to serve, selflessly and sincerely, a higher and common purpose. Not without earnest conscientiousness can we understand this purpose. Not without constant Divine help and increasing awareness of the Divine, can we undertake this journey besieged by ample trials and lined with the lure of recalcitrant wayside distractions:

إِيَّاكَ نَعْبُدُ وَإِيَّاكَ نَسْتَعِينُ ۝

It is You that we worship
It is You we beseech for help.

Surah Fatiha concludes with the personal and collective prayer for Divine Guidance and Divine Succor to help keep the compact. Not without earnest conscientiousness can we subordinate our own self-interest and self-gratification. Without constant Divine-guidance we are likely to lose our way:

اهْدِنَا الصِّرَاطَ الْمُسْتَقِيمَ ۝ صِرَاطَ الَّذِينَ أَنْعَمْتَ عَلَيْهِمْ غَيْرِ الْمَغْضُوبِ عَلَيْهِمْ وَلَا الضَّالِّينَ ۝

Guide us on the straight path {Sirat ul Mustaqeem},
The path of those whom You have blessed
Not of those who incur wrath and not of those who are lost in error

Within these seven verses lies the essence of the relationship between the two parties, unmistakably clear, plain, uncomplicated and direct. As God's eminent creation and His deputy on earth this is the oath-of-the-office if you will, with loyalty and surrender to God and God alone. Furthermore while the contract is collective, the accountability is several; with no arbitrator, intercessor, or any hierarchical or bureaucratic encumbrances. Even the state of conformance to the compact by an individual is a secret known to God alone, and is not the business of another human being!

$$إِنَّ رَبَّكَ هُوَ أَعْلَمُ بِمَن ضَلَّ عَن سَبِيلِهِۦ وَهُوَ أَعْلَمُ بِٱلْمُهْتَدِينَ ۝$$

Verily thy Sustainer alone is fully aware of who has strayed from His path,
just as He alone is fully aware of those who have embraced His guidance[113]

Equally noteworthy in the *Surah Fatiha* is the plural "we" and not the "I" in "*It is You that <u>we</u> worship*" and "*It is You we beseech for help*" and the plural "us" and not the "me" in "*Guide us on a path that leads to You {Sirat ul Mustaqeem}*", underscoring the fact that our relationship with God coexists with our communal and fraternal bonds. Good deeds do not happen in a vacuum but flow from our interaction with other human beings, with justice, compassion and love. God may be reached through the sincerity of relationships, just as our relationships will find their due and proper fulfillment through our sincerity of worship of God. The 'personal' God is first the God over *all*, *Rabbul Alameen*. The fraternity attributed to in the collective plea above, contemplates a wider rather than a narrower embrace, more inclusive than exclusive. As God's regent on earth this inclusiveness must indeed embrace all of God's creation on earth. Every life and every Divine creation is God's sacred Word.

$$۞ قُل لِّلَّهِ ٱلْمَشْرِقُ وَٱلْمَغْرِبُ يَهْدِى مَن يَشَآءُ إِلَىٰ صِرَٰطٍ مُّسْتَقِيمٍ ۝ وَكَذَٰلِكَ جَعَلْنَٰكُمْ أُمَّةً وَسَطًا$$

Say: "God's is the east and west;
He guides whom He wills onto a straight way
And thus have we willed you to be a community harmoniously centered
{Ummatan wasatan}[114]

The relationship between the individual and God and the resultant community is illustrated by the rich symbolism of the "Rope of God". "*Grasp firmly the rope of God, collectively. And break not into factions*[115]". Each individual must grasp the Divine Rope, directly and firmly. The firm grip on the rope is better than hanging on to another. One attaches to God *directly*, and not through an intermediary. The community is formed by individuals anchored along this Divine Life-Line. Togetherness comes from firm individual attachment to the One. The rope of Oneness is the connecting medium, not the castes or clans to

113 Al Quran 68:7
114 Al Quran 2:142 as interpreted by Muhammad Asad in The Message of the Quran
115 Al Quran 3:103

which these individuals belong.

And what is the Straight-Path, *Sirat ul Mustaqeem?* The straight-path is the direct and therefore the shortest distance between two points. The straightness of a path also reflects the distraction-free purposefulness of the journey itself. *Sirat ul Mustaqeem* is a creature's purposeful path to its Creator. The Quran addresses this purpose:

أَلَّا تُشْرِكُواْ بِهِۦ شَيْـًٔا وَبِٱلْوَٰلِدَيْنِ إِحْسَٰنًا وَلَا تَقْتُلُوٓاْ أَوْلَٰدَكُم مِّنْ إِمْلَٰقٍ نَّحْنُ نَرْزُقُكُمْ وَإِيَّاهُمْ وَلَا تَقْرَبُواْ ٱلْفَوَٰحِشَ مَا ظَهَرَ مِنْهَا وَمَا بَطَنَ وَلَا تَقْتُلُواْ ٱلنَّفْسَ ٱلَّتِى حَرَّمَ ٱللَّهُ إِلَّا بِٱلْحَقِّ ذَٰلِكُمْ وَصَّىٰكُم بِهِۦ لَعَلَّكُمْ تَعْقِلُونَ ۝ وَلَا تَقْرَبُواْ مَالَ ٱلْيَتِيمِ إِلَّا بِٱلَّتِى هِىَ أَحْسَنُ حَتَّىٰ يَبْلُغَ أَشُدَّهُۥ وَأَوْفُواْ ٱلْكَيْلَ وَٱلْمِيزَانَ بِٱلْقِسْطِ لَا نُكَلِّفُ نَفْسًا إِلَّا وُسْعَهَا وَإِذَا قُلْتُمْ فَٱعْدِلُواْ وَلَوْ كَانَ ذَا قُرْبَىٰ وَبِعَهْدِ ٱللَّهِ أَوْفُواْ ذَٰلِكُمْ وَصَّىٰكُم بِهِۦ لَعَلَّكُمْ تَذَكَّرُونَ ۝ وَأَنَّ هَٰذَا صِرَٰطِى مُسْتَقِيمًا فَٱتَّبِعُوهُ

Do not ascribe divinity, in any way, to aught beside Him
And [do not offend against but, rather,] do good unto your parents
And do not kill your children for fear of poverty
For it is We who shall provide sustenance for you as well as for them
And approach not indecency, outward or inward
And do not take any human being's life
[the life] which God has declared to be sacred- otherwise than in [the pursuit of] justice
This has He enjoined upon you so that you might use your reason
And do not touch the substance of an orphan
save to improve it — before he comes of age
And [in all your dealings] give full measure and weight with equity:
[however] We do not burden any human being with more than he is able to bear;
And when you voice an opinion be just, even though it be [against] one near of kin.
And [always] observe your bond with God:
This he has enjoined upon you, so that you keep it in mind.
And [know] that this is the way leading straight unto Me {sirati mustaqeeman fattabi uhu}[116]

Further more *Sirat ul Mustaqeem* is not a new path. It has been a path treaded by men of God before Muhammad. This is the path sought by and traversed by *all* prophets. There is mention of Abraham and Jesus on this path:

---

116 Al Quran 6:151-152 as interpreted by Muhammad Asad in The Message of the Quran

قُلْ إِنَّنِي هَدَىٰنِي رَبِّي إِلَىٰ صِرَٰطٍ مُّسْتَقِيمٍ دِينًا قِيَمًا مِّلَّةَ إِبْرَٰهِيمَ حَنِيفًا ۚ وَمَا كَانَ مِنَ ٱلْمُشْرِكِينَ

Say: "Behold, my Sustainer has guided me onto a Straight Way {siratim mustaqeeman} through an ever true faith—
The way of Abraham, who turned away from all that is false, and was not of those who ascribe divinity to aught beside Him[117]

وَمُصَدِّقًا لِّمَا بَيْنَ يَدَيَّ مِنَ ٱلتَّوْرَىٰةِ وَلِأُحِلَّ لَكُم بَعْضَ ٱلَّذِى حُرِّمَ عَلَيْكُمْ ۚ وَجِئْتُكُم بِـَٔايَةٍ مِّن رَّبِّكُمْ فَٱتَّقُوا۟ ٱللَّهَ وَأَطِيعُونِ ۝ إِنَّ ٱللَّهَ رَبِّي وَرَبُّكُمْ فَٱعْبُدُوهُ ۚ هَٰذَا صِرَٰطٌ مُّسْتَقِيمٌ ۝

"And (I Jesus) come) confirming that which was before me of the Torah, and to make lawful some of that which was forbidden unto you.
I come unto you with a sign from your Lord, so keep your duty to God and obey me.
Lo! God is my Lord and your Lord, so worship Him.
That is a straight path {siratum mustaqeeman}"[118]

And, yes, this road will offer its own trials and tribulations:

قَالَ فَبِمَآ أَغْوَيْتَنِى لَأَقْعُدَنَّ لَهُمْ صِرَٰطَكَ ٱلْمُسْتَقِيمَ ۝

[Whereupon Iblees] said: "Now that thou hast thwarted me,
I shall most certainly lie in ambush for them all along Thy straight Way {Sirat ul Mustaqeem}[119]

Satan {*Iblees*} who fell from Grace, disobeying God by refusing to bow to Adam personifies the "deluding force of self-centered intelligence"[120] that prods us to give in to our base passions, obscuring thereby, the path to the Source. Satan-hood encompasses our own false pride {*Mustakbir*} and our un-yielding self-interest that blocks us from recognizing and respecting the common lineage and Divine heritage of fellow men and women. Satan when asked by God as to why he refused to prostrate before Adam, responded, "I am better than he"[121]. Satan's arrogance, as any other arrogance, blinds the heart.

Just as darkness is the lack of light and 'coldness' comes from the lack of 'heat',

117 Al Quran 6:161 as interpreted by Muhammad Asad in The Message of the Quran
118 Al- Quran 3:50-51 as interpreted by Pickthal
119 Al Quran 7:16 as interpreted by Muhammad Asad in The Message of the Quran
120 *The Heart of the Quran* by Lex Hixon, p 77
121 Al Quran 7-12

evil (*sharr*) takes birth in the absence of active goodness (*khair*). Evil is not intrinsic to us. Only goodness and beauty are intrinsic to nature. Evil is a progressive disease of the heart that has lost its consciousness of God. Evil is insidiously proactive, cunning, enticing, conniving, luring; the neglectful heart will fall prey to its bait. Like cancer which grows from a single cell, evil can start with a single dark thought which can devour the soul. Satan, the degenerative being, and evil's foremost advocate whispers to a covetous heart. The heart in the void of darkness is only too eager to follow the lure of self gratifying whispers. Light negates darkness and God-consciousness vanquishes evil. Through Compassion, Mercy and companionship as Sustainer (*Rabb*), by Power, Right and Might as Sovereign {*Malik*} and as the Owner of all transcendentally Beautiful Attributes of Creation, Truth and Goodness {*Ellahie*}, God is One, Omnipresent and Omniscient radiance of the Heavens and earth; Only the blind of heart can live the lie of our independence or distance from God.

In his book, "*The Quran, a biography*" Bruce Lawrence, professor of Islamic Studies at Duke University, includes an illustrative interpretation of *Surah Fatiha* from Jalaluddin Rumi's *Divan-e Kabeer*[122]. Rumi, as only his heart can, hears a garden in prayer. The garden is innately aware that it cannot face alone the tribulations of its seasonal journeys; Only faith can sustain it in the lonesome-retreat (*Khalwa*) of its winter, and only Divine help can lighten the burden of its coming-out (*Jilwa*) in spring. The 'oft-repeated' *Surah Fatiha* sustains Rumi's garden as it cycles through the sea-shifts of its seasons:

In the winter pleads the garden: "*You alone do we worship*"

In the spring it says: "*And from You alone do we seek alleviation*"

"*You alone do we worship*" means: I have come to your door; Open the portal of joy, do not keep me any longer distressed.

"*And from You alone do we seek alleviation* means: From the wealth of fruits I have become broken. O Helper, watch me well. [123]

Rumi's garden is all heart, whose beauty transcends the seasons. It must not lose sight of its purpose in the frigid barrenness of its winter. It must persevere and keep its doubts at bay. In the bloom of its spring it must not slide into forgetfulness. The bounty of its summer wares, bear a burden too. Rumi's garden must not be lost in its seasons. It must seek, through sincerity, the fulfillment of its assigned purpose.

Sincerity is a quest, and before it is a quest, it is a thirst, much like the thirst and

---

122 Poem 2046
123 Extracted from The Quran, A biography by Bruce Lawrence, published in 2006 by Douglas & McIntyre, P. 120-121

quest for knowledge—never complete but transformational nonetheless. The sincere heart longs to cross the clear, if distant, horizon of purity—never reachable but forever beckoning. Through this endless journey it will progressively cleanse itself of doubt, seeking and projecting clarity of purpose and resolve. Sincerity is the approach towards 'single-heartedness'. God has not placed within any man two hearts, says the Quran (33:4).

The concise chapter of the Quran, one of the earlier revelations, called 'Sincerity' (*Surah Ikhlas*) is the clear horizon of the Quranic vision. Like the horizon, the four mighty verses of this chapter, project a meaning that is both inescapable and higher (and further) than its current vision. These verses hold within them the living essence of purity of belief and sincerity of purpose. It is noted in the Bukhari that Prophet Muhammad said "I swear by the One in whose hand is my life that Surah *Al-Ikhlas* is equivalent to a third of the Quran". This beautiful chapter is the second most recited chapter of the Quran (*Surah Fatiha* being the first):

قُلْ هُوَ ٱللَّهُ أَحَدٌ ۝ ٱللَّهُ ٱلصَّمَدُ ۝ لَمْ يَلِدْ وَلَمْ يُولَدْ ۝ وَلَمْ يَكُن لَّهُۥ كُفُوًا أَحَدٌۢ ۝

SAY: He is the One God {Ahad}:
God the Eternal, the Uncaused Cause of All Being {Samad}.
He begets not, and neither is He begotten;
And there is nothing that could be compared with Him[124].

Surah *Al-Ikhlas* portrays the compelling simplicity of Truth. God is not human or earthly. God is beyond dogma, beyond thought, beyond heresy, beyond the limits of our knowledge or imagination. There is no point in 'grappling' with God. 'Rest your mind', these verses seem to say, and 'open your heart and *contemplate* God's *signs*'.

These are spiritually emancipating verses, which shatter illusions for what they are. Reality will remain obscure to those who diminish God to a dogma or a sensory definition. Surah *Al-Ikhlas* establishes the unmitigated distinction between creation and the Supreme Creator. God cannot fit in the human mind. God must be found in and by the believing heart. Without the heart in the lead, the human mind would be busy cracking conundrums, spinning in circles, like a dog chasing its tail. And so that the heart may believe, the mind must submit.

The horizons of this surah, speak to Oneness in all its aspects. The Muslim must acknowledge Oneness *Tawheed* in the multiplicity of creation. An acknowledgement that bears a truly awesome responsibility: All creation is by God and God's alone. All mankind, the Muslim, the Pagan, the Jew and the Christian and all that there is in heaven and earth are God's creation.

---

124 Al Quran 112:1-4, as interpreted by Muhammad Asad

Indeed the practitioner of Oneness places a higher burden on himself or herself. If a father has three sons and only one knows that all three are brothers, his knowledge places the responsibilities of brotherhood squarely on him. This son must act with brotherliness towards the other two, because he is *charged* by knowledge. Are we then better off by being ignorant? Absolutely not! Ignorance is *not* bliss (as we sometimes say or hear), but it is an opportunity lost. We are all special creatures of One Creator. This knowledge bears mighty opportunities! A Single Creator sets the basis of equality, equity and commonality between the creations. The recognition of one God demands the recognition of equality amongst mankind and a reverence towards what we call Nature. Embrace of God, leads to the embrace of humanity, just as the embrace of humanity will lead to the embrace of God. The Divine Being is the Unity of Will and Purpose, Truth and Peace. Outside of this is nothing, but the fallacy of 'total freewill' and the emptiness of a callous or misguided soul. God is the Source and God is the Goal, of life's journey. If *Fatiha* is the journey's prayer, Surah *Ikhlas* is the journey's goal.

One beautiful meditative rendering of this surah by Lex Hixon in his work of immense love, "The Heart of the Quran" is worthy of reference:

> 'My beloved Muhammad, please transmit these unique Words of Truth as the purest essence of Islam: "The One Reality, Who calls itself Allah Most High, is peaceful Unity and harmonious Completeness. This Supreme Oneness has not been generated by any power more primordial, nor has any being ever come into being independent of the Only One, Who is beyond time and eternity and Who is the Single Source and Goal of Being. There is none equal to the One and there is nothing beside the One, for apart from the One Reality, nothing is."[125]'

Oneness declares that the other is not and must not be so different from the self. The external is not and cannot be so distant from the internal. The great Sufi Spiritualist of the twentieth century, Frithjof Schuon, who rested in Islam as "Isa Nur Al Din", distills the implication of Oneness with respect to our relationship with fellow man:

> Charity starts from the truth that my neighbor is not other than myself, since he is endowed with an ego; that in the sight of God he is neither more or less "I" than I am myself; that what is given to 'another' is given to myself; that my neighbor is also made in the image of God; that he carries within him the potentiality of the Divine presence and that this potentiality must be revered in him"[126]

There are three English renderings of this surah offered by Michael Sells. These renderings are based on the variations in meaning of the enigmatic Arabic word "*Samad*":

---

125 *The Heart of the Quran* by Lex Hixon
126 *Spiritual Perspectives and Human Facts* by Frithjof Schuon, part 1 chapter 3, P. 24

Say he is God, One
God forever
Not begetting, unbegotten, and having as an equal none[127]

Say he is God, One
God the refuge
Not begetting, unbegotten, and having as an equal none[128]

Say he is God, One
God the rock
Not begetting, unbegotten, and having as an equal none[129]

There is a rendering in English by Edwin Arnold that attempts to capture the rhythm of the Arabic Verse:

SAY: "He is God alone,
Eternal on the Throne.
Of none begotten, and begetting none,
Who hath not like unto Him any one!"[130]

In *Mathnavi*, I, Ch. 1176, Rumi's soul, with its separation exposed, aches to return to the Beloved:

O Thou Whose soul is free from "we" and "I",
O Thou Who art the essence of the spirit in men and women.
When men and women become one, Thou art that One;
When the units are wiped out lo, Thou art that Unity[131]

The Path to God has remained unchanged

Scripture does not change; Human practice of scripture changes. The "money changers", whose tables Jesus would overturn personified *deviance* from scripture. Jesus came to realign Judaism. Jesus had no quarrel with the message brought by Moses. He came to reinforce it. The chain of prophets is one. Muhammad is a link and the last link in the chain. Muhammad came to reinforce the message of Jesus and Moses and Abraham and Noah and Adam.

---

127 Al Quran 112:1- as interpreted by Michael Sells in *Approaching the Quran*
128 Al Quran 112:1- as interpreted by Michael Sells in *Approaching the Quran*
129 Al Quran 112:1- as interpreted by Michael Sells in *Approaching the Quran*
130 *Pearls of Faith* by Edwin Arnold
131 *Mathnavi I*, 1776, translated by R.A. Nicholson, Rumi Poet and Mystic, P. 33

نَزَّلَ عَلَيْكَ ٱلْكِتَـٰبَ بِٱلْحَقِّ مُصَدِّقًا لِّمَا بَيْنَ يَدَيْهِ وَأَنزَلَ ٱلتَّوْرَىٰةَ وَٱلْإِنجِيلَ ۞

He hath revealed unto thee (Muhammad) the Scripture with truth, confirming that which was (revealed) before it, even as He revealed the Torah and the Gospel[132]

Perhaps the most poignant present-day reminder underscoring the *reformist* aspect of the prophet's message is the Kaabah itself. For a pilgrim to the Kaabah, the symbolism of its *restoration* (as opposed to *recreation*) as the House of Abraham is inescapable. The Kaabah stands today (symbolically) as Abraham first stood it up, and so too continues to stand besides the Kaabah, the Station of Abraham, in memory of the prophet who built the House. There stands too on the north-west side of the Kaabah a small enclosure (called Hijr Ismaeel) delineated by a low semicircular wall, holding underneath its paved floor the graves of Ishmael and Hagar[133]. There is not a "Station of Muhammad" and neither is Muhammad buried there. Amongst the many doors leading to the Kaabah there is a "Door of the Prophet" —A fitting tribute to the Prophet who opened the final door. He wanted to be remembered for what he was, the last of *many* Messengers of God, faithful to the message in his own practice. The messenger who *restored* God's signs (even though some of his followers may have never received them before), one of them being the Kaabah itself.

The sincere Christian and the sincere Jew, states the Quran, cannot find it (the Quran) alien to his or her true faith and cannot resist its veracity except by his or her own duplicity. Divine Scripture has a 'native' quality, not lost upon the sincere of heart:

ٱلَّذِينَ ءَاتَيْنَـٰهُمُ ٱلْكِتَـٰبَ يَعْرِفُونَهُ كَمَا يَعْرِفُونَ أَبْنَآءَهُمُ ٱلَّذِينَ خَسِرُوٓاْ أَنفُسَهُمْ فَهُمْ لَا يُؤْمِنُونَ ۞

Those unto whom We gave the Scripture recognize (this revelation) as they recognize their sons.
Those who ruin their own souls will not believe.[134]

One of the biggest dogmas that divide the three monotheistic religions is related to Mary and her son Jesus. So what does the Quran say about Mary, mother of Jesus? The Negus too was curious. Jafar would then recite from the chapter of the Quran named after Mary, including this reference to her:

---

132 Al Quran (3:3) as interpreted by Pickthall
133 Hajar in Arabic
134 Al Quran 6:20

$$وَاذْكُرْ فِي الْكِتَابِ مَرْيَمَ إِذِ انتَبَذَتْ مِنْ أَهْلِهَا مَكَانًا شَرْقِيًّا ۝ فَاتَّخَذَتْ مِن دُونِهِمْ حِجَابًا$$

$$فَأَرْسَلْنَا إِلَيْهَا رُوحَنَا فَتَمَثَّلَ لَهَا بَشَرًا سَوِيًّا ۝ قَالَتْ إِنِّي أَعُوذُ بِالرَّحْمَٰنِ مِنكَ إِن كُنتَ تَقِيًّا$$

$$۝ قَالَ إِنَّمَا أَنَا رَسُولُ رَبِّكِ لِأَهَبَ لَكِ غُلَامًا زَكِيًّا ۝ قَالَتْ أَنَّىٰ يَكُونُ لِي غُلَامٌ وَلَمْ$$

$$يَمْسَسْنِي بَشَرٌ وَلَمْ أَكُ بَغِيًّا ۝ قَالَ كَذَٰلِكِ قَالَ رَبُّكِ هُوَ عَلَيَّ هَيِّنٌ ۖ وَلِنَجْعَلَهُ آيَةً لِّلنَّاسِ$$

$$وَرَحْمَةً مِّنَّا ۚ وَكَانَ أَمْرًا مَّقْضِيًّا ۝$$

Reflect on the record of Mary.
She withdrew from her family, into a solitary retreat to an eastern abode.
We then sent to her Our Spirit in the form of a perfect man.
She said: "May the Source of Mercy protect me from you, be you conscious of Him".
Replied (the Spirit) "I am but a messenger from your Sustainer, to bestow upon you a pure and perfect son."
Said she: "How can I have a son when no man has ever touched me and I am not unchaste".
Said he: "Thus it is" and your Sustainer conveys,
"It is easy for Me; and We intend to make him a sign for mankind and mercy from Us.
This act has been ordained"[135]

It has been said that upon hearing the Quranic recitation, the Negus welled up with tears, drew a line on the floor with his regal staff and said "Between your religion and ours there is no more difference than this line".

The Quran too records earnest tears welling up in the eyes of sincere people, not blinded by arrogance —priests and monks amongst them— when they hear the Recital:

$$وَإِذَا سَمِعُوا مَا أُنزِلَ إِلَى الرَّسُولِ تَرَىٰ أَعْيُنَهُمْ تَفِيضُ مِنَ الدَّمْعِ مِمَّا عَرَفُوا مِنَ الْحَقِّ$$

$$يَقُولُونَ رَبَّنَا آمَنَّا فَاكْتُبْنَا مَعَ الشَّاهِدِينَ ۝$$

And when they listen to the revelation received by the Messenger, you will see their eyes overflowing with tears, for they recognize the truth: They pray: "Our Sustainer! we believe; note us as among the witnesses.[136]

Does the Quran warn against the deviant practice of some Christians? Yes it certainly does:

---

135 Al Quran 19:16-21
136 Al Quran 5:83

يَـٰٓأَهْلَ ٱلْكِتَـٰبِ لَا تَغْلُوا۟ فِى دِينِكُمْ وَلَا تَقُولُوا۟ عَلَى ٱللَّهِ إِلَّا ٱلْحَقَّ إِنَّمَا ٱلْمَسِيحُ عِيسَى
ٱبْنُ مَرْيَمَ رَسُولُ ٱللَّهِ وَكَلِمَتُهُۥٓ أَلْقَىٰهَآ إِلَىٰ مَرْيَمَ وَرُوحٌ مِّنْهُ فَـَٔامِنُوا۟ بِٱللَّهِ وَرُسُلِهِۦ وَلَا
تَقُولُوا۟ ثَلَـٰثَةٌ ٱنتَهُوا۟ خَيْرًا لَّكُمْ إِنَّمَا ٱللَّهُ إِلَـٰهٌ وَٰحِدٌ سُبْحَـٰنَهُۥٓ أَن يَكُونَ لَهُۥ وَلَدٌ لَّهُۥ مَا
فِى ٱلسَّمَـٰوَٰتِ وَمَا فِى ٱلْأَرْضِ وَكَفَىٰ بِٱللَّهِ وَكِيلًا ﴿١٧١﴾

O People of the Scripture!
Do not exaggerate in your deen nor utter aught concerning God save the truth.
The Messiah, Jesus son of Mary, was only a messenger of God, and His word
which He conveyed unto Mary, and a Spirit from Him.
So believe in God and His messengers, and say not "Three" - Cease!
(It is) better for you! -
God is only One God.
Far is it removed from His Transcendent Majesty that He should have a son.
His is all that is in the heavens and all that is in the earth.
And God is sufficient as Defender {Wa kafa billahi Wakeela}. [137]

Though the dogma of Trinity is fundamentally repugnant to Islamic belief in the Oneness of God, noteworthy is the implicit message of tolerance in last of the preceding verses. '*God is sufficient as Defender {Wakeel}*'. The Quran does not exhort the believer to launch a 'crusade' against Christianity. A false-belief attributed to God is a dispute between God and the holder of the belief. A 'Muslim' cannot be so presumptuous as to believe that he or she is either required to or possesses the capacity to 'defend' God. God is his Own defender and trustee and a muslim's primary pre-occupation is to purify the Throne of God within the heart. The muslim shuns dogma, so that essence is pursued. The essence being that there is no other god but God. The idols to be purged are the idols *within* one's own heart.

The Quran holds Mary and Jesus in profound reverence, as amongst the closest to God. Mary, the blessed virgin is ranked highest amongst women, by God:

وَإِذْ قَالَتِ ٱلْمَلَـٰٓئِكَةُ يَـٰمَرْيَمُ إِنَّ ٱللَّهَ ٱصْطَفَىٰكِ وَطَهَّرَكِ وَٱصْطَفَىٰكِ عَلَىٰ نِسَآءِ ٱلْعَـٰلَمِينَ

And Lo! The angels said:
'O Mary Behold, God has elected you, and made you pure, and chosen you to be
foremost amongst all women[138].

And her son, God's chosen messenger, was given "clear signs" and

---

137 Al Quran 4 :171 as interpreted by Pickthall
138 Al Quran 3:42

"strengthened with the holy Spirit"[139], and spoke the word of God right from the cradle:

إِذْ قَالَتِ ٱلْمَلَـٰٓئِكَةُ يَـٰمَرْيَمُ إِنَّ ٱللَّهَ يُبَشِّرُكِ بِكَلِمَةٍ مِّنْهُ ٱسْمُهُ ٱلْمَسِيحُ عِيسَى ٱبْنُ مَرْيَمَ وَجِيهًا فِى ٱلدُّنْيَا وَٱلْـَٔاخِرَةِ وَمِنَ ٱلْمُقَرَّبِينَ ﴿٤٥﴾ وَيُكَلِّمُ ٱلنَّاسَ فِى ٱلْمَهْدِ وَكَهْلًا وَمِنَ ٱلصَّـٰلِحِينَ ﴿٤٦﴾

Lo the angels said:
"O Mary! Behold, God sends thee glad tiding, through a word from Him,
[of a son] who shall become known as Christ Jesus, son of Mary,
of great honor in this world and in the life to come
and [shall be] of those who are drawn near to God.
And he shall speak unto men in his cradle, and as a grown man, and shall be of the righteous."[140]

God has sent the signs of Truth through many messengers and in many ways. The signs change but the Truth does not. The same "Holy Spirit" that strengthened Jesus brought the revelation to Muhammad

تِلْكَ ءَايَـٰتُ ٱللَّهِ نَتْلُوهَا عَلَيْكَ بِٱلْحَقِّ وَإِنَّكَ لَمِنَ ٱلْمُرْسَلِينَ ﴿٢٥٢﴾ ۞ تِلْكَ ٱلرُّسُلُ فَضَّلْنَا بَعْضَهُمْ عَلَىٰ بَعْضٍ مِّنْهُم مَّن كَلَّمَ ٱللَّهُ وَرَفَعَ بَعْضَهُمْ دَرَجَـٰتٍ وَءَاتَيْنَا عِيسَى ٱبْنَ مَرْيَمَ ٱلْبَيِّنَـٰتِ وَأَيَّدْنَـٰهُ بِرُوحِ ٱلْقُدُسِ وَلَوْ شَآءَ ٱللَّهُ مَا ٱقْتَتَلَ ٱلَّذِينَ مِنۢ بَعْدِهِم مِّنۢ بَعْدِ مَا جَآءَتْهُمُ ٱلْبَيِّنَـٰتُ وَلَـٰكِنِ ٱخْتَلَفُوا۟ فَمِنْهُم مَّنْ ءَامَنَ وَمِنْهُم مَّن كَفَرَ وَلَوْ شَآءَ ٱللَّهُ مَا ٱقْتَتَلُوا۟ وَلَـٰكِنَّ ٱللَّهَ يَفْعَلُ مَا يُرِيدُ ﴿٢٥٣﴾

These are the signs of God which We recite to you (Muhammad) with Truth, and indeed you are from amongst the messengers;
Of messengers, some have We endowed above others,
And amongst them some to whom God spoke,
And some of them He raised in rank;
And We gave Jesus, son of Mary, clear proofs
And We supported him with the holy Spirit.
And if God had so willed it, those after them would not have fought one another after the clear proofs had come to them.
But they differed, some of them believing and some disbelieving.
And if God had so willed it, they would not have fought one with another; but God acts by what He wills [141]

---

139 Al Quran 2:253 and 2:87
140 Al Quran 3:45-46, as interpreted by Muhammad Asad

قُلْ نَزَّلَهُ رُوحُ ٱلْقُدُسِ مِن رَّبِّكَ بِٱلْحَقِّ لِيُثَبِّتَ ٱلَّذِينَ ءَامَنُوا۟ وَهُدًى وَبُشْرَىٰ لِلْمُسْلِمِينَ

Say, the Holy Spirit has brought the revelation from thy Lord in Truth,
In order to strengthen those who believe,
And as a Guide and Glad Tidings to those who submit to God[142]

God's messengers walk and show the path to God. As messengers they have not failed. It is by Divine Will, that men will fight each other over the meaning of the Message. The Absolute Truth does by definition stands on itself. It cannot ever be in danger. It is the heart that is in danger of missing it. Prophets are leaders of men, but it is between man and God that trust is kept or broken. Islam is the tryst between the inner heart and God. The same was conveyed to the prophet. He was not to be concerned with the sincerity of those who professed to the faith:

مَّن يُطِعِ ٱلرَّسُولَ فَقَدْ أَطَاعَ ٱللَّهَ ۖ وَمَن تَوَلَّىٰ فَمَآ أَرْسَلْنَٰكَ عَلَيْهِمْ حَفِيظًا ۞ وَيَقُولُونَ
طَاعَةٌ فَإِذَا بَرَزُوا۟ مِنْ عِندِكَ بَيَّتَ طَآئِفَةٌ مِّنْهُمْ غَيْرَ ٱلَّذِى تَقُولُ ۖ وَٱللَّهُ يَكْتُبُ مَا يُبَيِّتُونَ
فَأَعْرِضْ عَنْهُمْ وَتَوَكَّلْ عَلَى ٱللَّهِ ۚ وَكَفَىٰ بِٱللَّهِ وَكِيلًا ۞

Those who obey the messenger obey God,
And as for those who turn away,
We have not sent you (Muhammad pbuh) as a guard over them.
They profess obedience but when they depart from your presence, a party of
them, spend the night contemplating other than what thou say.
And God records what they contemplate
So let them be and put your trust in God
Sufficient is God as Guardian {Wakeel}.[143]

Stories in the Quran

The Arabic Quran reveals many stories and many parables. The stories of the Arabic Quran, specially the ones with a biblical context were revealed not as a single narrative, but as nuggets, on an 'as-needed' basis. These stories are the common fabric of all Scripture, though heretofore generally unknown to the Arabs. Some of these nuggets were timed to prepare the Prophet to answer questions (mostly posed to him by the Jews and Christians of the time). They therefore also served to dispel innovative dogmas that had taken hold (especially in relation to Mary and Jesus) and the resultant strife, ensuing from

141 Al Quran 2:252-253
142 Al Quran 16:102
143 Al Quran 4:80-81

and between the custodians of earlier scriptures. Other nuggets, recounting the rejection of earlier prophets, convey guidance and solace to the Prophet who faced his own early setbacks and rejection. For all these reasons and more, these nuggets are richly meditative and hold deep 'inner' meanings. For these very reasons alone, (leaving aside the Story Teller's vantage Seat—being First and Last; Hidden and Manifest), the Quran is unlike any other narrative text. A narrative account has chronology and continuity. The Quran on the other hand deemphasizes and even confronts time and tells its stories in the continuity of a *sea of signs* and the backdrop of the ever present Divine Will—all nuggets play out the Divine Will. Even the beautiful story of Joseph, though a narrative with detail and chronology, turns time from back to front. Here the chronology of the events unfolds from Joseph's dream. The dream is the Divine Plan, preordained and therefore not anchored in time. The substance of the story is the dream itself. Joseph's story seems to be telling us that life is neither accidental nor mundane. Every result is 'miraculous' in as much, even though it is freely willed, it moves us closer to a pre-determined end. Break the prison of time to sense an aspect of 'inevitability' which is attached to us and which is far more real than any aspect of incredibility that we attach to the mystery in these stories. God never fails to guide those who seek and follow His guidance. What is miraculous _is_ spiritually possible.

These scattered nuggets of narration become remembrances and in some inexplicable way they draw us in, bridging the chasm of time and dissipating the remoteness of our spiritual ancestors. Time takes the spatial form of a moving caravan to which we all belong.

These stories cannot be retold in mortal words, even though they have and will inspire a thousand Mathnavis. What can one really say of Divine Words? The mortal wordsmith can only scoop a vanishing palm-full from a running stream. And what if one were to reach the Sea? Mortal words cannot fold the Sea:

$$\text{قُل لَّوْ كَانَ ٱلْبَحْرُ مِدَادًا لِّكَلِمَٰتِ رَبِّى لَنَفِدَ ٱلْبَحْرُ قَبْلَ أَن تَنفَدَ كَلِمَٰتُ رَبِّى وَلَوْ جِئْنَا بِمِثْلِهِۦ مَدَدًا ۝}$$

Say: if the ocean were ink for the Words of my Sustainer
The ocean would exhaust before the Words of my Sustainer are exhausted, even if
We add another ocean to supplement[144]

Only the heart can fold the Sea unto itself, and unto its own measure.

Though these stories answered questions posed to the Prophet and as such have an outward meaning that dispel and refute man-made dogmas, they also

---

144 Al Quran 18:109

have an inner meaning. The outer meaning is for those who were (and those who still are) testing the Prophet's veracity. The inner meaning is for those who believe in God and His Messenger and hunger for Divine guidance and mercy:

$$لَقَدْ كَانَ فِى قَصَصِهِمْ عِبْرَةٌ لِّأُوْلِى ٱلْأَلْبَـٰبِ ۗ مَا كَانَ حَدِيثًا يُفْتَرَىٰ وَلَـٰكِن تَصْدِيقَ$$

$$ٱلَّذِى بَيْنَ يَدَيْهِ وَتَفْصِيلَ كُلِّ شَىْءٍ وَهُدًى وَرَحْمَةً لِّقَوْمٍ يُؤْمِنُونَ ۝$$

Indeed there is, in their stories a lesson for those with insight and understanding. It is not a tale invented, but a confirmation of what went before it — a detailed exposition of all things, and a Guide and a Mercy to people who believe. [145]

These stories remind us that nothing is 'miraculous' from the Divine perspective. What we understand to be "accidental' or "miraculous" is the certain 'becoming' of the Divine Word, 'BE". We live in a thin slice of time and a narrow tunnel of our sensory perception. Without the 'inner eye' and the 'inner ear', we have a poor perch to observe the Divine Will. Only the heart and mind _together_ can pass through the gates of mystical knowledge.

These stories remind us too that God *is* present on the scene and God understands the aspirations and struggles of a mortal. God has empathy for His creatures and for every hardship He promises ease. When something is impossible for the human being to change, Divine Hands intervene—the ways of Divine Mercy, contemplated in complete knowledge, are simply infinite. Like running streams meandering through a traveler's pathway, these stories too permeate almost every chapter of the Quran, offering rest and spiritual satiation to the earnest seeker:

$$۞ لَّقَدْ كَانَ فِى يُوسُفَ وَإِخْوَتِهِ ءَايَـٰتٌ لِّلسَّآئِلِينَ ۝$$

Verily In Joseph and His brethren are Signs for seekers. [146]

For devout mystics, like Rumi, the narrative nuggets and the parables of the Quran are the "*Manna*" and "*Salwa*" of the spirit and the living springs of their mysticism. Rumi, the best known of these poets illustrates the living richness in these stories. Those blind to it have their hearts closed. Rumi reminds his cynics, "let him (the cynic) know that to one who receives ideas (from God) all that is absent in the world is present." See how the inspired poet, Rumi takes off with the beautiful and well known story of Joseph in the Quran:

On the injustice and envy of his brothers, over which Joseph had no control, Joseph tells a visiting friend:

---

145 Al Quran 12:111
146 Al Quran 12:7

That was (like) a chain: and I was the lion.
The lion is not disgraced by the chain: I do not complain of God's destiny.
If a lion had a chain on his neck,
(yet) he was a prince over all the chain makers." [147]

On being left in the well and then locked in prison:

"Like the moon, in the interlunar period when she is on the wane
If in that period the new moon is bent double, does she not become the full moon
in the sky?
Though the seed-pearl is pounded in the mortar, it becomes the light of the eye
and heart and looks aloft.
They cast a grain of wheat under the earth, then from its earth they raised up ears
of corn;
Once more they crushed it with the mill: its value increased and it became soul-
invigorating bread;
Again they crushed the bread under their teeth: it became the mind and the spirit
and the understanding of one endowed with reason. [148]

I will venture to include in my book three stores from the Quran. I do
recognize that when it comes to explaining something mystical it is quite a
challenge, ably stated by Kabeer, "A dumb person who has tasted a sweet
thing—how shall it be explained"? I would not have ventured if I did not have
help from Rumi.

The Cave of Faith

This is the story, told in the chapter entitled 'The Cave', of young men who took
refuge in a cave to shield themselves from the misguided practices of their
people. When one's environment demands the compromise of Faith, people of
Faith seek refuge in God. God after all is the bestower of Faith, (*Al Mu'min*) and
its protector (*Al Muhaimin*). There is a refuge promised for all those who want to
preserve and purify their hearts. These young men were told to take refuge
within a cave. They would know later that their cave was placed under a time-
warp (easy to say so today). While these men had slept in the cave for a normal
night's sleep (or perhaps a little more), the time outside the cave, moving at a
much faster pace, had raced ahead—hundreds of years had transpired and
many generations had come and gone!

---

147 Mathnavi Book I verse 3160, Translated by Reynold A. Nicholson
148 Mathnavi Book I verse 3165, Translated by Reynold A. Nicholson

وَإِذِ ٱعْتَزَلْتُمُوهُمْ وَمَا يَعْبُدُونَ إِلَّا ٱللَّهَ فَأْوُۥٓاْ إِلَى ٱلْكَهْفِ يَنشُرْ لَكُمْ رَبُّكُم مِّن رَّحْمَتِهِۦ وَيُهَيِّئْ لَكُم مِّنْ أَمْرِكُم مِّرْفَقًا

*"And when you withdraw from them, and that which they serve in God's stead,
then seek refuge in the cave,
Your Sustainer will unfold for you His Mercy and will facilitate for you the
tools [to deal with] your matter [149]*

And though we do not know how much time actually passed (in the face of two
different realities), we are told that Faith reposed in God stays alive and vibrant;
though generations of men had come and gone, with their beliefs alongside
them, the sleepers awoke—staked to their Faith, deepened in God-
consciousness.

نَّحْنُ نَقُصُّ عَلَيْكَ نَبَأَهُم بِٱلْحَقِّ إِنَّهُمْ فِتْيَةٌ ءَامَنُواْ بِرَبِّهِمْ وَزِدْنَٰهُمْ هُدًى وَرَبَطْنَا عَلَىٰ قُلُوبِهِمْ

*We convey to you their story in its factual essence:
Indeed they were young men with faith in their Sustainer,
And We increased their Guidance and We fortified their hearts; [150]*

Veracity is rooted in the heart and not in the cleverness of the mind. Extraneous
details, such as numbers and time-lines, the specificity of names and places are
not important. These are human constructs, mostly meaningless to the heart;
they change and are subject to change. The worth of a thing is its quality and
not its form or quantitative aspects. For example, there would be no purpose
served if the Quran had said that a trillion and ten souls were to journey into life.
There would be too many opinions of too many wise men on this. The essential
truth, as the Quran does state, is that all souls will taste death. Likewise, it is not
important for us to know how many people took refuge in the Cave—this is
extraneous.

سَيَقُولُونَ ثَلَٰثَةٌ رَّابِعُهُمْ كَلْبُهُمْ وَيَقُولُونَ خَمْسَةٌ سَادِسُهُمْ كَلْبُهُمْ رَجْمًۢا بِٱلْغَيْبِ وَيَقُولُونَ سَبْعَةٌ وَثَامِنُهُمْ كَلْبُهُمْ قُل رَّبِّىٓ أَعْلَمُ بِعِدَّتِهِم مَّا يَعْلَمُهُمْ إِلَّا قَلِيلٌ فَلَا تُمَارِ فِيهِمْ إِلَّا مِرَآءً ظَٰهِرًا وَلَا تَسْتَفْتِ فِيهِم مِّنْهُمْ أَحَدًا

*(Some) Say they were three, the dog being the fourth among them;
(Others) Say they were five, the dog being the sixth, guessing at the unseen; (Yet
others) say they were seven, the dog being the eighth.*

---

149 Al Quran 18:15-16
150 Al Quran 18:13:14

Say: "My Lord knows best their number; none knows them but a few."
So do not dispute over them except what is evident nor solicit the opinion of another. [151]

Our rationality is conditioned by the 'effect' of a 'cause'. Were time to flow backwards 'effect' would precede 'cause', as when a dead man stands up to walk into a bullet in a movie being run in reverse. What would happen to our concept of 'cause and effect' if time were not running at the same pace for all of us? Without the forward flow of time we would not be able to acquire experience. Without the 'constancy' of time our reality would be in total chaos. The discourse between the subject and its object would be broken if time was fractured between them. Time, though it seems to flow forward in a constant manner is relative and though time seems to be tireless, it is a created thing. There is an end of time too, just as there was a beginning! God is aware of our mental roadblocks to the understanding of time warps:

أَمْ حَسِبْتَ أَنَّ أَصْحَٰبَ ٱلْكَهْفِ وَٱلرَّقِيمِ كَانُوا۟ مِنْ ءَايَٰتِنَا عَجَبًا ۝

Do you deem that companions of the Cave and their legend are amongst Our astonishing signs? [152]

The men who slept in the cave were as if in the zone of death, removed from all the sounds and other goings on in the world outside:

فَضَرَبْنَا عَلَىٰٓ ءَاذَانِهِمْ فِى ٱلْكَهْفِ سِنِينَ عَدَدًا ۝

So We cast out from their hearing (all sounds) in the cave for a number of years. [153]

Behold an aspect of the Divine Shield; it is not made of bricks or mortar, iron or copper, walls or moats. God preserves the faithful and their faith in the vulnerability of their sleep or death by means both powerful and subtle. God used a spider's web to serve as a protective shield between His Prophet and those who were thirsting for his blood. God bent light and slowed the march of time, to preserve men and enshrine their Faith, in an unsealed cave.

---

151 Al Quran 18:22
152 Al Quran 18:9
153 Al Quran 18:11

وَتَرَى ٱلشَّمْسَ إِذَا طَلَعَت تَّزَٰوَرُ عَن كَهْفِهِمْ ذَاتَ ٱلْيَمِينِ وَإِذَا غَرَبَت تَّقْرِضُهُمْ ذَاتَ ٱلشِّمَالِ وَهُمْ فِى فَجْوَةٍ مِّنْهُ ذَٰلِكَ مِنْ ءَايَٰتِ ٱللَّهِ مَن يَهْدِ ٱللَّهُ فَهُوَ ٱلْمُهْتَدِ وَمَن يُضْلِلْ فَلَن تَجِدَ لَهُۥ وَلِيًّا مُّرْشِدًا ۝

You would have seen the sun, when it rose, skirting the cave to its right, and when it set, turning away from them to the left, and they lay in the openness within.
These are the Signs of God. He, whom God guides, is guided;
But he whom God leaves stray, not will you find a Wali (guiding friend) to lead him aright. [154]

To an observer outside the cave, the visual distortions of a time-fracture would be a surreal scene. Imagine an eye-blink taking hours; sleepers suspended in various positions during their painstakingly slow roll from side to side.

وَتَحْسَبُهُمْ أَيْقَاظًا وَهُمْ رُقُودٌ وَنُقَلِّبُهُمْ ذَاتَ ٱلْيَمِينِ وَذَاتَ ٱلشِّمَالِ وَكَلْبُهُم بَٰسِطٌ ذِرَاعَيْهِ بِٱلْوَصِيدِ لَوِ ٱطَّلَعْتَ عَلَيْهِمْ لَوَلَّيْتَ مِنْهُمْ فِرَارًا وَلَمُلِئْتَ مِنْهُمْ رُعْبًا ۝

You would have deemed them awake, while they were asleep.
And we turned them on their right and their left sides,
And their dog with paws stretched out upon the threshold.
Had you observed them, you would certainly have turned back from them in flight, and would certainly have been filled with awe of them. [155]

Time is the medium of our consciousness and discourse. To the men in the warp, it had merely been a day or part of it:

وَكَذَٰلِكَ بَعَثْنَٰهُمْ لِيَتَسَآءَلُوا بَيْنَهُمْ قَالَ قَآئِلٌ مِّنْهُمْ كَمْ لَبِثْتُمْ قَالُوا لَبِثْنَا يَوْمًا أَوْ بَعْضَ يَوْمٍ قَالُوا رَبُّكُمْ أَعْلَمُ بِمَا لَبِثْتُمْ

From such (a state), we awakened them that they might question one another.
A speaker from among them said: "How long have you stayed (here)?"
They said: "We have stayed (perhaps) a day or part of a day."
Others said: "Your Lord (Alone) knows best how long you have stayed (here)"

One or more of them set out to bring back some food. They had a silver coin for its purchase:

فَٱبْعَثُوٓا۟ أَحَدَكُم بِوَرِقِكُمْ هَـٰذِهِۦٓ إِلَى ٱلْمَدِينَةِ فَلْيَنظُرْ أَيُّهَآ أَزْكَىٰ طَعَامًا فَلْيَأْتِكُم بِرِزْقٍ مِّنْهُ
وَلْيَتَلَطَّفْ وَلَا يُشْعِرَنَّ بِكُمْ أَحَدًا ۝ إِنَّهُمْ إِن يَظْهَرُوا۟ عَلَيْكُمْ يَرْجُمُوكُمْ أَوْ يُعِيدُوكُمْ فِى
مِلَّتِهِمْ وَلَن تُفْلِحُوٓا۟ إِذًا أَبَدًا ۝

"So send one of you with this silver coin of yours to the town, and let him find
clean fresh food, and bring from it provision for you.
And let him be careful so not to draw any one's attention.
For if they see through you they will stone you, or pull you back to their fold,
and then never will you attain spiritual success." [156]

The coin they possessed was no longer the currency of the realm! Though the men in the cave surmised they slept about a day, the townsfolk found the coin to be ancient—300 or 309 years old by their reckoning!

Man is not anchored in time. Man's only anchor is Faith. Faith is transcendental and lives in all conditions except by man's willful rejection of it; though time indeed had stopped (for many centuries by our reckoning), for the young men in the cave, their faith continued to grow—richer and purer than before. During the hours of wakefulness time is the medium of our free will; and during the hours of sleep, time eludes us; rehearsing the eventuality of its end, and with it, the termination of our free-will:

وَكَذَٰلِكَ أَعْثَرْنَا عَلَيْهِمْ لِيَعْلَمُوٓا۟ أَنَّ وَعْدَ ٱللَّهِ حَقٌّ وَأَنَّ ٱلسَّاعَةَ لَا رَيْبَ فِيهَآ

Thus did we make their case known to the people, that they might know that the
promise of Allah is True, and that there can be no doubt about the end of time. [157]

Outside the cave, in the 'real' world, under the impulse of our sensory fears and aspirations, we either fear or worship the form of the Artist's work instead of the Artist Himself:

إِذْ يَتَنَـٰزَعُونَ بَيْنَهُمْ أَمْرَهُمْ فَقَالُوا۟ ٱبْنُوا۟ عَلَيْهِم بُنْيَـٰنًا رَّبُّهُمْ أَعْلَمُ بِهِمْ قَالَ ٱلَّذِينَ غَلَبُوا۟
عَلَىٰٓ أَمْرِهِمْ لَنَتَّخِذَنَّ عَلَيْهِم مَّسْجِدًا ۝

Behold, they dispute among themselves as to the affair.
(Some) said, "Construct a building over them": their Lord knows about them:
those who prevailed over their affair said, "Let us surely build a place of
worship over them." [158]

The men in the cave surmised they had slept merely a day or part of it; as

156 Al Quran 18:19
157 Al Quran 18:20-21
158 Al Quran 18:20-21

indeed there were no physical changes in or around them, to suggest otherwise—a night's sleep after all does not bring any remarkable changes. Yet outside the cave was another reality—hundreds of years had passed with several generations having come and gone. The people on either side of the time-fracture had lived a different 'reality'. It was but by the evidence of a coin's obsolescence, that the chasm of time between them was exposed! The story of the Men of the Cave exposes the spider-web of a thread by which we hang our 'reality':

ثُمَّ بَعَثْنَٰهُمْ لِنَعْلَمَ أَىُّ ٱلْحِزْبَيْنِ أَحْصَىٰ لِمَا لَبِثُوٓا۟ أَمَدًا ۝

Then We awakened them so that We may make it known which of the two parties would best reckon the time they had tarried. [159]

Time, a medium of a creature's existence and experience, unfolds by Divine Will and Knowledge. We are a minute aspect of time. Man as a creature who lives *in* time cannot be an honest expert about matters that relate to the 'pre-beginning' and 'post-end' of time. Only God, *Al Awwal*, *Al Akhir* transcends time—a thing that He created. In the verses that precede this narration the Quran warns:

وَيُنذِرَ ٱلَّذِينَ قَالُوا۟ ٱتَّخَذَ ٱللَّهُ وَلَدًا ۝ مَّا لَهُم بِهِۦ مِنْ عِلْمٍ وَلَا لِءَابَآئِهِمْ ۚ كَبُرَتْ كَلِمَةً تَخْرُجُ مِنْ أَفْوَٰهِهِمْ ۚ إِن يَقُولُونَ إِلَّا كَذِبًا ۝

[This revelation] warns those who say, "God has begotten a son":
They have no knowledge of it, nor had their forefathers.
Dreadful is the word that comes out of their mouths.
They speak nothing but falsehood! [160]

When will man accept that fabrications related to God are the constructs of a deluded mind and diseased heart?

Mary, the foremost amongst women

The 'story' of Mary and her holy son, is revealed in many[161] nuggets. The nuggets in the chapters titled 'The Family of Imran' (Chapter 3) and 'Mary' (Chapter 19) are quoted here. The narratives of Mary reinforce the theme that all prophets have a common lineage and though they are, without exception, mortals like us, their spiritual purity, knowledge and enlightenment, elevate them to a station of transcendental insight. They have served and continue to serve as pure conduits of God's Will. These servants of God, men and women, were

---

159 Al Quran 18:12
160 Al Quran 18:4-5
161 I found 35 refrences to Mary using the 'topic search' feature in the Quran Search engine at
   http://www.islamicity.com/QuranSearch/

not spared the pain and grief that are part of the human regimen of life. They became greater by the experience of their tests. Faith does not take root without patience and perseverance.

Take to heart the unfolding of the Divine Will as it becomes the eternal destiny of the daughter of Imran, Mary, and her son Jesus, in their own words. Mary, who has been in seclusion, is ready to receive God's Message through an Angel in the form of a man. *"How can I have a son, when no man has touched me, nor am I unchaste?"* asks an incredulous Mary. The impossibility or improbability of an event only exposes the constricted view of human perspective. The impossible, God tells Mary *"is easy for Me."* Miracles are to be embraced and not explained. When words become meaningless silence too can become the symbol of Faith. In the same temple the aged Zachariah was speechless for three days and nights in the wake of his son Yahiya's arrival. Mary would be speechless after her miraculous child came to be.

Divine Will is Absolute and all 'beings' and their 'becoming', in the minutest of details, flow from the Divine Word. The trauma of 'becoming' is a mortal's part of this bargain. Mary, the foremost mother is human too; she too must go through the test of motherhood's mettle. Guarding her sacred trust, she would serve God, waiting, in the solitude:

قَالَتْ أَنَّىٰ يَكُونُ لِى غُلَٰمٌ وَلَمْ يَمْسَسْنِى بَشَرٌ وَلَمْ أَكُ بَغِيًّا ۝ قَالَ كَذَٰلِكِ قَالَ رَبُّكِ هُوَ عَلَىَّ هَيِّنٌ

وَلِنَجْعَلَهُۥ ءَايَةً لِّلنَّاسِ وَرَحْمَةً مِّنَّا وَكَانَ أَمْرًا مَّقْضِيًّا ۝ فَحَمَلَتْهُ فَٱنتَبَذَتْ بِهِۦ مَكَانًا قَصِيًّا

She [Mary] said: "How can I have a son, when no man has touched me, nor am I unchaste?" He [the angel] said: "This said your Sustainer:
'It is easy for Me—We shall appoint him as a Sign unto men; A blessing from Us.' It is a matter decreed and due."
So she conceived him, and she withdrew with him to a far place. [162]

No mother is ever alone and God lowers the rivers of Paradise under a mother's feet[163]. Water has broken the ground beneath Mary—streaming to be on offer. The date-palm too has readied its choicest offering. Laden, it is straining to shade the duo, waiting and wanting to release the ripest of its profuse fruit. Where there is hardship there is ease. There are no detached spectators here— only eager slaves of God in many forms, enraptured by the Divine Word "Be".

فَأَجَآءَهَا ٱلْمَخَاضُ إِلَىٰ جِذْعِ ٱلنَّخْلَةِ قَالَتْ يَٰلَيْتَنِى مِتُّ قَبْلَ هَٰذَا وَكُنتُ نَسْيًا مَّنسِيًّا ۝

---

162 Al Quran 19:20-22
163 A very famous saying of the Prophet

فَنَادَىٰهَا مِن تَحْتِهَآ أَلَّا تَحْزَنِي قَدْ جَعَلَ رَبُّكِ تَحْتَكِ سَرِيًّا ۩ وَهُزِّىٓ إِلَيْكِ بِجِذْعِ ٱلنَّخْلَةِ تُسَٰقِطْ
عَلَيْكِ رُطَبًا جَنِيًّا ۩ فَكُلِي وَٱشْرَبِي وَقَرِّى عَيْنًا

The pains of childbirth drove her to the trunk of a date-palm.
She said: "Would that I had died before this, and had been forgotten and out of
sight!" (A voice) cried to her from beneath her: "Grieve not! Your Sustainer has
provided a stream beneath you; Nudge the trunk of date-palm towards you,
It will let fall fresh ripe-dates upon you.
So eat and drink and savor the sight." [164]

This day the foremost mother bore the pure Word of God. Any other word is out of place for her. Mary need not heed the wagging tongues. The self-righteous do not hear, though their slanderous tongues always wag:

فَإِمَّا تَرَيِنَّ مِنَ ٱلْبَشَرِ أَحَدًا فَقُولِىٓ إِنِّى نَذَرْتُ لِلرَّحْمَٰنِ صَوْمًا فَلَنْ أُكَلِّمَ ٱلْيَوْمَ إِنسِيًّا ۩ فَأَتَتْ بِهِۦ
قَوْمَهَا تَحْمِلُهُۥ قَالُوا۟ يَٰمَرْيَمُ لَقَدْ جِئْتِ شَيْئًا فَرِيًّا ۩ يَٰٓأُخْتَ هَٰرُونَ مَا كَانَ أَبُوكِ ٱمْرَأَ سَوْءٍ وَمَا
كَانَتْ أُمُّكِ بَغِيًّا

And when you see any mortal, say, 'I have taken a vow of abstinence in
gratitude to God, The Beneficent. This day I will not talk to any one"
She went back to her people carrying the child.
They said: "O Mary! You have done a radical thing!
"O sister of Aaron! Your father was not an evil man; your mother was not
unchaste!" [165]

The Word of God had come through His devoted slave:

فَأَشَارَتْ إِلَيْهِ قَالُوا۟ كَيْفَ نُكَلِّمُ مَن كَانَ فِى ٱلْمَهْدِ صَبِيًّا ۩
قَالَ إِنِّى عَبْدُ ٱللَّهِ ءَاتَىٰنِىَ ٱلْكِتَٰبَ وَجَعَلَنِى نَبِيًّا ۩

Then she pointed to him.
They said: "How can we talk to an infant in the cradle?"
He [Jesus] said: "Verily! I am a slave of God;
He has given me the Scripture and made me a Prophet;" [166]

Do not be fooled into believing that life or anything decreed by God is

---

164 Al Quran 19:23-25
165 Al Quran 19:25-28
166 Al Quran 19:29-30

accidental, the Quran seems to be suggesting to us when we revisit the subject of Mary, this time from the perspective of Mary's mother, the wife of Imran. The wife of Imran too is living the mystery of the Divine "Be". She is taken aback when the child she seeks to consecrate to God, turns out to be a female. She need not be. In God's plan there are no accidents; the Divine Will transcends a slice of time—it is timeless. Without the vision of the 'inner eye', the spot light of time (which is our perspective) hides more than it reveals. When she was pregnant, the wife of Imran had prayed for God to enlist in His service the child she carried in her womb. Now after she has delivered her child, her words encompass more. She prays for her own new-born, Mary, and Mary's future offspring:

فَلَمَّا وَضَعَتْهَا قَالَتْ رَبِّ إِنِّي وَضَعْتُهَا أُنثَىٰ وَٱللَّهُ أَعْلَمُ بِمَا وَضَعَتْ وَلَيْسَ ٱلذَّكَرُ كَٱلْأُنثَىٰ ۖ وَإِنِّي سَمَّيْتُهَا مَرْيَمَ وَإِنِّي أُعِيذُهَا بِكَ وَذُرِّيَّتَهَا مِنَ ٱلشَّيْطَٰنِ ٱلرَّجِيمِ ۝

But when she had given birth to the child, she said: "O my Sustainer! Behold, I have given birth to a female" - the while God had been fully aware of what she would give birth to, and [fully aware] that no male child [she might have hoped for] could ever have been like this female - "and I have named her Mary. And, verily, I seek Thy protection for her and her offspring against Satan, the accursed." [167]

In the nugget of Al Imran (3:33-55), the stories of the miraculous births of Jesus and John the Baptist are interwoven as one integrated act contained in a timeless moment, anchored in the House of Imran. Intertwined are the common anxieties and hopes, fears and faith of Mary and Zachariah in anticipation of predestined miracles. The virginity of Mary and the barren age of Zachariah's wife, collapse into irrelevance as His Will is done; crystallizing in the prophecy of Jesus. The essence of the story, if it must be called a story, is the continuity of the signs of God and these signs, consistent in themselves, transcend time. All prophets, the signs of the story seem to be telling us, have a unified heritage and beckon to the Only Truth. Adam, Noah, the family of Abraham and the family of Imran are all descendents, one of the other, says the Quran (3:33).

The inspired poet, Rumi, cannot hold back. He sets aside the constraints of place and time and arranges a meeting between the mothers of John the Baptist and Jesus:

The mother of Yahya[168], before disburdening herself (of him) says in secret to Mary:

---

167 Al Quran 3:36 as interpreted by Muhammad Asad
168 John the Baptist

"I see with certainity, within thee is a king
who is possessed of firm purpose and is an Apostle
endowed with knowledge of (God).
When I happened to meet thee my burden at once bowed in deference.
This embroyo bowed in deference to that embryo,
so that pain arose in my body from its bowing."
Mary said, "I also felt within me a bowing performed by this babe in the
womb."[169]

Another nugget on the subject of Jesus advances the clock to the hour of reckoning and brings it to the present. Truth transcends time and the heart that lives to embrace Truth's timelessness need not wait for the hour of death. God and Jesus both witness the Truth, in the here and now of the Quran, for the heeding heart:

وَإِذْ قَالَ ٱللَّهُ يَعِيسَى ٱبْنَ مَرْيَمَ ءَأَنتَ قُلْتَ لِلنَّاسِ ٱتَّخِذُونِي وَأُمِّيَ إِلَهَيْنِ مِن دُونِ ٱللَّهِ قَالَ سُبْحَـٰنَكَ مَا يَكُونُ لِى أَنْ أَقُولَ مَا لَيْسَ لِى بِحَقٍّ إِن كُنتُ قُلْتُهُ فَقَدْ عَلِمْتَهُ تَعْلَمُ مَا فِى نَفْسِى وَلَآ أَعْلَمُ مَا فِى نَفْسِكَ إِنَّكَ أَنتَ عَلَّـٰمُ ٱلْغُيُوبِ ۝

AND LO! God said: O Jesus, son of Mary! Didst thou say unto men, `Worship me and my mother as deities beside God'?" [Jesus] answered: "Limitless art Thou in Thy glory! It would not have been possible for me to say what I had no right to [say]! Had I said this, Thou wouldst indeed have known it! Thou knowest all that is within myself, whereas I know not what is in Thy Self. Verily, it is Thou alone who fully knowest all the things that are beyond the reach of a created being's perception. [170]

Moses and Khidr

Then there are the two seas whose meeting place is the quest of Moses. The Quran tells this story of never-ending mystical take-aways, with its many facets and many dimensions in 22 verses. "I will not give up until I reach the point where the two seas meet, though I march on for ages" says the thirsting Moses to his aide. Moses may or may not have found the indiscernible boundary of two seas, but Moses does find the insightful man who lives in the meeting point of

---

169 Mathnavi Book I I verse 3605, Translated by Reynold A. Nicholson. Modified 'bowed in worship' in Nicholson's translation to 'bowed in deference' to correctly reflect the eastern muslim's custom of bowing to another human in deference. 'Bowing in worship' is reserved exclusively for God.
170 Al Quran 5:116 as interpreted by Muhammad Asad

two worlds. A fish packed by Moses and his aide to serve as their meal during that day's journey, instead leads Moses (and us) to an inexhaustible spiritual feast. It turns out that the place where the unattended fish bolts into the water (a place where Moses had paused for rest and then moved on, unaware) is the place Moses is seeking. Returning to this place, Moses finds Khidr. Moses the leader becomes the follower. Khidr the roving Servant of God is the reluctant teacher and Moses his avid student. Khidr allows Moses to accompany him on the condition that Moses would display his patience by not questioning Khidr's actions and wait for Khidr to volunteer the answers. Moses promises patience and stakes it on God's Will. With the journey on, we witness in complete awe the grooming of a man who has the perfection of a prophet. Moses the law-bearer learns the ways of the man who lives in this world with knowledge of the next. To our dismay the tryst between Moses and Khidr is too short; the student lacking his teacher's insight is too quick to question the moral and legal soundness of his teacher's acts. After only three incidents during the journey together, Moses and Khidr part company. The law-bearer and the sage have separate missions. God did not will Moses' patience (and this journey) to last any longer. Nevertheless the prophet in Moses has learned his lesson in obedience well enough. When it will come to be, Moses will not question the Divine Command and will walk his people into the sea. The man, who set out to find the meeting of two seas, would then part a sea in two.

وَإِذْ قَالَ مُوسَىٰ لِفَتَىٰهُ لَآ أَبْرَحُ حَتَّىٰٓ أَبْلُغَ مَجْمَعَ ٱلْبَحْرَيْنِ أَوْ أَمْضِيَ حُقُبًا ﴿٦٠﴾

Behold, Moses said to His aide, "I will not give up until I reach the place where the two seas meet, though I march on for ages" [171]

Though Moses has arrived at the place he is seeking, he does not know: All of God's creatures have their own special innate knowledge. The fish is no stranger to the invisible barrier between two waters:

فَلَمَّا بَلَغَا مَجْمَعَ بَيْنِهِمَا نَسِيَا حُوتَهُمَا فَٱتَّخَذَ سَبِيلَهُۥ فِى ٱلْبَحْرِ سَرَبًا ﴿٦١﴾ فَلَمَّا جَاوَزَا قَالَ لِفَتَىٰهُ ءَاتِنَا غَدَآءَنَا لَقَدْ لَقِينَا مِن سَفَرِنَا هَٰذَا نَصَبًا ﴿٦٢﴾ قَالَ أَرَءَيْتَ إِذْ أَوَيْنَآ إِلَى ٱلصَّخْرَةِ فَإِنِّى نَسِيتُ ٱلْحُوتَ وَمَآ أَنسَىٰنِيهُ إِلَّا ٱلشَّيْطَٰنُ أَنْ أَذْكُرَهُۥ وَٱتَّخَذَ سَبِيلَهُۥ فِى ٱلْبَحْرِ عَجَبًا ﴿٦٣﴾ قَالَ ذَٰلِكَ مَا كُنَّا نَبْغِ فَٱرْتَدَّا عَلَىٰٓ ءَاثَارِهِمَا قَصَصًا ﴿٦٤﴾

But as they arrived by the meeting of the two seas, they both forgot their fish; it made its way through to the sea, barreling into it.
And after they had passed ahead Moses said to his aide: "Bring us breakfast; indeed this journey of ours has extracted much toil".

Said he (the aide):"Did you notice when we rested by the rock? I was remiss to tend to the fish; none but callousness made me inattentive to it.
It improvised its way to sea in a fascinating manner.
Said he (Moses): "That is what we have been seeking." so they turned back retracing their footsteps. [172]

God's servants like Khidr are not to be found living in townships. They have no anchors and interests in the world. The world and this life to them are no more than the fields and means of servitude to God.

فَوَجَدَا عَبْدًا مِّنْ عِبَادِنَا ءَاتَيْنَهُ رَحْمَةً مِّنْ عِندِنَا وَعَلَّمْنَهُ مِن لَّدُنَّا عِلْمًا ۞ قَالَ لَهُۥ مُوسَىٰ هَلْ أَتَّبِعُكَ عَلَىٰ أَن تُعَلِّمَنِ مِمَّا عُلِّمْتَ رُشْدًا ۞ قَالَ إِنَّكَ لَن تَسْتَطِيعَ مَعِىَ صَبْرًا ۞ وَكَيْفَ تَصْبِرُ عَلَىٰ مَا لَمْ تُحِطْ بِهِۦ خُبْرًا ۞ قَالَ سَتَجِدُنِى إِن شَآءَ ٱللَّهُ صَابِرًا وَلَآ أَعْصِى لَكَ أَمْرًا ۞ قَالَ فَإِنِ ٱتَّبَعْتَنِى فَلَا تَسْـَٔلْنِى عَن شَىْءٍ حَتَّىٰ أُحْدِثَ لَكَ مِنْهُ ذِكْرًا ۞

So they found a slave from amongst our slaves, unto whom we had bestowed Mercy from Us, and unto whom we delivered knowledge from Us.
Moses said to him (Khidr) "May I follow you so that you may teach me from the righteous knowledge upon you?"
He (Khidr) said: "Know that you will not be able to cultivate patience with me! How can you be patient about what is not within your awareness?
(Moses) said: "You will find me patient, God willing, and I will not disobey you in any matter."
He (Khidr) said: "Follow me then if you will, but do not question me about anything until I relate to you its meaning." [173]

To Moses' view Khidr has endangered the safety of the people who ply the boat. Moses can see no reason for such behavior:

فَٱنطَلَقَا حَتَّىٰٓ إِذَا رَكِبَا فِى ٱلسَّفِينَةِ خَرَقَهَا قَالَ أَخَرَقْتَهَا لِتُغْرِقَ أَهْلَهَا لَقَدْ جِئْتَ شَيْـًٔا إِمْرًا ۞ قَالَ أَلَمْ أَقُلْ إِنَّكَ لَن تَسْتَطِيعَ مَعِىَ صَبْرًا ۞ قَالَ لَا تُؤَاخِذْنِى بِمَا نَسِيتُ وَلَا تُرْهِقْنِى مِنْ أَمْرِى عُسْرًا ۞

So they both went on until, when they embarked upon a boat he (Khidr) made a hole in it. (Moses) said: "Have you made a hole to drown its owners? Indeed you have committed a grievous act.
He (Khidr) said: "Did I not tell you, that you would not be able to have patience with me?"

172 Al Quran 18:61-64
173 Al Quran 18:65-70

(Moses) said: "Do not take me to task on account of my forgetfulness, and be not hard upon me for what I have done [174]

"Thou shall not murder" is one of the Ten Commandments. Moses cannot and must not remain silent.

فَانطَلَقَا حَتَّىٰ إِذَا لَقِيَا غُلَامًا فَقَتَلَهُ قَالَ أَقَتَلْتَ نَفْسًا زَكِيَّةً بِغَيْرِ نَفْسٍ لَّقَدْ جِئْتَ شَيْئًا نُّكْرًا ۝ ۞ قَالَ أَلَمْ أَقُل لَّكَ إِنَّكَ لَن تَسْتَطِيعَ مَعِيَ صَبْرًا ۝ قَالَ إِن سَأَلْتُكَ عَن شَيْءٍ بَعْدَهَا فَلَا تُصَاحِبْنِي ۖ قَدْ بَلَغْتَ مِن لَّدُنِّي عُذْرًا ۝

So the two went till they met a boy; he (Khidr) slew him. (Moses) said: "Have you taken an innocent soul who has taken no other soul? You have done a despicable thing."
(Khidr) said: "Did I not tell you that you cannot have patience with me?"
(Moses) said: "If now I question you over anything after this, keep me not in your company, you have already gotten an excuse from me." [175]

This time Khidr has not broken a law. Perhaps Moses must have thought to himself, "How could Khidr ever secure a meal for himself and how could he ever survive? Does he have no sense of the ways of the world?" Moses could not help asking:

فَانطَلَقَا حَتَّىٰ إِذَآ أَتَيَا أَهْلَ قَرْيَةٍ اسْتَطْعَمَا أَهْلَهَا فَأَبَوْا أَن يُضَيِّفُوهُمَا فَوَجَدَا فِيهَا جِدَارًا يُرِيدُ أَن يَنقَضَّ فَأَقَامَهُ ۖ قَالَ لَوْ شِئْتَ لَتَّخَذْتَ عَلَيْهِ أَجْرًا ۝ قَالَ هَٰذَا فِرَاقُ بَيْنِي وَبَيْنِكَ ۚ سَأُنَبِّئُكَ بِتَأْوِيلِ مَا لَمْ تَسْتَطِع عَّلَيْهِ صَبْرًا ۝

And so the two went on until when they came to the people of a town; they asked them for food, but they declined any hospitality to the two of them. Then they came upon a wall therein, about ready to collapse and he (Khidr) shored it up. (Moses) said: "If you had wished, surely, you could have taken wages for it!"
(Khidr) said: "This is the parting between me and you; now I will tell you the meaning in depth, for which you were unable to bear patience. [176]

Khidr is aware that a king was seizing all sea-worthy boats for his own needs. This is the kind of knowledge available in the worldly domain. A caring person must act. Khidr likewise acts on his own volition:

---

174 Al Quran 18:71-73
175 Al Quran 18:74-76
176 Al Quran 18:77-78

$$\text{أَمَّا ٱلسَّفِينَةُ فَكَانَتْ لِمَسَٰكِينَ يَعْمَلُونَ فِى ٱلْبَحْرِ فَأَرَدتُّ أَنْ أَعِيبَهَا وَكَانَ وَرَآءَهُم مَّلِكٌ يَأْخُذُ}$$

$$\text{كُلَّ سَفِينَةٍ غَصْبًا ﴿٧٩﴾}$$

"As for the boat, it belonged to a people without means, working in the sea. So I decided to make a defect in it, as there was a king ahead of them who was claiming all boats by force. [177]

The Sage shares knowledge from the Other World—the World where the knowledge of all of time already exists. This is God's Knowledge. The boy was to become his parents' tormentor. *"Persecution is worse than Killing"* [178] says the Quran. When persecution exceeds its bounds Divine Hands intervene. The Quran reminds the Muslims who had battled their enemies that they had been conduits of the Divine Will. *"Ye (Muslims) slew them not, but Allah slew them. And thou (Muhammad) threwest not when thou didst throw, but Allah threw".* [179] Khidr too by his act is a conduit of God's Will:

$$\text{وَأَمَّا ٱلْغُلَٰمُ فَكَانَ أَبَوَاهُ مُؤْمِنَيْنِ فَخَشِينَآ أَن يُرْهِقَهُمَا طُغْيَٰنًا وَكُفْرًا ﴿٨٠﴾ فَأَرَدْنَآ أَن}$$

$$\text{يُبْدِلَهُمَا رَبُّهُمَا خَيْرًا مِّنْهُ زَكَوٰةً وَأَقْرَبَ رُحْمًا ﴿٨١﴾}$$

"And as for the boy, his parents were believers, and we feared he would burden them by rebellion and disbelief.
"So we decided that their Sustainer should replace him for them with one more devout and more affectionate. [180]

Knowledge of the treasure came from God. It was not an open fact. Khidr is moved by the Divine Will. There can be no better reward than the reward of being willingly aligned to the Divine Will:

$$\text{وَأَمَّا ٱلْجِدَارُ فَكَانَ لِغُلَٰمَيْنِ يَتِيمَيْنِ فِى ٱلْمَدِينَةِ وَكَانَ تَحْتَهُ كَنزٌ لَّهُمَا وَكَانَ أَبُوهُمَا صَٰلِحًا}$$

$$\text{فَأَرَادَ رَبُّكَ أَن يَبْلُغَآ أَشُدَّهُمَا وَيَسْتَخْرِجَا كَنزَهُمَا رَحْمَةً مِّن رَّبِّكَ وَمَا فَعَلْتُهُ عَنْ أَمْرِى}$$

$$\text{ذَٰلِكَ تَأْوِيلُ مَا لَمْ تَسْطِع عَّلَيْهِ صَبْرًا ﴿٨٢﴾}$$

"And as for the wall, it belonged to two orphan boys in the town; and there was under it a treasure belonging to them; and their father was a righteous man, and your Sustainer intended that they should attain their age of full strength and take out their treasure as a Mercy from your Sustainer. I did it not of my own accord. That is the real meaning for which you could not bear patience." [181]

---

177 Al Quran 18:79
178 Al Quran 2:191
179 Al Quran 8:17 as interpreted by Pickthall
180 Al Quran 18:80-81
181 Al Quran 18:82

The story of Moses and Khidr is a story for all those who quest in God's Way. Though God is beyond anything that we can grasp, the quest for Him and his assent is a life-long thirst. Moses would seek him in the expanse of wilderness, away from his flock; Mary would seek Him in the remoteness of the temple; the Prophet would seek Him in the solitude and stillness of the night, by lips and limbs, and tears too. Says Rumi of Moses' quest:

By God do not tarry in anything or any station that thou has gained,
(But crave more) like one suffering from dropsy who is never satiated with water.
Learn from him with whom God spake,
O noble sir! See what Kaleem (Moses) says in his longing!
"Not withstanding such a dignity and such a prophetic office (as I possess),
I am seeker of Khidr, (I am) quit of self regard."
I will fare as far as the meeting-place of two seas,
(afterwards) I may be accompanied by the Sovereign of the time.
I will make Khidr a means to my purpose: either that
or *I will go onward* and journey by night *for a long while.*
I will fly with wings and pinions for years: what are years? For a thousand years.
Do not deem the passion of the Beloved to be less than the passion for bread."[182]

Spiritual Consciousness is the Gate-Way to Islam

The Quran has a special word for the spiritually-conscious—*Muttaqeen*. The *Muttaqeen* are people who are engaged in serious and earnest introspection at every step of their life's journey, always aspiring to a higher standard of personal morality and behavior. Spiritual consciousness takes root in the simple truism that life is a trust to be returned to its Source and rightful Owner:

كُلُّ نَفْسٍ ذَآئِقَةُ ٱلْمَوْتِ ثُمَّ إِلَيْنَا تُرْجَعُونَ ۝

Every soul must know the taste of death.
Then you will be sent back to Us[183].

It is understood that Divine Revelation is synchronized to the mortal needs of the hour. When there was a need for a parting verse, heralding the completion of the Prophet's mission, the Quran offered this never-to-be-forgotten reminder. This reminder exposes the other dimension to the trust of life; life is a test too with personal accountability:

وَٱتَّقُواْ يَوْمًا تُرْجَعُونَ فِيهِ إِلَى ٱللَّهِ ثُمَّ تُوَفَّىٰ كُلُّ نَفْسٍ مَّا كَسَبَتْ وَهُمْ لَا يُظْلَمُونَ ۝

Be conscious of the Day when you shall be brought back to God.

---

182 Mathnavi Book III verses 1960-1970, Translated by Reynold A. Nicholson
183 Al Quran 29:57

Then shall every soul be paid in full for what it has earned, and none shall be dealt with unjustly. [184]

Those who take their 'Return' seriously—seriously enough to make it the central aspect of their lives and consciousness—have placed themselves on the Right Path to God. This path is self-unfolding. God Himself leads the *Muttaqeen* to transcendental deliverance:

يَٰٓأَيُّهَا ٱلَّذِينَ ءَامَنُوٓاْ إِن تَتَّقُواْ ٱللَّهَ يَجْعَل لَّكُمْ فُرْقَانًا وَيُكَفِّرْ عَنكُمْ سَيِّـَٔاتِكُمْ وَيَغْفِرْ لَكُمْ وَٱللَّهُ ذُو ٱلْفَضْلِ ٱلْعَظِيمِ ۝

O you who have attained to faith! If you remain conscious of God, He will endow you with a standard by which to discern the true from the false, and will efface your bad deeds, and will forgive you your sins: for God is limitless in His great bounty. [185]

Human beings as mortals are both subjects and objects of change. We change our environment and our environment changes us. We can change our consciousness and our consciousness will in turn change us. We are both free-willed and pre-destined. Masters of our intent and aspirations, pre-destined to our time and space, pre-destined too to return to our Source. The essence of life is not material but the beauty of its purpose and the purity of its aspirations. In a changing world, only God is constant and Real and therefore the sole Judge and Recorder of beauty and purity. The material manifestations of human action and creativity will, like wilted straw be dispersed by the winds of time. Like water, the purity of our motivations contemplated in the awareness of the return will find transcendence:

وَٱضْرِبْ لَهُم مَّثَلَ ٱلْحَيَوٰةِ ٱلدُّنْيَا كَمَآءٍ أَنزَلْنَٰهُ مِنَ ٱلسَّمَآءِ فَٱخْتَلَطَ بِهِۦ نَبَاتُ ٱلْأَرْضِ فَأَصْبَحَ هَشِيمًا تَذْرُوهُ ٱلرِّيَٰحُ وَكَانَ ٱللَّهُ عَلَىٰ كُلِّ شَىْءٍ مُّقْتَدِرًا ۝

And propound for them the similitude of the life of this world:
It is as water that We usher from the skies,
And the earth's vegetation mingles with it
And by a morning it is straw for the winds to scatter.
God prevails over everything [186]

The Quran is a warning against false beliefs and therefore false pursuits. A false

---

184 Al Quran 2:281
185 Al Quran 8:29 as interpreted by Muhammad Asad
186 Al Quran 18:45

belief is anything that mis-aligns us with the Creator and breeds the false notion of superior selfhood. Idol worship in its literal or figurative form closes the inner eye of gnosis. Idol worship in its literal form compartmentalizes god to an object confined to the form and space that the worshipper assigns to it. The worshipper *defines* the deity, placing the worshipper's whims at the center. Idol worship in its figurative sense, and perhaps more insidious form, is the pursuit of a false obsession. It amounts to being fixated on a nonexistent oasis hosted by the desert sun:

$$\text{أَفَرَءَيْتَ مَنِ ٱتَّخَذَ إِلَٰهَهُۥ هَوَىٰهُ وَأَضَلَّهُ ٱللَّهُ عَلَىٰ عِلْمٍ وَخَتَمَ عَلَىٰ سَمْعِهِۦ وَقَلْبِهِۦ وَجَعَلَ عَلَىٰ بَصَرِهِۦ غِشَٰوَةً فَمَن يَهْدِيهِ مِنۢ بَعْدِ ٱللَّهِ أَفَلَا تَذَكَّرُونَ}$$

Hast thou seen him who has taken his caprice to be his god, and whom God has let go astray, out of knowledge, and set a seal upon his hearing and his heart, and placed a veil upon his eyes? Who shall guide him after God? Will you not then contemplate? [187]

God is above mortal whims and though God is omnipresent, God is the growing realization of a sincere quest—a quest not possible without struggle and patience, and a ceaseless aspiration for knowledge, both inwards and outwards. This quest must not be abandoned at the altar of an idol, nor compromised in the pursuit of the bubble of worldly profit. The Quran is a reminder; we mortals, need constant reminding that this existence is not the be-all and the end-all of being. Those who insist otherwise, in the face of undeniable signs, say so without knowledge:

$$\text{وَقَالُوا مَا هِيَ إِلَّا حَيَاتُنَا ٱلدُّنْيَا نَمُوتُ وَنَحْيَا وَمَا يُهْلِكُنَا إِلَّا ٱلدَّهْرُ وَمَا لَهُم بِذَٰلِكَ مِنْ عِلْمٍ إِنْ هُمْ إِلَّا يَظُنُّونَ}$$

And they say: "There is nothing but our present life; we die and we live, and nothing but time destroys us." Of that they have no knowledge; they merely guess. [188]

The reminder comes in the form of both a warning and promise of transcendental deliverance. God is loving and lovable but God must be feared. As agents of free-will we will be accountable. This we need to fear so that as conscientious creatures, imperfect as we are, we may be hopeful of Mercy.

The foremost message of the Quran is one of Mercy. Of all His attributes, that God reminds us of, He reminds us most abundantly of His Compassion, Forgiveness and Mercy. The Quran reveals a loving God pleased with a soul's

187 Al Quran 44:23
188 Al Quran 44:24

ascension towards light (enlightenment, if you will) and displeased with its falling into darkness. There are admonitions too along with reminders of pending accountability; Reminders of the obliteration of the haughty transgressors of the past and reminders of the burning loss of a wasted life. The awe-filled reminders of Divine punishment are brought home to us so that we may take account of ourselves *now*. Pharaoh and Moses are not mere historical figures. They represent the active opposing forces within our souls. The soul unanchored in the troubled and turbid tide that is civilization, like Noah, needs faith and perseverance to reach the highlands of safety. Man cannot live outside of, or away from God because God is Truth.

فَذَٰلِكُمُ ٱللَّهُ رَبُّكُمُ ٱلْحَقُّ ۖ فَمَاذَا بَعْدَ ٱلْحَقِّ إِلَّا ٱلضَّلَٰلُ ۖ فَأَنَّىٰ تُصْرَفُونَ ﴿٣٢﴾

So that is God for you: your Lord, the Truth.
And what is there after Truth but error?
Then why are you alienated?[189]

Man outside of faith is like Noah's son, outside of the Ark, lost in the turbulence of his own ego and the falsity of his self-sufficiency.

God wants the returning soul to return to His Presence in the Abode of Peace {*Dar es Salaam*}[190]. The Ark is the Quran.

---

189 Al Quran 10:32. Interpreted by Thomas Cleary
190 Al Quran 6:127

Sadequain Calligraphy. *The Kalima-e-Tayyeba*

Courtesy of Dr. Salman Ahmad at www.sadequainfoundation.com

[The *The Kalima-e-Tayyeba* original mural measures 20 x 12 feet. Sadequain's script and style, are uniquely his own, aptly called "Khatt-e-Sadequani".]

The Messenger

They don't know
that if the shadow of Muhammad's true form falls across a wall,
the wall will bleed!
And it will no longer have two sides!
What a blessing to be one thing. [191]

Verily God and His angels whelm in blessing the prophet.
O ye who believe, invoke blessings upon him, and give him greetings of Peace. [192]

The Prophet of History

The followers of Islam believe that Muhammad was the last messenger of God. This was a matter of belief then. Today, fourteen centuries later, the belief is a historical fact. What is equally factual is that Muhammad's prophethood took place in the "day light of history". His mission took many years to complete but it did reach its fruition during his life-time. The constancy of his companions, a sophisticated infrastructure of a nation that matured during his life-time, all contributed to the authenticity of his legacy. An authenticity that is far, far superior to that of any other prophet.

Unlike other prophets, Muhammad is also a historical figure. The Muhammad of history stands tall. He is ranked on the top of the list of the 100 most influential men in history by Michael H. Hart

My choice of Muhammad to lead the world's most influential persons may surprise some readers and may be questioned by others, but he was the only man in history who was supremely successful on both the religious and secular levels. Of humble origins, Muhammad founded and promulgated one of the world's great religions,

191 *The Soul of Rumi* by Coleman Barks. Published by Harper Collins 2002
192 Al Quran as interpreted by Martin Lings in *Muhammad, his life based on the earliest sources*

and became an immensely effective political leader. Today, thirteen centuries after his death, his influence is still powerful and pervasive. [193]

Explaining his decision to rank him so, Michael Hart states:

"How, then, is one to assess the overall impact of Muhammad on human history? Like all religions, Islam exerts an enormous influence upon the lives of its followers. It is for this reason that the founders of the world's great religions all figure prominently in this book. Since there are roughly twice as many Christians as Muslims in the world, it may initially seem strange that Muhammad has been ranked higher than Jesus. There are two principle reasons for that decision. First, Muhammad played a far more important role in the development of Islam than Jesus did in the development of Christianity. Although Jesus was responsible for the main ethical and moral precepts of Christianity (insofar as these differed from Judaism), St. Paul was the main developer of Christian theology, its principle proselytizer, and the author of a large portion of the New Testament. Muhammad, however, was responsible for both the theology of Islam and its main ethical and moral principles. In addition, he played the key role in proselytizing the new faith, and in establishing the religious practices of Islam." (Pages 38, 39)

Muhammad as prophet is an ongoing presence amongst his adoring believers to whom he is known by many other names. Explaining his decision to name him Muhammad, as opposed to the traditional method of naming a child after his ancestors, his grandfather Abd al-Muttalib explained: "I did do with the wish that my grandson would be praised by God in heaven and by men on earth[194]." Other names for the Prophet are *Ahmad* (co-rooted with "Muhammad" and also used in the Quran 61:6) *Mustafa* (the chosen), *Rasool Allah* (messenger of God) and *Rahamat-un-lil Alameen* (mercy for all people and on all planes).

The Messenger of God

Muhammad bore and lived the message of the Quran. The Quran is the direct unaltered word of God transmitted to and uttered by Muhammad in Arabic. True to God's promise, the Arabic Quran, the indelible Writ of God, stands intact and unchanged. It is and has been the supreme Holy Scripture amongst and across all the religious sects in Islam. Through the tradition of *Hifz* the entire Quran was memorized by many early Muslims during the prophet's life-time. This tradition has continued uninterrupted through the ages. Today, there are several hundred thousand *Huffaz*. Even so, the physical book, as it exists today, was compiled during the life-time of some of the prophet's contemporary companions. The highest spiritual practice of a Muslim continues to be the recitation of the Quran

---

193 *The 100. A Ranking of the Most Influential Persons in History. Updated for the Nineties* by Michael H. Hart. p33
194 *The Life of Muhammad* by Muhammad Husayn Haykal, 8th ed. translated by Ismail Ragi p 48

in its original Arabic. A study of the Quran in another language is a supplementary practice. The Quran in any other language is not the Quran per se.

The chronicles of the practice of Prophet Muhammad, {*Sunnah*} and his sayings {*Hadith*} are documents of great exemplary import and reference. These chronicles are supported and authenticated by documented chains of communication and corroboration leading up to a source amongst the prophet's companions and contemporaries {*Isnad*}. Hamza Yusuf, a contemporary Muslim scholar, who himself elected to embrace Islam, in his memoriam to Martin Lings, brings this point home:

> Dr. Martin Lings became a Muslim in 1938, partly, he told me, because he felt Islam was unique among the world religions in maintaining transmission in its revelation as well as in its sciences, through unbroken chains that involved a "handing down," the literal meaning of tradition[195]

Nevertheless, like the Gospels, these records are sourced by believing historians who lived 120 to 200 years after the prophet's death. The Arabic Quran was memorized and written *as it was revealed*. Chroniclers of Muhammad's history (and the Hadith) are mortals of their time. Any human expose` (of a record) is affected by the cultural and social mores of its author. The Quran is not a chronicle. It is a living and lasting *sign*. This is the essential differentiation between the *Hadith* and the Arabic Quran. The Hadith is anchored in time whereas the Quran is *not*. By this I mean that were the Prophet to be alive today, the words of the *Hadith* would be different, but the *signs* of the Quran would *not*.

Muhammad's mission was to receive and deliver and live the Quran. He, the prophet was the "Slave of God" first and the leader of his men second. It is God and not Muhammad who is the object of worship. It is for this reason that Muslims, throughout history have conscientiously refrained from giving form to Muhammad, lest he himself becomes an object of worship. There is no physical illustration of the prophet. Muhammad wanted it so. The evidence of this will not be lost upon the pilgrim to Mecca. The prophet as God's instrument *restored* the *Kaabah* and the station (*Maqaam*) of Abraham. The Kaabah does not house Muhammad, nor is there a physical monument to him. Fittingly, there is a gate at the Kaabah named after him, in remembrance of his usual approach to the Kaabah. Beseeching God, the pilgrim thirsts to walk in Muhammad's footsteps— Footsteps leading to the "straight path" {*Siratul Mustaqeem*}. A *Hadith* says as much: "Do not exalt me like the Christians exalted Jesus son of Mary".

What is not subjective is the fact that Muhammad, the unlettered prophet,

---

195 *A return to the Spirit*, In Memoriam, Hamza Yusuf

transformed an ignorant, superstitious, disparate and warring Arabian peninsula into a progressive, enlightened nation connected by values of equality, justice and equity heretofore not known to them. Through this transformation Muhammad did not accumulate any personal material benefits. He lived and died as poor as the poorest of his followers[196]. He restored the Kaabah, the House consecrated by Abraham to God, as the center of worship to the One God. He lived an open life by the very message that he preached. Muhammad, by God's command, is the human illustration of the Quran.

قُلْ يَٰٓأَيُّهَا ٱلنَّاسُ إِنِّي رَسُولُ ٱللَّهِ إِلَيْكُمْ جَمِيعًا ٱلَّذِى لَهُ مُلْكُ ٱلسَّمَٰوَٰتِ وَٱلْأَرْضِ لَآ إِلَٰهَ إِلَّا هُوَ يُحْىِۦ وَيُمِيتُ فَـَٔامِنُوا۟ بِٱللَّهِ وَرَسُولِهِ ٱلنَّبِىِّ ٱلْأُمِّىِّ ٱلَّذِى يُؤْمِنُ بِٱللَّهِ وَكَلِمَٰتِهِۦ وَٱتَّبِعُوهُ لَعَلَّكُمْ تَهْتَدُونَ ۝

Say "O mankind I am the messenger of God to all inclusive.
[God] who is the Sovereign of the heavens and earth
There is no god but God
Who grants life and brings death.
So believe in God and His messenger,--
the unlettered prophet who believes in God and His Words
Follow him so that you may be guided"[197]

The Divine Plan

Muhammad was born an orphan in 570 C.E a year after his parents were married. His father Abd'Allah had fallen ill and died in Yathrib, while returning to Mecca from a trading trip to Palestine and Syria. In his inimitable style and meticulous detail, Martin Ling in his must-read *Muhammad* gives an account of the expecting mother, Aminah, and the child's arrival:

'There was great grief in Mecca when Harith returned (with news of Abd'Allah's death). Aminah's one consolation was the unborn child of her dead husband, and her solace increased as the time of her delivery drew near. She was conscious of a light within her, and one day it shone forth from her so intensely that she could see the castle of Bostra in Syria. And she heard a voice say to her: "Thou carriest in thy womb the lord of this people; and when he is born say: 'I place him beneath the protection of the One, from the evil of evey envier'; then name him Muhammad". Some weeks later the child was born. Aminah was in the home of her uncle and sent word to Abd al-Muttalib, asking him to come see his grandson. He took the boy in his arms and carried him to the Sanctuary (Kaabah) and into the Holy House where he prayed a prayer of thanksgiving to God for this gift. Then he brought him once

---

196 The homeless in Medina were given shelter in the compound next to his apartment.
197 Al Quran 7:158

more to his mother, but on the way showed him to his household. He himself was shortly to have another son (Hamza), by Aminah's cousin Halah.[198] At the moment his youngest son was the three-year-old Abbas who now met him at the door of his house. "This is thy brother; kiss him," he said, holding out to him the new-born babe, and Abbas kissed him.'

Muhammad descended from the tribe of Quraish. The Quraish traced their lineage to Ishmael, Abraham's son from his bondmaid, Hagar. While no one foresaw the extraordinary events that would unfold from the destiny of Aminah's child, this still was no ordinary year for the Quraish. In contemporary lore it became known as the 'Year of the Elephant' for the induction of elephant(s) in the invading army of Abrahah; Abrahah, the Abyssinian vice-regent of Yemen, had marched upon Mecca, seeking the destruction of the Kaabah, so that Yemen could replace Mecca as the center of worship and the nexus of Arabian pilgrims and traders. When the army reached Mecca, and the Kaabah left to its own defense by the Meccans, was within sight, the lead elephant doggedly refused to advance. Abrahah's designs would come to a calamitous end, with his troops routed by swarms of birds. Years later when the Quraish would find improbable, Muhammad as God's chosen messenger, the Quran would remind them of the improbable decimation of a proud army by mere birds. The Divine plan is far-reaching and purposeful. In every aspect of life and living the Sustainer is manifested by Divine signs:

أَلَمْ تَرَ كَيْفَ فَعَلَ رَبُّكَ بِأَصْحَبِ ٱلْفِيلِ ۝ أَلَمْ يَجْعَلْ كَيْدَهُمْ فِي تَضْلِيلٍ ۝ وَأَرْسَلَ عَلَيْهِمْ طَيْرًا أَبَابِيلَ ۝ تَرْمِيهِم بِحِجَارَةٍ مِّن سِجِّيلٍ ۝ فَجَعَلَهُمْ كَعَصْفٍ مَّأْكُولٍ ۝

Have you not seen how Your Sustainer dealt with those with the Elephant?
Did He not thwart their plan? And sent against them birds, in swarms, striking
them with stones laden with Sijjil
And made them like famished straw [199]

لِإِيلَٰفِ قُرَيْشٍ ۝ إِۦلَٰفِهِمْ رِحْلَةَ ٱلشِّتَآءِ وَٱلصَّيْفِ ۝ فَلْيَعْبُدُواْ رَبَّ هَٰذَا ٱلْبَيْتِ ۝ ٱلَّذِىٓ أَطْعَمَهُم مِّن جُوعٍ وَءَامَنَهُم مِّنْ خَوْفٍ ۝

So that the Quraish might remain secure,
Secure by their winter and summer caravans,
So they should worship the Sustainer of this House
Who has given them sustenance against hunger, and security from fear.[200]

Customarily a tribe was subdivided into clans (extended households), named

---

198 Abd al-Muttalib was married to Halah the same day that his late son Abd'Allah was married to Aminah
199 Al Quran 105
200 Al Quran 106

after the clan's founder. Muhammad belonged to the clan of the Hashim, named after his great grandfather. His great-great-great grandfather, Qusayy, was the ruler of Mecca. At the center of Mecca and its chief attraction was the *Kaabah*. The Kaabah (meaning cube) was a sanctuary built by Abraham and Ishmael, dedicated to the One God. Today, as then, it was in the shape of a cube, with its four corners pointing towards the four points of the compass. Besides the Kaabah is the spring of *Zamzam*. A spring that sustained Hagar and her child, a spring whose water is still cherished by modern-day pilgrims. Today, as then, pilgrims circumambulate the Kaabah. Today, as then, violence was strictly forbidden in the Kaabah and its precincts. The Kaabah was held sacred by the descendents of both Ishmael and Isaac. As time passed and as descendents of Ishmael spread over the land, the annual pilgrimage began drawing an ever larger number of people. Neighboring pagan tribes and their idol worship also began to find their nexus in the Kaabah. Over time, there would also be violent wresting of the control of the Kaabah and during one of these violent episodes the spring of Zamzam was deliberately buried. It remained lost for centuries, until Muhammad's grandfather Abd Al Muttalib, guided by a dream, would recover and restore the spring of Zamzam. At the time of Muhammad's birth the Kaabah was at the centre of pagan rites and rituals. The clan of Hashim had charge of the spring of Zamzam and it had been their job to provide water for the pilgrims. In the desert, where water was everything, Muhammad's tribe of Quraish was at the centre, part and parcel of the Meccan nobility.

It was the custom of the Meccan nobility to send their newborns to the desert in the care of wet-nursing foster mothers. Muhammad would thus spend the early years away from his mother, with his foster mother Halimah. Halimah would nurse him for two whole years and then bring him back for a brief period to his mother in Mecca. He would remain with Halimah until the fifth year of his life. "These five years exerted upon Muhammad a most beautiful and lasting influence, as Halimah and her people remained the object of his love through out the length of his life"[201]

When he was six, his mother Aminah took him with her to Yathrib (later to be named *Medinatun Nabi*, meaning the City of the Prophet) to introduce him to her side of the family. It was also here that his father was buried. The child's loss was to be immeasurably compounded. During the return journey to Mecca after a month's stay in Yathrib, Aminah fell fatally sick and died on the way. She was buried in Abwa, a place midway between Mecca and Yathrib. A loss-ridden Muhammad would return to Mecca, in the care of his maid-servant Barakah (later known as Umm Ayman). Back in Mecca he would find much affection from his doting grandfather, Abd al Muttalib. This bond was to be short-lived too. Abd al Muttalib too would die in two years. Upon the death of his grandfather

---

201 *The Life of Muhammad* by Muhammad Husayn Haykal, 8th ed. translated by Ismail Ragi p 52

Muhammad was given to the care of his loving fraternal uncle Abu Talib and the latter's wife Fatimah. Abu Talib lived through the first nine years of Muhammad's prophethood. Although he (Abu Talib) did not formally profess Muhammad's new faith, he was unrelenting in offering tribal protection to Muhammad. Fatimah did all she could to soften the young orphan's loss. Muhammad would often recount in later years that "she (Fatimah) would have let her own children go hungry rather than him".

The tragic early losses in Muhammad's life would expand his heart (as pain and loss always do). It is poignant that this young orphan would later deliver the Quranic message of unrelenting compassion towards one's parents:

$$ وَوَصَّيْنَا ٱلْإِنسَـٰنَ بِوَالِدَيْهِ حُسْنًا $$

Now [among the best of righteous deeds which] We have enjoined upon man [is] the goodness towards his parents.[202]

Muhammad would also famously say that "Paradise lay at a mother's feet".

Al Amin

Muhammad would grow up fast. He had many child-hood playmates. He was particularly close to Hamza and Saffiyah, uncle and aunt in relation to him but of his age group. At age twelve he would widen his horizons by accompanying his uncle Abu Talib with a trading caravan to Al Sham (which is modern day Syria). This trading trip was not to deliver any significant material gains to him or his uncle and probably this lack of gain would force him to earn his immediate livelihood as a shepherd. The gain from trading would come later at the age of twenty five when he would undertake another trading mission with another caravan bound to Syria. This time in the service of a wealthy and honored Meccan tradeswoman, Khadijah. In the meantime the spartan vocation of a shepherd would inoculate him from material avarice and instill in him a sense of profoundness and an attitude of conscientiousness. These traits were to be the hallmarks of his life and as a young man he was known as *Al Amin*, in recognition of his Honesty, Trustworthiness and Reliability. The Quran, much later, would recall this same trait, when some of the very same people who now called him *Amin* would disbelieve and deride him over his claim of a Divine mission (81:21). The Quran would likewise ask rhetorically of the disbelievers' turning away from the Prophet they called *Al Amin*, *"Do they reject him because they know not their Messenger?"*(23:69)

Khadijah was about forty years old and as a wealthy widow she was wary of the marital proposals that came her way. Moved by Muhammad's integrity she

---

202 Al Quran 29:8

would take the initiative in marrying him. In marriage they cherished each other but there would be heartbreaks. Their two sons would die in childhood. This tragedy was not lost upon his opponents, steeped in a culture that regarded sons as a man's "roots" and a measure of his "legacy". As if by Providence, in a society that felt shamed by female-offspring and would often bury them alive, Muhammad would be a loving father to their four daughters, Zaynab, Ruqayyah, Umm Kulsum and Fatimah.

Slavery was common place if not rampant in pre-Islamic Arabia, but in the would-be prophet's household the dark shadows of this abominable practice were to find their early and the first of many retreats. Upon his marriage to Khadijah, Muhammad would free his own maid-servant Barakah and arrange for her to be married. As a married couple Khadijah and Muhammad would manumit Khadijah's recently acquired slave, Zayd Bin Harithah. Zayd now fifteen had come into slavery long before as an abducted child. Like the fated Joseph, Zayd too was destined for providence's honor. First, the nexus of the Meccan crossroads would afford Zayd being traced by his father. But then when it came time to choose between Muhammad and his father, Zayd chose the former. Muhammad likewise would proclaim Zayd to be his adopted son. Zayd Bin Muhammad as he would now be called would earn the distinct honor of being amongst the earliest followers of Muhammad the Prophet; being only behind Khadijah and Ali. The latter, Ali Ibn Abu Talib, Muhammad's cousin would be five years old when Muhammad and Khadijah would bring him home to alleviate his father, Abu Talib's financial hardship. Around this time too Khadijah would bear her last child. This Meccan household of Muhammad and his beloved Khadijah would consist of their four daughters, Ali Ibn Talib and Zayd.

As a young man in his thirties Muhammad would seek each year a period of retreat and contemplation—a tradition not uncommon amongst the Meccan spiritualists. Muhammad's place of retreat was a cave at the top of Mount Hira, about two miles north of Mecca, and the time of his retreat was usually the month of Ramadan. As an illiterate man Muhammad could not have studied the scriptures during his retreat. He must have instead contemplated the powerful signs of nature around him, a nature of spartan hills, the burning desert sun and the bright stars in the stillness of the night. This would be Muhammad's gateway to the Truth.

The Recital

In his fortieth year, during his retreat, occurred the first revelation. On a night in the trailing third period of Ramadan, an Angel appeared to him, saying "Recite". When Muhammad was at a loss to recite, the Angel whelmed Muhammad in his unbearably tight embrace and repeated his request again, and then again. After the third embrace the Angel delivered the recitation:

اَقْرَأْ بِٱسْمِ رَبِّكَ ٱلَّذِى خَلَقَ ۞ خَلَقَ ٱلْإِنسَـٰنَ مِنْ عَلَقٍ ۞ ٱقْرَأْ وَرَبُّكَ ٱلْأَكْرَمُ ۞ ٱلَّذِى عَلَّمَ بِٱلْقَلَمِ ۞ عَلَّمَ ٱلْإِنسَـٰنَ مَا لَمْ يَعْلَمْ ۞

Recite in the name of thy Sustainer who created
He created man from a clingy embryo.
Recite; and your sustainer is the most bountiful {Al Akram},
He who has taught by the pen. Taught man what he knew not [203]

Muhammad repeated these words as if they were etched in his heart.

Stricken with fear from what had just transpired Muhammad fled from the cave, and on his way downwards he heard a voice from above him "O Muhammad, thou art the messenger of God, and I am Gabriel". Around him over the horizon and in every direction the archangel filled the skies. Upon reaching his house he fell on his couch and still shaking, asked Khadijah to cover him. During the early days of fear and disbelief, it would be Khadijah and her elderly cousin Waraqah, a Coptic, who validated him. Divine validation would follow:

نٓ ۚ وَٱلْقَلَمِ وَمَا يَسْطُرُونَ ۞ مَآ أَنتَ بِنِعْمَةِ رَبِّكَ بِمَجْنُونٍ ۞ وَإِنَّ لَكَ لَأَجْرًا غَيْرَ مَمْنُونٍ ۞ وَإِنَّكَ لَعَلَىٰ خُلُقٍ عَظِيمٍ ۞

Nun, by the pen, and by that which they write,
You are not by the grace of your Sustainer under delusion,
Of certain yours shall be a meed unfailing, for indeed highly exalted is your
existence. [204]

A period of silence ensued before the revelations resumed. This must have been a period of intense introspection, the would-be prophet left to wondering if he had somehow fallen short. The revelation that finally broke the silence challenged Muhammad to contemplate upon the caring Hands of God in his own life:

203 Al Quran 96:1-5
204 Al Quran 68:1-4

وَالضُّحَىٰ ۝ وَالَّيْلِ إِذَا سَجَىٰ ۝ مَا وَدَّعَكَ رَبُّكَ وَمَا قَلَىٰ ۝ وَلَلْآخِرَةُ خَيْرٌ لَّكَ مِنَ الْأُولَىٰ ۝ وَلَسَوْفَ يُعْطِيكَ رَبُّكَ فَتَرْضَىٰ ۝ أَلَمْ يَجِدْكَ يَتِيمًا فَآوَىٰ ۝ وَوَجَدَكَ ضَآلاًّ فَهَدَىٰ ۝ وَوَجَدَكَ عَآئِلاً فَأَغْنَىٰ ۝ فَأَمَّا الْيَتِيمَ فَلَا تَقْهَرْ ۝ وَأَمَّا السَّآئِلَ فَلَا تَنْهَرْ ۝ وَأَمَّا بِنِعْمَةِ رَبِّكَ فَحَدِّثْ ۝

By the day's early light, and the night's dark stillness, your Sustainer has not forsaken you, nor is He displeased:
The future holds His promise over what was
your Sustainer will surely fill you with contentment.
Did He not find you an orphan and give you protection?
He found you wandering and gave you guidance
He found you needy and freed you from want
Therefore oppress not the orphan,
Or rebuff the needy and the dispossessed {Saail},
And by the bounty of your Sustainer be your discourse. [205]

The Passion of Prophethood

He began his mission by first confiding his message to the immediate family, and then later on to the extended family, including his aunts and uncles. His earliest followers were Khadijah, Ali, Zayd and his close friend Abu Bakr. There are fascinating chronicles of these early conversions and rejections; Person by person, soul by soul. Amongst his extended family, most of the younger members would embrace his message. The young Abbas and Hamza, who were roughly of the prophet's own age, were yet unaffected in these early days and offered no empathy. On the other hand none of his four paternal uncles accepted his message. Abu Talib and Abu Lahab were father figures to him and their rejection must have been heart-breaking. And although Abu Talib's love and affection for Muhammad remained un-muted and the protection afforded to Muhammad by Abu Talib as the chief of the clan remained active and intact, Abu Talib refused to forsake the religion of his forefathers. Abu Lahab was ridiculing and hostile at the outset and would remain so. The prophet was tortured by the emerging split in the house of Quraish.

These early days in Mecca were tortuous. The Quran etches a haunting image of the prophet alone and still, reaching the depths of his core to come to grips with the demands of his mission and the agony of rejection by the people he dearly loved. Moses was given Aaron as a companion. Muhammad's companion when there was no other was to be the Quran itself. The message would fill the messenger and there would be no turning back from the message

---

or the mission:

يَـٰٓأَيُّهَا ٱلْمُزَّمِّلُ ۝ قُمِ ٱلَّيْلَ إِلَّا قَلِيلًا ۝ نِّصْفَهُۥٓ أَوِ ٱنقُصْ مِنْهُ قَلِيلًا ۝ أَوْ زِدْ عَلَيْهِ
وَرَتِّلِ ٱلْقُرْءَانَ تَرْتِيلًا ۝ إِنَّا سَنُلْقِى عَلَيْكَ قَوْلًا ثَقِيلًا ۝

O thou wrapped up in thy raiment {Muzzammil}!
Keep vigil the night long, save a little -
Rise to pray in the night except a little,
A half thereof, or abate a little thereof
Or add (a little) thereto - and chant the Quran in measure,
For we shall charge thee with a word of weight.[206]

The stalemates of this life veil the vistas of spiritual breakthroughs. Worldly detachment frees the spirit and bares the truth. The prophet was to seek no gain except that which came from the purification of soul. He was to be the sincere and pure conduit of the Will of God:

يَـٰٓأَيُّهَا ٱلْمُدَّثِّرُ ۝ قُمْ فَأَنذِرْ ۝ وَرَبَّكَ فَكَبِّرْ ۝ وَثِيَابَكَ فَطَهِّرْ ۝ وَٱلرُّجْزَ فَٱهْجُرْ ۝
وَلَا تَمْنُن تَسْتَكْثِرُ ۝

O thou enveloped in thy cloak {Muddassir},
Arise and warn! Thy Lord magnify;
Thy raiment purify; Pollution shun!
And show not favour, seeking worldly gain! [207]

His message against idolatry and self-centeredness ran contrary to the material and social interests of the Meccan establishment. The Kaabah was the repository of many idols and the annual pre-Islamic pilgrimage drew many pilgrims from across Arabia, bringing with them the material benefits ensuing from trade and the veneration of the idols. To disown Muhammad and his message they launched a campaign to brand Muhammad as a "dangerous sorcerer" so that the visiting pilgrims would shun him. This, however, had the opposite effect, and Muhammad's message would find its way to spiritually earnest pilgrims. In the meantime, as the revelations grew so did the count of Muhammad's followers and therefore the number of people who committed the revelations to memory. In a society that was rigidly hierarchical and culturally iconic, the message had a special appeal to the disaffected, the slaves, the former slaves, the young and to women. In a way, not much had changed since the time of Noah. Human arrogance is recalcitrant and primordial like Satan's own. Like the Prophet now, Noah too back then was mocked by the big wigs of his time when they gloated, *"we (the chieftains) do not see that any follow thee*

---

206 Al Quran 73:1-5 As interpreted by Pickthal
207 Al Quran 74:1-6. As interpreted by Pickthal

save the most abject amongst us" (11:27).

The lines in the sand dug deeper as the stakes got higher. Often there were splits within the household. Those of the believers without protection would find increasing persecution. Slaves were out rightly tortured and a female slave died as a result of torture. Abu Bakr who was a man of means had already used his money to buy the freedom of many slaves, male and female. Amongst those whose freedom he would buy was Bilal. Bilal was often flogged and tortured by his Jewish master, because of his (Bilal's) unconcealed love of the prophet. Later in Medina, Bilal would become the first *muezzin* (one who loudly calls the people to formal prayers).

When, for some it became nearly impossible to practice their faith, Muhammad instructed them to emigrate to Abyssinia, where he believed, correctly so, that the Christian Negus was just and the land had "sincerity of religion". All together 80 adults and some small children emigrated to Abyssinia in small batches. The Negus granted asylum to the Muslims over the objections of the Quraish ambassadors, after finding empathy with the message of this new-found *deen*, conveyed to him (Negus) by Jafar ibn Abu Talib, the prophet's cousin.

At home in Mecca, the continuing persecution of the Muslims, would only serve to elevate the truth. Hamza had already embraced Islam and now the fearless maverick, Umar Ibn Khattab would embrace the call of Muhammad and he, Umar, would proclaim it openly. The Muslims had reached a critical mass and their practice was beginning to move out into the open. One of the few remaining options for the Quraish was to boycott the clan of Muttalib and the clan of Hashim (Abu Lahab exempted). All other clans signed a pledge not to trade with, or sell food to the clans of Muttalib and Hashim and forbade marriage to any of their women. The boycott was designed to force the clan of Hashim to disown Muhammad or better still to force Muhammad to renounce his mission. The Muslims persevered and this boycott slowly fizzled out, resulting in its formal annulment two years later.

Divine Succor

In 619 CE, Muhammad approaching 50 would suffer more personal losses. His cherished wife of 25 years and his close confidant and counselor, Khadijah would pass away. And so would the head of his clan and uncle, Abu Talib. Abu Lahab would succeed Abu Talib as the chief of the Hashim. With the protection of Abu Talib gone, Muhammad's enemies found him to be vulnerable and the insults and injuries intensified. Well aware of his passion regarding personal cleanliness, his opponents would defile his home and person, throwing refuse and animal discards. Abu Bakr, found himself in a similar position as the Muslims were lacking protection. The prophet no longer safe in Mecca would seek protection in neighboring Taif. Here, as other prophets before him, he would be severely tested. The leaders in Taif rejected his plea for protection and instead inundated him with rebukes and insults. They organized an unruly crowd that routed him from town. A few individual conversions during this ordeal must have been a small consolation.

Prophets never waver in their mission and rejection comes their way all too often. Running out of choices, he was able to return to Mecca under the protection of the clan of Muteem. Around this time of ebbing worldly fortunes, Providence would give succor to Muhammad, with more Signs. Muhammad had been primed for his most holy spiritual experience. The miraculous night journey {*Isra*} to the "Furthest Mosque", in Jerusalem, followed by his ascension to the luminous Heavens {*Mi'raj*} and his direct encounter with fellow prophets, the angels and, from our perspective, the unfathomable Grace of God. The Seer and Hearer of all things and words would fill the prophet's ready and wanting heart with the Signs of God:

سُبْحَٰنَ ٱلَّذِىٓ أَسْرَىٰ بِعَبْدِهِۦ لَيْلًا مِّنَ ٱلْمَسْجِدِ ٱلْحَرَامِ إِلَى ٱلْمَسْجِدِ ٱلْأَقْصَا ٱلَّذِى بَٰرَكْنَا حَوْلَهُۥ لِنُرِيَهُۥ مِنْ ءَايَٰتِنَآ إِنَّهُۥ هُوَ ٱلسَّمِيعُ ٱلْبَصِيرُ ۝

Glory to (God) Who did take His servant for a Journey by night from the Sacred Mosque to the farthest Mosque,
Whose precincts We did bless, - in order that We might show him some of Our Signs: for He is the One Who heareth and seeth (all things). [208]

The most cherished legacy of the prophet, the *Salaat* (the daily five devotional prayers), based on Hadith, has its origin in the *Mi'raj*. Like the *Mi'raj* the *Salaat* contemplates the presence of God and the assembly of prophets and angels. It is the "earthly forms of celestial adorations[209]" unfolded by the *Mi'raj*. At its core the *Salaat* is the Divine gift of spiritual healing and intimacy to each individual who yearns to follow in the way of Islam. It is a mystical union of intent and action, body and spirit, words and thought, moving progressively and cyclically towards the impossible "now" of time. In this "now" the rituals collapse into intimacy. The pleas for guidance, forgiveness, blessings for the present prophets, before and after the prostrations, are direct, and emanate from the amorphous core of the body and spirit, words and deeds. The *Salaat* represents the rhythm of mortal existence, between the self and God. It is the spiritual exercise by which the soul renews its mandate from God as it is an acknowledgement that the self submits and stands by the Will of God.

The author is moved to yield to the eloquence of others to convey the Beauty, the Grace, and the Blessing which is *Salaat*. In their must-read expose' on the

---

208 Al Quran 17:1
209 *The illuminated Prayer, The five-times prayer of the Sufis* by Coleman Barks and Michael Green.

Salaat "*The illuminated Prayer, The five- times prayer of the Sufis*" by Coleman Barks and Michael Green, quoting, the Sufi teacher Bawa Muhaiyadden, they offer:

> For those who have come to grow, the whole world is a garden.
> For those who wish to remain in a dream, the whole world is a stage.
> For those who have come to learn, the whole world is a university.
> For those who have come to know God, the whole world is a prayer mat.

In the cross-hairs—Emigration

Later in 621 CE, during the annual pilgrimage the Prophet would also meet six men from Yathrib (Medina) who would embrace his message and pledge to recognize the Unity of God, respect life and property and be cognizant of the impending reckoning with God. This would be called the first pledge of Aqabah. Providence had sown the seeds for the second emigration.

Yathrib was a city populated by the idol-worshipping tribes of Al Aws and Al Khazraj, living alongside Jewish tribes and often at odds with each other. The less numerous Jews, having been warred against previously, by a coalition of Christians from Al Sham and the tribes of Al Aws and AL Khazraj, now found advantage in the strife between the Al Aws and AL Khazraj. The six men from Yathrib had already been exposed to monotheism and Muhammad's Islam to them had an instant appeal. Amongst other reasons, not the least of which was providence itself, there was also the reason that Muhammad's message, unlike Judaism which claimed an "exclusive and chosen" status for its people, was decidedly inclusive. Islam to them was the panacea for their worn-torn city. The pilgrims would return to Yathrib, after the encounter with Muhammad, and the message of the new faith spread with great rapidity and a wide-spread enthusiasm.

The following year would bring a batch of 12 pilgrims who would now go back with a Meccan Muslim Musab Ibn Umair, as their Quranic teacher. The next year, 622 CE, seventy three men and two women would come for the pilgrimage. The pilgrims would conclude a treaty of mutual support and solidarity amongst the Muslims, irrespective of their domicile. There would also be a collective pledge by the Yathrib pilgrims to protect Muhammad as they would their own family. The Muslims of Mecca and the Muslims of Yathrib were one community bound by their faith and led by Muhammad. There would no more be delineation by tribal heritage, domicile, rank or status. This agreement would be known as the second pledge of Aqabah. Arabia had shed the yoke of tribal polity. The seed of pan-humanism had taken root.

The stage was set for the second emigration and the news of the pledge had leaked out. In Mecca it would be unsettling to the Quraysh. In Yathrib itself, the chronic feud between the Aws and the Khazraj, was to the strategic advantage of the Jewish tribes. The amalgamation of these warring factions into a new unified community was worth their note.

The Muslims would begin the emigration process discreetly and in small batches, though there would be some, who would be apprehended and blocked by the Quraish. The prophet himself would stay behind, waiting for others to safely leave. Sensing that time was running out, the Quraish would devise a plan to collectively assassinate Muhammad. Fashioned after the senatorial assassins of Julius Caesar, one member of each clan would take a strike at Muhammad. A collective strike, they thought, would inoculate them from blame and retaliation. But it was not to be. Muhammad would walk away from right under the noses of his would be assassins:

وَإِذْ يَمْكُرُ بِكَ ٱلَّذِينَ كَفَرُوا لِيُثْبِتُوكَ أَوْ يَقْتُلُوكَ أَوْ يُخْرِجُوكَ ۚ وَيَمْكُرُونَ وَيَمْكُرُ ٱللَّهُ ۖ وَٱللَّهُ خَيْرُ ٱلْمَـٰكِرِينَ ۝

{Recall} that those who resisted the truth,
plotted to confine you, kill you, or to banish you.
They plan and God has His Plan. And God is the best of planners.[210]

The *Hijra* (emigration from Mecca to Medina, on the night of his intended assassination by a coalition of Meccan tribes) had begun. With a bounty of 300 camels on his head, accompanied by his close companion Abu Bakr, the dangerous journey across 400 miles of barren hilly terrain, to Medina was under way. About 70 of his followers who had faced similar persecution in Mecca had already preceded him.

Providence would guide Muhammad and Abu Bakr out of Mecca to a tumultuous welcome into Medina. Thirteen years of perseverance had paid off. In Medina, Muhammad's dilemma was the opposite. In Mecca he was running out of clans that would protect him. In Medina his followers, cutting across tribal lines of the Aws and Khazraj, were competing over hosting him! The prophet would cede this decision to his camel. His abode would be the spot where his camel stopped. The camel kneeled at a yard belonging to two orphans. Justly purchased, this place of the camel's choosing would be the ground of Masjid-e-Nabawi — the mosque of Medina and the abode of the prophet. The covered area of the mosque ("*Suffah*") would also provide shelter for the homeless amongst them.

The tide had turned and with it came the advent of a new phase of the Message. The Meccans had resisted change and the people of Medina welcomed it. In Mecca the message was delivered to a people who, despite having known him

---

210 Al Quran 8:30

as a trustworthy man, had been reluctant, adversarial, antagonistic and oppressive. The Quraish must have believed, in the days of Islam's infancy, that the movement would fizzle away or that it could be contained. The Muslims were commanded then to bear and endure the persecution and injustices with patience and forbearance. Towards the end of the Meccan period the Quraish had contemplated fratricide and elimination, not containment. The Muslims were then commanded to leave Mecca. Despite the *Hijra* (emigration from Mecca), the unrelenting Quraish were an existential threat. In Medina Muhammad had found general support and enthusiasm. The community of Muslims had heretofore been a collection of courageous individuals who had defied Meccan authority. Now the community had been transformed, with rapid growth, both in numbers and diversity. *Al Amin* was rapidly being pulled to the center of power in Medina. In the mix of those who looked up to him as a trustworthy and wise leader, were non-muslims too. Muhammad's vision of peace and justice had to be translated into a new social order, fitting the new secular challenges of Medina. The Messenger would also become a statesman and within him there was no conflict between the two roles. The Quran commanded a strict ethical code of conduct, transcending communal or religious lines:

$$\text{يَٰٓأَيُّهَا ٱلنَّاسُ إِنَّا خَلَقْنَٰكُم مِّن ذَكَرٍ وَأُنثَىٰ وَجَعَلْنَٰكُمْ شُعُوبًا وَقَبَآئِلَ لِتَعَارَفُوٓا۟ إِنَّ أَكْرَمَكُمْ}$$
$$\text{عِندَ ٱللَّهِ أَتْقَىٰكُمْ إِنَّ ٱللَّهَ عَلِيمٌ خَبِيرٌ ۝}$$

O Mankind, We have created you from (the same pair of) male and female and have dispersed you into nations and tribes so that you may know and cooperate with each other. God ranks you by your piety alone
God is all knowing {Aleem}, all-aware {Khabeer}. [211]

His message was one of universal peace and justice with religious tolerance. Non-muslims could not be coerced into the new faith:

$$\text{لَآ إِكْرَاهَ فِى ٱلدِّينِ قَد تَّبَيَّنَ ٱلرُّشْدُ مِنَ ٱلْغَىِّ}$$

"Deen takes root without coercion".
"The truth (as willing seekers will discern) stands clear of error" [212]

And further more:

$$\text{قُلْ يَٰٓأَيُّهَا ٱلْكَٰفِرُونَ ۝ لَآ أَعْبُدُ مَا تَعْبُدُونَ ۝ وَلَآ أَنتُمْ عَٰبِدُونَ مَآ أَعْبُدُ ۝ وَلَآ}$$
$$\text{أَنَا۠ عَابِدٌ مَّا عَبَدتُّمْ ۝ وَلَآ أَنتُمْ عَٰبِدُونَ مَآ أَعْبُدُ ۝ لَكُمْ دِينُكُمْ وَلِىَ دِينِ ۝}$$

Say to those in hindrance to your faith

---

211 Al Quran 49:13
212 Al Quran 2 :256

I do not worship that which you worship
Nor do you worship what I worship
Never shall I worship that which you worship
And you will not worship that which I worship
Unto you your way and unto me my way.[213]

He would make treaties with the various tribes of Medina, including the dominant Jewish tribes, to establish the code of civil conduct, guaranteeing the freedom of religion for Muslims and non-muslims alike. His integrity and principled fairness would propel his rapid political ascendancy.

In the cross-hairs—Wars

Power like water does not grow organically. It flows from one point to another. The accumulation of political power is not through its organic growth but through its shift from one or more power-centers to another. Those who found their power diminishing, the Quraish of Mecca, the lip-service converts of Medina and the powerful Jewish tribes of Medina had a common cause. Muhammad, in their opinion, still short of critical mass had to be stopped. Their calculus had a mortal flaw. Their equation ignored the decisive power of Faith.

There would be three major wars, the wars of *Badr*, *Uhud* and *Khandaq* (trench), each increasingly threatening the complete annihilation of the Muslims. The reluctant prophet was commanded by the Quran to fight. The first battle, the battle of Badr was sanctioned by the Quran and was substantially an act of faith, given that the 313 Muslims prevailed over an enemy vastly superior in armaments and numbers (1000 plus). The Quran asserts the power of belief:

يَـٰٓأَيُّهَا ٱلنَّبِىُّ حَرِّضِ ٱلْمُؤْمِنِينَ عَلَى ٱلْقِتَالِ إِن يَكُن مِّنكُمْ عِشْرُونَ صَـٰبِرُونَ يَغْلِبُوا۟ مِا۟ئَتَيْنِ
وَإِن يَكُن مِّنكُم مِّا۟ئَةٌ يَغْلِبُوٓا۟ أَلْفًا مِّنَ ٱلَّذِينَ كَفَرُوا۟ بِأَنَّهُمْ قَوْمٌ لَّا يَفْقَهُونَ ۝

O Prophet! Inspire the faithful to fight.
If there be of you twenty steadfast they shall overcome two hundred,
and if there be of you a hundred steadfast they shall overcome a thousand of
those hostile to faith, because they are a people without the capacity to
grasp.[214]

At the battle of Uhud, a force of about 700 Muslims would encounter an army of over 3000 blood-thirsty Quraish, seeking to erase the disgrace of Badr. At Uhud, although they would survive, the Muslims would taste their first military defeat. The Prophet himself was bodily wounded but the pain of a deeper wound awaited him on the spent battlefield. Not only had the brave and bold Hamza Ibn

---

213 Al Quran 109
214 Al Quran 8:65

Abd Al Muttalib fallen in battle but in their despicable vengeance the Quraish mutilated his remains. In deep despair over the dishonor to his bosom friend and uncle, Muhammad would bury Hamza where the body lay. He was also to bury the hatchet of revenge. The Quran would call the Prophet to the power of forbearance:

وَإِنْ عَاقَبْتُمْ فَعَاقِبُوا بِمِثْلِ مَا عُوقِبْتُم بِهِ ۖ وَلَئِن صَبَرْتُمْ لَهُوَ خَيْرٌ لِّلصَّابِرِينَ ۝ وَاصْبِرْ
وَمَا صَبْرُكَ إِلَّا بِاللَّهِ ۚ وَلَا تَحْزَنْ عَلَيْهِمْ وَلَا تَكُ فِي ضَيْقٍ مِّمَّا يَمْكُرُونَ ۝

If ye punish, then punish with the like of that wherewith ye were afflicted.
But if ye endure patiently, verily it is better for the patient.
Endure thou patiently (O Muhammad).
Thine endurance is only by (the help of) Allah.
Grieve not for them, and be not in distress because of that which they devise. [215]

In the encounter of Khandaq, a coalition of almost all of Muhammad's enemies and contenders to his power would lay siege to the city of Medina. The coalition led by the Quraish of Mecca at the behest of the Banu al Nadir, and including the tribes of Banu Saad and Banu Asad would field a force of over 10,000. This was the largest army ever assembled and seen in Arabia. A stalemated enemy would lose heart and eventually withdraw.

The prophet was a reluctant warrior and never did he begin the hostilities. He was the pivot of social change in a violent Arabia, and his new order would have to survive the violent onslaught of his enemies. War is a constant condition in human history and most of history's radical social or political changes have had to march through the gate of war. The Quran has explicit commandments relating to war. The most resonant and explicit, instructs muslims to eschew aggression. But in the defense of his community, a muslim must take up arms and not be afraid to die. War is an abominable business that must come to a speedy end, without triggering a new cycle. This demands fearlessness with restraint, and peace with justice. It is summed up so inimitably in the Quranic edict:

وَالْفِتْنَةُ أَشَدُّ مِنَ الْقَتْلِ

Persecution is worse than killing [216]

The strategy and tactics of war are a human construct; How and where to face the enemy is a decision to be made by those engaged in war. The prophet would strategize with his comrades and many critical decisions such as the venue of Badr or the trench of the battle of Khandaq were ideas not of the

215 Al Quran 16:126-127 as interpreted by Pickthall
216 Al Quran 2:191

prophet, but those of his comrades. The conduct was a different matter. The Quran would radically transform the rules of engagement and rules in war's aftermath, commanding humane treatment of prisoners of war and swift cessation of hostilities.

The unarmed soldier of peace, conqueror of hearts

Six years had passed in Medina and Muhammad had a vision that he would enter the holy sanctuary of Mecca and perform the pilgrimage in peace. Fully aware, though unperturbed, by the potential danger of such a mission, he would lead a group of about 1400 Muslim and non-muslim pilgrims, appropriately attired, and in possession of sacrificial cattle. Studiously avoiding any violence, Muhammad's caravan would approach from the south and stop at Hudaybiyah. Here he was at the door-step of Mecca, fully vulnerable to his enemy. By any ordinary imagination this was a risky undertaking. In this remarkable act, a testament to faith and fearlessness no doubt, Muhammad, now a pilgrim, was telling his mortal enemies that hearts could be healed and trust could be won by dropping the sword. The pilgrim was saying in effect that stalemates of the heart could only be broken with peace and not wars. [217]

The Quraish, dumb-founded, would block the commonly used accesses to Mecca. The Muslims though, had come in peace and had already foreclosed any options to defy the Quraish. The opportunity to reverse distrust was at hand. Muhammad was here to show the Quraish that there was another way. He would negotiate with the Quraysh the treaty of Hudaybiyah, by which Muhammad would be prohibited to enter Mecca on this occasion but would be allowed to return the following year. As an additional concession to the Quraysh any person of the Quraysh emigrating to the Muslims in Medina would be returned to Mecca whereas any new Muslim emigrating from Medina to Mecca would not be under any obligation to be returned to Medina. Superficially, this was a setback for the Muslims and many Muslims would see it as such, but not the prophet. Unable to circumambulate the Kaaba, he would nevertheless perform the concluding rites of the pilgrimage in Hudaybiyah and be ever so grateful to God. On the return trip to Medina he would receive the revelation which would confirm both the acceptance of his pilgrimage and the bestowal of victory:

إِنَّا فَتَحْنَا لَكَ فَتْحًا مُّبِينًا ۞ لِّيَغْفِرَ لَكَ ٱللَّهُ مَا تَقَدَّمَ مِن ذَنۢبِكَ وَمَا تَأَخَّرَ وَيُتِمَّ نِعْمَتَهُ عَلَيْكَ وَيَهْدِيَكَ صِرَٰطًا مُّسْتَقِيمًا ۞

We have granted to you victory, an unmitigated victory,
So that God may forgive you of your past sins and those to come,

---

217 Karen Armstrong's *Muhammad* has a whole chapter on this, appropriately called "Holy Peace"

and may complete His blessing on you,
and may guide you on a righteous path {Siraat um Mustaqeem}[218]

At Hudaybiyah, Muhammad chose peace over war at the apparent expense of his prestige. At the outset he undertook a dangerous mission, meeting unarmed with his enemy, at the enemy's doorstep. If there was to be a perception that he had been slighted by the ban on his entry into Mecca, he showed that he did not care. He concluded his pilgrimage without completing the customary rites at the Kaabah. Per the terms of the treaty he would leave behind in Mecca those that converted on this occasion (significant amongst them Abu Jandal ibn Suhail, son of the very person negotiating on behalf of the Quraish with Muhammad). He would also agree to offer no hindrance to those in Medina who would want to revert from faith, and go back to Mecca. The first was emotionally heart-wrenching, the second, an imbalanced concession as it may appear, was nevertheless agreeable to his message. Muhammad was not averse to paying a price for peace and civility. Significant in the treaty however was the clause of non-aggression towards each other, and each others allies.

The rewards of unmitigated victory started pouring in and were incessant. The Muslim émigrés in Abyssina returned and the next year, 7 A.H., 629 C.E. Muhammad would return with 2000 pilgrims as per the terms of the treaty. The Muslims would joyously fulfill the rites at Kaabah and perform their congregational prayers. The Meccans watching this marvelous display of spirituality and brotherhood from the adjoining hilltops could not help being affected. Here-in was another victory without battle. The fearless warrior and brilliant strategist of the Quraysh, Khalid Bin Waleed, who displayed his prowess at Uhud was foremost amongst the notables to embrace Islam and would follow Muhammad to Medina. He left the principals of Quraysh telling them that he was ready for submission having seen the truth unfold before his very eyes. Many more would follow him.

The treaty of Hudaybiyah was broken when the Quraysh aided their allies, the tribe of Banu Bakr, against the non-Meccan Muslim tribe of Khuzaah. Routed from their homes, the latter sought Muhammad's intervention. This time Muhammad marched towards Mecca with an army of 10,000 and the dominoes began to fall. The defectors from the Quraysh heretofore prohibited from joining him, would leave Mecca to join up with him along the way. Abu Sufyan himself would set out to secure the terms of surrender. His persecutors at his mercy, Muhammad issued the proclamation of general amnesty. "Whoever enters the house of Abu Sufyan shall be secure. Whoever remains in his or her home shall be secure and whoever enters the Mosque shall be secure." Under stern orders of disengagement and restraint, the victorious entry into Mecca was bloodless.

---

218 Al Quran 48:1-2

Standing by the door of the Kaabah, Muhammad reminded the diverse multitudes of their common lineage, urging them to respect their equality and cherish their diversity, recalling from the Quran:

يَـٰٓأَيُّهَا ٱلنَّاسُ إِنَّا خَلَقْنَـٰكُم مِّن ذَكَرٍ وَأُنثَىٰ وَجَعَلْنَـٰكُمْ شُعُوبًا وَقَبَآئِلَ لِتَعَارَفُوٓا۟ إِنَّ أَكْرَمَكُمْ

عِندَ ٱللَّهِ أَتْقَىٰكُمْ إِنَّ ٱللَّهَ عَلِيمٌ خَبِيرٌ ۝

O Mankind, We have created you from (the same pair of) male and female
and have dispersed you into nations and tribes
so that you may know and cooperate with each other
God ranks you by your piety alone
God is all knowing {Aleem}, all-aware {Khabeer}.[219]

It is note-worthy that the preceding Quranic verse encompasses the human race and not just the community of Muslims; Temporal equality and respect cuts across lines of race, religion, sex, or social status. The Prophet had lived these words. By these very principles, during the Prophet's very lifetime (short from a political perspective) the Arabian Peninsula was transformed from a land of disparate and warring tribes, driven by revenge and vendettas, into a nation abiding in brotherhood.

Family

As was customarily the case in the Arabia of those times, Muhammad was polygamous. He was neither different in this respect than the previous prophets such as Abraham, Moses, Jacob, David or Solomon. For twenty eight years, from age 23 to the age of 50 he was married to Khadijah. His other marriages took place after Khadijah's death. Marriage in Islam is not only a means to sanctify a relationship between a man and a woman, but also a means to provide social respect and contractual security to women and their children from the current or previous marriages. In a male-dominated society, marriage is not about lust, it is in fact about the rights of the woman. Karen Armstrong, a leading religious scholar of our times, notes "[The Quran] gave women legal rights of inheritance and divorce; most Western women had nothing comparable until the nineteenth century".[220]

The wives of the Prophet were awarded the highest respect that was due to them both inside and outside their homes. The Quran calls them the "Mothers of the Believers":

219 Al Quran 49:13
220 *A History of God*, Karen Armstrong, Ballantine Books, New York 1993 pg 158

اَلنَّبِيُّ أَوْلَىٰ بِالْمُؤْمِنِينَ مِنْ أَنفُسِهِمْ ۖ وَأَزْوَٰجُهُۥ أُمَّهَـٰتُهُمْ

The Prophet is closer to the Believers than their own selves,
and his wives are their mothers.[221]

Marriage is that private, living plane on which one can discover the beauty that is goodness, and tranquility that is security, love, commitment and compassion. It is a plane, spiritually fertile, because the "signs" of God permeate this plane:

وَمِنْ ءَايَٰتِهِۦٓ أَنْ خَلَقَ لَكُم مِّنْ أَنفُسِكُمْ أَزْوَٰجًا لِّتَسْكُنُوٓا۟ إِلَيْهَا وَجَعَلَ بَيْنَكُم مَّوَدَّةً وَرَحْمَةً

إِنَّ فِى ذَٰلِكَ لَءَايَٰتٍ لِّقَوْمٍ يَتَفَكَّرُونَ ۝

And among the signs of God is this that He created for you mates
that you might live in tranquility with them;
and He has put love and mercy between your hearts.
Behold there are signs for those who contemplate.[222]

In pre-Islamic Arabia, females were considered liabilities and often female infants were killed at birth. An arbitrary form of estrangement called *zihar* allowed the husband to deprive his wife of all marital rights and at the same time prevent her from remarrying. Widows themselves were considered as bad omens and marriage to a widow was considered a curse.

Other contemporary societies and religions did not accord just rights to women either. In the Mosaic law, women did not have the right to seek divorce. The vow of a woman was reversible by her father or husband. The guilt or innocence of a wife accused of adultery was subject to trial by the ordeal of the bitter water. Daughters could inherit only in the absence of sons.

Women did not fare well under Roman law either, despite some relief in the Justinian-I era of the 6th century. Under Roman law, a woman was the property of her father and when married she became the purchased property of her husband and was thus no different from a slave. Even her own property passed to the husband. She could not be a witness to or enter into a contract. Adultery was punished with death by Constantine. Justinian reduced the penalty to banishment to a convent. A woman condemned for adultery could not re-marry. A marriage between a Christian and a Jew rendered the parties guilty of adultery. Women under Hindu law had only limited rights of inheritance, and were disqualified as witnesses. Widows were not allowed to remarry and were treated as social outcasts. The practice of "*sati*" would require them to be immolated on their husband's funeral pyre

---

221 Al Quran 33:6
222 Al Quran 30:21

Marriage, in Islam, is that intimate union in which the husband is the wife's raiment, as is the wife to the husband[223]. It is that private domain of two people, where the union is under the shade of Divine sanction. At the root of this union is a voluntary commitment that must renew itself with love, caring, forgiveness and trust. Relationships are the only context in which virtue can exist. The spousal relationship is the foremost of all. Mates are from the single soul and bonds between the separated souls are offered by God. The sacrosanct bond of marriage lives under the watchful presence of God Himself.

يَٰٓأَيُّهَا ٱلنَّاسُ ٱتَّقُواْ رَبَّكُمُ ٱلَّذِى خَلَقَكُم مِّن نَّفْسٍ وَٰحِدَةٍ وَخَلَقَ مِنْهَا زَوْجَهَا وَبَثَّ مِنْهُمَا رِجَالًا كَثِيرًا وَنِسَآءً ۚ وَٱتَّقُواْ ٱللَّهَ ٱلَّذِى تَسَآءَلُونَ بِهِۦ وَٱلْأَرْحَامَ ۚ إِنَّ ٱللَّهَ كَانَ عَلَيْكُمْ رَقِيبًا ۞

O mankind be conscious of your Lord
Who created you from a single soul;
And created from it mates
And thereby countless men and women.
Be conscious of God by Whom you bond and develop kinship
God is watching you {Raqeeb}[224]

With a few exceptions, (Ayesha and Mariah the Copt being amongst the exceptions), all of Muhammad's wives were widows. These women would not have a second chance in pre-Islamic Arabia or anywhere else for that matter. There are differing accounts of the story and marital status of Mariah. According to Husayn Haykal in *The Life of Muhammad*, Mariah and her sister Sirin were sent as gifts to the Prophet by the Coptic Archbishop of Egypt. The Prophet married Mariah and Sirin was given in marriage to Hassan Ibn Thabit.[225] Mariah is different from the other wives in that she did not and does not enjoy the rank and incumbent responsibility of being one of the 'Mothers of the Believers'.

The Prophet need not have married her if he had followed the prevailing norms. Martin Lings whose account suggests that Mariah was a bondmaid states that the "law revealed to Moses has corroborated such rights, and the Quran expressly allowed a master to take his bondmaid as a concubine on condition of her free consent"[226]. The differing accounts of history aside, the Quran, which the Prophet exemplified, repeatedly exhorts the believers to move away from exploitive relations between men and women. God is minutely aware of our innermost desires and motivations; including the compassion with which we treat others less fortunate than ourselves:

---

223 Al Quran 2:187
224 Al Quran 4:1
225 *The life of Muhammad* by Muhammad Husayn Haykal. Translated from the 8th edition by Ismail, Ragi A al Faruqi. pg376
226 *Muhammad*, his life based on the earliest sources by Martin Lings pg 277

وَتُوبُوٓا۟ إِلَى ٱللَّهِ جَمِيعًا أَيُّهَ ٱلْمُؤْمِنُونَ لَعَلَّكُمْ تُفْلِحُونَ ۞ وَأَنكِحُوا۟ ٱلْأَيَٰمَىٰ مِنكُمْ
وَٱلصَّٰلِحِينَ مِنْ عِبَادِكُمْ وَإِمَآئِكُمْ إِن يَكُونُوا۟ فُقَرَآءَ يُغْنِهِمُ ٱللَّهُ مِن فَضْلِهِۦ وَٱللَّهُ وَٰسِعٌ عَلِيمٌ
۞

Turn to God in repentance, — all of you — O believers,
So that you might attain spiritual success
And marry the single from amongst you and the pious of your slaves and maid-
servants.
If they be poor, God will enrich them of His bounty.
God is without limits, Aware.[227]

Muhammad Asad regards the preceding verse and 4-25 as conclusive evidence of the Quran's clear-cut forbiddance of the taking of women as secret concubines. "The above verse rules out all forms of concubinage and postulates marriage as the only basis of lawful sexual relations between a man and a female slave."[228] Marriage accords honor to a relationship:

ٱلْيَوْمَ أُحِلَّ لَكُمُ ٱلطَّيِّبَٰتُ وَطَعَامُ ٱلَّذِينَ أُوتُوا۟ ٱلْكِتَٰبَ حِلٌّ لَّكُمْ وَطَعَامُكُمْ حِلٌّ لَّهُمْ
وَٱلْمُحْصَنَٰتُ مِنَ ٱلْمُؤْمِنَٰتِ وَٱلْمُحْصَنَٰتُ مِنَ ٱلَّذِينَ أُوتُوا۟ ٱلْكِتَٰبَ مِن قَبْلِكُمْ إِذَآ ءَاتَيْتُمُوهُنَّ
أُجُورَهُنَّ مُحْصِنِينَ غَيْرَ مُسَٰفِحِينَ وَلَا مُتَّخِذِىٓ أَخْدَانٍ وَمَن يَكْفُرْ بِٱلْإِيمَٰنِ فَقَدْ حَبِطَ
عَمَلُهُۥ وَهُوَ فِى ٱلْءَاخِرَةِ مِنَ ٱلْخَٰسِرِينَ ۞

This day are (all) good things made lawful for you.
The food of those who have received the Scripture is lawful for you, and your
food is lawful for them.
And so are the virtuous women of the believers and the virtuous women of those
who received the Scripture before you (lawful for you).
When ye give them their marriage portions and live with them in honor, not in
fornication, nor taking them as secret concubines.
Whoso denieth the faith, his work is vain and he will be among the losers in the
Hereafter.[229]

The worldly havens of relationships are portals to Heaven itself. The commitment to the other is through the commitment to God; and the commitment to God is through commitment to the other. God is the third in a sacred bond between two. The Quran offers a moving vision of men and women joined in a common purpose. Each soul, male and female, is here to cherish the

227 Al Quran 24:31-32
228 *The Message of The Quran* by Muhammad Asad in footnote 43 to 24:32
229 Al Quran 5:5 as interpreted by Pickthall

other, relationships being not ends in themselves but pathways to transcendence. What is asked of one gender is asked equally of the other. By the other person, one knows oneself. True giving aligns us with the Truth, just as the Arabic words for giving and truth spring from the same root-word. By giving, the soul defines itself. True 'gain', profuse and for keeps, comes from *giving* in the way of God. By restraining the self (*sawm*, common expression being 'fasting'), the soul frees itself. The household of Muhammad lived by and for the transcendental assent of God:

إِنَّ ٱلْمُسْلِمِينَ وَٱلْمُسْلِمَٰتِ وَٱلْمُؤْمِنِينَ وَٱلْمُؤْمِنَٰتِ وَٱلْقَٰنِتِينَ وَٱلْقَٰنِتَٰتِ وَٱلصَّٰدِقِينَ وَٱلصَّٰدِقَٰتِ وَٱلصَّٰبِرِينَ وَٱلصَّٰبِرَٰتِ وَٱلْخَٰشِعِينَ وَٱلْخَٰشِعَٰتِ وَٱلْمُتَصَدِّقِينَ وَٱلْمُتَصَدِّقَٰتِ وَٱلصَّٰٓئِمِينَ وَٱلصَّٰٓئِمَٰتِ وَٱلْحَٰفِظِينَ فُرُوجَهُمْ وَٱلْحَٰفِظَٰتِ وَٱلذَّٰكِرِينَ ٱللَّهَ كَثِيرًا وَٱلذَّٰكِرَٰتِ أَعَدَّ ٱللَّهُ لَهُم مَّغْفِرَةً وَأَجْرًا عَظِيمًا ۝

Lo! men in submission to God, and women in submission to God,
and men in peace of faith, and women in peace of faith,
and men devout and obedient, and women devout and obedient,
and men who speak and live the truth, and women who speak and live the truth,
and men persevering and patient, and women persevering and patient,
and men who are humble, and women who are humble,
and men who give alms, and women who give alms,
and men who fast and restrain themselves, and women who fast and restrain themselves,
and men who guard their modesty, and women who guard,
and men who remember and contemplate God frequently and abundantly,
and women who remember and contemplate,
God has prepared for them forgiveness and a recompense immense.[230]

Muhammad's wives were his equals and he had earned their faith in him. They shared him as their husband as his followers shared him as their leader. He would say in his last sermon:

Do treat your women well and be kind to them for they are your partners and committed helpers

After Khadijah, he first married Sawdah (who came to be known as the Mother of the believers). Sawdah was the widow of Sakran Ibn Amr ibn Abd Shams, an early convert to Islam, who was also one of the emigrants to Abyssinia and had died upon his return to Mecca. About three years later, in the year 622, he married Ayesha daughter of Abu Bakr, one of his closest companions. He then married Hafsah widowed daughter of Umar, another one of his close

---

230 Al Quran 33:35

companions. Others included Zaynab daughter of Khuzaymah, widow of Ubaydah ibn al Harith, ibn al Muttalib who died in the battle of Badr; Umm Salamah daughter of Umayyah ibn al Mughira, widow of Abu Salamah who also died of wounds suffered in the battle of Uhud; Zaynab daughter of Jash, ex-wife of his adopted son, Zayd.

The Return

Muhammad was a king who ruled over men's hearts. He was a king who disdained a crown and who preferred a hut over a palace. There never was food in his house for the following day. This king slept on a reed mat. He slept little, preferring to be awake in prayer. His passionate application of his message to his own life is poignantly illustrated by Hussayn Haykal in his story of Muhammad's last days. Stoically enduring the pains of an illness that he fully understood to be fatal he would go about the business of winding up his life. This would include visitation to the graves of the slain Muslims buried in the graveyard of *Baqi*, not very far from his house. He would also make some visits, which he knew to be farewell visits, to the mosque during prayer times. He must have derived some comfort to see his emotionally fraught followers learning to cope with the ritual of prayers without his presence. One of his final quests was to assure the dissemination of every penny of his personal belongings. At the advent of his sickness, he had instructed his beloved wife, Ayesha to give unto charity seven coins that were his. Now towards the end he wanted confirmation. Upon finding that Ayesha was remiss he asked her to place the coins on his open outstretched palm. With seven coins, all of this king's worldly wealth on his palm, he asked aloud "What spectacle is this of Muhammad, if I were to meet God in this repose"? The seven dinars were promptly given away. The mortal messenger departed the next day, just as he had come into this world—with no material wealth to his name. He was buried where he died, in his small house inside the compound of the mosque of Medina.

His blessed wife Ayesha related his saying: "This world is the dwelling of him who has no dwelling and the property of him who has no property". He is also reported to have said "What have I to do with the world? In relation to the world, I am just a rider who shades himself under a tree, then goes off and leaves it.

The congregation at the mosque shocked into denial, were not open to receiving the news of Muhammad's death. Umar would have none of it. It was then Abu Bakr, the would-be first caliph of Medina, who would announce Muhammad's death to the congregation thusly:

"O people, if you have been worshipping Muhammad, then know that Muhammad is dead. But if you have been worshipping God, then know that God is living and never will God die". He then went on to recite from the Quran:

وَمَا مُحَمَّدٌ إِلَّا رَسُولٌ قَدْ خَلَتْ مِن قَبْلِهِ ٱلرُّسُلُ أَفَإِين مَّاتَ أَوْ قُتِلَ ٱنقَلَبْتُمْ عَلَىٰ أَعْقَـٰبِكُمْ وَمَن
يَنقَلِبْ عَلَىٰ عَقِبَيْهِ فَلَن يَضُرَّ ٱللَّهَ شَيْئًا وَسَيَجْزِى ٱللَّهُ ٱلشَّـٰكِرِينَ ﴿١٤٤﴾

Muhammad is but a messenger before whom many messengers have passed
Should he die or be killed, will you then turn away?
Know that detraction does not diminish God,
And requited by God are those who are thankful to Him"[231]

The Quran also instructs Muhammad to proclaim his mission thusly:

قُل لَّآ أَمْلِكُ لِنَفْسِى نَفْعًا وَلَا ضَرًّا إِلَّا مَا شَآءَ ٱللَّهُ وَلَوْ كُنتُ أَعْلَمُ ٱلْغَيْبَ لَٱسْتَكْثَرْتُ مِنَ
ٱلْخَيْرِ وَمَا مَسَّنِيَ ٱلسُّوٓءُ إِنْ أَنَا۠ إِلَّا نَذِيرٌ وَبَشِيرٌ لِقَوْمٍ يُؤْمِنُونَ ﴿١٨٨﴾

Say [O Prophet]: "It is not within my power to bring benefit to, or avert harm
from, myself, except as God may please.
And if I knew that which is beyond human perception, abundant good fortune
would surely have fallen on my lot, and no more evil would ever have touched
me. I am nothing but a warner and a herald of good tidings unto people who will
believe"[232]

The Last Sermon of Prophet Muhammad [233]

This sermon was delivered on the Ninth day of Dhul-Hijjah, 10 A.H. (623CE) in the
Uranah valley of Mount Arafat in Mecca. It was the occasion of the annual rites of
Hadj. It is also known as the Farewell Pilgrimage.
After praising and thanking God the Prophet (peace be upon him) began with the
words:
"O People! Lend me an attentive ear, for I know not whether after this year I shall
ever be amongst you again. Therefore, listen carefully to what I am saying and take
these words to those who could not be present here today."
"O People! just as you regard this month, this day ,this city as sacred ,so regard the
life and property of every Muslim as a sacred trust. Return the goods entrusted to
you to their rightful owners. Hurt no one so that no one may hurt you. Remember
that you will indeed meet your Lord, and that he will indeed reckon your deeds."
"God has forbidden you to take usury; therefore all interest obligations shall
henceforth be waived. Your capital is yours to keep .You will neither inflict nor
suffer any inequality. God has judged that there shall be no interest, and that all
interest due to Abbas Ibn 'Aal-Muttalib be waived."

---

231 Al Quran 3:144
232 Al Quran 7:188 as interpreted by Muhammad Asad in The message of the Quran
233 Also known as the "Farewell Sermon" of the Prophet

"Every right arising out of homicide in pre-Islamic days is henceforth waived, and the first such right that I waive is that arising from the murder of Rabiah ibni al-Harithiah."

"O men! the unbelievers indulge in tampering with the calendar in order to make permissible that which God forbade, and to prohibit what God has made permissible. With God the months are twelve in number. Four of them are holy, these are successive, and one occurs singly between the months of Jumada and Shaban."

"Beware of Satan, for the safety of your Deen. He has lost all hope that he will be able to lead you astray in big things so beware of following him in small things."

"O People it is true that you have certain rights with regard to your women but they also have rights over you. Remember that you have taken them as your wives only under God's trust and with His permission. If they abide by your right then to them belongs the right to be fed and clothed in kindness. Do treat your women well and be kind to them for they are your partners and committed helpers. And it is your right that they do not make friends with any one of whom you do not approve, as well as never to be unchaste."

"O People! listen to me in earnest, worship God, say your five daily prayers (Salaat), fast during the month of Ramadan, and give your wealth in Zakat .Perform Hadj if you can afford it."

"All mankind is from Adam and Eve, an Arab has no superiority over a non-Arab nor a non-Arab has any superiority over an Arab; also a White has no superiority over a Black nor does a Black have any superiority over a White except by piety and good action. Learn that every Muslim is a brother to every Muslim and that the Muslims constitute one brotherhood. Nothing shall be legitimate to a Muslim which belongs to a fellow Muslim unless it was given freely and willingly."

"Do not therefore do injustice to yourselves. Remember one day you will meet God and answer your deeds. So beware, do not stray from the path of righteousness after I am gone."

"O People! No Prophet or apostle will come after me and no new faith will be born. Reason well, therefore O People! and understand words that I convey to you. I leave behind me two things, the Quran and the Sunnah and if you follow these you will never go astray."

"All those who listen to me shall pass on my words to others and those to others again; and may the last ones understand my words better than those who listen to me directly."

"O God, be my witness, that I have conveyed your message to Your people."

As part of this sermon, the prophet recited to them a revelation from God, which he had just received, and which completed the Quran, for it was the last passage to be revealed:

ٱلۡيَوۡمَ يَئِسَ ٱلَّذِينَ كَفَرُواْ مِن دِينِكُمۡ فَلَا تَخۡشَوۡهُمۡ وَٱخۡشَوۡنِ ۚ ٱلۡيَوۡمَ أَكۡمَلۡتُ لَكُمۡ دِينِكُمۡ
وَأَتۡمَمۡتُ عَلَيۡكُمۡ نِعۡمَتِى وَرَضِيتُ لَكُمُ ٱلۡإِسۡلَٰمَ دِينًا ۚ

This day the disbeliever's despair of prevailing against your deen, so fear them
not, but fear Me (God)!
This day have I perfected for you, your deen and fulfilled My favor unto you, and
it hath been My good pleasure to choose Islam for you as your deen. (Al Quran
5:3)

The sermon was repeated sentence by sentence by Safwan's brother Rabiah (May God be pleased with him), who had a powerful voice, at the request of the Prophet and he faithfully, proclaimed to over ten thousand gathered on the occasion. Towards the end of his sermon, the Prophet asked "O people, have I faithfully delivered unto you my message?" A powerful murmur of assents "O God! yes!" arose from thousands of pilgrims and the vibrant words "*Allahumma Na'm*," rolled like thunder throughout the valley. The Prophet raised his forefinger and said: "O God bear witness that I have conveyed your message to your people." [234]

---

234 Reproduced from: http://www.isna.net/Resources/articles/general/The-Last-Sermon-Of-Prophet-Muhammad.aspx

Sadequain Calligraphy. [*And He has raised high the bounds of the sky, and set the Balance.*]

Courtesy of Dr. Salman Ahmad at www.sadequainfoundation.com

[In 1969 Sadequain painted thirty individual panels of refrains from "*Surah Rahman.*"]

The Scales of Justice

اَلرَّحْمَٰنُ ۞ عَلَّمَ ٱلْقُرْءَانَ ۞ خَلَقَ ٱلْإِنسَٰنَ ۞ عَلَّمَهُ ٱلْبَيَانَ ۞ ٱلشَّمْسُ وَٱلْقَمَرُ بِحُسْبَانٍ ۞ وَٱلنَّجْمُ وَٱلشَّجَرُ يَسْجُدَانِ ۞ وَٱلسَّمَآءَ رَفَعَهَا وَوَضَعَ ٱلْمِيزَانَ ۞ أَلَّا تَطْغَوْا۟ فِى ٱلْمِيزَانِ ۞ وَأَقِيمُوا۟ ٱلْوَزْنَ بِٱلْقِسْطِ وَلَا تُخْسِرُوا۟ ٱلْمِيزَانَ ۞

He is the Source of Mercy,
and the Source of the knowledge of the Quran,
Who created mankind
And endowed man with the power of expression and articulation
To Him are the sun and moon unerringly compliant
And the stars and the trees are in His adoring servitude
And He has raised high the bounds of the sky, and set the scale
So do not transgress the scale
Live by the measure of equity and do not diminish the scale's balance 235

Justice and Equity are Divine Pathways

Every element of creation is an essential cog in the form of the whole. The sun and the moon and the stars and the trees, from the fiery to the cool, the large to the small, the far-off to the close-by, are indispensable elements of a single tapestry. There is a harmonious interdependence between and amongst creation. The harmony of the universe flows from the balance of interdependence. Only God is truly independent. Every human soul must respect and exist within this balance. The path to internal peace is through the gate of external harmony and therefore demands an equitable and just interaction with all of creation. The pursuit of equity and justice is an aspect of God Consciousness. God commands us to be active and dispassionate witnesses to the truth:

---

235 Al Quran 55:1-9

يَٰٓأَيُّهَا ٱلَّذِينَ ءَامَنُوا۟ كُونُوا۟ قَوَّٰمِينَ لِلَّهِ شُهَدَآءَ بِٱلْقِسْطِ ۖ وَلَا يَجْرِمَنَّكُمْ شَنَـَٔانُ قَوْمٍ عَلَىٰ
أَلَّا تَعْدِلُوا۟ ۚ ٱعْدِلُوا۟ هُوَ أَقْرَبُ لِلتَّقْوَىٰ

*O you who believe! Be steadfast witnesses for God in equity, and let not hatred
of any people seduce you to deviate from justice. Be just, this is an aspect of God
Consciousness.* [236]

An injustice to a fellow human-being is a contravention of the Divine Edict and
therefore breaks one's faith. As witnesses, we are fore sworn to God Himself.
Any act or testimony must withstand the highest scrutiny; the supreme scrutiny
of God Himself. Testimony in the dispensation of justice is a sacred trust:

❁ يَٰٓأَيُّهَا ٱلَّذِينَ ءَامَنُوا۟ كُونُوا۟ قَوَّٰمِينَ بِٱلْقِسْطِ شُهَدَآءَ لِلَّهِ وَلَوْ عَلَىٰٓ أَنفُسِكُمْ أَوِ ٱلْوَٰلِدَيْنِ
وَٱلْأَقْرَبِينَ ۚ إِن يَكُنْ غَنِيًّا أَوْ فَقِيرًا فَٱللَّهُ أَوْلَىٰ بِهِمَا ۖ فَلَا تَتَّبِعُوا۟ ٱلْهَوَىٰٓ أَن تَعْدِلُوا۟ ۚ وَإِن تَلْوُۥٓا۟ أَوْ
تُعْرِضُوا۟ فَإِنَّ ٱللَّهَ كَانَ بِمَا تَعْمَلُونَ خَبِيرًا ﴿١٣٥﴾

O, you who have embraced faith in God
Uphold equity (qist) and be God's witnesses [to the truth]
Even though it be against your own selves or your parents
or those close to you, whether rich or poor
Superior is God's claim over both (claimants)
Do not be driven by desire or bias lest you sway from justice (adl)
And if you distort the truth or withhold it,
Know that God is fully aware of all that you do [237]

Amongst the Divine Names are *Al Adl* (The Just) and *Al Muqsit* (The Equitable).
To be unjust or inequitable is to be misaligned with God. Justice, so that it may
lead to enduring peace, should be anchored in ethics and equity. The Quran
expounds justice and equity as amongst the finest of moral values, and issues
repeated reminders. Islamic practice repeats these reminders, most tellingly
during the opening sermon of Friday's congregational-prayers[238]. The Friday-
sermon, typically a discourse on issues and conditions of local and global
interest, provides the perspective of the Quran and the *Hadith* on these issues
and conditions. It is traditional, that these sermons conclude with this reminder
from the Quran:

---

236 Al Quran 5:8
237 Al Quran 4:135
238 The largest weekly gathering of a Muslim locality, is opened with a sermon.

* إِنَّ ٱللَّهَ يَأْمُرُ بِٱلْعَدْلِ وَٱلْإِحْسَانِ وَإِيتَآئِ ذِى ٱلْقُرْبَىٰ وَيَنْهَىٰ عَنِ ٱلْفَحْشَآءِ وَٱلْمُنكَرِ وَٱلْبَغْىِ يَعِظُكُمْ لَعَلَّكُمْ تَذَكَّرُونَ ۝

Behold, God enjoins justice (adl) and the doing of good,
and generosity towards [one's] fellow-men; and He forbids all that is shameful
and all that runs counter to reason, as well as envy;
[and] He exhorts you [repeatedly] so that you might bear [all this] in mind.[239]

Life is sacrosanct

The sanctity of human-life resonates repeatedly in the Quran. In Surah *Al Takwir* (The Overthrowing), the Day of Reckoning is brought to the fore and within this haunting depiction of the cataclysmic end of the Universe, the horrible crime of infanticide finds context and equivalence. When, declares the Quran, the sky is torn open and the fury of hell is ablaze, the record book will lay bare its pages. The meekest who were muzzled in life, would in turn find their voice. The crime of the taking of an innocent life will come to the fore even when every thing around us, that by which we reference our reality, is brought to naught:

إِذَا ٱلشَّمْسُ كُوِّرَتْ ۝ وَإِذَا ٱلنُّجُومُ ٱنكَدَرَتْ ۝ وَإِذَا ٱلْجِبَالُ سُيِّرَتْ ۝ وَإِذَا ٱلْعِشَارُ عُطِّلَتْ ۝ وَإِذَا ٱلْوُحُوشُ حُشِرَتْ ۝ وَإِذَا ٱلْبِحَارُ سُجِّرَتْ ۝ وَإِذَا ٱلنُّفُوسُ زُوِّجَتْ ۝ وَإِذَا ٱلْمَوْءُۥدَةُ سُئِلَتْ ۝ بِأَىِّ ذَنۢبٍ قُتِلَتْ ۝

When the sun folds,
And when the stars fall
And when the mountains are moved
And when the camel mature in term is abandoned
And when the beasts are assembled
And when the seas boil over
And when the souls are matched
And when the girl-child who was buried alive is asked
For what sin she was slain?[240]

He who takes a life has mortally wounded all of humanity, and he that saves a life has saved all of humanity. God forcefully declares all human life as sacrosanct and he, who takes blood, bleeds the Divine Plan and he who stops the bleeding aligns himself with the Divine Healer. Violence is the capital symptom of the soul ridden by the disease of its ego. Fratricide appears within

---

239 Al Quran 16:90
240 Al Quran 81:1-9

the first generation of humans, with Cain's slaying of his brother Abel. The Quran re-warns and re-exhorts:

مِنْ أَجْلِ ذَٰلِكَ كَتَبْنَا عَلَىٰ بَنِىٓ إِسْرَٰٓءِيلَ أَنَّهُۥ مَن قَتَلَ نَفْسًۢا بِغَيْرِ نَفْسٍ أَوْ فَسَادٍ فِى ٱلْأَرْضِ فَكَأَنَّمَا قَتَلَ ٱلنَّاسَ جَمِيعًا وَمَنْ أَحْيَاهَا فَكَأَنَّمَآ أَحْيَا ٱلنَّاسَ جَمِيعًا

Because of this We did ordain unto the children of Israel
That if anyone slays a human being—unless it be (in punishment) for another life
taken or for spreading strife and discord {fasaad} on earth—it shall be as though
he had slain all mankind. Whereas, if anyone saves a life, it shall be as though
he saved the lives of all mankind.[241]

Life is among the foremost of Divine gifts. The Quran lifts whatever prohibitions it proscribes when life is at risk. Food that is normally forbidden is allowed under the distress of incapacitating hunger, requirements of ablution taught by the Quran are relaxed in sickness. Submission is always about the sincerity of the intent and never about 'throwing away' a life:

فَمَنِ ٱضْطُرَّ فِى مَخْمَصَةٍ غَيْرَ مُتَجَانِفٍ لِّإِثْمٍ فَإِنَّ ٱللَّهَ غَفُورٌ رَّحِيمٌ ۝

Whoso is forced by hunger, not by will, to sin: (for him) lo! God is Forgiving,
Merciful.[242]

God ranks by heart not nationality

To be sure human history is full of blood, shed in the name of God, each side claiming to be the true partisans of God, belonging to His "chosen" religion. The Crusades are one such sad and sadly enduring example. These bloody wars, sanctimoniously called the 'Crusades' were drenched in the politics of religion and were anathema to the very Faith, they claimed to represent and defend. The Crusades were and are a testament to the sanguinary nature of those who lusted (and still lust) for power; sought (and still seek) glory through slaughter and subjugation. The teachings of Christ or those of Islam were (and are) not at fault.

God creates us as equals and this equality cuts across lines of race, religion, sex, or social rank. Human diversity is nature's rich gift and is to be cherished as such. A person's stature is measured by the person's conscientiousness and goodness, matters known fully to God alone. Human justice must be blind and the family of Adam and Eve should live together in harmony. Diversity itself is to be accepted as part of God's scheme and provides the medium within which to test and hone our piety:

---

241 Al Quran 5:32
242 Al Quran 5:3 as interpreted by Pickthall

يَـٰٓأَيُّهَا ٱلنَّاسُ إِنَّا خَلَقْنَـٰكُم مِّن ذَكَرٍ وَأُنثَىٰ وَجَعَلْنَـٰكُمْ شُعُوبًا وَقَبَآئِلَ لِتَعَارَفُوٓا۟ إِنَّ أَكْرَمَكُمْ

عِندَ ٱللَّهِ أَتْقَىٰكُمْ إِنَّ ٱللَّهَ عَلِيمٌ خَبِيرٌ ۝

O Mankind, We have created you from (the same pair of) male and female and
have dispersed you into nations and tribes so that you may know and cooperate
with each other. God ranks you by your piety alone.
God is all knowing {Aleem} , all-aware {Khabeer}.[243]

God ranks us by our piety and peacefulness. God does not love the aggressor.

Lo! God loveth not aggressors[244]

Prophets are charged with a Divine Mission, not the same as ours

Yes there is blood that is necessarily shed to bring about social change and
sometimes so as to successfully plant a "new" message. Moses knew that the
seas parted by his staff would close upon his pursuers. "Deliverance" would
come at the cost of the enemy's annihilation. There is also this story of an
enraged Moses demanding death for those of his people who in his absence
turned away from the One God and reverted to idol-worship. This example of an
intra-religious purge is recorded in the book of Exodus (also alluded to in the
Quran 2: 54):

> Moses stood in the gate of the camp, and said, "Whoever is on Yahweh's side, come
> to me!" All the sons of Levi gathered themselves together to him.
> He said to them, "Thus says Yahweh, the God of Israel, 'Every man put his sword
> on his thigh, and go back and forth from gate to gate throughout the camp, and every
> man kill his brother, and every man his companion, and every man his neighbor.'"
> The sons of Levi did according to the word of Moses: and there fell of the people
> that day about three thousand men.[245]

A prophet, like any other mortal must confront existential issues, but unlike other
mortals, the prophet's preoccupation is primarily other-worldly. A muslim
therefore views prophetic action with reverence, even on those occasions when
the wisdom of the action is not immediately obvious to him or her. Those closest
to God have different levels and degrees of spiritual knowing and insightfulness,
having cast away many of the veils that obscure True Reality.

---

243 Al Quran 49-13
244 Al Quran 2:190
245 Exodus 32:26-28

عَلِمُ ٱلْغَيْبِ فَلَا يُظْهِرُ عَلَىٰ غَيْبِهِۦ أَحَدًا ۝ إِلَّا مَنِ ٱرْتَضَىٰ مِن رَّسُولٍ فَإِنَّهُۥ يَسْلُكُ مِنۢ بَيْنِ يَدَيْهِ وَمِنْ خَلْفِهِۦ رَصَدًا ۝

He [alone] knows that which is beyond the reach of a created being's perception, and to none does He disclose aught of the mysteries of His Own unfathomable knowledge, unless it be to an apostle whom He has been pleased to elect [there for]: and then He sends forth [the forces of heaven] to watch over him in whatever lies open before him and in what is beyond his ken [246]

God's chosen Messengers see what we ordinary people do not see and their actions, even the pre-emptory ones, defy human purview. Theirs is the 'other worldliness' befuddling to those of us still mired and enmeshed, even if necessarily, in the trappings of this world. Moses the eager roving student seeking the literal meeting point of two seas finds instead the mystical Khidr; the roving devotee of the Divine, blessed with mercy and clairvoyant knowledge. [247] Khidr's life is an errand of mercy, though not so obvious to Moses. The man seeking the meeting of two seas cannot understand, much less judge the man seeking the meeting of this and the other life. So it was that Moses could not help but ask. Why would Khidr disable a boat and thus endanger future travelers after having availed it himself to cross the river? Why would Khidr repair a breach in the wall that belonged to a community that refused them basic food? Why would Khidr slay a youth who had no blood on his hands?

قَالَ هَٰذَا فِرَاقُ بَيْنِى وَبَيْنِكَ سَأُنَبِّئُكَ بِتَأْوِيلِ مَا لَمْ تَسْتَطِع عَّلَيْهِ صَبْرًا ۝ أَمَّا ٱلسَّفِينَةُ فَكَانَتْ لِمَسَٰكِينَ يَعْمَلُونَ فِى ٱلْبَحْرِ فَأَرَدتُّ أَنْ أَعِيبَهَا وَكَانَ وَرَاءَهُم مَّلِكٌ يَأْخُذُ كُلَّ سَفِينَةٍ غَصْبًا ۝ وَأَمَّا ٱلْغُلَٰمُ فَكَانَ أَبَوَاهُ مُؤْمِنَيْنِ فَخَشِينَآ أَن يُرْهِقَهُمَا طُغْيَٰنًا وَكُفْرًا ۝ فَأَرَدْنَآ أَن يُبْدِلَهُمَا رَبُّهُمَا خَيْرًا مِّنْهُ زَكَوٰةً وَأَقْرَبَ رُحْمًا ۝ وَأَمَّا ٱلْجِدَارُ فَكَانَ لِغُلَٰمَيْنِ يَتِيمَيْنِ فِى ٱلْمَدِينَةِ وَكَانَ تَحْتَهُۥ كَنزٌ لَّهُمَا وَكَانَ أَبُوهُمَا صَٰلِحًا فَأَرَادَ رَبُّكَ أَن يَبْلُغَآ أَشُدَّهُمَا وَيَسْتَخْرِجَا كَنزَهُمَا رَحْمَةً مِّن رَّبِّكَ وَمَا فَعَلْتُهُۥ عَنْ أَمْرِى ذَٰلِكَ تَأْوِيلُ مَا لَمْ تَسْطِع عَّلَيْهِ صَبْرًا ۝

[The sage] replied: "This is the parting of ways between me and thee.
[And now] I shall let thee know the real meaning of all [those events] that thou wert unable to bear with patience:

---

246 Al Quran 72:26-27 as interpreted by Muhammad Asad
247 Al Quran 18:65 -82

"As for that boat, it belonged to some needy people who toiled upon the sea -and I desired to damage it because (I knew that] behind them was a king who is wont to seize every boat by brute force.
"And as for that young man, his parents were [true] believers - whereas we had every reason to fear that he would bring bitter grief upon them by [his] overweening wickedness and denial of all truth:
and so we desired that their Sustainer grant them in his stead [a child] of greater purity than him, and closer [to them] in loving tenderness.
And as for that wall, it belonged to two orphan boys [living] in the town, and beneath it was [buried] a treasure belonging to them [by right]. Now their father had been a righteous man, and so thy Sustainer willed it that when they come of age they should bring forth their treasure by thy Sustainer's grace. "
And I did not do (any of] this of my own accord: this is the real meaning of all [those events] that thou wert unable to bear with patience.".[248]

Those with knowledge and those without it, tarry on different planes. Without clairvoyance, Khidr's actions seem unreasonable and criminal. With knowledge the same actions reveal their merciful and compassionate motivations. The non-prophets, which mean all of us after the last prophet, neither can fully comprehend the motivations of those chosen by God, nor do we have a license to act like them. We do not have the license of Moses to order a purge of those who reject the Divine message. Neither do we have the license of Khidr, to take a life to pre-empt evil.

Islam is the last cycle of revelation. Muhammad is the *seal* of the prophets. The Revelation to Muhammad, the Quran <u>is</u> complete and divinely protected. There are no enemies of Islam who can roll-back the Quran. There is no further need or requirement on the part of any individual to 'safeguard' the Message. The only thing that needs saving is the soul. The only thing that needs physical defending is the community. The most inspired action is one that contemplates restraint, moving towards peace, with justice and mercy. War and peace are therefore matters subject to diligent purview, and must pass informed and deliberative consensus, along with the clear tests of restraint, morality, and fairness as dictated by the Quran.

The heart does not yield to force

The Quran is very specific about its opposition to violence stemming from a difference in faith or belief. There is first the clear warning that God does not love aggressors. There is then also the instruction that any message of faith, specially the message that stands on Truth, demands discernment and sincerity of the heart. Islam is the state of a sincere heart. The heart cannot be won by the sword. Any such attempt would be against the Divine Writ and quite

---

[248] Al Quran 18:78-82 Interpreted by Muhammad Asad

obviously, counter-productive:

$$لَآ إِكْرَاهَ فِى ٱلدِّينِ قَد تَّبَيَّنَ ٱلرُّشْدُ مِنَ ٱلْغَىِّ$$

"Deen takes root without coercion".
"The truth (as willing seekers will discern) stands clear of error" [249]

$$وَلَوْ شَآءَ رَبُّكَ لَأَمَنَ مَن فِى ٱلْأَرْضِ كُلُّهُمْ جَمِيعًا أَفَأَنتَ تُكْرِهُ ٱلنَّاسَ حَتَّىٰ يَكُونُوا۟ مُؤْمِنِينَ ۞ وَمَا كَانَ لِنَفْسٍ أَن تُؤْمِنَ إِلَّا بِإِذْنِ ٱللَّهِ$$

Now if your Lord had willed, everyone of earth would have believed;
Are you then going to compel the people to become believers?
For no soul can believe except by God's permission;[250]

Further more the prophet is constantly reminded about the nature of his mission and responsibility:

$$فَذَكِّرْ إِنَّمَآ أَنتَ مُذَكِّرٌ ۞ لَّسْتَ عَلَيْهِم بِمُصَيْطِرٍ ۞$$

And so, [O prophet,] exhort them;
Your task is only to exhort; You cannot compel them [to believe][251]

And as to whose side, God is on, that too is quite clear. God does not stand with the aggressor. From a muslim's perspective, as aggression is not allowed, there can be no initiation of a "holy" war. Holy-war (when there are to be no *new* Divine messages) is a spiritual oxymoron. Yes there can be and sometimes must be "holy" resistance. "Islamic resistance" is condoned, allowed and, yes, sometimes enjoined. Nevertheless, in the echelon of spiritual and moral values, restraint is amongst the finest. Restraint from being unjust, restraint from being provocative, restraint from being disrespectful, and even restraint in exacting lawful retribution. In fact the Quran is quite explicit about the "trip-line" that justifies taking up arms. Arms are to be taken when muslims are being physically and systematically persecuted for their faith and there is no other recourse. To deter violence, muslims must organize and be ready to stand against it:

249 Al Quran 2:256
250 Al Quran 10:99-100. Interpreted by Thomas Cleary
251 Al Quran 88:21 -22 as interpreted by Muhammad Asad

$$\text{إِنَّمَا يَنْهَىٰكُمُ ٱللَّهُ عَنِ ٱلَّذِينَ قَٰتَلُوكُمْ فِى ٱلدِّينِ وَأَخْرَجُوكُم مِّن دِيَٰرِكُمْ وَظَٰهَرُوا۟ عَلَىٰٓ إِخْرَاجِكُمْ أَن تَوَلَّوْهُمْ}$$

God only forbids you to turn in friendship towards such as fight against you because of your faith and drive you forth from your homes, or aid others in driving you out[252]

A Muslim must coexist harmoniously with all those who will let them be. Those of a different faith, amongst whom a Muslim is free to practice his or her faith, provide the grounds for testing one's sense of justice and fair-play:

$$\text{لَّا يَنْهَىٰكُمُ ٱللَّهُ عَنِ ٱلَّذِينَ لَمْ يُقَٰتِلُوكُمْ فِى ٱلدِّينِ وَلَمْ يُخْرِجُوكُم مِّن دِيَٰرِكُمْ أَن تَبَرُّوهُمْ وَتُقْسِطُوٓا۟ إِلَيْهِمْ إِنَّ ٱللَّهَ يُحِبُّ ٱلْمُقْسِطِينَ ۝}$$

As for such who do not fight you on account of your faith, and neither drive you from your homes, God does not forbid you to show them kindness and to behave towards them with full equity: God loves those who act equitably[253]

Inner and Outer Jihad

A conflict, to which a Muslim is drawn, can therefore be rooted only in injustice. In a world where self-interest is often the overriding motivation behind people's actions, peace and justice are the first casualties. Raw, unbridled human envy is the primal force of aggression, leading to certain oppression of the weak by the strong. A Muslim must not be a party to a system of oppression and must struggle against oppression in the framework of his moral and contractual obligations and capacity. Herein lies the concept of *Jihad*. *Jihad* is the struggle to *resist injustice and oppression together with the* <u>struggle</u> *to* <u>resist</u> *justly*. This struggle to resist, before it ever becomes an armed struggle, must pass the phase of an internal struggle to persevere and forbear. When the sword is to be raised, it must be commanded only by those who have cultivated the temperament of restraint:

$$\text{۞ لَتُبْلَوُنَّ فِىٓ أَمْوَٰلِكُمْ وَأَنفُسِكُمْ وَلَتَسْمَعُنَّ مِنَ ٱلَّذِينَ أُوتُوا۟ ٱلْكِتَٰبَ مِن قَبْلِكُمْ وَمِنَ ٱلَّذِينَ أَشْرَكُوٓا۟ أَذًى كَثِيرًا وَإِن تَصْبِرُوا۟ وَتَتَّقُوا۟ فَإِنَّ ذَٰلِكَ مِنْ عَزْمِ ٱلْأُمُورِ ۝}$$

Assuredly ye will be tried in your property and in your persons,
And ye will hear much wrong from those who were given the Scripture before
you, and from the idolaters. But if ye persevere and ward off (evil),

---

252 Al Quran 60:9
253 Al Quran 60:8

Then that is of the steadfast heart of things. [254]

When *Jihad* does take the form of an armed struggle its proper aim is and must always be to move towards justice. *Jihad* cannot be invoked to bring about the forcible change of belief or creed of the opponent. 'Forcible conversion' lacks both common and spiritual sense. Those misaligned with the Truth are best known to and dealt with by God Himself:

$$وَقُلِ ٱلْحَقُّ مِن رَّبِّكُمْ ۖ فَمَن شَآءَ فَلْيُؤْمِن وَمَن ۚ شَآءَ فَلْيَكْفُرْ ۚ إِنَّآ أَعْتَدْنَا لِلظَّٰلِمِينَ نَارًا أَحَاطَ بِهِمْ سُرَادِقُهَا$$

The Truth is from the Sustainer of all.
Whosoever will, let him believe, and whosoever will, let him disregard
For We have appointed for those in denial (of the Truth) a milieu of fire.[255]

Because a Muslim is clearly instructed in the Quran not to dwell upon or stand in judgment over another's creed, *Jihad* cannot ever be a 'holy war'—the 'holy instrument' of punishment 'deserved' by the 'infidels'. The Quran has no such concept. *Jihad* as 'holy war' is a misplaced notion; Religion has often been exploited by power hungry leaders, for a rationale and reasons that are blatantly irreligious. Misguided men, by their actions, do not, cannot and must not, speak for any religion. There is no concept of "war against the infidels". Indeed there is no equivalent of the English "infidel" in the Quranic lexicon, although some translations, poor if not dishonest, translate the Arabic word *Kafir* as 'infidel'. Our discussion on this term in the preface is worth recalling: *Kafir* is a person in the state of *Kufr*. To be in *Kufr* is to be misaligned with God. Nominally, it is to be outside His message, un-heedful of final accountability. Yes, the state becomes deeper with callousness, doubt, rejection and hostility, but even a 'Muslim' can and is likely to find his or her self in the un-heedful state. It has been attributed to Umar, son of Khattab, the second caliph of Medina, and a companion of the prophet that every verse revealing the torment awaiting the *Kafir* has a relevance to the disobedient 'Muslim'.

The root-word for *Jihad* is *JHD*. It implies an inner effort that is spiritual and physical, moral and intellectual to move towards sincerity, demanding justness, peace, restraint, and the purging of hatred. A related word *Tahajjud* refers to the most earnest contemplation of God in the solitude of the night's stillness, an exercise no doubt in sincere introspection, reaching the innermost self. True honor, says the Quran may unfold for the soul that approaches God by the portal of *Tahajjud*.

---

254 Al Quran 3:186 as interpreted by Pickthall
255 Al Quran 18:29

Likewise, the men who led Muslims into battle were no ordinary men. These were men who were drilled in patience and perseverance. They did not seek the glory of the battlefield; their glory was inward and the path to it was through the restraint of piety:

يَٰأَيُّهَا ٱلَّذِينَ ءَامَنُواْ ٱصْبِرُواْ وَصَابِرُواْ وَرَابِطُواْ وَٱتَّقُواْ ٱللَّهَ لَعَلَّكُمْ تُفْلِحُونَ ۝

O you who believe! Be patient, vie with one another in patience, be vigilant, And observe your pious duty to God, in order that you may become spiritually prosperous.[256]

The Arabic language has other words for war and battle. Arabic for war is *harb* and for battle is *ma'araka*.[257] A well-known Hadith (tradition of the prophet) has him saying upon returning from a battle that the "greater *jihad*" lay ahead. This was the *jihad* of selflessness, personal-restraint and piety. It is also true that Muhammad's greatest victory, the embrace of Islam by the multitudes and their subsequent un-resisted march to Mecca, came through the auspices of a truce and not of war. The true meaning of the word 'victory' in Arabic, '*Fath*', is exposed by its co-rooted words *Fatiha* (meaning 'opening') and *Muftah* (meaning 'key'). True victory does not mean conquest over another; in its truest sense victory means the 'unlocking' of a stalemate and the opening of doors—doors to personal, communal and universal peace. Victory necessarily involves the purging of hatred from one's own heart so that others hearts' may be won. An enemy is truly neutralized only when his heart has been won. To the Muslims, after they had prevailed over their enemies, the Quran issues its warning against the seduction of 'power' and the blindness of hatred:

وَلَا يَجْرِمَنَّكُمْ شَنَئَانُ قَوْمٍ أَن صَدُّوكُمْ عَنِ ٱلْمَسْجِدِ ٱلْحَرَامِ أَن تَعْتَدُواْ وَتَعَاوَنُواْ عَلَى ٱلْبِرِّ وَٱلتَّقْوَىٰ وَلَا تَعَاوَنُواْ عَلَى ٱلْإِثْمِ وَٱلْعُدْوَٰنِ وَٱتَّقُواْ ٱللَّهَ إِنَّ ٱللَّهَ شَدِيدُ ٱلْعِقَابِ ۝

And let not your hatred of a folk who (once) stopped your going to the inviolable place of worship seduce you to transgress; but help ye one another unto righteousness and pious duty. Help not one another unto sin and transgression, but keep your duty to God. Lo! God is severe in punishment.[258]

The triggers of War

Knowing that God's love is reserved for those who avoid aggression and deal equitably, a Muslim can be drawn into battle for very specific purposes. For

---

256 Al Quran 3:200
257 Karen Armstrong's discussion on this is a must-read.
258 Al Quran 5:2 as interpreted by Pickthall

these purposes a Muslim is duty-bound. Turning the cheek is not an option; good defensive strategy aside, a Muslim is morally bound to standup against oppression and persecution.

وَمَا لَكُمْ لَا تُقَـٰتِلُونَ فِى سَبِيلِ ٱللَّهِ وَٱلْمُسْتَضْعَفِينَ مِنَ ٱلرِّجَالِ وَٱلنِّسَآءِ وَٱلْوِلْدَٰنِ ٱلَّذِينَ يَقُولُونَ رَبَّنَآ أَخْرِجْنَا مِنْ هَـٰذِهِ ٱلْقَرْيَةِ ٱلظَّالِمِ أَهْلُهَا وَٱجْعَل لَّنَا مِن لَّدُنكَ وَلِيًّا وَٱجْعَل لَّنَا مِن لَّدُنكَ نَصِيرًا ۝

How should ye not fight for the cause of Allah and of the feeble among men and of the women and the children who are crying: Our Lord! Bring us forth from out this town of which the people are oppressors! Oh, give us from Thy presence some protecting friend! Oh, give us from Thy presence some defender! [259]

It is the sad truth about the human condition and human history that no radical social change has come about without the use or the threat of the use of force. In fact none of the three monotheistic religions were to be spared the task of physical struggle. Were there not men and women ready to die for their right and duty to live their faith, there would not be a Synagogue, Church or Mosque today:

ٱلَّذِينَ أُخْرِجُوا۟ مِن دِيَـٰرِهِم بِغَيْرِ حَقٍّ إِلَّآ أَن يَقُولُوا۟ رَبُّنَا ٱللَّهُ ۗ وَلَوْلَا دَفْعُ ٱللَّهِ ٱلنَّاسَ بَعْضَهُم بِبَعْضٍ لَّهُدِّمَتْ صَوَٰمِعُ وَبِيَعٌ وَصَلَوَٰتٌ وَمَسَـٰجِدُ يُذْكَرُ فِيهَا ٱسْمُ ٱللَّهِ كَثِيرًا ۗ وَلَيَنصُرَنَّ ٱللَّهُ مَن يَنصُرُهُۥٓ ۗ إِنَّ ٱللَّهَ لَقَوِىٌّ عَزِيزٌ ۝

[Permission to fight is given to] those who have been driven from their homelands against all right for no other reason than their saying. "Our Sustainer is God!" For, if God had not enabled people to defend themselves against one another, [all] monasteries and churches and synagogues and mosques - in [all of] which Gods name is abundantly extolled - would surely have been destroyed [ere now]. And God will most certainly succor him who succors His cause: for, verily, God is most powerful, almighty. [260]

The triggers of war are often material and sometimes simply megalomaniacal. Aggression does not take its color from a specific creed. The stand against aggression is secular as is the demand for justice. A Muslim stands against aggression, even when it rears its head within the community of Muslims:

---

259 Al Quran 4:75
260 Al Quran 22:40

وَإِن طَآئِفَتَانِ مِنَ ٱلْمُؤْمِنِينَ ٱقْتَتَلُوا۟ فَأَصْلِحُوا۟ بَيْنَهُمَا ۖ فَإِنۢ بَغَتْ إِحْدَىٰهُمَا عَلَى ٱلْأُخْرَىٰ
فَقَـٰتِلُوا۟ ٱلَّتِى تَبْغِى حَتَّىٰ تَفِىٓءَ إِلَىٰٓ أَمْرِ ٱللَّهِ ۚ فَإِن فَآءَتْ فَأَصْلِحُوا۟ بَيْنَهُمَا بِٱلْعَدْلِ وَأَقْسِطُوٓا۟ ۖ إِنَّ
ٱللَّهَ يُحِبُّ ٱلْمُقْسِطِينَ ۝

If two factions of believers fight each other, make peace between them;
If thereafter one transgresses the other, fight the transgressor until there is
compliance to God's commandment; and upon compliance, enjoin peace with
justice, and equity. Verily God loves those who act equitably.[261]

Islam abhors oppression. A Muslim must always take a practical strand against injustice. When faced with the option of War, a Muslim, if unsure, must always err on the side of peace rather than on the side of war. Peace after all is the goal and war, was it to happen, never must be more than a means to the goal. War is a thing to be avoided, but if undertaken for the pursuit of peace and justice, it is a thing condoned. The first Quranic sanction of physical struggle in the face of persecution and physical displacement is in fact a 'condonation':

أُذِنَ لِلَّذِينَ يُقَـٰتَلُونَ بِأَنَّهُمْ ظُلِمُوا۟ ۚ وَإِنَّ ٱللَّهَ عَلَىٰ نَصْرِهِمْ لَقَدِيرٌ ۝ ٱلَّذِينَ أُخْرِجُوا۟ مِن
دِيَـٰرِهِم بِغَيْرِ حَقٍّ إِلَّآ أَن يَقُولُوا۟ رَبُّنَا ٱللَّهُ

Leave is given to those who fight because they were wronged
Surely God will help them
Those that were expelled from their homes unjustly because they said
Our sustainer is God[262]

The wars during the prophet's time were always of an existential nature. Not standing up and fighting the enemy would have meant annihilation. A telling Quranic verse, underscoring this peril instructs the Muslims to divide into groups during prayer times, so that one group of Muslims would stand guard over the other, providing protection during the vulnerable position of prostration. These early Muslims armed themselves to protect their sheer existence as men and women in a new faith. They were no different, as we know from Luke, than those two disciples of Jesus who carried swords to protect their person.

It is also very clear that arms were to be taken up for self-defense and self-preservation and *not* for the purpose of spreading Islam. The Quranic verse, 2:256, *forbidding the use of force to promote the faith of Islam* was revealed *subsequent* to the verse permitting the Muslims to take up arms. This latter verse does not abrogate the previous one. It simply draws a line between what is permissible and what is not. The sword is picked up for self-defense. It is

---

261 Al Quran 49:9-10
262 Al Quran 22:39

categorically the wrong instrument to change hearts or minds. The enemy's faith or lack thereof is not worth fighting for. Defending one's faith is to defend one's own right to *follow* the faith. The preoccupation is to stay rooted *within* the faith.

وَلَا يَزَالُونَ يُقَٰتِلُونَكُمْ حَتَّىٰ يَرُدُّوكُمْ عَن دِينِكُمْ إِنِ ٱسْتَطَٰعُواْ وَمَن يَرْتَدِدْ مِنكُمْ عَن
دِينِهِۦ فَيَمُتْ وَهُوَ كَافِرٌ فَأُوْلَٰٓئِكَ حَبِطَتْ أَعْمَٰلُهُمْ فِى ٱلدُّنْيَا وَٱلْأَخِرَةِ

[Your enemies] will not cease to fight against you till they have turned you away from your faith, if they can. But if any of you should turn away from his faith and die as a denier of Truth, they are those whose works will go to naught in this world and in the world to come.[263]

The three major wars in Islamic history, in which the Prophet participated, were all existential from the Muslims' perspective. Yet these battles were at the Prophet's directive, measured, tactical and restrained; even respectful of the enemy, so that the option of reconciliation was never fore-closed. The guiding principle in any action is accountability to God. A Muslim is accountable for wanton killing, and a Muslim is also accountable for not standing up against persecution.

The triggers of Peace

Jihad is first a spiritual struggle of restraint, peace being always preferable over hostilities and an opportunity of peace (bleak or unreliable as it may be) must always be pursued. It takes faith, forgiveness and perseverance to pursue peace with an enemy:

۞ وَإِن جَنَحُواْ لِلسَّلْمِ فَٱجْنَحْ لَهَا وَتَوَكَّلْ عَلَى ٱللَّهِ إِنَّهُۥ هُوَ ٱلسَّمِيعُ ٱلْعَلِيمُ ۝ وَإِن يُرِيدُوٓاْ أَن
يَخْدَعُوكَ فَإِنَّ حَسْبَكَ ٱللَّهُ هُوَ ٱلَّذِىٓ أَيَّدَكَ بِنَصْرِهِۦ وَبِٱلْمُؤْمِنِينَ ۝

But if they seek peace then you must seek peace too
Place your trust in God who alone hears all and sees all
If they intend deception, be certain that God protects you
He it is who has fortified you with his Help and the believers[264]

Just resistance requires one to be conscious of the prescribed bounds. The 'end' does not justify all means. A Muslim must at all times, in peace as well as in war, guard against anger and hatred. Anger, the prophet is recorded to have said, "Consumes good deeds just as fire consumes up dry wood." A just fight must preclude a disproportional response, staying clear of aggression, persecution, torture, anger and hatred so that the chances of peaceful resolution

---

263 Al Quran 2:217
264 Al Quran 8:61-62

are kept alive. God does not love transgressors:

وَقَٰتِلُوا۟ فِى سَبِيلِ ٱللَّهِ ٱلَّذِينَ يُقَٰتِلُونَكُمْ وَلَا تَعْتَدُوٓا۟ إِنَّ ٱللَّهَ لَا يُحِبُّ ٱلْمُعْتَدِينَ ۝

Resist in the way of God against those who fight against you,
But do not transgress or commit aggression.
Behold! God does not love transgressors[265]

Retribution—when it is called for—must not exceed the initial injury even though there may be a risk of the perpetrator repeating the offence. What one risks or loses by exercising restraint is not lost upon God:

۞ ذَٰلِكَ وَمَنْ عَاقَبَ بِمِثْلِ مَا عُوقِبَ بِهِۦ ثُمَّ بُغِىَ عَلَيْهِ لَيَنصُرَنَّهُ ٱللَّهُ إِنَّ ٱللَّهَ لَعَفُوٌّ غَفُورٌ

And whosoever retaliates proportionate to their injury, and then is wronged
again, God will help him. For God is the Pardoner and the Forgiver.[266]

The objective of war is not conquest or gain but the establishment of peace or even a half-fair truce. The conduct of the war and the conduct of the truce must be such that the cycle of violence does not renew itself.

وَٱقْتُلُوهُمْ حَيْثُ ثَقِفْتُمُوهُمْ وَأَخْرِجُوهُم مِّنْ حَيْثُ أَخْرَجُوكُمْ وَٱلْفِتْنَةُ أَشَدُّ مِنَ ٱلْقَتْلِ وَلَا
تُقَٰتِلُوهُمْ عِندَ ٱلْمَسْجِدِ ٱلْحَرَامِ حَتَّىٰ يُقَٰتِلُوكُمْ فِيهِ فَإِن قَٰتَلُوكُمْ فَٱقْتُلُوهُمْ كَذَٰلِكَ جَزَآءُ
ٱلْكَٰفِرِينَ ۝ فَإِنِ ٱنتَهَوْا۟ فَإِنَّ ٱللَّهَ غَفُورٌ رَّحِيمٌ ۝ وَقَٰتِلُوهُمْ حَتَّىٰ لَا تَكُونَ فِتْنَةٌ وَيَكُونَ
ٱلدِّينُ لِلَّهِ فَإِنِ ٱنتَهَوْا۟ فَلَا عُدْوَٰنَ إِلَّا عَلَى ٱلظَّٰلِمِينَ ۝

And engage them in battle wherever ye find them, and drive them out of the
places from where they drove you out, for persecution is worse than slaughter.
And fight not with them at the Inviolable Place of Worship but if they attack
you (there) then battle them. Such is the reward of disbelievers.
But if they desist, then lo! God is Forgiving, Merciful
And fight them until persecution is no more, and subjugation is to God alone.
But if they desist, then let there be no hostility except against wrong-doers.[267]

A Muslim must uphold his or her oath, promise, or treaty, conscientiously. A pact between human beings has God as a witness.

265 Al Quran 2:190
266 Al Quran 22:60
267 Al Quran 2:191-193

$$\text{وَأَوْفُوا بِالْعَهْدِ ۖ إِنَّ الْعَهْدَ كَانَ مَسْئُولًا ۝}$$

And be true to every promise for verily you will be called to account for every promise which you have made.[268]

A Muslim undertakes anything consequential "*In the Name* of God". This must not be a meaningless attribution. God's Name cannot be taken in vain or in consecration of anything that is misaligned with the Truth. And so too when a Muslim makes a pledge he calls upon God to witness his good faith. Good faith does not just bind the Muslim to his pledge; it also demands sincerity of motive:

$$\text{وَأَوْفُوا بِعَهْدِ اللَّهِ إِذَا عَاهَدْتُمْ وَلَا تَنقُضُوا الْأَيْمَانَ بَعْدَ تَوْكِيدِهَا وَقَدْ جَعَلْتُمُ اللَّهَ عَلَيْكُمْ كَفِيلًا ۚ إِنَّ اللَّهَ يَعْلَمُ مَا تَفْعَلُونَ ۝}$$

And be true to your bond with God whenever you bind yourselves by a pledge,
And do not break [your] oaths after having [freely] confirmed them and having
called upon God to be witness to your good faith:
Behold, God knows all that you do[269]

In all that a muslim undertakes, the goal is to find God's assent here and God's Presence in the hereafter.

$$\text{فَمَا أُوتِيتُم مِّن شَيْءٍ فَمَتَاعُ الْحَيَاةِ الدُّنْيَا ۖ وَمَا عِندَ اللَّهِ خَيْرٌ وَأَبْقَىٰ لِلَّذِينَ آمَنُوا وَعَلَىٰ رَبِّهِمْ يَتَوَكَّلُونَ ۝ وَالَّذِينَ يَجْتَنِبُونَ كَبَائِرَ الْإِثْمِ وَالْفَوَاحِشَ وَإِذَا مَا غَضِبُوا هُمْ يَغْفِرُونَ ۝ وَالَّذِينَ اسْتَجَابُوا لِرَبِّهِمْ وَأَقَامُوا الصَّلَاةَ وَأَمْرُهُمْ شُورَىٰ بَيْنَهُمْ وَمِمَّا رَزَقْنَاهُمْ يُنفِقُونَ ۝ وَالَّذِينَ إِذَا أَصَابَهُمُ الْبَغْيُ هُمْ يَنتَصِرُونَ ۝ وَجَزَاءُ سَيِّئَةٍ سَيِّئَةٌ مِّثْلُهَا ۖ فَمَنْ عَفَا وَأَصْلَحَ فَأَجْرُهُ عَلَى اللَّهِ ۚ إِنَّهُ لَا يُحِبُّ الظَّالِمِينَ ۝}$$

And remember whatever you are given [now] is but for the [passing] enjoyment of the life in this world whereas that which is with God is far better and more enduring. [It shall be given to all] who attain to faith and in their Sustainer place their trust; and who shun more heinous sins and abominations; and who whenever they are moved to anger, readily forgive; and who respond to [the call of] their Sustainer and are constant in prayer; and whose rule [in matters of common concern] is consultation among themselves; and who spend out of what We provide for them as sustenance; and who whenever tyranny afflicts them, defend themselves. But [remember] that an attempt at requiting evil may, too,

---

268 Al Quran 17:34 as interpreted by Muhammad Asad
269 Al Quran 16:91

become an evil: hence, whoever pardons [his foe] and makes peace; his reward rests with God- for verily, He does not love transgressors {Zalimeen} [270]

The Quran reminds us that to fight adversity, the weapons of choice are patience and forgiveness:

وَلَمَن صَبَرَ وَغَفَرَ إِنَّ ذَٰلِكَ لَمِنْ عَزْمِ ٱلْأُمُورِ ۝

But withal, if one is patient in adversity and forgives — this behold is indeed to set one's heart upon [271]

Ahmad and Bayhaqi record the prophet's saying that "a (true) warrior is one who exerts himself in the worship of God."

'Eye for an eye' squanders the opportunity to wash away ones own sins

Islam recognizes the need for just punishment. Punishment is a necessary deterrence against crime. The biblical adage of "an eye for an eye" makes for mathematically balanced punishment, but this zero-sum give and take is to a muslim a lost opportunity!

وَكَتَبْنَا عَلَيْهِمْ فِيهَا أَنَّ ٱلنَّفْسَ بِٱلنَّفْسِ وَٱلْعَيْنَ بِٱلْعَيْنِ وَٱلْأَنفَ بِٱلْأَنفِ وَٱلْأُذُنَ بِٱلْأُذُنِ
وَٱلسِّنَّ بِٱلسِّنِّ وَٱلْجُرُوحَ قِصَاصٌ فَمَن تَصَدَّقَ بِهِۦ فَهُوَ كَفَّارَةٌ لَّهُۥ وَمَن لَّمْ يَحْكُم
بِمَآ أَنزَلَ ٱللَّهُ فَأُوْلَٰٓئِكَ هُمُ ٱلظَّٰلِمُونَ ۝

And We ordained therein [Torah] for them:
A Life for a life, and an eye for an eye, and a nose for a nose, and an ear for an ear, and a tooth for a tooth, and for wounds equal retribution.
But he, who forgoes retribution by way of charity, shall mitigate his own sins.
And whosoever do not judge by that which God has revealed are steeped in error and injustice {Zalimoon} [272]

Not all crimes are to be forborne. The sanctity of life is supreme, and across class as it is across gender. No life is worth more than another. There must be a price to be paid for the taking of a life, here and now. Capital punishment, heart-wrenching as it is to the muslim-heart, must be on the table. It is the severest deterrent against murder. Yet, here too is a path for mercy. There is reprieve from capital punishment predicated on a pardon from the victim's 'brother' (the closest and able of survivors or trustee) plus an effective and meaningful

---

270 Al Quran 42:36-40. Interpreted by Muhammad Asad
271 Al Quran 42:43. Interpreted by Muhammad Asad
272 Al Quran 5:45

restitution—Restitution that is both affectively compensatory (for the victim's trustee) as it is effectively punitive (for the perpetrator of the crime). The perpetrator, if a master must pay more than if the perpetrator was a servant. The trustee, if a woman without means, must receive more than a man were he the trustee. Compassionate justice calls for both a judge and a jury or peers. The measure of relief for the aggrieved is subjective as is the measure of punishment for the perpetrator. There are multiple considerations and applications of law and morality, equity and compassion, involving both the victim and the accused. The Quran invites people with vision and discernment (*yaa ulil albaab*), the would-be jurists in this case, to contemplate this issue from all sides and perspectives:

يَٰٓأَيُّهَا ٱلَّذِينَ ءَامَنُوا۟ كُتِبَ عَلَيْكُمُ ٱلْقِصَاصُ فِى ٱلْقَتْلَى ٱلْحُرُّ بِٱلْحُرِّ وَٱلْعَبْدُ بِٱلْعَبْدِ وَٱلْأُنثَىٰ بِٱلْأُنثَىٰ فَمَنْ عُفِىَ لَهُۥ مِنْ أَخِيهِ شَىْءٌ فَٱتِّبَاعٌۢ بِٱلْمَعْرُوفِ وَأَدَآءٌ إِلَيْهِ بِإِحْسَٰنٍ ذَٰلِكَ تَخْفِيفٌ مِّن رَّبِّكُمْ وَرَحْمَةٌ فَمَنِ ٱعْتَدَىٰ بَعْدَ ذَٰلِكَ فَلَهُۥ عَذَابٌ أَلِيمٌ ۝ وَلَكُمْ فِى ٱلْقِصَاصِ حَيَوٰةٌ يَٰٓأُو۟لِى ٱلْأَلْبَٰبِ لَعَلَّكُمْ تَتَّقُونَ ۝

O YOU who have come to faith!
Just retribution is decreed for the taking of a life.
[dispense justice] master by [the rights and obligations of] the master,
and the servant by [the rights and obligations of] of the servant,
and the woman by [the rights and obligations of] the woman
And if there be remittance, to whatever extent, by the brother [trustee]
Be bound by fairly instituted dispensations {bil maaroof}[273]
and offer [restitution and remission] with grace and goodness
This is a reprieve from your Sustainer, by His Mercy.
And for him who thereafter violates the bounds of propriety, there awaits
agonizing reckoning.
In just retribution, O people with insight, there is preservation of life,
so that you remain piously conscious of God[274]

Rush to justice, and hasty condemnation, reflect lack of dispassionate deliberation, so the Quran directs the muslim to be wary of rumors and demagoguery:

---

273 Maaroof literally means something "known, recognized, distinguished, honourable, good, befitting"
274 Al Quran 2:178-179

$$\text{يَـٰٓأَيُّهَا ٱلَّذِينَ ءَامَنُوٓا۟ إِن جَآءَكُمْ فَاسِقٌۢ بِنَبَإٍ فَتَبَيَّنُوٓا۟ أَن تُصِيبُوا۟ قَوْمًۢا بِجَهَـٰلَةٍ فَتُصْبِحُوا۟ عَلَىٰ مَا}$$
$$\text{فَعَلْتُمْ نَـٰدِمِينَ ﴿٦﴾}$$

Believers, if a vicious person brings any news, try to get the facts, lest you afflict people ignorantly and become regretful for what you have done[275].

Judgment is by God

It cannot be over emphasized, from the Quranic perspective, that the quest for righteousness from the perspective of a mortal (not chosen by God to be a prophet) is to be directed inwards. Divine Judgment (God being outside of time) has already gone forth. We as mortals, living inside of time, must discover and find refuge in Divine Compassion, best by being compassionate ourselves. Righteousness too, the one focused within, manifests outwardly as compassion. Witness Abraham's reaction when he finds what is in store for Lot's people.

$$\text{فَلَمَّا ذَهَبَ عَنْ إِبْرَٰهِيمَ ٱلرَّوْعُ وَجَآءَتْهُ ٱلْبُشْرَىٰ يُجَـٰدِلُنَا فِى قَوْمِ لُوطٍ ﴿٧٤﴾ إِنَّ إِبْرَٰهِيمَ لَحَلِيمٌ}$$
$$\text{أَوَّٰهٌ مُّنِيبٌ ﴿٧٥﴾ يَـٰٓإِبْرَٰهِيمُ أَعْرِضْ عَنْ هَـٰذَآ إِنَّهُۥ قَدْ جَآءَ أَمْرُ رَبِّكَ وَإِنَّهُمْ ءَاتِيهِمْ عَذَابٌ غَيْرُ}$$
$$\text{مَرْدُودٍ ﴿٧٦﴾}$$

And when the awe departed from Abraham, and the glad news[276] *reached him,*
he pleaded with Us on behalf of the folk of Lot.
Lo! Abraham was mild, imploring, and penitent.
(It was said) O Abraham! Forsake this! Lo! thy Lord's commandment hath gone forth, and lo! there cometh unto them a doom which cannot be repelled. [277]

Muhammad, the last prophet, too personifies compassion and mercy. A messenger with a fair warning, leaving judgment (in matters of the pursuit of faith and belief) to the Divine purview:

---

275 Al Quran 49:6
276 News of a son by Sarah
277 Al Quran 11:73-76 as interpreted by Pickthall.

وَمَآ أَرْسَلْنَٰكَ إِلَّا رَحْمَةً لِّلْعَٰلَمِينَ ۝ قُلْ إِنَّمَا يُوحَىٰ إِلَيَّ أَنَّمَآ إِلَٰهُكُمْ إِلَٰهٌ وَٰحِدٌ

فَهَلْ أَنتُم مُّسْلِمُونَ ۝ فَإِن تَوَلَّوْا۟ فَقُلْ ءَاذَنتُكُمْ عَلَىٰ سَوَآءٍ وَإِنْ أَدْرِىٓ أَقَرِيبٌ أَم

بَعِيدٌ مَّا تُوعَدُونَ ۝ إِنَّهُۥ يَعْلَمُ ٱلْجَهْرَ مِنَ ٱلْقَوْلِ وَيَعْلَمُ مَا تَكْتُمُونَ ۝ وَإِنْ

أَدْرِىٓ لَعَلَّهُۥ فِتْنَةٌ لَّكُمْ وَمَتَٰعٌ إِلَىٰ حِينٍ ۝ قَٰلَ رَبِّ ٱحْكُم بِٱلْحَقِّ وَرَبُّنَا ٱلرَّحْمَٰنُ ٱلْمُسْتَعَانُ

عَلَىٰ مَا تَصِفُونَ ۝

We have not sent you (Muhammad pbuh) but as mercy to all beings
Say "It has been revealed to me that your god is The One God"
"Will you then submit to Him"?
If they turn away say, "I have delivered to you a fair warning though I do not
know whether the promised reckoning is near or far. God knows your spoken
words and hidden thoughts.
This may be a test or short reprieve"
Say "My Sustainer judge You by the truth
Our Sustainer is the Source of Mercy {Rahman} and the Shield {Musta'an} against
what you concoct and assert"[278]

War is vainglorious. Submission to the Master is the essence.

Human history recounts the glory of conquerors. The Arabs too prized fables of
men and horses charging bravely into enemy lines. Fluttering flags raised above
charging horses (marching boots and rolling tanks, in our time) are captivating,
though erroneous symbolisms of power and glory. War and conquest are
vainglorious pursuits. Through the captivating sound rhythms of its verses, the
Quran evokes the war-scene to expose the delusion. In man's vainglorious
pursuits of conquest and wealth, nature loyally and dutifully yields to him. Iron
yields to the fire and is agreeably pliant to its mold, surrendering its strength to
the smith. The atom yields its inner power by annihilating its core, surrendering
its innate secrets to the human mind. Likewise, the trusting steeds charge at
their masters' command, into the thicket of death— consummately fearless,
passionately loyal, surrendering their all to their mounted masters. Man,
intoxicated by power and wealth, forgets his own Master, Who bestows upon
him his ability to command as well as the resources to exploit. Man mistakes
nature's dependable submission with his own mastery and control. What will he
use this mastery and control for? Will it be for self aggrandizement or will it be
for a purpose higher than his own? Is he or she an instrument or is he or she the
purpose? Man too, though apt to forget, is part of nature and will soon enough
yield to the grave; reduced to dust. His 'substance' and worth will lie in the

---

278 Al Quran 21:107-112

lifelong yearnings cultivated within his heart and manifested by his deeds. Was he ever his Master's willing slave?

وَٱلْعَـٰدِيَـٰتِ ضَبْحًا ۝ فَٱلْمُورِيَـٰتِ قَدْحًا ۝ فَٱلْمُغِيرَٰتِ صُبْحًا ۝ فَأَثَرْنَ بِهِۦ نَقْعًا ۝ فَوَسَطْنَ بِهِۦ جَمْعًا ۝ إِنَّ ٱلْإِنسَـٰنَ لِرَبِّهِۦ لَكَنُودٌ ۝ وَإِنَّهُۥ عَلَىٰ ذَٰلِكَ لَشَهِيدٌ ۝ وَإِنَّهُۥ لِحُبِّ ٱلْخَيْرِ لَشَدِيدٌ ۝ ۞ أَفَلَا يَعْلَمُ إِذَا بُعْثِرَ مَا فِى ٱلْقُبُورِ ۝ وَحُصِّلَ مَا فِى ٱلصُّدُورِ ۝ إِنَّ رَبَّهُم بِهِمْ يَوْمَئِذٍ لَّخَبِيرٌۢ ۝

By the snorting coursers
Striking sparks of fire
And scouring to the raid at dawn,
Then, therewith, with their trail of dust,
Cleaving, as one, the centre (of the foe),
Lo! man is an ingrate unto his Lord
And lo! he is a witness unto that;
And lo! in the love of wealth he is violent.
Knoweth he not that, when the contents of the graves are poured forth
And the secrets of the breasts are made known,
On that day will their Lord be perfectly informed concerning them. [279]

---

279 Al Quran 100:1-11

Sadequain Calligraphy. *Lord of the Two Easts and Two Wests*

Courtesy of Dr. Salman Ahmad at www.sadequainfoundation.com

Relationship with God

The grapes of my body can only become wine after the winemaker tramples me.
I surrender my spirit like grapes to his trampling so my inmost heart can blaze and dance with joy.
Although the grapes go on weeping blood and sobbing: "I cannot bear any more anguish, and more cruelty"
The trampler stuffs cotton in his ears: "I am not working in ignorance.
You can deny Me if you want, you have every excuse, but it is I who am the Master of this work.
And when through My Passion you reach perfection you will never be done praising My Name."[280]

Relationship with God is the quest for awareness

Why seek a relationship with God? This is equivalent to asking why open one's eyes. The heart is the sacred space of God, and the heart oblivious of this space is unaware, closed and therefore blind.

وَمَنْ أَعْرَضَ عَن ذِكْرِى فَإِنَّ لَهُۥ مَعِيشَةً ضَنكًا وَنَحْشُرُهُۥ يَوْمَ ٱلْقِيَٰمَةِ أَعْمَىٰ ﴿۱۲٤﴾

But as for him who shall turn away from remembering Me
his shall be a life of narrow scope
And on the day of resurrection, we shall raise him up blind.[281]

Paradise the ultimate fulfillment of pure aspirations for a correct relationship with the Divine is the pinnacle of awareness that unveils the presence of God. The blind heart squanders paradise.

Paradise is described in the Quran in terms that are physical, but this physicality is rich with symbolism. The spiritual transcendence is never too obscure for the

---

280 Maulana Jalaludin Rumi
281 Al Quran 20:124 (as interpreted by Muhammad Asad, 'The Message of the Quran')

'seeing' heart. The bounteous gardens over streams of water provide a vision that would not be lost to the people of the desert, the first audience of the Quran, but these are not just gardens to which is available the abundance of water. These are gardens with *subservient* streams. The streams serve at the pleasure of the garden in a creative cycle of infinitude, just as the fountain of Kafur yields to its drinker, increasing its flow by the drinker's want. The streams of paradise likewise, serve at the garden's pleasure, yielding to its fancy!

The gardens of Paradise are, beyond their physical vision, mystical states of being—without scarcity, without denial, without limits, without measure, and outside of want. The Quran refers to Paradise, variously and inclusively, as the garden of purity, *{Jannatu Adn}*, bliss *{Jannatun Naeem}*, rest and peace *{Jannatul Maawa}* and the Garden of gardens *{Jannatul Firdaus}*—The station of security, where loss or longing do not exist *{Maqaamin Ameen}*.

At the literal level Paradise promises solace to the mortal. There is promise of love and comfort; peace and pleasure; beauty and purity; and reunion with the family and loved ones. It is a place of no unfulfilled desires and a place without loss. To be sure, Paradise has a sensory appeal just as Hell holds physical pain. How else to get our attention? The mystical cannot and does not exclude the literal. "Does man think that We shall not assemble his bones?" asks the Quran and then reminds the doubters "Yes, Yes Indeed. We are Able to restore his very fingers" (75:3-4)

But there is more. What are insatiable obsessions on earth now satiate the spirit. The drink in Paradise is not inebriating. The wine does not overfill the body, it illumines the soul. It does not induce sleep or blabber, instead it awakens the heart. Companions are in human form, though the beauty of the companions of paradise *{hoor}* is characterized by the earnestness of their gaze and the radiance of their eyes. This beauty, formless, emanates from the soul, radiating inner sincerity. Companionship is now the meeting of souls. The ambiance of grandeur is no longer decadent; it is soothing because covetousness is no more.

It is the spirit that is being invited to its Wholeness. From this mystical perspective, Paradise is a state of enlightened awareness and therefore a station of the conscientious soul— the spirit *(Ruh)* conscious and reposed in peace. The soul's knowledge in terms of its awareness does not preclude the sensory. And so could, Hell be viewed , as a state of emptiness; the station of a callous and arrogant soul, mired in the false ego of selfhood and materiality; unconscious of its spirit, grievously penned outside the gate of Peace. The *Ruh* itself is not physical and is therefore neither male or female and perhaps not even separate. The pleasures are not of the body but of the ecstatic spirit. Paradise transcends any one or many and all perspectives. Absolute knowledge belongs to God alone. Knowledge, in any form, and more meaningfully as insight and consciousness is known to us by degrees and stages. Above every one with knowledge is one who knows more (12:76). Paradise, like anything else in the hereafter is unfathomable. It may be said though that by its purity its beauty becomes congruent with goodness—a state of peace or a station of peaceable repose of the conscious spirit.

It should therefore suffice that Paradise is the attainment of the *realization* of the presence of God. I say 'realization' because God is always present in any thing and by any act that is intrinsically good and beautiful. Outside of paradise, most of us cannot realize the Divine presence, primordial as it is. The roadblocks to this realization will not yield to cerebral intellect, only the seeking heart can eviscerate them. The knowledge being sought is mystical and so the quest must be spiritual. The vision of paradise is not for the eyes of the face. It is for the eye of the heart. Rumi partakes of the "pure wine" promised in 83:24 to awaken the heart in paradise to the presence of God—the truest of aspirations:

$$يُسْقَوْنَ مِن رَّحِيقٍ مَّخْتُومٍ ۝ خِتَمُهُ مِسْكٌ وَفِي ذَٰلِكَ فَلْيَتَنَافَسِ ٱلْمُتَنَافِسُونَ ۝$$

They shall be given, to slake their thirst, pure wine—sealed
Its seal—musk. And for that let those who aspire, aspire[282]

This belief at this level is far beyond the scope and limitations of a dogma. It has been said that "water takes the color of the vessel that holds it". The heart is the vessel and the water is the faith the heart holds. Paradise too resides in the heart. The appeal of Paradise therefore must size itself to the heart in which it reposes; an appeal with both literal and mystical decibels. The garden and its streams must bloom and flow in the heart. They will not fail the loyal heart. The loyal heart is certain too:

$$جَنَّٰتِ عَدْنٍ ٱلَّتِي وَعَدَ ٱلرَّحْمَٰنُ عِبَادَهُ بِٱلْغَيْبِ إِنَّهُ كَانَ وَعْدُهُ مَأْتِيًّا ۝$$

[Theirs will be the] gardens of perpetual bliss {Jannat Adn}
which the Most Gracious has promised unto his servants,
in a realm which is beyond the reach of human perception.
Verily, his promise is ever sure of fulfillment[283]

One mystical interpretation of the Quran, footed in the concept of a single Reality, considers Hell and Paradise (as well as our earthly life) to be the same "place", though different stations of consciousness. The spiritually aware basking in God's Light while the spiritually unaware and unprepared, "burning" by their own blindness.

---

282 Al Quran 83:25-26
283 Al Quran 19:61 (as interpreted by Muhammad Asad, 'The Message of the Quran')

وَمَنْ أَعْرَضَ عَن ذِكْرِى فَإِنَّ لَهُۥ مَعِيشَةً ضَنكًا وَنَحْشُرُهُۥ يَوْمَ ٱلْقِيَٰمَةِ أَعْمَىٰ ۝

But as for him who shall turn away from remembering Me,
his shall be a life of narrow scope
And on the day of resurrection, we shall raise him up blind.[284]

To be in Paradise is to embrace the only Reality that ever was, primordial and eternal. The ego of the self surrendered to the Self. Adam and Eve restored to the Abode of Peace {*Dares Salaam*} in the presence of God.

Spiritual harmony—the alignment of our will with God's Will

It is one of the fundamental laws of Nature that matter moves towards a stable-equilibrium. A rock falls until it can fall no more. A river flows in the path of least resistance until it reaches the sea. Equilibrium is a state of harmony created by the perfect balance of forces. Matter will transform itself or its state until it reaches a state of equilibrium, transitory as it may be. There is a quality of "giving-in" or "ungrudging submission" (surrendering if you will) inherent in nature. Without this quality a stable equilibrium would not be attainable. Nature is driven by a defined and regulated "need" conditioned by a cohesive "inter-dependence". It has been said that nature does not protect the weak from the strong, but that is from the perspective of man who sees himself as a separate "self". Nature sees itself as a whole and therefore always in harmony.

Man on the other hand is disinclined to accept the status-quo, howsoever harmonious it may be. That much is clear in the story of Adam in Eden. Man is driven by need and desire. A need can be fulfilled but desire by definition must perpetuate itself. A fulfilled desire ceases to be. Need expresses a lacking while desire expresses aspiration. Islam does not quibble with man's needs and desires. In matters of need it simply discourages waste and encourages civility, justice and restraint and tells us (as if to scoff those who concoct convoluted and meaningless lists of 'DOs' and 'DON'Ts') not to call forbidden that which "God has allowed". The weight of our base earthly instincts can and will anchor us down, and we need to be watchful. We as human beings are fully capable of discernment. In matters of aspiration it urges no less than reaching for the Absolute Truth. We are God's eminent creation. We preserve and reclaim our spiritual eminence through faith *and* righteous deeds. They are both severally necessary. Together they are not just sufficient, but complementary. Faith and righteous deeds feed each other. To act righteously is to practice faith and to purify faith is to add grace and beauty to behavior:

---

284 Al Quran 20:124 (as interpreted by Muhammad Asad, 'The Message of the Quran')

وَٱلتِّينِ وَٱلزَّيْتُونِ ۝ وَطُورِ سِينِينَ ۝ وَهَـٰذَا ٱلْبَلَدِ ٱلْأَمِينِ ۝ لَقَدْ خَلَقْنَا ٱلْإِنسَـٰنَ فِى أَحْسَنِ تَقْوِيمٍ ۝ ثُمَّ رَدَدْنَـٰهُ أَسْفَلَ سَـٰفِلِينَ ۝ إِلَّا ٱلَّذِينَ ءَامَنُوا۟ وَعَمِلُوا۟ ٱلصَّـٰلِحَـٰتِ فَلَهُمْ أَجْرٌ غَيْرُ مَمْنُونٍ ۝ فَمَا يُكَذِّبُكَ بَعْدُ بِٱلدِّينِ ۝ أَلَيْسَ ٱللَّهُ بِأَحْكَمِ ٱلْحَـٰكِمِينَ ۝

By the Fig by the Olive, by the Mountain of Sinai, by the expanse of this city,
We create man in the finest mold then lower him to the lowest station
except those who seek faith and righteous deeds.
Their reward cannot be stopped.
So what hereafter can belie you regarding the judgment
Is it is not God who is the Supreme of all judges.[285]

A relationship without 'I', 'me' and 'mine'

The Truth is not evasive. The mortal is apt to forget it, even though it is manifestly pervasive:

فَأَيْنَمَا تُوَلُّوا۟ فَثَمَّ وَجْهُ ٱللَّهِ

Wherever you turn is the face of God[286]

Islamic spirituality is about the pursuit of the transcendental Truth. It is therefore the pursuit of God for Truth's sake. It is a transcendental quest to embrace the hereafter from the 'here' and 'now'. It is a quest to embrace eternity from within the station of mortality. It is the mystical exercise to "die before you die[287]". To "die" now is *not* to waste the gift of life, but to put life and Truth in its proper perspective. It is to live fully, without fear, without avarice, givingly, and to belong *now* to the Truth that is One and Transcendental and to which we shall return.

Unfettered selfhood, (ego if you will) displaces the centrality of God, obscuring the Truth. Piety, the practice of "taming" worldly desire for its wantonness, is not meant to make our experience poor but to keep our priorities in check. All goals must rest within the only transcendental Goal. All reality must find its validation in the Only Reality. The perception of 'me' and 'mine' must find its proper perspective:

A sojourning Dervish finds himself struggling to move on. At his current locale, his hosts had generously opened their homes and hearts to him. He had come to know them well—well enough to be privy to their deepest fears and dearest desires. Each time the Dervish would hint about moving on, his hosts would have none of it and

---

285 Al Quran 95
286 Al Quran 2:115
287 A very famous saying of the Prophet

convince him to stay another week. Their sincerity had deeply moved the Dervish. Yet and therefore, being the Dervish that he was, he was anxious to cast off his anchor. Finally one night, when the moon was full, having packed his spartan sundries, he informed his hosts: "There is a time to leave and mine is now. I do not have the means to return your hospitality in kind" "I will", he continued "in gratitude and all sincerity pray that you be granted that which you seek most. I will be along to the place called the Dwelling of the Liars". With this short goodbye, he left, just as he came, without a trace.

In the wake of the Dervish's exit, the village began to change. Before long it was awash in prosperity. Tall homes—two, three, four stories tall, lined the narrow alleys. Busy billboards hung from the new and half-finished structures and large cloth banners stretched across the crowded streets, touting the wares on offer. Goods from overflowing shops cluttered the pavements. Everyone who was anyone important was always present on the prestigious main-street—-The village had become a busy bustling town. It was obvious to the ex-villagers that their transformation was by the aegis of the departed Dervish. Every villager's desire was coming to be. They would surely thank the Dervish, only if he could be found. Then, one day, years later, long after they had given up hope of ever finding the "Dwelling of Liars" and their Dervish, an old villager stumbled upon him. He could not believe himself! "Our people looked for you everywhere and across all horizons. We enquired in all villages and townships and of every wayfarer. No one has heard of this Dwelling of Liars. And now here you are in this nameless and abandoned graveyard"! The Dervish looked up. His famished state had not dulled the brightness of his gaze. He grasped his excited complainant's hand to help himself up. "Come see this", he said as he pointed to a wind-worn grave. "Here lies a man who claimed that the tall green building yonder was his". Moving along, he continued, "Here lies the man who claimed that he owned the most abundant well in the village, and here lies the man who fenced the orchards that he said were his". Then looking down at the dry and parched land and after a pause and a sigh he continued, "They have no claim, they said false. Were they all not liars?"

The Truth

What is Reality? What is the Truth? Though neither is within our grasp, we must persevere with our quest. We live in the realm of temporality so how are we to grasp something of another realm? The Quran undertakes this mystical task:

$$ ٱلْحَآقَّةُ ۝ مَا ٱلْحَآقَّةُ ۝ وَمَآ أَدْرَىٰكَ مَا ٱلْحَآقَّةُ ۝ $$

The Reality
What is the Reality?
What will teach thee what the Reality is? [288]

---

288 Al Quran 69:1-3

To turn to the Truth we must burnish our consciousness of God, because God Alone is the transcendent Truth and Reality. God consciousness takes hold in a heart that is earnest and open. A heart blinded by self-pride, arrogance, power and obsessive attachments to wealth and fame closes and hardens to a point of no return. It has squandered Reality.

The Quran reminds us persistently about those who have perished while still under the spell of falsehood and therefore unconscious of God. The worldly security that we craft for ourselves by fortifying our dwellings—raising our roofs on mammoth columns (like the people of Tahmud) or by hewing them in hardened hillocks (like the people of Aad), does not stop the march of time nor the Truth that time bears. The Tahmud and the Aad are no more; they have left behind no remnants of themselves. Likewise, Pharaoh, the king who played god, judging by whim, which amongst his people would live or die, could muster no resistance to the fury of a parted sea. The symbols of his might, armor and armaments, yielded silently to the crashing walls of water. Noah's scoffers, the rich and sure-footed, were swept away by a soaring tide while a laughable craft that would serve as a mother ship rode the surge to the highlands of safety. What is temporary is not Real; Temporality breeds an illusion; when it perishes it exposes the lie of its 'reality'. The Truth is the he or she who ridicules and rejects God's Messengers and their message will awaken to a fiery chastisement; not the least of it would be the burning agony of their own regrets:

يَٰلَيْتَهَا كَانَتِ ٱلْقَاضِيَةَ ۝ مَآ أَغْنَىٰ عَنِّى مَالِيَهْ ۝ هَلَكَ عَنِّى سُلْطَٰنِيَهْ ۝

Ah! Would that (Death) had been the end of me!
My wealth has not availed me, gone is my authority from me! 289

The Word of God is an aspect of Reality. Messengers are the teachers bearing the Word of God. The Word of God that is the Arabic Quran is the mystical key to unlock the doors to the Truth and the Reality that it (the Truth) holds and unfolds. This Word is not the ornate speech of man. It is the profound and primordial Speech of God, guiding us into a journey that is beyond our perception.

فَلَآ أُقْسِمُ بِمَا تُبْصِرُونَ ۝ وَمَا لَا تُبْصِرُونَ ۝ إِنَّهُ لَقَوْلُ رَسُولٍ كَرِيمٍ ۝ وَمَا هُوَ
بِقَوْلِ شَاعِرٍ قَلِيلًا مَّا تُؤْمِنُونَ ۝ وَلَا بِقَوْلِ كَاهِنٍ قَلِيلًا مَّا تَذَكَّرُونَ ۝ تَنزِيلٌ مِّن رَّبِّ
ٱلْعَٰلَمِينَ

No! I swear by that you see, and by that you do not see, it is a speech of a noble
Messenger. It is not the speech of a poet—little do you believe; nor the speech of

---

a soothsayer— little do you remember. A sending down from the Lord of all Being [290]

The Truth cannot be changed by us. What can be changed is by definition, not the truth. The Truth cannot be suppressed by us. What can be suppressed is by definition, not the truth. The Truth does not depend on us. We are from it and perish by disinheriting it. We can choose to heed the Truth by letting it into willing hearts; when we choose to ignore or reject it, we live and nurture the delusion that comes from spiritual blindness. The choice we make affects none other but ourselves. God is self sufficient and therefore *without* need. Man is instructed to worship God Alone. This is not God's need as God has none. Man would be in error if man was any other way. To praise God or to worship God is man's necessary acknowledgement of the Truth. That which we fail to acknowledge we cannot embrace:

$$\text{يَـٰٓأَيُّهَا ٱلنَّاسُ أَنتُمُ ٱلۡفُقَرَآءُ إِلَى ٱللَّهِ ۖ وَٱللَّهُ هُوَ ٱلۡغَنِيُّ ٱلۡحَمِيدُ ۞}$$

O mankind it is you that have need of God
But God is Free of all needs, {Ghani}, worthy of all Praise {Hameed} [291]

God {Al Haqq} is The Truth so God is all that *really* is. Man contemplates this Truth by the many signs (*ayahs*) which are God's manifestation and by the many attributes that God assigns to Himself. The Truth is truly embraced when it is the same inwards and outwards, when actions match words:

$$\text{يَـٰٓأَيُّهَا ٱلَّذِينَ ءَامَنُواْ لِمَ تَقُولُونَ مَا لَا تَفۡعَلُونَ ۞ كَبُرَ مَقۡتًا عِندَ ٱللَّهِ أَن تَقُولُواْ مَا لَا تَفۡعَلُونَ ۞}$$

O ye who believe! Why say ye that which ye do not?
It is most hateful in the sight of God that ye say that which ye do not. [292]

Seeking the Truth

There can be no 'free-will' in the direct presence of God—only submission. Adam's free-will cost him the loss of Transcendental Reality to an illusory reality of forms and phenomena; a displacement from Eden to a station whence God can neither be 'seen' nor 'sensed'. In this station our sensibilities are tuned to what God *manifests*, not to what God *is*. Here we are veiled from the Creator by a 'reality' rooted in our multifaceted perceptions of The Reality. We can have no 'direct knowledge' of God. God is outside our realm of perception, though the

---

290 Al Quran 69:39-43 as interpreted by A.J. Arberry
291 Al Quran 35:15
292 Al Quran 61:2-3 as interpreted by Pickthall

signs of his presence are everywhere. God is to be 'found' by the 'seeker'. God is to be 'sought'—contemplating the creative manifestations of the 'Hidden Creator'.

The very first commandment borne by Gabriel to Muhammad in the cave of Hira has a quality of God being 'found by the seeker', in as much as it begins to answer the aspirations of an earnestly contemplative soul. Muhammad, the man not yet prophet, was of spartan tastes with minimal needs, already known as *Al Amin* for his honesty and truthfulness. He would retreat to the cave of Hira, away from the din of worldliness, to contemplate in the earnestness of solitude the nature of the transcendental Truth. *"Recite: In the name of thy Sustainer Who createth[293]"*, the unlettered would-be messenger was commanded. *"Createth man from a clot", "Recite: And thy Sustainer is the Most Bounteous {al Akram}"*. The bounty about to be laid on him was the bounty of Knowledge. The knowledge of Truth, so profound, that it could not be set upon a mountain, so vast and rich that if all the seas were ink, there wouldn't be enough ink to characterize it.

Muhammad's recital was to be *"in the name"* of his Sustainer, implying the Sustainer's Will, and Presence. God's presence however transcends sensory perception, as the Quran would reveal later:

$$\text{لَّا تُدۡرِكُهُ ٱلۡأَبۡصَٰرُ وَهُوَ يُدۡرِكُ ٱلۡأَبۡصَٰرَ}$$

"No Vision comprehends God, but God comprehends all vision"[294]

Within the collective enigma of *"Wherever you turn is the face of God[295]"* and *"No Vision comprehends God, but God comprehends all vision"*[296] is the mystical quest of the soul.

What better way of contemplation (to remove the veils) than by the attributes that God has chosen for Himself. God's attributes mentioned by God in the Quran exceed one hundred and they are 'The Most Beautiful Names'[297] (*Al-Asma'-Ul-Husna*). These are primordial names (attributes, if you will) that He imparted to Adam. The Beautiful Names are the Names of Goodness. What is good is beautiful and true beauty exudes from goodness.

In the Quran these attributes are widely used, separately and often in juxtaposition to each other.

---

293 Al Quran 96:1-3
294 Al Quran 6:103
295 Al Quran 2:115
296 Al Quran 6:103
297 It is noteworthy that in Arabic, beauty and goodness are derivatives of the same root-word.

$$\text{هُوَ ٱللَّهُ ٱلْخَلِقُ ٱلْبَارِئُ ٱلْمُصَوِّرُ لَهُ ٱلْأَسْمَآءُ ٱلْحُسْنَىٰ يُسَبِّحُ لَهُۥ مَا فِى ٱلسَّمَٰوَٰتِ وَٱلْأَرْضِ}$$

$$\text{وَهُوَ ٱلْعَزِيزُ ٱلْحَكِيمُ ﴿٢٤﴾}$$

He is God, the Creator, the Originator, The Fashioner,
To Him belong the most beautiful names:
Whatever is in the heavens and on earth, do declare His praises and glory.
And He is boundless in Might, complete Wisdom. [298]

$$\text{وَلِلَّهِ ٱلْأَسْمَآءُ ٱلْحُسْنَىٰ فَٱدْعُوهُ بِهَا}$$

The most beautiful names belong to God: so call on Him by them [299]

Remembering God

Just as our five senses provide the framework of our bodily existence and our physical awareness, the attributes of God provide the framework of spiritual reflection. The Quran invites the believer to engage in the *"Dhikr"* of Allah. *Dhikr* is the "pronouncement", "invocation", "remembrance" and "contemplation" of God. *Dhikr*, serves to remove the veils of illusion, and as embodied by the Sufi tradition, aspires to touch the state of awareness where the word, the mind and the heart meld together to embrace the harmony of the single Truth, thereby making a 'religious duty' an act of love. Says the Quran of *Dhikr*:

$$\text{أَلَا بِذِكْرِ ٱللَّهِ تَطْمَئِنُّ ٱلْقُلُوبُ ﴿٢٨﴾}$$

Verily in the remembrance of God, hearts find peace, security and rest [300]

This is the essence of 'Spirituality'. Religion to a certain extent is the 'fear' of God so that our relationship with fellow man is correct. We must submit to Divine Commandments. The body of the violator will burn. Spirituality to that same extent is the 'love' of God so that our relationship with God is based on the Truth. We cannot but want to submit to that which we love. The spirit of the lover seeks the bliss of repose in the beloved. Fear of God now takes a new meaning. Love and fear become the two sides of the same coin. Having found True love, the lover fears abandonment. Punishment is now other than corporeal.

God is both personal and universal

The sea may be described as a mass of water or may be described variously and inclusively as green and blue; shallow and deep; sparkling and dull; calm

---

298 Al Quran 59:24
299 Al Quran 7:180
300 Al Quran 13:28

and violent; life threatening and life-sustaining. The first description is a common-ground description. The second description is a personal perspective. The first is precise, the second is a beginning. The first is a definition. The second is an experience.

Dhikr is to experience God and like all experience it is within oneself, personal and intimate, and therefore defiant of uniform expression. At a minimum it is the richly laden process of connection to our Source and the ensuing discovery of our belonging to It.

Dhikr of God is a temporal act but it promises transcendence. On a basic level it is a reminder of who we are and who we are not, so that we may find our proper place and perspective—a discernment of what is beautiful and what is not and of what is real and what is not. On a higher level *Dhikr* is the thirst for God so that our distance from God when God is evident falls within the borders of Paradise. *Dhikr* purifies *Dhakireen* (men immersed in *Dhikr*) and *Dhakiraat* (women immersed in *Dhikr*) and their fulfillment awaits them (33:35). It is by our hands and feet and tongues that we earn or spurn our proximity to God. *Dhikr* tethers us to the Truth.

يَوْمَ تَشْهَدُ عَلَيْهِمْ أَلْسِنَتُهُمْ وَأَيْدِيهِمْ وَأَرْجُلُهُم بِمَا كَانُواْ يَعْمَلُونَ ۞   يَوْمَئِذٍ يُوَفِّيهِمُ ٱللَّهُ دِينَهُمُ ٱلْحَقَّ وَيَعْلَمُونَ أَنَّ ٱللَّهَ هُوَ ٱلْحَقُّ ٱلْمُبِينُ ۞

On the Day when their tongues, their hands and their feet will bear witness to their deeds
On that day, God will pay them fully and justly, their due
And they will know that God is the Truth {Al Haq}, Evident {Mobeen} [301]

Pathways to Truth

The attributes of God are the medium of contemplating the Divine as well as the self. Names such as *Al Haq* (The Truth), *Al Quyyum* (The Eternal), *Al Ahad* (The One and Only), *Al Qahhaar* (The Irresistible) are the Essence of The Divine. Other such as *Ar Rabb* (The Lord) and *Al Malik* (The Sovereign) encompass a plurality portraying the relationship between the Lord and His creation and between the Sovereign and His subjects. This relationship with the Divine, can only begin to exist (from the human perspective) in the presence of a persistent and sustained effort to put God at the center of life. In practical terms it starts by staying within proscribed limits of earthly behavior and conduct so that the egocentric self may give way to the consciousness of the spirit. The relationship with God is through the spirit. The spirit cannot free itself unless the ego is tethered. The spiritual

---

301 Al Quran 24 :24-25

plane rests on a harmonious and balanced temporal plane. Tacit knowledge and awareness are anchored in an individual's intentions, ideals and value-structure. Furthermore, when all creation is God's alone, our relationship with God must be preceded with the correct relationship with all that God is manifested by, i.e. all of God's creatures. Our earthly relationships must be constructed on justice and equity and restraint and this framework is clearly laid down in the Quran. To violate this framework is to foreclose the path to spiritual ascension and to an intimate relationship with God.

The spiritual path is progressive and calls one beyond correctness to Grace. Compassion, forgiveness and mercy which are inspired qualities move beyond justice and equity. Whereas justice and equity have proscribed minimum standards, compassion and forgiveness reach beyond the necessary and towards sufficiency. The pursuit of Grace {*Ehsan*} is to move towards the Divine Attributes and to participate in them.

Man moves closer to God by being close to fellow man. An act of grace will invite God into the act. Giving without social acclaim is giving for the acclaim of God. Giving something material away—the transaction between the giver and the needy—becomes a spiritual transaction between man and God.

إِن تُبْدُواْ ٱلصَّدَقَٰتِ فَنِعِمَّا هِىَ ۖ وَإِن تُخْفُوهَا وَتُؤْتُوهَا ٱلْفُقَرَآءَ فَهُوَ خَيْرٌ لَّكُمْ ۚ وَيُكَفِّرُ عَنكُم مِّن سَيِّـَٔاتِكُمْ ۗ وَٱللَّهُ بِمَا تَعْمَلُونَ خَبِيرٌ ۝

If overtly, you give unto charity, this too is fine,
but if you covertly give to the poor, it will be better for you,
and will atone for some of your ill-deeds. God is informed of what ye do. [302]

The quest for God, oral, material, physical, emotional, all is *Dhikr*. The quest for God is on God's terms, so it encompasses an evolving reality that does not lend itself to being conveyed. It is a journey of intimate and subjective experiences. It is the quest for the Essential Truth, "*Al Haqq*", by way of The Guide {*Al Haadi*}. The Expander {*Al Basit*} will open the constricted heart, Divine Bounty {*Al Akram*} shall bring fulfillment and Divine Wisdom {*Al Hakeem*} will determine how and when.

The Trust

Our relationship with the Divine has another aspect. God vests man with power on earth. Said the Sustainer to the angels:

إِنِّى جَاعِلٌ فِى ٱلْأَرْضِ

I will place a deputy upon the earth[303]

---

302 Al Quran 2:171

God's attributes serve as a dual reminder to man. One reminder, that man as God's vicegerent can and must aspire to embrace the Divine attributes, consistent with the pre-eminent stature of his creation. Man draws his power from God and rules in God's name. A perfect man would parallel himself to the Divine qualities. He will find these attributes as guide-posts. Through them we must discover who and what we are. As an agent of free-will we must choose wisely. The second reminder, inherent in the Divine Attributes, is that dominion is conferred upon man by Divine Will and is of a limited term, with the ultimate power and dominion residing with God alone.

هُوَ ٱلَّذِى جَعَلَكُمْ خَلَٰئِفَ فِى ٱلْأَرْضِ فَمَن كَفَرَ فَعَلَيْهِ كُفْرُهُۥ وَلَا يَزِيدُ ٱلْكَٰفِرِينَ كُفْرُهُمْ عِندَ

رَبِّهِمْ إِلَّا مَقْتًا وَلَا يَزِيدُ ٱلْكَٰفِرِينَ كُفْرُهُمْ إِلَّا خَسَارًا ۝

He it is who deputizes you on earth
So those in denial of the truth only delude themselves.
The denial of the deniers gains them with God only His abhorrence
The denial of the deniers gains them only loss and emptiness[304]

Through these attributes we must discover who and what we are *not*. We do not have a claim on life nor to any of life's offerings. Life and its offerings are a Divine Trust. Every thing that we think *belongs* to us does not. The selfhood labels of "I" and "me" and "mine" are ephemeral and can engender spiritual opacity. By giving and sharing we live by the Trust. By withholding and amassing we live outside of the Trust and diminish 'ourselves'. Knowledge based on the Truth *must* inspire humbleness, humility and gratitude. That which inspires arrogance is ignorance, caused by the heart's blindness. Any pretensions of self sufficiency on the part of man are false, any arrogance is misguided, and any existence outside of God's Will is an illusion:

أَفَرَءَيْتُم مَّا تُمْنُونَ ۝ ءَأَنتُمْ تَخْلُقُونَهُۥ أَمْ نَحْنُ ٱلْخَٰلِقُونَ ۝

Have you ever considered that [seed] which you emit?
Is it you who create it—or are We the source of its creation?[305]

He who hoards tomorrow's food while his neighbor goes hungry has forgotten the Trust:

أَفَرَءَيْتُم مَّا تَحْرُثُونَ ۝ ءَأَنتُمْ تَزْرَعُونَهُۥ أَمْ نَحْنُ ٱلزَّٰرِعُونَ ۝

have you ever considered the seed which you cast upon the soil?

---

303 Al-Quran 2:30
304 Al-Quran 35:39
305 Al Quran 56:58-59

Is it you who cause it to grow — or are We the cause of its growth[306]

As he who guards a well to keep the wayfarer away

أَفَرَءَيْتُمُ ٱلْمَآءَ ٱلَّذِى تَشْرَبُونَ ۞ ءَأَنتُمْ أَنزَلْتُمُوهُ مِنَ ٱلْمُزْنِ أَمْ نَحْنُ ٱلْمُنزِلُونَ ۞

Have you ever considered the water which you drink?
Is it you who cause it to come down from the clouds?
Or are We the cause of it coming down?[307]

As he who is ensconced in the warmth of comfort, oblivious of others in the cold of discomfort:

أَفَرَءَيْتُمُ ٱلنَّارَ ٱلَّتِى تُورُونَ ۞ ءَأَنتُمْ أَنشَأْتُمْ شَجَرَتَهَآ أَمْ نَحْنُ ٱلْمُنشِئُونَ ۞

Have you ever considered the fire which you kindle?
Is it you who have brought it into being the tree that serves as its fuel?
Or are We the cause of its coming into being?[308]

Knowledge based on Truth must inspire humbleness, humility and gratitude. God's deputy on earth, empowered to harness a plenitude of resources, must not lose sight of the fact that the universe in not anthropocentric. The universe is the expression of the immanent Creator; the footstool of the Divine Throne. Man is a new comer to this unfathomably complex parade of forms and phenomena:

هَلْ أَتَىٰ عَلَى ٱلْإِنسَٰنِ حِينٌ مِّنَ ٱلدَّهْرِ لَمْ يَكُن شَيْئًا مَّذْكُورًا ۞

Has there [not] been an endless span of time before man [appeared - a time]
when he was not yet a thing to be thought of[309]

This fact is not lost upon paleontologists, astronomers and anthropologists. The science of it, and speculation aside, there is enough evidence that man is a very late regent. Based on radiometric dating of zircon crystal found in Western Australia scientists put the age of the earth at 4.4 billion years, give or take a few million years. Knowing man, Homo sapiens came on earth sometime between 100 to 250 thousand years ago (give or take a few tens of thousands of years)! This fact is brought home with amazing resonance by psychologist Robert Ornstein and his co-author Paul Ehrlich in their book *New World New Mind*:

> "Suppose the earth's history was charted on a single calendar year, with Jan. 1 representing the origin of the Earth and midnight December 31 the present. Then

---

306 Al Quran 56:63-64
307 Al Quran 56:68-69
308 Al Quran 56:71-72
309 Al Quran 76:1 interpreted by Muhammad Asad

each day of the earths "year" would represent 12 million years of actual history. On that scale the first form of life, a simple bacterium, would arise sometime in February. More complex forms, however, come much later; the first fishes appear around November 20. The dinosaurs arrive around December 10 and disappear on Christmas Day. The first of our ancestors recognizable as human would not show up until the afternoon of December 31. Homo sapiens—our species—would emerge around 11:45 P.M. All that has occurred in recorded history would occur in the final minute of the year."

As God's appointed viceroy on earth man must *seek* guidance from God. Life is not an accident. It is the flawless expression of the Divine Word and therefore entirely purposeful. This is the purpose that we must seek and need. The sincerity of this quest will lead us in the right direction. As Rumi says "Wherever a difficult question is the answer flows." Man cannot live outside of, or away from God because God is Truth.

فَذَٰلِكُمُ ٱللَّهُ رَبُّكُمُ ٱلْحَقُّ فَمَاذَا بَعْدَ ٱلْحَقِّ إِلَّا ٱلضَّلَٰلُ فَأَنَّىٰ تُصْرَفُونَ ﴿٣٢﴾

So that is God for you: Your Lord, The Truth.
And what is there after Truth but error?
Then why are you alienated?[310]

It is noteworthy as it is instructive that of all His attributes, God reminds us foremost of Divine Compassion, Forgiveness and Mercy. Imperfect as we are, callous and often remiss, it is never too late. The Divine Hands, by which we were designed, are ours to grasp. There can be no better security than the one that flows from the Hands of the Creator.

Let us not forget.

Accountability to God entails more than mere ritual practice of religion. A soul, untouched and unmoved by the physical and emotional needs of others less fortunate than himself, though often seen on his or her prayer mat, is merely a religious exhibitionist. One cannot aspire towards God without reaching out to fellow human beings. A heart that cannot feel the pain of others seeks God in vain. True worship of God, demands as well as fosters, compassion, love and caring towards our fellow human beings. God has made us neighbors of each other so that we may discover that true wealth—ours to keep—is gained by giving, sharing and reaching-out to others. A person does not become a *Mumin* until he or she has made room in his or her heart for others. The tender sapling of spirituality is fed and nurtured with courteous deeds motivated by compassion, kindness, and sharing—all the little things that constitute good-neighborliness. The Quran recalls the Arabic word "*Ma'oon*", connoting the daily

310 Al Quran 10:32. Interpreted by Thomas Cleary

ration of general necessities and niceties like salt and sugar, in the beautiful short Surah called by the same name to remind us all—aspirants to Divine Blessings—of the insidiousness that comes from a sanctimonious attitude towards the practice of religion. We cannot grow spiritually by rote recitals or robotic rituals. To grow spiritually, we must learn not to withhold our active and consistent participation in the care and well-being of others:

أَرَءَيْتَ ٱلَّذِى يُكَذِّبُ بِٱلدِّينِ ۝ فَذَٰلِكَ ٱلَّذِى يَدُعُّ ٱلْيَتِيمَ ۝ وَلَا يَحُضُّ عَلَىٰ طَعَامِ ٱلْمِسْكِينِ ۝ فَوَيْلٌ لِّلْمُصَلِّينَ ۝ ٱلَّذِينَ هُمْ عَن صَلَاتِهِمْ سَاهُونَ ۝ ٱلَّذِينَ هُمْ يُرَآءُونَ ۝ وَيَمْنَعُونَ ٱلْمَاعُونَ ۝

Have you observed he who is in denial of Deen
It is he who pushes away the orphan
And participates not in the feeding of the needy
Woeful are they in prayer
They who in their prayers are detached
They who make a display of it
Though they withhold even small neighborly assistance and courtesies [311]

Sadequain Calligraphy. The Sun and Moon in adoring servitude

Courtesy of Dr. Salman Ahmad at www.sadequainfoundation.com

The Most Beautiful Rosary

Like the oil in the kernel and the spark in the flint-stone
Your Lord is within. Wakeup if you can. Wakeup![312]

Empowerment of the heart

The Arabic Quran is not a mere book. It is God's speech, living and transformational, directed to the spiritual heart. In every earnest heart it will awaken a quest and for every quest it offers its own pace and own mileposts. God beckons the heart to reflect, or as Rumi would say, "sell your cleverness and buy bewilderment":

لَوْ أَنزَلْنَا هَـٰذَا ٱلْقُرْءَانَ عَلَىٰ جَبَلٍ لَّرَأَيْتَهُۥ خَـٰشِعًا مُّتَصَدِّعًا مِّنْ خَشْيَةِ ٱللَّهِ ۚ وَتِلْكَ ٱلْأَمْثَـٰلُ نَضْرِبُهَا لِلنَّاسِ لَعَلَّهُمْ يَتَفَكَّرُونَ ۝

Had We revealed this Quran upon a mountain
you would see it humble itself and implode in awe of God
We propound such analogies so that they may reflect

Sincerity is single-heartedness. There cannot be duplicity of purpose or desire; one longing above all longings. The cleansed and emptied heart, places itself at the mercy of the beloved! Leave trepidation behind because this Beloved is the Fount of Mercy.

هُوَ ٱللَّهُ ٱلَّذِى لَآ إِلَـٰهَ إِلَّا هُوَ ۖ عَـٰلِمُ ٱلْغَيْبِ وَٱلشَّهَـٰدَةِ ۖ هُوَ ٱلرَّحْمَـٰنُ ٱلرَّحِيمُ ۝

God is God and there is no other
Knower of the hidden and imperceptible {Ghaib} and the evident

---

312 Kabir's Doha. Jaise til mein tel hai, jyon chakmak mein aag; Tera Sain tujh mein hai, tu jaag sake to jaag

The Source of Compassion {Rahman}, The Merciful {Raheem}

A mystical tryst, like no other is on offer. A drop of water is being called by the sea. Can the drop offer any terms of surrender? Can its journey end any other way?

$$\text{هُوَ ٱللَّهُ ٱلَّذِى لَآ إِلَٰهَ إِلَّا هُوَ ٱلْمَلِكُ ٱلْقُدُّوسُ ٱلسَّلَٰمُ ٱلْمُؤْمِنُ ٱلْمُهَيْمِنُ ٱلْعَزِيزُ ٱلْجَبَّارُ ٱلْمُتَكَبِّرُ ۚ سُبْحَٰنَ ٱللَّهِ عَمَّا يُشْرِكُونَ ٢٣}$$

God is God and there is no other
The Sovereign {Malik}, The Holy {Quddus}, The Source of Peace {As Salaam},
The Guardian of Faith {Mumin}, The Giver of Safety {Muhaimin}, The Almighty
{Azeez}, The Compeller {Jabbar}, The Overwhelming {Muttakabir}
Exalted is God, above any partners they may associate (with Him).[313]

The kaleidoscopic forms and colors of life are expressions of Divine Artistry, which moulds us, shapes us, and moves us. The heart is moved by beauty though it will need guidance and wisdom to discern between what is truly beautiful and what merely poses for beauty. True beauty flows from the Divine. The contemplation of this beauty in an expressed or silent form is the remembrance of God (*Dhikr*).

$$\text{هُوَ ٱللَّهُ ٱلْخَٰلِقُ ٱلْبَارِئُ ٱلْمُصَوِّرُ ۖ لَهُ ٱلْأَسْمَآءُ ٱلْحُسْنَىٰ ۚ يُسَبِّحُ لَهُۥ مَا فِى ٱلسَّمَٰوَٰتِ وَٱلْأَرْضِ وَهُوَ ٱلْعَزِيزُ ٱلْحَكِيمُ ٢٤}$$

This is God, the Creator {Khaliq}, The Originator {Bari}, The Shaper {Mussawwir}
To Him refer the Most Beautiful Names
Celebrated by all there is in the Heavens and the earth
And He is boundless in Might {Azeez}, complete in Wisdom {Hakeem} [314]

The "Most Beautiful Names" (of God) are Arabic Names sprinkled throughout the Quran. They are often used to conclude a verse, imprinting the context with a contemplative residue. These Divine Names are also referred to as Divine Attributes. Sometimes a Name is used by itself and often it is used in juxtaposition with another Name (such as *Barrun Raheem, Ghafoorul Raheem*). Some of these Attributes are just shades apart (*Al Khaliq, Al Bari, Al Musawwir*) and some are 'opposites' such as *AZ Zahir* and *AL Batin, Al Awwal* and *AL-Aakhir*. Together, the union of shades and the union of opposites leave nothing out, enfolding all contemplation, phenomena and time, space and physicality. Contemplation of

---

313 Al Quran 59:21-23
314 Al Quran 59:24

these names yields no vision. The imagination trying to tie God to a form is quickly frustrated; much like the eye probing the sky for its limit or imperfections withdraws unto itself tired, defeated and dazzled. Creation, leaving the Creator aside, is beyond imagination. How then to imagine the Creator? One cannot. No vision can comprehend God.

God transcends, time and magnitude. The magnitude of *Al Kabeer* and *Al Wasi* is not static, not physical and is limited by our own capacity. Contemplation of His Names will humble the mind and thus soften the heart. This is the *Dhikr* of God. The *Dhikr* of God challenges the false 'complacency of knowing' so that we make room for the Truth. It confronts the self so that it aligns to the Self. It expounds Unity, so that we may participate in It. Says, Rumi, the eloquent participant in Unity, there is no use being a swimmer when the ocean has no edges. It is time to let the ocean move you and mould you.

The journey of *Dhikr* is towards the Real, towards transcendence and towards the Source. *Dhikr* is also the pursuit of beauty as His are the most Beautiful Names. For some like Rumi, *Dhikr* exposes their separation from our Source, so that they long for re-union.

God is the Beginning and the End, the First and the Last, the Caring and the Stern, the Just and the Forgiving, the Conceiver and the Creator, the King and the Master, the Source and the Goal, the Giver and the Taker, the Forbearing and the Compeller. We seek refuge in God, in His Mercy and away from His Wrath. God is both near to us (by the attributes of *Tasbih*,[315] (attributes in which we can participate in this life) and far from us (by attributes of *Tanzih*, attributes in which we can have no participation). The attributes of God convey both his *Jamal* (beauty and compassion) and *Jalal* (majesty and sternness). Said the Prophet, "Peace of Faith (*Emaan*) reposes between fear and hope[316]".

The Divine Word "Be" {*Kun*} is the singular and absolute cause of all causes. Within this Word is the knowledge of all that will be caused to happen and it is free of any impediments, including the impediment of time. All phenomena and time (the latter being the medium in which phenomena exists) flow from *Kun*. Each being (and its allotted time) *is* the Divine Word. Time circumscribes human life and knowledge and therefore serves as the medium in which human experience exists. Time is extraneous to the fulfillment of the Divine Command. Being and its knowledge *is* the Divine command "Be". The Divine knowledge is complete and has always been complete. Divine knowledge of the Day of Reckoning is as complete as the knowledge of the Day of Creation. Human experience and knowledge emanate from events, or simply said, events make

---

315 Tasbih and Tanzih are discussed in great depth in *The Vision of Islam* by Murata and Chittick
316 Hadith, Bukhari

news. With God events emanate from Knowledge.

$$\text{مَآ أَصَابَ مِن مُّصِيبَةٍ فِى ٱلْأَرْضِ وَلَا فِىٓ أَنفُسِكُمْ إِلَّا فِى كِتَٰبٍ مِّن قَبْلِ أَن نَّبْرَأَهَآ ۚ إِنَّ ذَٰلِكَ عَلَى ٱللَّهِ يَسِيرٌ ۝}$$

No affliction befalls in the earth or in yourselves but it is in a Book before We bring it into being. Indeed that is easy for God [317]

It may be said that from the Divine perspective, before and after, cause and effect are coincident. To the human experience, which must exist and operate in time, this is paradoxical. *Dhikr* invites contemplation outside of this paradox, to a state of awareness (or understanding, if you will) in which the paradox begins to fade and disintegrate. *Dhikr* nurtures a 'supra logic' within which rests 'analytical logic'—un-impaired, un-hindered, and fully reconciled. This is not mere polemics. Were it so then the science of Physics would not be any less polemical or baffling even to the scientist. Consider that we are all made of atoms, *same* as those that make up the wooden and plastic wares around us. Our atomic construct is no different than that of a table! And atoms too are mostly empty space. The nucleus of an atom, its solid core, is like a ball in a coliseum, far, far smaller than the empty space that forms its outer boundary. An indeterminate cloud is the outer non-substance of our physical 'form'. We and our world *are* a physical paradox. It should suffice, to stay clear of the pre-destination versus the free-will conundrum that while our physical existence flows from the Divine Word, our free-willed *intentions* (as they relate to our participation (sincere or otherwise) in the Divine Plan) are *fully autonomous*. Through our sincere participation in the Divine Plan we find ourselves inside the stated purpose of the Divine Word—Mercy. And yes, God does invite us to participate in the Divine Plan of beauty.

$$\text{وَمَن يَقْتَرِفْ حَسَنَةً نَّزِدْ لَهُۥ فِيهَا حُسْنًا}$$

Anyone who fosters goodness and beauty,
We will add goodness and beauty to it [318]

By skirting or fighting the Divine Plan we merely foster an illusion. A heart that does not consistently remind itself both of its dependence upon God and accountability to Him becomes the host of its own vanity and gratification. It lives in denial, hoisting more veils between itself and Reality. Our fixation on ourselves, fostered too by modern life's insulation from Nature, is spiritually cancerous. *Dhikr* helps to scrub, renew and realign the heart, rolling up the veils that cloister it from true and abiding peace and harmony. One purpose of *Dhikr* is

---

317 Al Quran 57:22
318 Al Quran 42:23

to move ones 'center' from the self to the Absolute Reference that is God. Without this Absolute Reference we are wayward and ill-prepared for the Return. *Dhikr* is an effort to approach and embrace *Tawheed* (Oneness)—an effort and a journey without limits and beyond words—perhaps akin to the journey of a rain-drop back to the sea.

God has absolute primacy over each of His attributes. "There is no god but God" may be amplified to "There is no god but *Rahman*" and-or "There is no mercy except God's Mercy."[319]   Beauty, Power, Control, Mercy, Creativity and Forgiveness belong to God alone. God invites his deputy to participate in these attributes, in compliance (*Islam*), conscientiously (with *Emaan*) and with the purity of devotion (*Ehsan*). *Dhikr* is to discover our bond with God. A bond that is both universal and personal, within and outside of time, on earth and in heaven.

"Try to gain one moment in which you see only God in heaven and earth."[320]

According to a mystic tradition, ninety-nine Divine Names hold the key to a transformational spiritual awakening. The following list is compiled to present the Name in reference of a selected verse. The verses are trans-interpreted. Their rendering here, far from being sufficient, is intended to encourage the reader to seek and recite the Arabic Source. The Most Beautiful Names are the beads of a meditative rosary; Whisper often upon these beads. The Most Beautiful Names are also the breath-taking patterns of a spiritual kaleidoscope. Contemplate, because the kaleidoscope holds, for Adam and Eve on earth, the beauty of Paradise. The Prophet was reported to have said that the people in Paradise will have no regrets except for the regret of those moments on earth which passed without the *Dhikr of Allah*.

The musings of the author, alongside each Divine Name, are mere gravel at the starting point of the meditative path. God {*Al Haadi*} is the Guide. The Divine Attributes are "pathways of the heart[321]". The journey of the heart is on wings. The Destination is within:

وَلَقَدْ خَلَقْنَا ٱلْإِنسَـٰنَ وَنَعْلَمُ مَا تُوَسْوِسُ بِهِۦ نَفْسُهُۥ ۖ وَنَحْنُ أَقْرَبُ إِلَيْهِ مِنْ حَبْلِ ٱلْوَرِيدِ ۝

Truly We have created man
And We know the whispers within his innermost being,
And We are closer to him than his jugular vein.[322]

---

319 *The Vision of Islam* by Murata and Chittick
320 Abu Yazid al-Bistami, translated and quoted in "The Enlightened Mind" An anthology of Sacred Prose
    edited by Stephen Mitchell
321 *The Sufi Book of Life, 99 Pathways of the Heart for the Modern Dervish,* by Neil Douglas-Klotz
322 Al Quran 50:16

Asma ul Husna

1.   *ALLAH*   God.

The word Allah is pre-Islamic and is the Arabic name of God. There are various opinions on the exegesis of the word. A common opinion explains the word as a fusion of two root words, *Al* and *Ilah*, meaning "*The* Deity".

وَمَآ أَرْسَلْنَـٰكَ إِلَّا رَحْمَةً لِّلْعَـٰلَمِينَ ۝ قُلْ إِنَّمَا يُوحَىٰ إِلَىَّ أَنَّمَآ إِلَـٰهُكُمْ إِلَـٰهٌ وَٰحِدٌ
فَهَلْ أَنتُم مُّسْلِمُونَ ۝

We have not sent you (Muhammad) except as [bearer of] mercy for all beings
Say "It is revealed to me that your deity is God Alone {Illahun-Waahid}
Do you then surrender unto Him?"[323]

The significance though, of God referring to Himself by this pre-existing name in the Arabic Quran, is that God is willing to adopt the name adopted by His creatures. Allah is the essence of existence and not the existence that we know; an existence that defies both form and term and human understanding. "The Essence Whose Existence is Incumbent" and yet it is *not* that which we can conceive. Incumbent upon man is submission to *Allah* as there is no other worthy of submission.

إِنِّىٓ أَنَا۠ رَبُّكَ فَٱخْلَعْ نَعْلَيْكَ إِنَّكَ بِٱلْوَادِ ٱلْمُقَدَّسِ طُوًى ۝ وَأَنَا ٱخْتَرْتُكَ فَٱسْتَمِعْ لِمَا
يُوحَىٰ ۝ إِنَّنِىٓ أَنَا ٱللَّهُ لَآ إِلَـٰهَ إِلَّآ أَنَا۠ فَٱعْبُدْنِى وَأَقِمِ ٱلصَّلَوٰةَ لِذِكْرِىٓ ۝

"(Moses) I am your Lord.[324]
Cast off your shoes for you are in the sacred valley of Tuwa.
I have chosen you so hear and receive what is being revealed.
I am Allah, there is no other god.
So worship Me alone and observe prayer for My remembrance[325]

2.   *Ar Rahman*   The All-Merciful

This Divine attribute defies a simple translation. It has been translated variously, though inclusively, as "The Most Gracious", "The All-Merciful", "The Most Compassionate", "The Beneficent". The root word "*R-H- M*" carries the meaning "origin", "womb", "kinship", "mercy", and "compassion". Likewise, *Rahman* assumes a symbolic dynamism in its meaning. *Rahman* is a Name of Divine Essence {*Ism-e-Dhaat*}. God is Mercy, God is Compassion and God is

---

323 Al Quran 21:107-108
324 God speaking to Moses by the fire
325 Al Quran 20:12-15

Beneficence. Creation, singly and in its entirety, manifests its Creator, *Rahman*. Mercy is therefore The Divine theme of creation. *Rahman* is the Absolute and Singular Source of all mercy and His mercy is universal. Mercy flows to the sinful too. Did God not enlighten Khidr so that the goodness in the free-will of Khidr would pre-empt the evil in the free-will of others?

Mercy flows from the powerful to the less powerful and infinite ways. Every soul therefore returns to the Beneficent Master. The conscientious soul returns to Divine Love:

إِن كُلُّ مَن فِى ٱلسَّمَٰوَٰتِ وَٱلْأَرْضِ إِلَّآ ءَاتِى ٱلرَّحْمَٰنِ عَبْدًا ۞ لَّقَدْ أَحْصَىٰهُمْ وَعَدَّهُمْ عَدًّا ۞ وَكُلُّهُمْ ءَاتِيهِ يَوْمَ ٱلْقِيَٰمَةِ فَرْدًا ۞ إِنَّ ٱلَّذِينَ ءَامَنُوا۟ وَعَمِلُوا۟ ٱلصَّٰلِحَٰتِ سَيَجْعَلُ لَهُمُ ٱلرَّحْمَٰنُ وُدًّا ۞

There is none in the heavens and the earth but cometh unto the Beneficent {Rahman} as a slave. Verily He knoweth them and numbereth them with (right) numbering. And each one of them will come unto Him on the Day of Resurrection, alone. Lo! those who believe and do good works, the Beneficent will appoint for them love. [326]

قُلِ ٱدْعُوا۟ ٱللَّهَ أَوِ ٱدْعُوا۟ ٱلرَّحْمَٰنَ أَيًّا مَّا تَدْعُوا۟ فَلَهُ ٱلْأَسْمَآءُ ٱلْحُسْنَىٰ وَلَا تَجْهَرْ بِصَلَاتِكَ وَلَا تُخَافِتْ بِهَا وَٱبْتَغِ بَيْنَ ذَٰلِكَ سَبِيلًا ۞

Say: "Call upon Allah, or call upon Rahman by whatever name ye call upon Him, (it is well) for to Him belong the Most Beautiful Names.
Neither speak thy Prayer aloud, nor speak it in a low tone, but seek a middle course between." [327]

3. *Ar Raheem*   Dispenser of Mercy.

Rahman and *Raheem* share the same root word. Unlike *Rahman*, an attribute in which the creature has no share, *Raheem* is a Divine attribute that invites human participation. Man must seek Divine Mercy and so should man deliver mercy to others who depend upon him.

Mercy is an attribute which shows itself within the context of a relationship or relationships. It is that which operates beyond the framework of justice and equity. It is that without which there would be no sympathy, no empathy, no forgiveness, no healing and no love. Mercy is what makes the universe Whole.

---

326 Al Quran 19:93-96
327 Al Quran 17:110

Mercy flows from the offended to the offender, from the strong to the weak, from the satiated to the hungry, from the master to the subject. Its quality rises with the degree of the offence, or the degree of inequality. God is therefore *"The Most Merciful of those who show mercy"*[328]

Mercy, from the human perspective is the qualitative aspect of forgiveness, compassion, forbearance and patience. It is at once the giving of one's self to the other, and the taking in of the other into the self. It is more meaningful and significant, in the context of the relationship with the enemy, than with the friend. So as to signify the importance of reconciliation and compassion, in the aftermath of the last revelation, Muhammad, the last prophet, is declared by the Quran to be *"Rahamat-un-lil Alameen"*[329], meaning the bearer of mercy for *all* beings.

This attribute of God has been recalled numerously in the Quran as well as in the opening verse (known as *'Basmallah'* or *'Bismillah*[330]*'*) of all chapters:

بِسْمِ ٱللَّهِ ٱلرَّحْمَٰنِ ٱلرَّحِيمِ ۝

In the name of God, The Beneficent {Ar Rahman}, The Merciful {Raheem}[331]

رَبَّنَا وَسِعْتَ كُلَّ شَيْءٍ رَّحْمَةً وَعِلْمًا

Our Lord! You comprehended all things in mercy and knowledge[332]

وَكَانَ بِٱلْمُؤْمِنِينَ رَحِيمًا ۝

He is Merciful to the believers[333]

وَرَحْمَتِى وَسِعَتْ كُلَّ شَيْءٍ

My Mercy has embraced all things[334]

كَتَبَ رَبُّكُمْ عَلَىٰ نَفْسِهِ ٱلرَّحْمَةَ

Your Lord has prescribed for Himself Mercy[335]

۞ نَبِّئْ عِبَادِىٓ أَنِّىٓ أَنَا ٱلْغَفُورُ ٱلرَّحِيمُ ۝

Inform My devotees that I am the Forgiving, the Merciful {Ghafoor ur Raheem}[336]

---

328 Al Quran 12:64
329 Al Quran 21:107
330 'Basmallah' is its alphabetical representation in English, though the correct pronunciation is 'Bismillah'
331 Opening verse of every Surah (save the 9th) in the Quran
332 Al Quran 40:7
333 Al Quran 33:43
334 Al Quran 7:156
335 Al Quran 6:54
336 Al Quran 15:49

$$وَهُوَ ٱلْغَفُورُ ٱلرَّحِيمُ$$

He is The Forgiving, The Merciful {Ghafoor ur Raheem} [337]

4. *Al Malik*   The Sovereign.

Spiritual contemplation is a continuous though regenerative process. It is an approach towards the Sovereign, by the Sovereign's Will. God grants to the patient seeker, increasing awareness and deeper understanding.

$$وَكَذَٰلِكَ أَنزَلْنَٰهُ قُرْءَانًا عَرَبِيًّا وَصَرَّفْنَا فِيهِ مِنَ ٱلْوَعِيدِ لَعَلَّهُمْ يَتَّقُونَ أَوْ يُحْدِثُ لَهُمْ ذِكْرًا ۝$$

$$فَتَعَٰلَى ٱللَّهُ ٱلْمَلِكُ ٱلْحَقُّ ۗ وَلَا تَعْجَلْ بِٱلْقُرْءَانِ مِن قَبْلِ أَن يُقْضَىٰٓ إِلَيْكَ وَحْيُهُۥ ۖ وَقُل رَّبِّ زِدْنِى عِلْمًا ۝$$

AND THUS have We bestowed from on high this [Divine writ] as a discourse in the Arabic tongue, and have given therein many facets to all manner of warnings, so that men might remain conscious of Us, or that it give rise to a new awareness in them. [Know,] then, [that] God is sublimely exalted, the Ultimate Sovereign, the Ultimate Truth {Malikul Haqq}: and [knowing this,] do not approach the Quran in haste, ere it has been revealed unto thee in full, but [always] say: "O my Sustainer, cause me to grow in knowledge" [338]

The Sovereign is to be obeyed and sought, until the subject is ready and worthy to be invited into the Sovereign's presence in the station of Paradise:

$$وَكُلُّ شَىْءٍ فَعَلُوهُ فِى ٱلزُّبُرِ ۝ وَكُلُّ صَغِيرٍ وَكَبِيرٍ مُّسْتَطَرٌ ۝ إِنَّ ٱلْمُتَّقِينَ فِى جَنَّٰتٍ وَنَهَرٍ ۝$$

$$فِى مَقْعَدِ صِدْقٍ عِندَ مَلِيكٍ مُّقْتَدِرٍۭ ۝$$

All their deeds are recorded in the book
Every deed, small and big, alike are noted
The righteous shall dwell in gardens and running streams
in the seat of Truth by the Omnipotent Sovereign {Maleek im Muqtadir} [339]

5. *Al Quddoos*   The Holy

God is absolute Purity beyond the realm of human conception—beyond being, Whose essence is Itself. Whose reference is Itself; beyond the imperfections of form and the impurities of substance, lacking nothing and wanting nothing;

---

337 Al Quran 10:107
338 Al Quran 20:113-114 as interpreted by Muhammad Asad
339 Al Quran 54:52-55

Completeness within and by Itself. *Al Quddoos* is an essential attribute of Divine Essence {*Ism-e-Dhaat*}. Known to us by Its Attributes, which by Its purity, are without fault or flaw.

The beauty of an act lies in the purity of intent, known (besides God) only to the heart itself. *Al Quddoos* has the power to purify the believer's heart so that it may approach the Truth.

6.   *As Salaam*   The Peace.

The Whole; The One who displaces doubt, fear and anxiety with Peace; The One who satiates the seeker's heart. *Salaam, Islam* and *muslim* share the same root word. The promise of Islam is peace. Peace has no walls, only possibilities. No strife, only healing. No fear, only strength. No limits, only transcendence. No separation, only Unity. God wants the returning soul to return to The Divine Presence in the Abode of Peace {*Dar es Salaam*}[340]. The Word of God is Divine Will and the 'state of being' of Divine Creation. To those who have attained the paradise of proximity to their Sustainer, in the Abode of Peace, the Divine Word expressing the Divine Will shall be Peace![341]

7.   *Al-Mu'min*   The bestower of Faith.

The One who has placed the Divine Spark within each one of us. The One who illuminates our spiritual awareness. The One who pours faith in the spiritual heart of the seeker. *Mu'min* and *Emaan* share the same root word. *Al Mumin* plants the seed of Faith that leads to the Wholeness of *As Salaam*.

8.   *Al Muhaimin*   The Preserver.

The One who preserves the spiritual heart of the seeker. If *As Salaam* is the Light that fills the heart, *Al Mumin* is the Divine Flame and *Al Muhaimin* is its lamp. God preserves us and our faith in sleep and death too, as He preserved the young men and their faith in 'The Cave'.

9.   *Al Azeez*   The Almighty.

The Absolute Authority by right and might. Power and honor belong only to God, and to Him are accountable all those who exercise power. The root word ' *'IZZ*' connotes might, power, supremacy of rank and honor, etc. A related word is *Izzat*, often translated as honor or high-standing. A man's standing is intrinsic and does not rest upon his material or social status, or of those mortals that he associates with. One's true rank and honor rests in his proximity to God.

---

340 Al Quran 6:127
341 Al Quran 36:58

ٱلَّذِينَ يَتَّخِذُونَ ٱلْكَفِرِينَ أَوْلِيَآءَ مِن دُونِ ٱلْمُؤْمِنِينَ ۚ أَيَبْتَغُونَ عِندَهُمُ ٱلْعِزَّةَ فَإِنَّ ٱلْعِزَّةَ لِلَّهِ

جَمِيعًا ۝

Those who take for allies people who are hostile to faith, leaving aside the faithful: is it honor and rank {Izzat} that they seek among them?
Though without a doubt, all honor and rank {Izzat} is with God.[342]

10. *Al Jabbar*   The Compeller.

In God's compliance is the universe. God is the absolute Sovereign of Order. *Jabbar* is derived from the word *Jabr*, both a verb and a noun that means 'coercion' and 'coercive force' respectively. *Jabr*, by a human-being amounts to oppression. *Jabr*, by the Source of Peace, Pure and Self-Glorious, Protector of all, implies the force that restores a broken thing or a degenerative process to its beauteous form or proper state. *Al Jabbar* the superlative of *Jabr* keeps the Universe in the harmony of its balance. There is no such thing as a 'chance' or 'randomness' from the Divine perspective. Scientific Laws of Nature that unravel the mystery of nature, only confirm the existence of a "Supreme Force" that guarantees pre-determined compliance by all things. It may be said that life too is a manifestation of compliance. Each heart beat manifests compliance to the Compeller.

11. *Al Mutakabbir*   The Self-Glorious.

This name is related to the co-rooted words, *Kibriya* (applicable to God) and *Takabbur* (applicable to humans). The former means transcendental sovereignty, arising from and resting in unknowable wisdom, irresistible strength, absolute independence and pure Wholeness. *Takabbur*, in a human, who is dependent, mortal and flawed, amounts to arrogance and exposes vanity. Pride is too burdensome for the human and it disfigures the soul. Pride and Glory belong to God alone.

12. *Al Khaliq*   The Creator.

Who creates by Will and from nothing else. Life therefore is the mysterious (from the human perspective) Will of the Creator and it is to be so understood. The link between the Creator and creation is constant and permanent. The creature is forever dependent on its Creator and the Creator is forever the Willing Keeper.

13. *Al Bari'*   The Evolver

---

342 Al Quran 4:139

The Inventor, The Shaper out of naught, The Maker. The One who gives each creature its distinct existence and identity and places it in the larger Scheme. The One Who gives life its course and instinct. The One who grants self-hood.

14. *Al Musawwir*   The One Who gives form and shape to life.

Who fashioned time, matter and motion and placed one in the other; Who gave property to matter and who gave speed to motion; Who formed time and gave it yesterday and made hope and provision for tomorrow; Who brought color to sight and music to hearing.

The distinction between *Khaliq*, *Bari* and *Musawwir* is rather blurred. *Bari* alone has been translated as 'The Inventor', 'The Shaper out of naught', 'The Evolver' and the 'The Maker' by Mohsin Khan, Pickthall, Yusuf Ali and Asad respectively. To be mired in these nuances is to miss the point. *Khaliq*, *Bari* and *Musawwir* are Onc, to the exclusion of all others. In the many conditions that we find ourselves in- - in any shape and form and at any stage in our lives, we exist and live and die by the Single Divine Will and by no other.

All creation is by the Beneficent and exists in Mercy. We are God's handiwork, constrained by his Writ, individual and special by His purpose. God is Overwhelming, Almighty, and Unfathomable. There can be no earnest contemplation of God outside of complete submission. A humbled mind constructs a deistic belief. An awakened heart surrenders to the Only Reality. God is the Absolute Ground of Being. "*Allah Hu*", "*Allah Hu*", is the heart-beat of the Universe. The Universe comes into being by the Divine-word "Be" .Still unfolding still becoming. Time still unfurling, stars still breaking, planets still forming, matter still pulsating. All time and space, life and matter, discrete and individual, together and connected are facets of the Single Word of the Sole Creator, All Mighty, Pure Wisdom and Pure Mercy:

لَوْ أَنزَلْنَا هَـٰذَا ٱلْقُرْءَانَ عَلَىٰ جَبَلٍ لَّرَأَيْتَهُۥ خَـٰشِعًا مُّتَصَدِّعًا مِّنْ خَشْيَةِ ٱللَّهِ ۚ وَتِلْكَ ٱلْأَمْثَـٰلُ نَضْرِبُهَا لِلنَّاسِ لَعَلَّهُمْ يَتَفَكَّرُونَ ۝ هُوَ ٱللَّهُ ٱلَّذِى لَآ إِلَـٰهَ إِلَّا هُوَ ۖ عَـٰلِمُ ٱلْغَيْبِ وَٱلشَّهَـٰدَةِ ۖ هُوَ ٱلرَّحْمَـٰنُ ٱلرَّحِيمُ ۝ هُوَ ٱللَّهُ ٱلَّذِى لَآ إِلَـٰهَ إِلَّا هُوَ ٱلْمَلِكُ ٱلْقُدُّوسُ ٱلسَّلَـٰمُ ٱلْمُؤْمِنُ ٱلْمُهَيْمِنُ ٱلْعَزِيزُ ٱلْجَبَّارُ ٱلْمُتَكَبِّرُ ۚ سُبْحَـٰنَ ٱللَّهِ عَمَّا يُشْرِكُونَ ۝ هُوَ ٱللَّهُ ٱلْخَـٰلِقُ ٱلْبَارِئُ ٱلْمُصَوِّرُ ۖ لَهُ ٱلْأَسْمَآءُ ٱلْحُسْنَىٰ ۚ يُسَبِّحُ لَهُۥ مَا فِى ٱلسَّمَـٰوَٰتِ وَٱلْأَرْضِ ۖ وَهُوَ ٱلْعَزِيزُ ٱلْحَكِيمُ ۝

Had We revealed this Quran upon a mountain you would see it humble itself and implode in awe of God. We propound such analogies so that they may reflect.

God is God and there is no other —
Knower of the hidden and imperceptible {Ghaib} and the evident.
The Source of Compassion {Rahman}, The Merciful {Raheem}.
God is God and there is no other —
The Sovereign {Malik}, The Holy {Quddus}, The Source of Peace {As Salaam},
The Guardian of Faith {Mumin}, The Giver of Safety {Muhaimin},
The Almighty {Azeez},The Compeller {Jabbar}, The Overwhelming {Muttakabir.}
Exalted is God, above any partners they may associate (with Him).[343]
This is God — The Creator {Khaliq}, The Originator {Bari}, The Shaper {Mussawwir}.
To Him refer the Most Beautiful Names.
Celebrated by all there is in the Heavens and the earth.
And He is boundless in Might {Azeez}, complete in Wisdom {Hakeem} [344]

15. *Al Ghaffar*   The Forgiver, from Whom flows all forgiveness.

Derived from the root-word *GH-F-R,* meaning 'veiling', 'pardoning', 'protecting', 'preserving', etc. He is the One who forgives, has the propensity to forgive and is the ultimate Source and Arbiter of forgiveness. With Him is the complete knowledge of any act, replete with the associated thought and intent. Forgiveness is therefore an attribute of His Grace, and the ultimate forgiveness is in His jurisdiction alone. Forgiveness is "here" and "now" ready to cleanse the heart that opens itself through repentance, remorse and its own willing readiness to forgive others. He forgives by accepting repentance.[345]

Forgiveness is an invitation to reflection and remorse and not a license to callousness. The "arrogant and self-exalting" heart is sealed[346] and deprives itself from receiving His forgiveness. Forgiveness of others is a recurring theme[347] in the Quran:

$$﴿ وَسَارِعُوٓا۟ إِلَىٰ مَغْفِرَةٍ مِّن رَّبِّكُمْ وَجَنَّةٍ عَرْضُهَا ٱلسَّمَـٰوَٰتُ وَٱلْأَرْضُ أُعِدَّتْ لِلْمُتَّقِينَ ﴾$$

$$ٱلَّذِينَ يُنفِقُونَ فِى ٱلسَّرَّآءِ وَٱلضَّرَّآءِ وَٱلْكَـٰظِمِينَ ٱلْغَيْظَ وَٱلْعَافِينَ عَنِ ٱلنَّاسِ ۗ وَٱللَّهُ يُحِبُّ$$

$$ٱلْمُحْسِنِينَ ﴿﴾$$

And vie with each other to attain your Sustainer's forgiveness {maghfira} and to a Paradise as vast as the heavens and the earth, which has been readied for the God-conscious. Who spend [in His way] in time of plenty and in time of

---

343 Al Quran 59:21-23
344 Al Quran 59:24
345 Al Quran 40:1-3
346 Al Quran 40:35
347 Al Quran 2:109; 3:159; 4 v-149; 5:13; 15:85; 24:22; 42:40

hardship, and hold in check their anger and pardon their fellow-men because God loves those who show grace.[348]

All prophets have carried the persistent message of Divine mercy and forgiveness. They have made their call passionately, loyally and in every possible way—pleading and warning, privately and openly, quietly and loudly. The gates of Divine Forgiveness are always open. The arrogant heart spurns the offer:

وَإِنِّي كُلَّمَا دَعَوْتُهُمْ لِتَغْفِرَ لَهُمْ جَعَلُوٓاْ أَصَٰبِعَهُمْ فِىٓ ءَاذَانِهِمْ وَٱسْتَغْشَوْاْ ثِيَابَهُمْ وَأَصَرُّواْ وَٱسْتَكْبَرُواْ ٱسْتِكْبَارًا ۝ ثُمَّ إِنِّي دَعَوْتُهُمْ جِهَارًا ۝ ثُمَّ إِنِّيٓ أَعْلَنتُ لَهُمْ وَأَسْرَرْتُ لَهُمْ إِسْرَارًا ۝ فَقُلْتُ ٱسْتَغْفِرُواْ رَبَّكُمْ إِنَّهُۥ كَانَ غَفَّارًا ۝

Every time I (Noah) called unto them that You may forgive them, they stuck their fingers in their ears and covered themselves with their cloaks puffed in pride, unmoved. I made the call loudly and pleaded in the open and have appealed to them in private. I said to them 'Ask for forgiveness of your Lord, God is the Fount of Forgiveness {Ghaffar}'[349]

16. *Al Qahhaar*   The Irresistible.

Overpowering. The One with the power to bring every thing and every creature to its proper place and rank. *Qahr* is the state of decimation and devastation. To overpower someone with *Qahr* is to completely decimate or reorder. The One with the power to clear darkness with Light, fear with hope, and falsehood with Truth. The supreme Creator and the absolute Master.

قُلْ مَن رَّبُّ ٱلسَّمَٰوَٰتِ وَٱلْأَرْضِ قُلِ ٱللَّهُ قُلْ أَفَٱتَّخَذْتُم مِّن دُونِهِۦٓ أَوْلِيَآءَ لَا يَمْلِكُونَ لِأَنفُسِهِمْ نَفْعًا وَلَا ضَرًّا قُلْ هَلْ يَسْتَوِى ٱلْأَعْمَىٰ وَٱلْبَصِيرُ أَمْ هَلْ تَسْتَوِى ٱلظُّلُمَٰتُ وَٱلنُّورُ أَمْ جَعَلُواْ لِلَّهِ شُرَكَآءَ خَلَقُواْ كَخَلْقِهِۦ فَتَشَٰبَهَ ٱلْخَلْقُ عَلَيْهِمْ قُلِ ٱللَّهُ خَٰلِقُ كُلِّ شَىْءٍ وَهُوَ ٱلْوَٰحِدُ ٱلْقَهَّٰرُ ۝

Say "Who is the Lord of the Heavens and the earth?"
Say "God."
Say "Do you then choose protectors other than Him—those that cannot bring good or harm to even themselves?"
Say "Is the blind the same as the seeing?
Or are darknesses the same as light?"

348 Al Quran 3:133-134
349 Al Quran 71:7-10

Have their improvised gods created the like of God's creation such that both
creations appear to them to be the same?
Say "God is the Creator of all things, The One {Waahid},
The Irresistible" {Qahhaar} [350]

Qahhaar is the intense form of Qahir which implies mastery and lordship. Qahir manifests the action of Qahhaar; the latter as "Absolute Power" being an attribute of Divine Essence {Ism-e-Dhaat}.

وَإِن يَمْسَسْكَ ٱللَّهُ بِضُرٍّ فَلَا كَاشِفَ لَهُۥ إِلَّا هُوَ ۖ وَإِن يَمْسَسْكَ بِخَيْرٍ فَهُوَ عَلَىٰ كُلِّ شَىْءٍ قَدِيرٌ

وَهُوَ ٱلْقَاهِرُ فَوْقَ عِبَادِهِۦ ۚ وَهُوَ ٱلْحَكِيمُ ٱلْخَبِيرُ

If God brings upon an affliction, none that can remove it save Him, and if He
brings upon good fortune (none that can impair it save Him). He has Power over
all things. God reigns supreme {Qahir} over His servants,
He is All-wise, All-aware [351]

17. *Al Wahhaab*   The Bestower.

Wahhaab is co-rooted with the noun Hibah and the verb yahib, defining the object and action of transferring ownership of a possession to another, free of compensation. Wahib is the one who gifts and manifests the action of Wahhaab. Al Wahhaab is the bestower of all that is of value. Foremost is the gift of life, filled with temporal gifts of love and companionship, comfort and affluence, power and influence. These are gifts meant to be wisely used and gratefully shared. The transcendental gift is God's guidance through revelation. The gift at the journey's end is for keeps.

رَبَّنَا لَا تُزِغْ قُلُوبَنَا بَعْدَ إِذْ هَدَيْتَنَا وَهَبْ لَنَا مِن لَّدُنكَ رَحْمَةً ۚ إِنَّكَ أَنتَ ٱلْوَهَّابُ رَبَّنَآ

إِنَّكَ جَامِعُ ٱلنَّاسِ لِيَوْمٍ لَّا رَيْبَ فِيهِ ۚ إِنَّ ٱللَّهَ لَا يُخْلِفُ ٱلْمِيعَادَ

"Our Sustainer do not let our hearts deviate after You have guided us.
And grant us Your Mercy
You are the Most Generous Bestower {Wahhaab}"
"Our Sustainer you are the one who will gather {Jaame'} mankind
On a day of which there is no doubt
For God never contravenes His promise" [352]

350 Al Quran 13:16
351 Al Quran 6:17-18
352 Al Quran 3:8-9

Any temporal gift is wasted if it is not used in the service of man and in the servitude of God. A wasted life is a wasted gift, akin to a dead king seated on the throne. It is the giving and caring king who elevates the throne. The throne cannot elevate a dead king. We are meant to be conduits of God's gifts and not their reservoir.

وَلَقَدْ فَتَنَّا سُلَيْمَنَ وَأَلْقَيْنَا عَلَىٰ كُرْسِيِّهِۦ جَسَدًا ثُمَّ أَنَابَ ۞ قَالَ رَبِّ أَغْفِرْ لِى وَهَبْ لِى

مُلْكًا لَّا يَنۢبَغِى لِأَحَدٍ مِّنۢ بَعْدِىٓ إِنَّكَ أَنتَ ٱلْوَهَّابُ ۞ فَسَخَّرْنَا لَهُ ٱلرِّيحَ تَجْرِى بِأَمْرِهِۦ

رُخَآءً حَيْثُ أَصَابَ ۞ وَٱلشَّيَٰطِينَ كُلَّ بَنَّآءٍ وَغَوَّاصٍ ۞ وَءَاخَرِينَ مُقَرَّنِينَ فِى ٱلْأَصْفَادِ

۞ هَٰذَا عَطَآؤُنَا فَٱمْنُنْ أَوْ أَمْسِكْ بِغَيْرِ حِسَابٍ ۞ وَإِنَّ لَهُۥ عِندَنَا لَزُلْفَىٰ وَحُسْنَ مَـَٔابٍ

۞

We tested Solomon, and set upon his throne a body.
Then he turned to God, saying, "My Sustainer forgive me and bestow on me a
kingdom beyond the reach of any one after me.
Verily, You are the Bestower {Wahhaab}."
We made subservient to him the wind, so it moved dutifully in his compliance
And the untamed forces, operating high above and deeply submerged
And some others too, bound with fetters.
This is Our gift, so give unto whosoever, or withhold from whosoever, without
measure. And surely he has with Us nearness, and a beautiful station.[353]

18. *Ar Razzaq*   The Nourisher.

The Provider — The One who sustains us by nourishing our spirits and feeding our bodies. *Razzaq* is co-rooted with the noun *rizq* which describes that which sustains a creature. At the very basic level of life, *rizq* is basic food for the body. On a higher level, *rizq* is also that which sustains the spirit. *Raziq* is the one who provides *rizq*, and manifests the action of *Razzaaq*. *Raziq* refers to the Divine Will (action), while *Razzaq* refers to the Divine Essence {*Ism-e-Dhaat*}. From God flows all, as by God is apportioned the *rizq* for every needful creature.

۞ وَمَا مِن دَآبَّةٍ فِى ٱلْأَرْضِ إِلَّا عَلَى ٱللَّهِ رِزْقُهَا وَيَعْلَمُ مُسْتَقَرَّهَا وَمُسْتَوْدَعَهَا كُلٌّ فِى كِتَٰبٍ

مُّبِينٍ ۞

And there is not a creature on the earth but whose sustenance {rizq} depends on
God.

---

353 Al Quran 38:34-40

He knows its habitation and its repository.
All is in a clear Record. 354

Sharing our *rizq* and *Hibah* with others is therefore to participate in the Divine Design.

وَمَا خَلَقْتُ ٱلْجِنَّ وَٱلْإِنسَ إِلَّا لِيَعْبُدُونِ ۝ مَآ أُرِيدُ مِنْهُم مِّن رِّزْقٍ وَمَآ أُرِيدُ أَن يُطْعِمُونِ

۝ إِنَّ ٱللَّهَ هُوَ ٱلرَّزَّاقُ ذُو ٱلْقُوَّةِ ٱلْمَتِينُ ۝

I have created the Jinn and Humans to serve Me
I do not want from them any sustenance
I do not want them to feed Me
For God is The Provider {Razzaq}
*Unbreakable in Might {quwwatil Mateen}*355

19. *Al Fattah*   The Opener (of Truth), The Victory-Giver.

Fattah is co-rooted with *Fatiha* (Opening), *Fath* (victory) and *Muftah* (key). *Al Fattah* opens all doors as He opens all hearts. The un-locked heart is aware that its innermost desires and motivations, fears and tribulations are in God's knowledge. The purity of its inner sincerity is the singular object of its concern as it is the foremost object of God's scrutiny. A heart un-locked is blissfully conscious of the knowledge that it too manifests God's omnipresence. This awareness is the flame of its inner struggle, its 'greater *jihad*'.

قُل لَّا تُسْـَٔلُونَ عَمَّآ أَجْرَمْنَا وَلَا نُسْـَٔلُ عَمَّا تَعْمَلُونَ ۝ قُلْ يَجْمَعُ بَيْنَنَا رَبُّنَا ثُمَّ يَفْتَحُ

بَيْنَنَا بِٱلْحَقِّ وَهُوَ ٱلْفَتَّاحُ ٱلْعَلِيمُ ۝

Say, "Not accountable will you be of our misdeeds
Nor shall we be held accountable for what you do"
Say, "Our Sustainer will gather us all
And will lay open between us what is real."
*He is the Opener (of all true doors) and All Knowing {Fattah ul Aleem}*356

The purified heart finds strength and security in the realization that the heart that welcomes God can never be locked again. The solace it seeks takes root in the realization that it never is and never was alone.

---

354 Al Quran 11:6
355 Al Quran 51:56-58
356 Al Quran 34:25-26

$$مَّا يَفْتَحِ ٱللَّهُ لِلنَّاسِ مِن رَّحْمَةٍ فَلَا مُمْسِكَ لَهَا وَمَا يُمْسِكْ فَلَا مُرْسِلَ لَهُ مِنْ بَعْدِهِ وَهُوَ الْعَزِيزُ ٱلْحَكِيمُ ۝$$

The [doors of] mercy that God opens (yaftahil lahu) for mankind,
None can obstruct and that which He obstructs none can pass thereafter.
He is the Mighty, the Wise. [357]

True and lasting victory is to be sought and can necessarily be achieved only by the heart. It must start its quest in faith and through submission. With God are the keys to its victorious journey.

$$۞ وَعِندَهُۥ مَفَاتِحُ ٱلْغَيْبِ لَا يَعْلَمُهَآ إِلَّا هُوَ$$

With Him are the keys of the unknown (mafathul ghaybi)
None has knowledge thereof but He[358]

20. *Al Aleem*   The All-Knowing.

Aleem is the superlative of *Alim* (one with knowledge) and is co-rooted with the words *ilm* (knowledge) and *alam* (state of being or awareness). The state of being depends upon knowledge and knowledge is both information and understanding. Human consciousness and awareness are relative to human knowledge. Our consciousness and knowledge evolve; Time and space, being the necessary mediums for this evolution. *Al Aleem's* knowledge and awareness is the unqualified Truth, transcendentally Complete and unconditionally Absolute.

Our temporal reality is anchored in space and time although both are relative. The East and West are relative to our position on earth just as the past and future are relative to our position in time. God, Transcendental, is the Absolute Anchor.

$$وَلِلَّهِ ٱلْمَشْرِقُ وَٱلْمَغْرِبُ فَأَيْنَمَا تُوَلُّوا فَثَمَّ وَجْهُ ٱللَّهِ إِنَّ ٱللَّهَ وَٰسِعٌ عَلِيمٌ ۝$$

"To God belongs the East and West.
Everywhere you turn is the Presence of God.
God is Omnipresent {Waasi} and All-Knowing {Aleem}.[359]

Another Divine name, *Al Khabeer*, diffuses with *Al Aleem*. *Al Aleem's* knowledge is absolute with no dependencies. Creation is a component of this knowledge but it does not change it. *Khabeer's* knowing is associated with what transpires.

357 Al Quran 35:2
358 Al Quran 6:59
359 Al Quran 2:115

Creation is a component of this knowledge and it also affects it. *Khabeer* is often translated as 'fully aware' or 'fully informed'. In the following verse, *Al Khabeer* and *Al Ameen* are used together, in a context that covers transcendental knowledge (The Creator's exclusive knowledge, outside of the context of creation) and knowledge of the human condition and the details and complexities of its experience:

إِنَّ ٱللَّهَ عِندَهُۥ عِلْمُ ٱلسَّاعَةِ وَيُنَزِّلُ ٱلْغَيْثَ وَيَعْلَمُ مَا فِى ٱلْأَرْحَامِ ۖ وَمَا تَدْرِى نَفْسٌ مَّاذَا تَكْسِبُ غَدًا ۖ وَمَا تَدْرِى نَفْسٌۢ بِأَىِّ أَرْضٍ تَمُوتُ ۚ إِنَّ ٱللَّهَ عَلِيمٌ خَبِيرٌۢ ۝

It is God who has the knowledge of the end of time
And who showers the rain
And who knows what is in the wombs.
No soul knows what it will earn tomorrow
And no soul knows in what land it will die
But God is Omniscient, completely Aware {Aleem un Khabeer}[360]

The sincerity of a deed lies in the heart. The relationship with God is from the heart. The heart, when it offers itself, does so with self-less love. The heart when it with-holds itself does so in self-delusional deceit. The veil between us and God is an illusion that we foster by our own forgetfulness:

أَلَآ إِنَّهُمْ يَثْنُونَ صُدُورَهُمْ لِيَسْتَخْفُوا۟ مِنْهُ ۚ أَلَا حِينَ يَسْتَغْشُونَ ثِيَابَهُمْ يَعْلَمُ مَا يُسِرُّونَ وَمَا يُعْلِنُونَ ۚ إِنَّهُۥ عَلِيمٌۢ بِذَاتِ ٱلصُّدُورِ ۝

Behold how they twist their hearts to hide from Him.
Even when they cover themselves with their cloaks
God knows that what they conceal and what they expose
God is Aware {Aleem} of what is in their hearts[361]

21. *Al Qaabid*   The One Who Constricts (provision or guidance).

Qaabid is rooted in the verb *qabd*, which means to 'firmly seize', 'to grip' and as a variation 'to forcibly take away', 'withhold' or 'constrict'. Paired with the complementary attribute *Al Basit* it conveys God's control over the cyclical rhythms of life and being. The Universe pulsates, at all levels, and in the rhythm defined by God. At the core of every particle, as at the core of every cell, living and lifeless is the energy of pulsation. The physical particle is its wave.

From God is abundance and from God is penury. God wills the heart to expand for whom He wills as God wills the heart to be constricted for whom He wills.

360 Al Quran 31:34
361 Al Quran 11:5

The pulse of being belongs to God. And to God belong the pulsations of the beating heart. He who constricts and withholds is He who expands and bestows. *Al Qaabid* and *Al Basit* as complementary attributes underscore change as an aspect of Divine design. Changing conditions and circumstances bear opportunities of growth and learning. They are reminders too of the approaching return.

22. *Al Baasit*   The One Who Expands (provision or guidance).

The tide lives by its 'ebb and flow'. With its flow it brings in the pearls and the nutrients that adorn and nourish the lagoon. In it's ebb it lays bare its treasures. Without the ebb and flow there would be no tide. Without the tide the lagoon would be dead and barren. There is also a "tide in the affairs of men". In its flow is God's bounty and in its ebb it expands the heart. Of this tide says the Quran:

فَإِنَّ مَعَ ٱلْعُسْرِ يُسْرًا ۝ إِنَّ مَعَ ٱلْعُسْرِ يُسْرًا ۝

And behold, with hardship comes ease: verily with hardship comes ease." [362]

Life renews itself with every heart-beat. To Him belongs every heart-beat. As to Him belongs every breath. Yet God will consider our spending in God's way an eternal debt!

مَّن ذَا ٱلَّذِى يُقْرِضُ ٱللَّهَ قَرْضًا حَسَنًا فَيُضَٰعِفَهُۥ لَهُۥٓ أَضْعَافًا كَثِيرَةً ۚ وَٱللَّهُ يَقْبِضُ وَيَبْصُۜطُ وَإِلَيْهِ تُرْجَعُونَ ۝

Who will loan to God an excellent loan
Which He will pay back many times over
God constricts and enlarges {Wallaahu yaqbizu wa yab-sut}
And to Him you return [363]

What is given to us in this life will be taken away, except that which we submit to God. What is taken away is meant to remind us that this life is a journey and the traveler who packs lightly covers more ground:

ٱللَّهُ يَبْسُطُ ٱلرِّزْقَ لِمَن يَشَآءُ وَيَقْدِرُ ۚ وَفَرِحُوا۟ بِٱلْحَيَوٰةِ ٱلدُّنْيَا وَمَا ٱلْحَيَوٰةُ ٱلدُّنْيَا فِى ٱلْءَاخِرَةِ إِلَّا مَتَٰعٌ ۝

God expands the provision {Allahhu yabsutur-Rizqa} for anyone He wills, and limits (at will)
And they rejoice in the life of the world,

---

362 Al Quran 94:5-6
363 Al Quran 2:245

Whereas the life of the world, compared with the Hereafter is but a brief interlude.[364]

23. *Al Khafiz*   The Abaser.

The One who humbles, softens, diminishes His creatures. *Al Khafiz* and *Al Rafi* are complementary attributes that underscore the spiritual truth that 'worldly ranking' is transitory. The ebb and flow of worldly fortunes are learning opportunities (tests) for the perceptive heart. Misfortune tests the perseverance of faith and good fortune tests conscientiousness. The accumulated value of the soul is not measured by what life offers it, but by the beauty of *how* it deals with its circumstances. The retained value of a soul is ranked by the heart's alignment with God. The determination of this final, and therefore the only real rank, is in God's hands—*Al Khafiz* and *Al Rafi*.

وَٱلْعَصْرِ ۝ إِنَّ ٱلْإِنسَٰنَ لَفِى خُسْرٍ ۝ إِلَّا ٱلَّذِينَ ءَامَنُوا۟ وَعَمِلُوا۟ ٱلصَّٰلِحَٰتِ وَتَوَاصَوْا۟ بِٱلْحَقِّ وَتَوَاصَوْا۟ بِٱلصَّبْرِ ۝

As certain as a day's waning,
Man faces decline and diminishment
Except in the pursuit of faith and righteous deeds,
steeped in truth, justice and patience.[365]

True rank is based on the sincerity of submission. This sincerity, never *hidden* from the individual soul, comes to the fore when materiality is pulverized. Souls will *self-sort* by their respective stations of submission. In three groups we will assemble in the Divine Court. The Quran portrays these groups in the symbolism of the Divine Throne:

To the group of the 'foremost' will belong many of the older generation, progressively fewer from succeeding generations; facing the Throne—incandescent hearts, without a speck of doubt; selfless, pure spirits, in total harmony with Unity, properly placed under God's direct gaze.

Then those, with hearts ajar, open just enough to keep the flame alive. Flawed and unfit for the foremost station, but within the fold of redemption; Saved by even the atom's weight of grace. Seekers of Divine Mercy and Forgiveness, grouped on the Throne's Right—The Right Hand, by its natural dominance, symbolizing Divine Largesse by predisposition.

Then those of us dismissive of *Aakhira* (the determination of harmony with Unity),

---

364 Al Quran 13:26
365 Al Quran 103

locked hearts, blinded by arrogance, tethered by our ego, now ill-prepared to stand in the Light of The Divine Presence. Lost souls, fearful spirits, ignorant of Divine Largesse, like herds corralled on the Divine Left, the symbol of Divine Wrath. Neglectful we were then, neglected are we now. Many will be from amongst us, the unrelenting worshippers of the idols named "I", "Me" and "Mine"; unfit and ill-prepared to face the Throne, gazing enviously at the group across:

إِذَا وَقَعَتِ ٱلْوَاقِعَةُ ۝ لَيْسَ لِوَقْعَتِهَا كَاذِبَةٌ ۝ خَافِضَةٌ رَّافِعَةٌ ۝ إِذَا رُجَّتِ ٱلْأَرْضُ رَجًّا ۝ وَبُسَّتِ ٱلْجِبَالُ بَسًّا ۝ فَكَانَتْ هَبَآءً مُّنۢبَثًّا ۝ وَكُنتُمْ أَزْوَٰجًا ثَلَٰثَةً ۝ فَأَصْحَٰبُ ٱلْمَيْمَنَةِ مَآ أَصْحَٰبُ ٱلْمَيْمَنَةِ ۝ وَأَصْحَٰبُ ٱلْمَشْـَٔمَةِ مَآ أَصْحَٰبُ ٱلْمَشْـَٔمَةِ ۝ وَٱلسَّٰبِقُونَ ٱلسَّٰبِقُونَ ۝ أُو۟لَٰٓئِكَ ٱلْمُقَرَّبُونَ ۝

When arrives the event
None, its happening will dispute
Abasing (some), exalting (others) {kafizatur rafiah};
When the earth is shaken with a shock
And the hills are pulverized, scattered as dust.
You will be of three kinds:
Those on the right hand; what of those on the right hand?
And those on the left hand; what of those on the left hand?
and those in the forefront , the foremost [366]

24. *Ar Rafi*   The Exalted and the One who exalts.

God is the One who made a stuttering Moses overcome the mighty Pharaoh. God is the One who made the child Jesus speak from his cradle. God is the One who chose the unlettered prophet to bear the Book of Wisdom.

رَفِيعُ ٱلدَّرَجَٰتِ ذُو ٱلْعَرْشِ يُلْقِى ٱلرُّوحَ مِنْ أَمْرِهِۦ عَلَىٰ مَن يَشَآءُ مِنْ عِبَادِهِۦ لِيُنذِرَ يَوْمَ ٱلتَّلَاقِ ۝

Most Exalted in rank {Rafi ud darajat}, the Lord of The Throne
He sends the Spirit by His command upon whosoever He chooses amongst His servants, so that He may warn of the Day of reckoning. [367]

25. *Al Muizz*   The One who bestows power and true honor.

Al Muizz and *Al Muzill* are complementary attributes that underscore the fact that worldly stature is only relative. *Al Muizz* shares the same root word as *Al Azeez*. *Al Muizz* is the expression of *Al Azeez*, the latter being an attribute of the Divine Essence. Honor is the test of power's purpose. The might of power does not lie in its physical magnitude, but in its qualitative sincerity. Words too are mighty and the sincere word bears honor. The meek and poor may arrive at the threshold of Grace with the beauty of the sincere word, deserving no less than a beneficent king. The king however carries a heavier burden. Power exercised overtly or surreptitiously, for purposes other than in the service of fellow human beings is dishonorable and misdirected might. It shall bear the agony of emptiness. Power is a Divine Trust and its iniquitous use will face severe and certain accountability.

مَن كَانَ يُرِيدُ ٱلْعِزَّةَ فَلِلَّهِ ٱلْعِزَّةُ جَمِيعًا ۚ إِلَيْهِ يَصْعَدُ ٱلْكَلِمُ ٱلطَّيِّبُ وَٱلْعَمَلُ ٱلصَّـٰلِحُ يَرْفَعُهُ ۚ وَٱلَّذِينَ يَمْكُرُونَ ٱلسَّيِّئَاتِ لَهُمْ عَذَابٌ شَدِيدٌ ۖ وَمَكْرُ أُوْلَـٰئِكَ هُوَ يَبُورُ ۝

Whoever seeks power and honor {yuridul izzata} — to God belongs all honor and power {izzatu jamia}. To Him ascend the heart-felt words and deeds of righteousness, He exalts. Those who attempt deceit and evil, for them awaits intense agony and their deceit will come to naught.[368]

26. *Al Muzill*   The One who withdraws power and honor.

Power used to oppose the merciful purpose of God or the merciful mission of His messengers, is power exercised to debase one's own soul; the arrogant heart free-falls in the abyss of its delusion, mistaking futility for might and debasement for stature. God dishonors those who abuse power assigned to them. The Truth can never be buried.

إِنَّ ٱلَّذِينَ يُحَآدُّونَ ٱللَّهَ وَرَسُولَهُۥ أُوْلَـٰئِكَ فِى ٱلْأَذَلِّينَ ۝ كَتَبَ ٱللَّهُ لَأَغْلِبَنَّ أَنَا۠ وَرُسُلِىٓ ۚ إِنَّ ٱللَّهَ قَوِىٌّ عَزِيزٌ ۝

Know that those who oppose God and His messenger,
they are the most abject {azileen}
God has written: Prevail I shall, I and My messengers.
Verily God is The Force, Almighty.[369]

God brings Muhammad to *Kawthar* (the fountain of the Eternal Peace of Paradise) as He awards oblivion to those who taunted Muhammad for being bereft of a legacy by not having a son. The heart empowers itself through the

368 Al Quran 35:10
369 Al Quran 58:20-21

sincerity of its quest. Life's vicissitudes are mere guideposts of learning. Lasting benefits, those that make us whole and elevate us, flow from our consciousness of God.

قُلِ ٱللَّهُمَّ مَٰلِكَ ٱلْمُلْكِ تُؤْتِى ٱلْمُلْكَ مَن تَشَآءُ وَتَنزِعُ ٱلْمُلْكَ مِمَّن تَشَآءُ وَتُعِزُّ مَن تَشَآءُ وَتُذِلُّ مَن تَشَآءُ بِيَدِكَ ٱلْخَيْرُ إِنَّكَ عَلَىٰ كُلِّ شَىْءٍ قَدِيرٌ ۝

Say: "O God. Lord of all dominion, You give dominion to whom You Will,
And You strip dominion from whom You Will
You grant honor to whomsoever You Will, {wa tu izzu man-tashaa u}
And You abase whom You Will {wa tu zillu man-tashaa u}
In Your Hands is all good.
Verily, over all things You have power[370].

27. *As Sami*   The All-Hearing.

Our innermost self is never hidden from God. God is never far from us. God's judgment and award are delivered in full knowledge of the truth.

وَٱللَّهُ يَقْضِى بِٱلْحَقِّ وَٱلَّذِينَ يَدْعُونَ مِن دُونِهِۦ لَا يَقْضُونَ بِشَىْءٍ إِنَّ ٱللَّهَ هُوَ ٱلسَّمِيعُ ٱلْبَصِيرُ ۝

And God will judge by the Truth
Whereas those they beseech besides Him cannot judge at all
Verily God alone is all hearing, all seeing {Sami ul Baseer}.[371]

God joins us in bonds of marriage and kinship. God is a Witness to our conduct at all times. Our relationships are open to God. God is the 'third' in the bond between two creatures.

فَاطِرُ ٱلسَّمَٰوَٰتِ وَٱلْأَرْضِ جَعَلَ لَكُم مِّنْ أَنفُسِكُمْ أَزْوَٰجًا وَمِنَ ٱلْأَنْعَٰمِ أَزْوَٰجًا يَذْرَؤُكُمْ فِيهِ لَيْسَ كَمِثْلِهِۦ شَىْءٌ وَهُوَ ٱلسَّمِيعُ ٱلْبَصِيرُ ۝

The Originator of the heavens and the earth;
He has made for you mates from yourselves,
And mates for grazing creatures too,
Spreading you thereby;
Nothing there is in likeness of Him;
The Hearing, the Seeing {Sami ul Baseer}[372]

---

370 Al Quran 3:26
371 Al Quran 40:20
372 Al Quran 42:11

God hears those who beseech Him and responds with Divine Wisdom and purpose:

$$هُنَالِكَ دَعَا زَكَرِيَّا رَبَّهُ ۖ قَالَ رَبِّ هَبْ لِي مِن لَّدُنكَ ذُرِّيَّةً طَيِّبَةً ۖ إِنَّكَ سَمِيعُ الدُّعَاءِ ٣٨ فَنَادَتْهُ الْمَلَائِكَةُ وَهُوَ قَائِمٌ يُصَلِّي فِي الْمِحْرَابِ أَنَّ اللَّهَ يُبَشِّرُكَ بِيَحْيَىٰ مُصَدِّقًا بِكَلِمَةٍ مِّنَ اللَّهِ وَسَيِّدًا وَحَصُورًا وَنَبِيًّا مِّنَ الصَّالِحِينَ ٣٩$$

There Zachariah called upon his Lord and said:
My Lord! Bestow upon me good progeny from You.
For You are the Hearer of prayer {Sami ud duaa}
And the angels called to him as he stood praying in the sanctuary
"God gives you glad tidings of John {Yahya},
Confirming the truth of God's Word,
noble, chaste, a prophet, one of the righteous[373]

28. *Al Baseer*   The All-Seeing One.

God is He who sees the intention before the act; the thought before the word. God sees the inside of the heart. He sees the Truth in the silence and the hypocrisy in the speech. God sees what we desire. God sees what we give and what we withhold. He sees through our plans and He sees when we conspire. He is the Witness to every kept pledge as He is Witness to every broken promise. God is the judge of Truth.

$$وَاللَّهُ يَقْضِي بِالْحَقِّ ۖ وَالَّذِينَ يَدْعُونَ مِن دُونِهِ لَا يَقْضُونَ بِشَيْءٍ ۗ إِنَّ اللَّهَ هُوَ السَّمِيعُ الْبَصِيرُ$$

And God will judge by the Truth
Whereas those they beseech besides Him cannot judge at all
Verily God alone is all hearing, all seeing {Sami ul Baseer}.[374]

True seeing is not merely 'optical'. The world is full of optical illusions. Gripped with fear we are likely to 'see the worst' and steeped in delusion we see only 'what we want to see'. True vision, far reaching, is through the eye of the heart cleansed with faith. And for those with faith and hope, the darkest clouds bear a silver lining:

373 Al Quran 3:38 -39
374 Al Quran 40:20

قَدْ كَانَ لَكُمْ ءَايَةٌ فِى فِئَتَيْنِ ٱلْتَقَتَا ۖ فِئَةٌ تُقَـٰتِلُ فِى سَبِيلِ ٱللَّهِ وَأُخْرَىٰ كَافِرَةٌ يَرَوْنَهُم مِّثْلَيْهِمْ رَأْىَ ٱلْعَيْنِ ۚ وَٱللَّهُ يُؤَيِّدُ بِنَصْرِهِۦ مَن يَشَآءُ ۗ إِنَّ فِى ذَٰلِكَ لَعِبْرَةً لِّأُوْلِى ٱلْأَبْصَـٰرِ

There has already been a sign for you in the two armies that met;
one party fought in the way of God, while the other was a group of scoffers;
it seemed to them that they saw twice their own number.
And God strengthens whomever God will by Divine assistance.
Surely there is a lesson in that for those who have eyes {ulil absar}[375]

زُيِّنَ لِلنَّاسِ حُبُّ ٱلشَّهَوَٰتِ مِنَ ٱلنِّسَآءِ وَٱلْبَنِينَ وَٱلْقَنَـٰطِيرِ ٱلْمُقَنطَرَةِ مِنَ ٱلذَّهَبِ وَٱلْفِضَّةِ وَٱلْخَيْلِ ٱلْمُسَوَّمَةِ وَٱلْأَنْعَـٰمِ وَٱلْحَرْثِ ۗ ذَٰلِكَ مَتَـٰعُ ٱلْحَيَوٰةِ ٱلدُّنْيَا ۖ وَٱللَّهُ عِندَهُۥ حُسْنُ ٱلْمَـَٔابِ ۞ قُلْ أَؤُنَبِّئُكُم بِخَيْرٍ مِّن ذَٰلِكُمْ ۚ لِلَّذِينَ ٱتَّقَوْا۟ عِندَ رَبِّهِمْ جَنَّـٰتٌ تَجْرِى مِن تَحْتِهَا ٱلْأَنْهَـٰرُ خَـٰلِدِينَ فِيهَا وَأَزْوَٰجٌ مُّطَهَّرَةٌ وَرِضْوَٰنٌ مِّنَ ٱللَّهِ ۗ وَٱللَّهُ بَصِيرٌ بِٱلْعِبَادِ

Made to seem pleasing to humanity is the love of desires for women
And children and heaps of and hoards of gold and silver,
And domesticated horses, and cattle and fields.
Those are conveniences for the life of the world,
while the finest resort is the presence of God.
Say: Shall I tell you of something better that what you have?
For those who are conscientious there are gardens in the presence of the Lord,
below which rivers flow, where they will abide;
And pure spouses,
And acceptance from God.
And God sees {Baseer} the devoted.[376]

29. *Al Hakam*   The Supreme Judge.

All judgment is for God who will judge all other judgements and whose judgment is based on complete knowledge and is final.

Hakam is co-rooted with *Hakeem*. The former attribute is one of Divine expression of fairness and justice and the latter, meaning wisdom, is an attribute of Divine Essence. The noun *Hukm* can mean both judgment and command. Divine

---

375 Al Quran 3:13 as interpreted by Thomas Cleary
376 Al Quran 3:14-15 as interpreted by Thomas Cleary

Judgment, based on full knowledge and in complete wisdom *is* the Divine Command.

وَرَبُّكَ يَعْلَمُ مَا تُكِنُّ صُدُورُهُمْ وَمَا يُعْلِنُونَ ۞ وَهُوَ ٱللَّهُ لَآ إِلَٰهَ إِلَّا هُوَ ۖ لَهُ ٱلْحَمْدُ فِى ٱلْأُولَىٰ وَٱلْآخِرَةِ ۖ وَلَهُ ٱلْحُكْمُ وَإِلَيْهِ تُرْجَعُونَ ۞

Your sustainer has full knowledge of what their hearts conceal
and what they make known
And He is God. There is no god but He.
To Him be praise, foremost and last,
to Him belongs the Judgment {wa lahul hukmu},
And to Him shall you return.[377]

30. *Al Adl*   The Just.

Absolute Justice is Divine. Injustice and oppression are alien to God.

An unjust heart is repugnant to God. The heart that aspires to be just, never stops growing because justice like beauty is not single layered nor is it within a single plane. Like beauty, justice has depth beyond what is apparent and a quality of aspiration by which the current plane reveals a higher one.

The Quran, in Surah 21 verse 78, alludes to an established Arabian tradition that highlights this characteristic of justice, via separate awards of justice by David and Solomon over the same issue. The Arabian tradition:

> A shepherd's flock strays in the night into a neighboring field completely destroying its crop. The aggrieved farmer files his claim against the shepherd in King David's court: David known for his objective justice takes account of the loss to the farmer and determines that the value of the lost crop is equal to the value of the shepherd's entire flock. Objectivity demands that the shepherd's entire flock be given to the farmer as compensation for the loss of his crop. Having come to this conclusion, a just-settlement, no doubt, David invites his son, Solomon, to arrive at his own verdict.
> The would-be king is in agreement with his father over the valuation of the lost crop. The farmer is owed compensation. In his verdict he awards the farmer the flock and flock's milk and further orders the shepherd to work the land, so that its crop is restored. But when, declares Solomon, the land bears its new crop, the shepherd is free and the farmer must return the flock to its shepherd.[378]

Justice embraces equity, compensation, compassion and forgiveness. The justice contemplated by law is about settlement. A compensatory framework alleviates an injustice; it cannot always restore the status-quo-ante. The justice

---

377 Al Quran 28:69-70
378 Paraphrased from Muhammad Asad's foot note related to Al Quran 21:78

of the heart is about inspired giving; Acts of compassion, kindness and mercy have no end! These are inspired actions of the heart.

So it is stated, plainly, and affectively that true giving is without reluctance and without measure:

وَيَسْـَٔلُونَكَ مَاذَا يُنفِقُونَ قُلِ ٱلْعَفْوَ

And they ask thee as to what they should spend in [in God's pleasure].
Say "what-ever you can spare"[379]

31. *Al Lateef*   The Subtle and unfathomable

لَّا تُدْرِكُهُ ٱلْأَبْصَـٰرُ وَهُوَ يُدْرِكُ ٱلْأَبْصَـٰرَ ۖ وَهُوَ ٱللَّطِيفُ ٱلْخَبِيرُ ۝

No vision comprehends Him but He comprehends all vision
He is the Most Subtle {Lateef} and Most Aware.[380]

Lateef is a derivative of the root word "*Lutf*". To experience "*lutf*" is to be touched and moved ever so deeply and subtly by the power of grace, love, kindness and intrinsic beauty. *Al Lateef* encompasses these qualities and the power behind these qualities. This purposeful power is both subtle and overwhelming. Consider the subtle purposefulness and resolution by which the tender shoot of a seed, its plumule, pushes the soil asunder—a phenomena that is at once subtle, intricate, firm and irresistible. The process and its phenomena, both manifest the Subtlety of the Sole Creator.

God helps in subtle ways. The "Divine Hand" holds the piously earnest soul through its journey. Joseph's, hand was held by God, throughout his odyssey, from abandonment at the well by his brothers, to the full family reunion at the palace where Joseph was master of Egypt's granaries. The abandoned child, sold for a few coins was God's instrument of mercy for both the people of Egypt and his own people of the desert, during a seven year drought. The sincere heart trusts the subtle purpose of God in every unavoidable adversity and uncontrollable setback. Life's turning points, those *beyond* our control, unfold new vistas for the God-fearing and steadfast soul.

---

379 Al Quran 2:219
380 Al Quran 6:103

وَرَفَعَ أَبَوَيْهِ عَلَى ٱلْعَرْشِ وَخَرُّوا۟ لَهُۥ سُجَّدًا ۖ وَقَالَ يَـٰٓأَبَتِ هَـٰذَا تَأْوِيلُ رُءْيَـٰىَ مِن قَبْلُ قَدْ

جَعَلَهَا رَبِّى حَقًّا ۖ وَقَدْ أَحْسَنَ بِىٓ إِذْ أَخْرَجَنِى مِنَ ٱلسِّجْنِ وَجَآءَ بِكُم مِّنَ ٱلْبَدْوِ مِنۢ بَعْدِ أَن

نَّزَغَ ٱلشَّيْطَـٰنُ بَيْنِى وَبَيْنَ إِخْوَتِىٓ ۚ إِنَّ رَبِّى لَطِيفٌ لِّمَا يَشَآءُ ۚ إِنَّهُۥ هُوَ ٱلْعَلِيمُ ٱلْحَكِيمُ ۝

And he [Joseph] elevated his parents on the throne,
And they fell down prostrate before him.
And he said, "Father, this is the explanation of my dream before;
My Lord has made it real and has been good to me,
getting me out of prison and bringing you from the desert after Satan had
alienated me and my brothers.
Truly my Lord is subtle in design {Lateef},
He is the All-Knowing, Complete Wisdom {Aleem ul Hakeem} 381

32. *Al Khabeer*   The Aware.

The muslim draws peace from God's complete awareness. There is no wrong that is not known to Him as there is no right that He does not note. He is aware of what is in the heart. God does not need an explanation or a confession, God is privy to the innermost struggle of the soul. God is aware of the ebb and flow in our lives as God is familiar with our fears and aspirations. We are in God's knowledge at all times {*Al Aleem*} and He is fully aware {*Al Khabeer*} of our station and condition.

ٱلْحَمْدُ لِلَّهِ ٱلَّذِى لَهُۥ مَا فِى ٱلسَّمَـٰوَٰتِ وَمَا فِى ٱلْأَرْضِ وَلَهُ ٱلْحَمْدُ فِى ٱلْءَاخِرَةِ ۚ وَهُوَ ٱلْحَكِيمُ ٱلْخَبِيرُ

۝ يَعْلَمُ مَا يَلِجُ فِى ٱلْأَرْضِ وَمَا يَخْرُجُ مِنْهَا وَمَا يَنزِلُ مِنَ ٱلسَّمَآءِ وَمَا يَعْرُجُ فِيهَا ۚ وَهُوَ

ٱلرَّحِيمُ ٱلْغَفُورُ ۝

Praise be to God to whom belongs all there is in the heavens and earth
And to Him is due all Praise in the hereafter
And He is All- Wise {Hakeem} and All-Aware {Khabeer}
He knows what goes into the earth and what comes out of it,
and what descends from the sky and what ascends to it
And He is Most Merciful {Raheem} and ever Forgiving {Ghafoor}. 382

33. *Al Haleem*   The Forbearing.

381 Al Quran 12:100. Interpreted by Thomas Cleary in *The Quran. A new Translation*
382 Al Quran 34:1-2

God does not exact immediate punishment but allows the time and opportunity to repent. Time itself is a manifestation of God's forbearance, bearing the opportunity to learn and grow; Bearing too, the opportunity of introspection, contemplation, repentance and the opportunity to grasp the rope of God while we are still free-willed. The opportunity of a willing submission, and the promise of Divine Forgiveness and Mercy

تُسَبِّحُ لَهُ ٱلسَّمَٰوَٰتُ ٱلسَّبْعُ وَٱلْأَرْضُ وَمَن فِيهِنَّ ۚ وَإِن مِّن شَيْءٍ إِلَّا يُسَبِّحُ بِحَمْدِهِۦ وَلَٰكِن لَّا تَفْقَهُونَ تَسْبِيحَهُمْ ۗ إِنَّهُۥ كَانَ حَلِيمًا غَفُورًا ﴿٤٤﴾

The seven heavens and the earth and all therein worship Him relentlessly
There is not a thing but celebrates His praise
Yet you cannot grasp how they worship Him
God is forbearing {Haleem} and forgiving {Ghafoor} [383]

---

34. *Al Azeem*   The Tremendous. The Most Grand. The Loftiest.

The 'Throne Verse' is a reminder of the difference between the Real and the illusory, the Creator and the creature. The creature is circumscribed, physically, spatially and chronologically. The Creator is not. The creature is dependent. The Creator is not. The creature can fathom no more what it can sense, experience or imagine. The Creator wills and holds all knowledge. The creature has no say in the cosmos although it is of it. The cosmos humbles the creature. The cosmos is the foot-stool of the Creator's throne. Only the Creator is *Azeem.*

ٱللَّهُ لَآ إِلَٰهَ إِلَّا هُوَ ٱلْحَيُّ ٱلْقَيُّومُ ۚ لَا تَأْخُذُهُۥ سِنَةٌ وَلَا نَوْمٌ ۚ لَّهُۥ مَا فِى ٱلسَّمَٰوَٰتِ وَمَا فِى ٱلْأَرْضِ ۗ مَن ذَا ٱلَّذِى يَشْفَعُ عِندَهُۥٓ إِلَّا بِإِذْنِهِۦ ۚ يَعْلَمُ مَا بَيْنَ أَيْدِيهِمْ وَمَا خَلْفَهُمْ ۖ وَلَا يُحِيطُونَ بِشَيْءٍ مِّنْ عِلْمِهِۦٓ إِلَّا بِمَا شَآءَ ۚ وَسِعَ كُرْسِيُّهُ ٱلسَّمَٰوَٰتِ وَٱلْأَرْضَ ۖ وَلَا يَـُٔودُهُۥ حِفْظُهُمَا ۚ وَهُوَ ٱلْعَلِىُّ ٱلْعَظِيمُ ﴿٢٥٥﴾

GOD - there is no deity save Him,
The Ever-Living, The Self-Subsistent Fount of All Being {Hayyul Qayyum}.
Neither slumber overtakes Him, nor sleep.
His is all that is in the heavens and all that is on earth.
Who is there that could intercede with Him, unless it be by His leave?
He knows all that lies open before them and all that is hidden from them,
Whereas they cannot attain to aught of His knowledge

---

383 Al Quran 17:44

Save that which He wills [them to attain].
His Throne extends over the heavens and the earth,
And their upholding wearies Him not.
And he alone is truly Exalted, Tremendous {Aliyyul Azeem}.[384]

35. *Al Ghafoor*   The Oft Forgiving.

Forgiveness washes and rejuvenates the earnest heart, just as the earth, after it has embraced the rain, explodes with the abundance of its wares and bares the rich hues of its colors. We too are like the pixels of a Divine tapestry; each being special and therefore forgivable. By treating the other as we would like to be treated ourselves, we honor both our diversity and individuality. By forgiving the other we forgive ourselves. Divine forgiveness relieves the burdened heart.

أَلَمْ تَرَ أَنَّ ٱللَّهَ أَنزَلَ مِنَ ٱلسَّمَآءِ مَآءً فَأَخْرَجْنَا بِهِۦ ثَمَرَٰتٍ مُّخْتَلِفًا أَلْوَٰنُهَا ۚ وَمِنَ ٱلْجِبَالِ جُدَدٌ

بِيضٌ وَحُمْرٌ مُّخْتَلِفٌ أَلْوَٰنُهَا وَغَرَابِيبُ سُودٌ ۝ وَمِنَ ٱلنَّاسِ وَٱلدَّوَآبِّ وَٱلْأَنْعَٰمِ مُخْتَلِفٌ

أَلْوَٰنُهُۥ كَذَٰلِكَ ۗ إِنَّمَا يَخْشَى ٱللَّهَ مِنْ عِبَادِهِ ٱلْعُلَمَٰٓؤُاْ ۗ إِنَّ ٱللَّهَ عَزِيزٌ غَفُورٌ ۝

Do you reflect that God pours water from the sky
Whereby we produce fruits of varied colors
And in the mountains are tracts of white and red in varied shades
And jet-black rocks
And so among men and beasts and cattle are differing colors
Amongst His servants, those in awe of God are the knowledgeable.
For God is Mighty {Azeez} and Forgiving {Ghafoor}[385]

36. *Ash Shakur*   The Appreciative.

A Master who lavishly rewards His seeking servant. God returns manifold what His servant may have willingly expended in God's way. Selfless giving enriches us. We are poorer by withholding. The calculus of beauty is not like the give and take of the bazaar. It is that of a seed planted in fertile soil. Giving is most beautiful when it is offered in devotion to God. It is a 'beautiful loan' advanced to God. The creature obligates the Creator!

384 Al Quran 2:255 as interpreted by Muhammad Asad in *The Message of the Quran*
385 Al Quran 35:27-28

$$\text{فَٱتَّقُوا۟ ٱللَّهَ مَا ٱسْتَطَعْتُمْ وَٱسْمَعُوا۟ وَأَطِيعُوا۟ وَأَنفِقُوا۟ خَيْرًا لِّأَنفُسِكُمْ ۗ وَمَن يُوقَ شُحَّ نَفْسِهِۦ}$$
$$\text{فَأُو۟لَـٰٓئِكَ هُمُ ٱلْمُفْلِحُونَ ۝ إِن تُقْرِضُوا۟ ٱللَّهَ قَرْضًا حَسَنًا يُضَـٰعِفْهُ لَكُمْ وَيَغْفِرْ لَكُمْ ۚ وَٱللَّهُ}$$
$$\text{شَكُورٌ حَلِيمٌ ۝}$$

So be conscious of God as best as you can,
and listen, and heed, and give, for your own good.
For those who are saved from their own greed and avarice, are the successful.
If you obligate God by a beautiful obligation, God will magnify and enhance it
for you and will forgive you
God is most appreciative, Clement[386]

Paradise too is designed for the servant's fulfillment. The servant is His Master's permanent guest. *Shukr* which shares its root word with *Shakur* means gratitude. Gratitude to God takes root in faith (*Emaan*) and its depth is a measure of its beauty (*Ehsan*)

$$\text{فَٱذْكُرُونِىٓ أَذْكُرْكُمْ وَٱشْكُرُوا۟ لِى وَلَا تَكْفُرُونِ ۝}$$

So remember Me; I will remember you.
Be grateful to Me {wa shukruli}, and deny Me not.[387]

$$\text{جَنَّـٰتُ عَدْنٍ يَدْخُلُونَهَا يُحَلَّوْنَ فِيهَا مِنْ أَسَاوِرَ مِن ذَهَبٍ وَلُؤْلُؤًا ۖ وَلِبَاسُهُمْ فِيهَا حَرِيرٌ ۝}$$
$$\text{وَقَالُوا۟ ٱلْحَمْدُ لِلَّهِ ٱلَّذِىٓ أَذْهَبَ عَنَّا ٱلْحَزَنَ ۖ إِنَّ رَبَّنَا لَغَفُورٌ شَكُورٌ ۝}$$

Gardens of Eternity will they enter wearing bracelets of gold and pearls
and their clothing therein of silk.
And they will say,
"Praise be to God Who has taken our grief away from us.
For Our Lord is Forgiving, Appreciative {Shakur}[388]

Another co-rooted word *Shaakir* means one who is grateful. Some lists include *Ash-Shaakir* as a Divine attribute

$$\text{۞ إِنَّ ٱلصَّفَا وَٱلْمَرْوَةَ مِن شَعَآئِرِ ٱللَّهِ ۖ فَمَنْ حَجَّ ٱلْبَيْتَ أَوِ ٱعْتَمَرَ فَلَا جُنَاحَ عَلَيْهِ أَن يَطَّوَّفَ}$$
$$\text{بِهِمَا ۚ وَمَن تَطَوَّعَ خَيْرًا فَإِنَّ ٱللَّهَ شَاكِرٌ عَلِيمٌ ۝}$$

Know that As-Safa and Al-Marwah are among the indications of God.

---

386 Al Quran 64:16-17
387 Al Quran 2:152
388 Al Quran 35:33-34

So he who performs Hadj or other visits to the House,
it is no sin to go around them
And he who does good of his own accord, God is Grateful {Shaakir}, Knowing. 389

37.   *Al Aliyy*   The Sublime, The High, The Exalted.

God is the highest in Rank and Essence. A related word is *Illiyyun* that refers to a place or book of records in which deeds of the righteous are recorded; our collective consciousness if you will. Good deeds are received and preserved in heaven and define the basis of ranking amongst mankind.

اللّهُ لَا إِلَٰهَ إِلَّا هُوَ ٱلْحَىُّ ٱلْقَيُّومُ ۚ لَا تَأْخُذُهُ سِنَةٌ وَلَا نَوْمٌ ۚ لَّهُ مَا فِى ٱلسَّمَٰوَٰتِ وَمَا فِى ٱلْأَرْضِ ۗ مَن ذَا ٱلَّذِى يَشْفَعُ عِندَهُۥٓ إِلَّا بِإِذْنِهِۦ ۚ يَعْلَمُ مَا بَيْنَ أَيْدِيهِمْ وَمَا خَلْفَهُمْ ۖ وَلَا يُحِيطُونَ بِشَىْءٍ مِّنْ عِلْمِهِۦٓ إِلَّا بِمَا شَآءَ ۚ وَسِعَ كُرْسِيُّهُ ٱلسَّمَٰوَٰتِ وَٱلْأَرْضَ ۖ وَلَا يَـُٔودُهُۥ حِفْظُهُمَا ۚ وَهُوَ ٱلْعَلِىُّ ٱلْعَظِيمُ ۝

GOD - there is no deity save Him,
The Ever-Living, The Self-Subsistent Fount of All Being {Hayyul Qayyum}.
Neither slumber overtakes Him, nor sleep.
His is all that is in the heavens and all that is on earth.
Who is there that could intercede with Him, unless it be by His leave?
He knows all that lies open before them and all that is hidden from them,
Whereas they cannot attain to aught of His knowledge
Save that which He wills [them to attain].
His Throne extends over the heavens and the earth,
And their upholding wearies Him not.
And he alone is truly Exalted, Tremendous {Aliyyul Azeem}. 390

A related and co-rooted name is *Al Aalaa,* The Most High; The Essence of every thing beautiful; The Essence of Essence; Singularly worthy of *Sajjida* (the prostration of surrender).

In the course of the five daily prayers (*Salaat*), a Muslim, starts each cycle of prayer, standing upright, asking for strength and guidance from his or her *Rabb*, then bows in contemplation of *Al-Azeem*, and finally drops on his or her hands and knees in prostration to *Al-Aalaa*. The standing-stance symbolizes the 'self' charged and deputed by God. The bowing-stance is the slave's

---

389 Al Quran 2:158
390 Al Quran 2:255 as interpreted by Muhammad Asad in *The Message of the Quran*

acknowledgment of the Master. The prostration, ego surrendered, is the soul's attempt to gain proximity to the beauty (essence of goodness, if you will) that is God, the most Exalted. The *Salaat* mirrors the rhythm of existence, between the self and Self.

There is an intrinsic essence and purposefulness to all natural forms, although the purpose transcends the form. The caterpillar will become the butterfly and each blade of green grass will turn brown to surrender itself to its intrinsic purpose assigned to it by its Creator. There is no 'accident' in nature, only purpose and the beauty of obedience. Existence is possible because each particle of the cosmos surrenders to the transcendentally Supreme Purpose.

سَبِّحِ ٱسْمَ رَبِّكَ ٱلْأَعْلَى ۞ ٱلَّذِى خَلَقَ فَسَوَّىٰ ۞ وَٱلَّذِى قَدَّرَ فَهَدَىٰ ۞ وَٱلَّذِىٓ أَخْرَجَ ٱلْمَرْعَىٰ ۞ فَجَعَلَهُۥ غُثَآءً أَحْوَىٰ ۞

Praise the name of your Lord, the Highest {Aalaa}
Who has created all things in order and proportion and prescribed their destinies
and their paths. And Who brings forth the pasture and turns it to hay. [391]

38. *Al Kabeer*   The Transcendentally Great[392].

God is infinitely, infinitesimally, unfathomably and quintessentially Great. There is no greatness outside of God as there is no greatness outside of the Divine Will.

Greatness in man is achieved with the attainment of paradise. This, for man is the quintessential success[393]. The path to this success is between man and God alone. When the Truth of God's word will be laid bare there will be no more denial. Sovereignty, absolutely, completely and exclusively belongs to God and no other.

قُلِ ٱدْعُوا۟ ٱلَّذِينَ زَعَمْتُم مِّن دُونِ ٱللَّهِ ۖ لَا يَمْلِكُونَ مِثْقَالَ ذَرَّةٍ فِى ٱلسَّمَٰوَٰتِ وَلَا فِى ٱلْأَرْضِ وَمَا لَهُمْ فِيهِمَا مِن شِرْكٍ وَمَا لَهُۥ مِنْهُم مِّن ظَهِيرٍ ۞ وَلَا تَنفَعُ ٱلشَّفَٰعَةُ عِندَهُۥٓ إِلَّا لِمَنْ أَذِنَ لَهُۥ ۚ حَتَّىٰٓ إِذَا فُزِّعَ عَن قُلُوبِهِمْ قَالُوا۟ مَاذَا قَالَ رَبُّكُمْ ۖ قَالُوا۟ ٱلْحَقَّ ۖ وَهُوَ ٱلْعَلِىُّ ٱلْكَبِيرُ ۞

Say "Call upon them who you fancy beside God"

---

[391] Al Quran 87:1-5
[392] *Kabeer* and *Akbar* share the same root word. The latter means 'greater'.
[393] Al Quran 85:11

Not sovereign (are they) over the smallest particle within the heavens and the earth.
And therein without claim or portion are they
And God has no supporter among them.
Without avail will be any intercession with God except whom He allows
So much so that when having gathered themselves from the terror in their hearts, they will ask
"What did your Lord say?"
They will reply "The Truth"
He is he Most Elevated, The Supremely Great {Kabeer} [394]

39. *Al Hafeez*   The Preserver. The Protector.

The Protector of Faith and the faithful; The One who preserves the order of the Universe; The Protector of the Arabic Quran, its bearer and its first reciter. *Hafeez* is an attribute of Divine Essence {*Ism-e-Dhaat*}. *Hafeez* is manifested as *Haafiz* (the protector of His creatures). *Hafeez* makes the Truth triumphant; *Haafiz* brings the Truth into the heart. Man cannot be outside of God's message, he can only ignore it. The Truth never changes. It is possessed or dispossessed.

$$\text{فَإِن تَوَلَّوْا فَقَدْ أَبْلَغْتُكُم مَّآ أُرْسِلْتُ بِهِۦٓ إِلَيْكُمْ ۚ وَيَسْتَخْلِفُ رَبِّي قَوْمًا غَيْرَكُمْ وَلَا تَضُرُّونَهُۥ شَيْـًٔا ۚ إِنَّ رَبِّي عَلَىٰ كُلِّ شَىْءٍ حَفِيظٌ ۝}$$

If you (people of Aad) turn away,
I (Hud) still have conveyed the Message with which I was sent to you
And my Sustainer will replace you by another people
And you will not cause Him any harm
Indeed my Sustainer is the Guardian over everything {Hafeez} [395]

The believing heart is aware that God and not man is its final Protector.

$$\text{قَالَ هَلْ ءَامَنُكُمْ عَلَيْهِ إِلَّا كَمَآ أَمِنتُكُمْ عَلَىٰٓ أَخِيهِ مِن قَبْلُ ۖ فَٱللَّهُ خَيْرٌ حَٰفِظًا ۖ وَهُوَ أَرْحَمُ ٱلرَّٰحِمِينَ ۝}$$

He (Joseph's father, Jacob) said (to his sons)
"Can I entrust him to you as I entrusted to you his brother (Joseph) before?"
God is the Supreme Guardian {Khairun Haafizan}
and in mercy God is foremost {Arhamur Rahimeen}. [396]

---

394 Al Quran 34:22-23
395 Al Quran 11:57
396 Al Quran 12:64

40. *Al Muqeet*   The Maintainer of Resources.

The Controller of things[397]. The root word for Muqeet is *Q-W-T* which connotes strength, power and resourcefulness. The co-rooted noun *Aqwata* means that which is required (sustenance and other material or non-material resources) by a dependent creature. Creation is whole and harmonious. God has assigned order to the universe. It is forever in His submission, abiding by His laws. The universe exists by the perfect harmony and the symbiotic connection of its constituent parts.

Man harnesses nature. He does not have a share in its creation or design. Man harnesses the power of the atom, he does not create it. Man harnesses the power of the genes; he does not create their intrinsic property. Man transforms matter into energy, but he did not create the relationship between energy and matter. Science is the great open-source instruction manual that teaches man how to harness nature. And Science too in turn depends on that marvelous Divine Resource—the human intellect.

وَجَعَلَ فِيهَا رَوَٰسِيَ مِن فَوْقِهَا وَبَٰرَكَ فِيهَا وَقَدَّرَ فِيهَآ أَقْوَٰتَهَا فِىٓ أَرْبَعَةِ أَيَّامٍ سَوَآءً لِّلسَّآئِلِينَ ۞

And [He] raised therein anchored mountains, towering above,
And placed therein a bounty of resources {Aqwata}, by Divine measure,
in four days apportioned for every needy and seeking creature[398]

That harnessing which works to honor the fair apportionment of God's bounty is aligned to the pathway of *Muqeet*. Greed, arrogance and indifference to our environment and fellow creatures, are manifestations of ignorance and darkness.

مَّن يَشْفَعْ شَفَٰعَةً حَسَنَةً يَكُن لَّهُۥ نَصِيبٌ مِّنْهَا ۖ وَمَن يَشْفَعْ شَفَٰعَةً سَيِّئَةً يَكُن لَّهُۥ كِفْلٌ مِّنْهَا ۗ
وَكَانَ ٱللَّهُ عَلَىٰ كُلِّ شَىْءٍ مُّقِيتًا ۞

Whoever intercedes for good owns a share in it,
And whoever intercedes for evil owns responsibility of it
And God controls and oversees all things {Muqeet}.[399]

41. *Al Haseeb*   The Reckoner.

---

397 Some 'lists' of 99 names substitute the name with Al Mughees, meaning "The one who rescues or provides relief". The word Mughees does not occur as a noun in the Quran
398 Al Quran 41:10
399 Al Quran 4:85

211 | *The Most Beautiful Rosary*

Al Haseeb keeps account of every creature, deed and every happening. *Haseeb* is co-rooted with the *Hisaab* which means accounting, reconciling, calculating, keeping a ledger, etc. The subjects of mathematics are also called *Hisaab*. *Al Haseeb* diffuses into another Divine attribute called *Al Muhsi*, translated as 'The Appraiser'. The Supreme Reckoner is a generous appraiser of goodness and beauteous deeds. Goodness and beauty are Divine and transcendental, and are amplified by God. Deeds devoid of goodness and beauty, sinful and ugly, are in a figurative sense merely deflected back:

مَن جَآءَ بِالْحَسَنَةِ فَلَهُ عَشْرُ أَمْثَالِهَا وَمَن جَآءَ بِالسَّيِّئَةِ فَلَا يُجْزَىٰ إِلَّا مِثْلَهَا وَهُمْ لَا يُظْلَمُونَ

Whoever brings a beauteous deed, he shall have ten-fold like it,
And whoever brings an evil deed, not shall he be recompensed, but by its like
And upon none would be an impropriety[400]

Accountability to God is deeper than the physical act. It lies at the core of the act's motivation and the earnestness of intent and execution. The integrity and beauty of our relationship with fellow human beings is integral to our relationship with God. An act of grace must not be left unreciprocated. God notes and appraises our responsiveness to a good deed, as well as the conscientiousness with which we reciprocate:

وَإِذَا حُيِّيتُم بِتَحِيَّةٍ فَحَيُّوا بِأَحْسَنَ مِنْهَا أَوْ رُدُّوهَا إِنَّ اللَّهَ كَانَ عَلَىٰ كُلِّ شَيْءٍ حَسِيبًا

When you are graced by a greeting, greet back with more grace, or return the
same. Yes God keeps count of all things [Haseeb][401].

God also notes and appraises the conscientiousness with which we deliver our trusts and execute our obligations. In our relationships we must deliver against obligations incumbent upon us, with increasing diligence over matters related to the trust and rights of those who lack the power of assertion or enforcement:

وَابْتَلُوا الْيَتَامَىٰ حَتَّىٰ إِذَا بَلَغُوا النِّكَاحَ فَإِنْ ءَانَسْتُم مِّنْهُمْ رُشْدًا فَادْفَعُوا إِلَيْهِمْ أَمْوَالَهُمْ وَلَا
تَأْكُلُوهَا إِسْرَافًا وَبِدَارًا أَن يَكْبَرُوا وَمَن كَانَ غَنِيًّا فَلْيَسْتَعْفِفْ وَمَن كَانَ فَقِيرًا فَلْيَأْكُلْ
بِالْمَعْرُوفِ فَإِذَا دَفَعْتُمْ إِلَيْهِمْ أَمْوَالَهُمْ فَأَشْهِدُوا عَلَيْهِمْ وَكَفَىٰ بِاللَّهِ حَسِيبًا

Keep guard over the orphans until they have reached the age of marriage
If you find them of sound judgment then hand over their property to them
And do not use it in extravagance or in haste before they grow up

---

400 Al Quran 6:160
401 Al Quran 4:86

And one who has the means should abstain
While the one without the means must use it fairly
Then when hand over their property to them, have it witnessed for them,
Though sufficient is God, in taking account. {Haseeb}[402]

42. *Al Jaleel*   The Majestic.

The One who holds all beauty, splendor, wonderment, grandeur, honor, and goodness. A derivative of the root word *J-L-L*, *Jaleel* is not specifically used in the Quran. A related and co-rooted name *Jalaal*, the expression of *Jaleel* is recalled in the Quran.

The end of time (*Aakhira*) is the end of manifestation, Reality unveiled, illusions eviscerated. No selfhood, just Truth. No deeds, just Knowledge—Nothing, but the overwhelming Power and Truth of *Jalaal*.

كُلُّ مَنْ عَلَيْهَا فَانٍ ۝ وَيَبْقَىٰ وَجْهُ رَبِّكَ ذُو ٱلْجَلَٰلِ وَٱلْإِكْرَامِ ۝

All that is in (existence) is to perish
But forever will remain the Face of your Sustainer
Lord of Majesty and Grace {Dhul Jalaali wal Ikraam}[403]

To be aware is to make possible. To be conscious is to experience. To be conscientious is to seek. Paradise, the promised place for the aware, the conscious and the conscientious, is akin to lifting all veils; Majesty and Grace revealed. Peace and Beauty; Honor and Truth; Love and Mercy, now Real and secured from time. Separation no-more! 'I' and 'me' and 'mine' returned to the Divine Will.

فِيهِنَّ خَيْرَٰتٌ حِسَانٌ ۝ فَبِأَيِّ ءَالَآءِ رَبِّكُمَا تُكَذِّبَانِ ۝ حُورٌ مَّقْصُورَٰتٌ فِى ٱلْخِيَامِ ۝
فَبِأَيِّ ءَالَآءِ رَبِّكُمَا تُكَذِّبَانِ ۝ لَمْ يَطْمِثْهُنَّ إِنسٌ قَبْلَهُمْ وَلَا جَآنٌّ ۝ فَبِأَيِّ ءَالَآءِ رَبِّكُمَا
تُكَذِّبَانِ ۝ مُتَّكِئِينَ عَلَىٰ رَفْرَفٍ خُضْرٍ وَعَبْقَرِيٍّ حِسَانٍ ۝ فَبِأَيِّ ءَالَآءِ رَبِّكُمَا تُكَذِّبَانِ
۝ تَبَٰرَكَ ٱسْمُ رَبِّكَ ذِى ٱلْجَلَٰلِ وَٱلْإِكْرَامِ ۝

Within them (gardens of Paradise) will be (attributes of) goodness and beauty
Which of the blessed favors of your Sustainer do you two deny?
Companions (with radiant gazes) lodged therein
Which of the blessed favors of your Sustainer do you two deny?
Whom no human or Jinn has touched before
Which of the blessed favors of your Sustainer do you two deny?

---

402 Al Quran 4:6
403 Al Quran 55:26-27

Reclined on (lush) green spreads, ornate and beauteous
Which of the blessed favors of your Sustainer do you two deny?
Blessed is the name of your Sustainer, Lord of All Majesty {Jalaal},All Grace
{Ikram}[404]

43. *Al kareem*   The One who gives generously without being asked.

The Benevolent, Whose portions of giving are beyond expectations; The One Whose largesse does not cease or diminish. Co-rooted words are *Karam* and *Akram*. *Karam* is that which when given or received, provides peace, fulfillment, satiation, healing etc. *Ikraam* is plural and the collective variety of *Karam*. *Kareem* as an adjective is used in the Quran to qualify Gabriel the Arch Angel, *{Malakun Kareem}* (12:31), the worthiness of words *{Kitabun Kareem}* (27:29), Prophet Muhammad *{Rasool un Kareem}* (44:17), the Quran itself *{Quran un Kareem}* (56:77), the lasting recompense of a good deed *{ajar un kareem}* (57:11), graceful words *{qaulan kareem}* (17:23), holistic species or pairs *{zaujin kareem}* (26:7) and the Bountiful Sustainer Himself *{Rabbik al Kareem}* (82:6). Amongst the first attributes revealed in the Quran are *Rahman, Raheem* and *Akram*

اقْرَأْ بِاسْمِ رَبِّكَ الَّذِى خَلَقَ ۞ خَلَقَ الْإِنسَـٰنَ مِنْ عَلَقٍ ۞ اقْرَأْ وَرَبُّكَ الْأَكْرَمُ ۞ الَّذِى عَلَّمَ بِالْقَلَمِ ۞ عَلَّمَ الْإِنسَـٰنَ مَا لَمْ يَعْلَمْ ۞

Recite in the name of your Sustainer, He who created.
Created mankind from a clot
Recite for your Sustainer is the most Bountiful {Al Akram}
Who taught by the pen
And taught man what he did not know[405]

God offers His bounty as a test. On the other hand, to the Self-Sufficient Being, the only offering that can be made by a mortal is one of gratitude. The soul when it is remiss perpetuates its own delusion. This is not lost upon Solomon, the mighty King, and the mortal, closest to becoming self-sufficient:

[404] Al Quran 55:70-78
[405] Al Quran 96:1-5

$$\text{هَـٰذَا مِن فَضْلِ رَبِّى لِيَبْلُوَنِى ءَأَشْكُرُ أَمْ أَكْفُرُ وَمَن شَكَرَ فَإِنَّمَا يَشْكُرُ لِنَفْسِهِۦ وَمَن كَفَرَ فَإِنَّ رَبِّى غَنِىٌّ كَرِيمٌ}$$

"This is by the Grace of my Lord!- to test me whether I am grateful or ungrateful!
And if any is grateful, truly his gratitude is (a gain) for his own soul;
But if any is ungrateful, truly my Lord is Free of all Needs {Ghani},
Fount of all bounty {Kareem}!"[406]

44. *Ar Raqeeb*   The Watchful. The Caretaker.

That which is goodness is a facet of beauty. With the exception of God Who is Self Sufficient, beauty must necessarily exist within the context of a relationship. The beauty that is compassion, kindness and justice exists or is absent only within the confines of a human thought or act. There can be no act of justice or injustice, no love or hate, any honesty or dishonesty, if there were not another being to interact with. We cannot cultivate forgiveness if there is no one to forgive. Beauty is nurtured or abused, recognized or ignored, only inside a relationship. Human relationships are Divine gifts that serve as the fertile planes on which to cultivate beauty. The family is such a fertile landscape—the immediate, tangible, nexus of love, kindness and compassion. The prophet was reported to have said that half of one's religious duty is to love and serve his family. To cherish the gift of parents, spouse, offspring, siblings, and the neighbors, is to move closer to the Creator. *Ar Raqeeb* is watchful of our give and take amongst ourselves.

$$\text{يَـٰٓأَيُّهَا ٱلنَّاسُ ٱتَّقُواْ رَبَّكُمُ ٱلَّذِى خَلَقَكُم مِّن نَّفْسٍ وَٰحِدَةٍ وَخَلَقَ مِنْهَا زَوْجَهَا وَبَثَّ مِنْهُمَا رِجَالًا كَثِيرًا وَنِسَآءً وَٱتَّقُواْ ٱللَّهَ ٱلَّذِى تَسَآءَلُونَ بِهِۦ وَٱلْأَرْحَامَ إِنَّ ٱللَّهَ كَانَ عَلَيْكُمْ رَقِيبًا}$$

O humankind, be conscious of your Lord
Who created you from one soul and created its mate from it,
and propagated from the two many men and women.
And be conscious of God, by Whom you ask of each other; and of relationships;
for God is watching you {Raqeeb}[407]

God's watchfulness makes worship possible. And even the mundane act, performed in the awareness of Divine watchfulness, presents an opportunity of worship. Responding to Arch Angel Gabriel's question as to the meaning of *Ehsan* (literally translated as beauty), the Prophet replied. "*Ehsan* means that you should worship God as if you see Him, for even if you do not see Him, *He sees*

406 Al Quran 27:40
407 Al Quran 4:1 as interpreted by Thomas Cleary

you".

45. *Al Mujeeb*   The Responsive. The One who responds to a call.

The root word for *Mujeeb* is *JWB* which encompasses a rich spectrum in its meaning, including, 'to answer,' 'to respond', 'to cut through' and 'to pierce'. *Mujeeb* responds by fulfilling a need, alleviating a suffering, healing a wound, overcoming a doubt, clearing a hurdle, opening the way, and filling the heart. Any one who undertakes any of this is therefore walking this Divine Pathway.

There is an inner voice between us, too often lost to arrogance. To be deaf to the inner voice is akin to being blind to the Creator, enmeshed in the transcendental error of living outside the sanctity of Truth. The inner voice is the Source talking to us:

$$وَقَالَ رَبُّكُمُ ٱدْعُونِىٓ أَسْتَجِبْ لَكُمْ ۚ إِنَّ ٱلَّذِينَ يَسْتَكْبِرُونَ عَنْ عِبَادَتِى سَيَدْخُلُونَ جَهَنَّمَ دَاخِرِينَ ۝$$

And your Lord says: "Call on Me; I will respond to you {astajib}
but those who are too arrogant to serve Me will surely find themselves in Hell,
humiliated[408]

The Creator is nigh. "God is closer than one's jugular vein.". Every where we turn is the Face of God.

"What separates man from Divine Reality is the slightest of barriers: God is infinitely close to man, but man is infinitely far from God. This barrier, for man, is a mountain; man stands in front of the mountain which he must remove with his own hands. he digs away the earth, but in vain, the mountain remains; man however goes on digging, in the name of God. And the mountain vanishes. It was never there"[409]

$$۞ وَإِلَىٰ ثَمُودَ أَخَاهُمْ صَٰلِحًا ۚ قَالَ يَٰقَوْمِ ٱعْبُدُوا۟ ٱللَّهَ مَا لَكُم مِّنْ إِلَٰهٍ غَيْرُهُۥ ۖ هُوَ أَنشَأَكُم مِّنَ ٱلْأَرْضِ وَٱسْتَعْمَرَكُمْ فِيهَا فَٱسْتَغْفِرُوهُ ثُمَّ تُوبُوٓا۟ إِلَيْهِ ۚ إِنَّ رَبِّى قَرِيبٌ مُّجِيبٌ ۝$$

To the Thamud (we sent as messenger) their brother Salih
Who said to them "O my people worship God
You have no other god
He is the one who created and settled you on earth
So seek His forgiveness and turn to Him in repentance
My Lord is always close {Qareeb} and Most Responsive." {Mujeeb}[410]

---

408 Al Quran 40:60
409 *The Stations of Wisdom*, Frithjof Schuon
410 Al Quran 11:61

Deep within the listening heart is the call of God, inviting it to its peaceful Union. The heart too must respond:

يَٰٓأَيُّهَا ٱلَّذِينَ ءَامَنُوا۟ ٱسْتَجِيبُوا۟ لِلَّهِ وَلِلرَّسُولِ إِذَا دَعَاكُمْ لِمَا يُحْيِيكُمْ ۖ وَٱعْلَمُوٓا۟ أَنَّ ٱللَّهَ يَحُولُ بَيْنَ ٱلْمَرْءِ وَقَلْبِهِۦ وَأَنَّهُۥٓ إِلَيْهِ تُحْشَرُونَ ۝

O believers, respond {tajibu} to God and His messenger who call you to that
which gives you life
and know that God comes between a man and his heart,
and unto God will you be gathered[411]

46. *Al Wasi*   The Boundless. The All Pervading and All Embracing.

The One Who can stretch open the limits of the heart. Some co-rooted words are *Wasia* (having the capacity to comprehend and absorb), *Wasiat* (having the capacity to include or embrace) and *Wasa'at* (with the quality or state of abundance and plenitude)

Wherever the heart turns in sincerity, it will find the face of God.

وَلِلَّهِ ٱلْمَشْرِقُ وَٱلْمَغْرِبُ ۚ فَأَيْنَمَا تُوَلُّوا۟ فَثَمَّ وَجْهُ ٱللَّهِ ۚ إِنَّ ٱللَّهَ وَٰسِعٌ عَلِيمٌ ۝

"To God belongs the East and West.
Everywhere you turn there is the Presence of God.
God is All Embracing {Waasi} and All-Knowing {Aleem}.[412]

The face of God is Mercy, and the seeking heart will find in it security and fulfillment:

وَرَحْمَتِى وَسِعَتْ كُلَّ شَىْءٍ

My mercy embraces {wasiat} all things[413]

۞ وَمَن يُهَاجِرْ فِى سَبِيلِ ٱللَّهِ يَجِدْ فِى ٱلْأَرْضِ مُرَٰغَمًا كَثِيرًا وَسَعَةً ۚ وَمَن يَخْرُجْ مِنۢ بَيْتِهِۦ مُهَاجِرًا إِلَى ٱللَّهِ وَرَسُولِهِۦ ثُمَّ يُدْرِكْهُ ٱلْمَوْتُ فَقَدْ وَقَعَ أَجْرُهُۥ عَلَى ٱللَّهِ ۗ وَكَانَ ٱللَّهُ غَفُورًا رَّحِيمًا ۝

Who ever must endure dislocation to walk in God's pathway,
Will find on earth many a refuge and plenitude {Wasa'at}[414]

Unable to grasp the vastness of the universe in units of length, we state it in light years. It exceeds every observation and it exceeds every imagination. We

---

411 Al Quran 8:24
412 Al Quran 2:115
413 Al Quran 7:156
414 Al Quran 4:100

pierce a limit to encounter another. Existence is governed by limits. Only God Himself is transcendentally limitless —*Al Wasi*. Embracing all and with all; Beyond magnitude, yet nearer than the jugular vein and the spark in the niche of the heart.

The real measure of human rank and worthiness is by the conscious quality of the heart.

وَقَالَ لَهُمْ نَبِيُّهُمْ إِنَّ ٱللَّهَ قَدْ بَعَثَ لَكُمْ طَالُوتَ مَلِكًا ۚ قَالُوٓا۟ أَنَّىٰ يَكُونُ لَهُ ٱلْمُلْكُ عَلَيْنَا

وَنَحْنُ أَحَقُّ بِٱلْمُلْكِ مِنْهُ وَلَمْ يُؤْتَ سَعَةً مِّنَ ٱلْمَالِ ۚ قَالَ إِنَّ ٱللَّهَ ٱصْطَفَىٰهُ عَلَيْكُمْ وَزَادَهُۥ

بَسْطَةً فِى ٱلْعِلْمِ وَٱلْجِسْمِ ۖ وَٱللَّهُ يُؤْتِى مُلْكَهُۥ مَن يَشَآءُ ۚ وَٱللَّهُ وَٰسِعٌ عَلِيمٌ ﴿٢٤٧﴾

Their prophet said to them;
"God has appointed Talut (Saul[415]) to be king over you."
They said "How could he be king over us when we are more worthy of being king than he and since he lacks in wealth?"
He said, "God has chosen him above you and has magnified him in knowledge and physical stature. God bestows sovereignty on whom He wills.
God is incomparably resourceful and All Embracing {Wasiun},
All-Knowing {Aleem}[416]

47. *Al Hakeem*   Complete Wisdom. The Fount of wisdom. The Healer.

Hakeem shares the root-word '*HKM*' with *Hakam*. *Hakam* is the expression of *Hakeem*. '*HKM*' means 'to be wise and in full knowledge of the essence of things' 'to pass judgment with awareness', 'to turn someone back from wrongdoing or ignorance'. The noun *Hikmat* means wisdom which bears healing and intrinsic wellness—wisdom that cures a disease instead of merely managing its symptoms.

There is no doubt or uncertainty in the plan of *Al Hakeem*. *Hakeem* is often paired with *Azeez* (Divine Might or Will). It follows therefore that the universe, or anything in it, is *not* the outcome of an accident. "God does not roll dice", Einstein famously said, even though for the wrong reason.[417] The universe and everything in it exists by Divine Will and Wisdom. *Hakeem* is also paired with *Aleem*. It follows therefore that no one is outside of Divine Knowledge or outside of God's plan. The Universe and life within it is the purposeful manifestation of Divine Wisdom, Divine Will and Divine Knowledge, mirroring the Wholeness that is Divine Unity.

---

415 Al Quran Per Pickthall and Thomas Cleary
416 Al Quran 2:247
417 Einstein reportedly said this in rejection of Heisenbergs Theory of Uncertainty.

هُوَ ٱلَّذِى يُصَوِّرُكُمْ فِى ٱلْأَرْحَامِ كَيْفَ يَشَآءُ ۚ لَا إِلَٰهَ إِلَّا هُوَ ٱلْعَزِيزُ ٱلْحَكِيمُ ۞

He it is who shapes you in the wombs as He wills.
There is no deity save Him,
The Almighty, The Truly Wise {Azeez ul Hakeem} [418]

This attribute bears an invitation to man to participate in The Plan. Wisdom in a person, that which discriminates between right and wrong and contemplates the Truth, is from God:

يُؤْتِى ٱلْحِكْمَةَ مَن يَشَآءُ ۚ وَمَن يُؤْتَ ٱلْحِكْمَةَ فَقَدْ أُوتِىَ خَيْرًا كَثِيرًا ۗ وَمَا يَذَّكَّرُ إِلَّا أُو۟لُوا۟ ٱلْأَلْبَٰبِ ۞

He grants wisdom to whom He pleases;
And he to whom wisdom is granted receives indeed a benefit overflowing;
But none will grasp the Message but men of understanding. [419]

True wisdom comes from the oneness of heart and soul. Abraham was only too aware that the burdened and broken heart needed to find refuge and find repair in a sanctuary blessed by the Divine Wisdom of the All Mighty:

وَإِذْ يَرْفَعُ إِبْرَٰهِۦمُ ٱلْقَوَاعِدَ مِنَ ٱلْبَيْتِ وَإِسْمَٰعِيلُ رَبَّنَا تَقَبَّلْ مِنَّآ ۖ إِنَّكَ أَنتَ ٱلسَّمِيعُ ٱلْعَلِيمُ ۞ رَبَّنَا وَٱجْعَلْنَا مُسْلِمَيْنِ لَكَ وَمِن ذُرِّيَّتِنَآ أُمَّةً مُّسْلِمَةً لَّكَ وَأَرِنَا مَنَاسِكَنَا وَتُبْ عَلَيْنَآ ۖ إِنَّكَ أَنتَ ٱلتَّوَّابُ ٱلرَّحِيمُ ۞ رَبَّنَا وَٱبْعَثْ فِيهِمْ رَسُولًا مِّنْهُمْ يَتْلُوا۟ عَلَيْهِمْ ءَايَٰتِكَ وَيُعَلِّمُهُمُ ٱلْكِتَٰبَ وَٱلْحِكْمَةَ وَيُزَكِّيهِمْ ۚ إِنَّكَ أَنتَ ٱلْعَزِيزُ ٱلْحَكِيمُ ۞

And remember Abraham and Ishmael raised the foundations of the House
"Our lord accept (our sincere offering). You are the All-Hearing and the All-
Knowing. Our Lord may in submission to You we be and may our progeny be a
nation in submission to You. Show us the rites of worship (by this House).
Grace us with your Mercy. You are Most Forgiving and Merciful {Tawwab-ur-
Raheem}. Our Lord raise amongst them a messenger who will expound to them
Your signs and unfold for them the Divine Wisdom of the Book and elevate them.
Indeed You are the Most Exalted and You are the Most Wise {Azeez ul Hakeem) [420]

48. *Al Wadud*   The Loving

---

[418] Al Quran 3:6
[419] Al Quran 2:269
[420] Al Quran 2:127-129

The co-rooted word *wudd* means love, caring and friendship. There can be no love without a relationship and there can be no relationship without the other being special. This attribute applies to the relationship between God and His creation and exists in the context of creation. Love is predisposed to forgiveness and is the antithesis of hate and rancor. God is a compassionate Sovereign who makes allowance for man's ego and self-centeredness. It is therefore never too late to align oneself with His Way. For every sin there is repentance. The repenting heart will not fail to receive His loving mercy. Hate obscures the Truth. Love of God for His creatures, the love of His creatures for God, and the love of His creatures for each other do not exist separately. They are different facets of the same. God endears Himself to those who turn to Him and to their fellow beings:

إِنَّ ٱللَّهَ يُحِبُّ ٱلْمُحْسِنِينَ

God loves those who act with grace and kindness {Mohsineen}. [421]

إِنَّ ٱللَّهَ يُحِبُّ ٱلْمُقْسِطِينَ

God loves those who act justly. {Muqsiteen} [422]

وَٱللَّهُ يُحِبُّ ٱلصَّـٰبِرِينَ

God loves those who are patient in adversity {Sabireen}. [423]

إِنَّ ٱللَّهَ يُحِبُّ ٱلْمُتَوَكِّلِينَ

God loves those who trust (Him) {Mutawakileen} [424]

Love can only grow along the Divine Pathways (*Sabeel Allah*):

إِنَّ ٱلَّذِينَ ءَامَنُوا۟ وَعَمِلُوا۟ ٱلصَّـٰلِحَـٰتِ سَيَجْعَلُ لَهُمُ ٱلرَّحْمَـٰنُ وُدًّا

Verily, them who attain to faith and act righteously, on them the Beneficent bestows love. [425]

As a community too, we must find and struggle for the common-cause:

إِنَّ ٱللَّهَ يُحِبُّ ٱلَّذِينَ يُقَـٰتِلُونَ فِى سَبِيلِهِۦ صَفًّا كَأَنَّهُم بُنْيَـٰنٌ مَّرْصُوصٌ

Surely God loves those who struggle in His way in ranks
As if they were a firm and solid wall. [426]

---

421 Al Quran 5:13
422 Al Quran 5:42 & 49:9
423 Al Quran 3:146
424 Al Quran 3:159
425 Al Quran 19:96
426 Al Quran 61:4

In love, the separated self yearns to merge with the beloved and even differences become bridges. To love God is to know that one is never alone; our separateness from Him is from the perspective of our own station. We journeyed from Him, and the return journey to Him is the end of separation. God does not reject man. Man chooses to reject God. God is ever so ready to embrace, should man turn towards Him. The Quran recalls *Wadud* with Mercy {*Raheem*} and Forgiveness {*Ghafoor*} to qualify the essence of love. Love is rediscovered through introspection and repentance:

$$\text{وَٱسْتَغْفِرُوا۟ رَبَّكُمْ ثُمَّ تُوبُوٓا۟ إِلَيْهِ ۚ إِنَّ رَبِّى رَحِيمٌ وَدُودٌ}$$

(Prophet Shuaib said to his people)
"Ask forgiveness of your Lord and then turn to Him in repentance
For my Lord is Most Merciful, Most Loving {Raheem un Wadud}"[427]

Love is rediscovered too by those who persevere against hate:

$$\text{إِنَّ ٱلَّذِينَ فَتَنُوا۟ ٱلْمُؤْمِنِينَ وَٱلْمُؤْمِنَٰتِ ثُمَّ لَمْ يَتُوبُوا۟ فَلَهُمْ عَذَابُ جَهَنَّمَ وَلَهُمْ عَذَابُ}$$
$$\text{ٱلْحَرِيقِ ۝ إِنَّ ٱلَّذِينَ ءَامَنُوا۟ وَعَمِلُوا۟ ٱلصَّٰلِحَٰتِ لَهُمْ جَنَّٰتٌ تَجْرِى مِن تَحْتِهَا ٱلْأَنْهَٰرُ ۚ ذَٰلِكَ}$$
$$\text{ٱلْفَوْزُ ٱلْكَبِيرُ ۝ إِنَّ بَطْشَ رَبِّكَ لَشَدِيدٌ ۝ إِنَّهُۥ هُوَ يُبْدِئُ وَيُعِيدُ ۝ وَهُوَ ٱلْغَفُورُ}$$
$$\text{ٱلْوَدُودُ ۝}$$

Those who persecute believing men and believing women and do so without remorse or repentance, they choose Hell, and the agony of fire.
For those who believe and act with goodness, will be in the Gardens of Paradise; with subservient rivers. That is the transcendental attainment.
Surely your Sustainer's grip is exceedingly strong!
Surely He it is Who originates and reproduces,
And He is the Forgiving, the Loving {Ghafoor ul Wadud}[428],

49.   *Al Majeed*   The Owner of glory. The most Noble and Venerable.

Majeed is an attribute of Essence. Its root word *MJD* encompasses meanings of 'glory', 'nobility', 'majesty', 'honor', and 'generosity'. This root word is shared with the Divine name, *Al Maajid*, which is the expression (Divine Will) of *Al Majeed*.

Glory belongs to God alone. Contemplation of Divine Glory softens the heart. Glory does not attach itself to those who pursue it for its own sake. It is glamour and not glory that rests in physical stature or material station. Glamour is fleeting. Glory is abiding. Glamour is illusory; glory is Real and can only be

---

427 Al Quran 11:90
428 Al Quran 85:10-14

found in the Divine Pathways (*Sabeel Allah*). The Quran attaches this attribute to itself—'By the Quran *Majeed*, is God's Oath (50:1). True glory seeks the humble and it shuns the arrogant. It embraces those who, like Abraham, are engaged in selfless giving, placing the other before the self. Nobility is a quality of the heart. It is not an inherited entitlement of worldly wealth. Abraham 'the clement' and 'tender- hearted',[429] though the banished and dispossessed son was to become God's chosen patriarch of the prophetic chain.

وَلَقَدْ جَآءَتْ رُسُلُنَآ إِبْرَٰهِيمَ بِٱلْبُشْرَىٰ قَالُوا۟ سَلَٰمًا ۖ قَالَ سَلَٰمٌ ۖ فَمَا لَبِثَ أَن جَآءَ بِعِجْلٍ حَنِيذٍ ۝ فَلَمَّا رَءَآ أَيْدِيَهُمْ لَا تَصِلُ إِلَيْهِ نَكِرَهُمْ وَأَوْجَسَ مِنْهُمْ خِيفَةً ۚ قَالُوا۟ لَا تَخَفْ إِنَّآ أُرْسِلْنَآ إِلَىٰ قَوْمِ لُوطٍ ۝ وَٱمْرَأَتُهُۥ قَآئِمَةٌ فَضَحِكَتْ فَبَشَّرْنَٰهَا بِإِسْحَٰقَ وَمِن وَرَآءِ إِسْحَٰقَ يَعْقُوبَ ۝ قَالَتْ يَٰوَيْلَتَىٰٓ ءَأَلِدُ وَأَنَا۠ عَجُوزٌ وَهَٰذَا بَعْلِى شَيْخًا ۖ إِنَّ هَٰذَا لَشَىْءٌ عَجِيبٌ ۝ قَالُوٓا۟ أَتَعْجَبِينَ مِنْ أَمْرِ ٱللَّهِ ۖ رَحْمَتُ ٱللَّهِ وَبَرَكَٰتُهُۥ عَلَيْكُمْ أَهْلَ ٱلْبَيْتِ ۚ إِنَّهُۥ حَمِيدٌ مَّجِيدٌ ۝

There came Our messengers to Abraham, bearing glad tidings
"Peace" they said and "Peace" he responded and without delay set out a roasted calf. But when they did not approach the meal Abraham felt fearful.
"Fear not" they said "We have been sent against the people of Lot"
And his wife, standing by, laughed when We gave her the good news of Isaac and of Jacob after Isaac. She said "Alas, how shall I bear a child when I am old in years and my husband is old too? This would be a strange thing!"
They said "Do you marvel at the ways of God?
The mercy and blessing of God are upon you, and this household
He is Owner of Praise, Owner of Glory {Hameed um Majeed}[430]

50. *Al Ba'ith*   The Resurrector. The Awakener.

The One who awakens the heart and raises a soul's rank by measure of its consciousness. *Al Ba'ith* is not specifically mentioned in the Quran by its name, but its verb form is. The co-rooted verb *yabasu* means to raise or to awaken. To be raised is to be ushered into Reality—the presence of God. God invites the earnest and sincere heart to arrive at the place of its True honor:

429 Al Quran 11:75
430 Al Quran 11:69-73

وَمِنَ ٱلَّيْلِ فَتَهَجَّدْ بِهِۦ نَافِلَةً لَّكَ عَسَىٰ أَن يَبْعَثَكَ رَبُّكَ مَقَامًا مَّحْمُودًا ۝

And in the night break free to God's worship {Tahajjud}, by the will of your devotion. May it be that your lord will raise you {yabasaka} to the honored station {Maqaamam Mahmooda}. [431]

وَأَنَّ ٱلسَّاعَةَ ءَاتِيَةٌ لَّا رَيْبَ فِيهَا وَأَنَّ ٱللَّهَ يَبْعَثُ مَن فِى ٱلْقُبُورِ ۝

And the hour will arrive off which there is no doubt.
So will God raise {yabasu} (the dead) from their graves [432]

51. *Al Shaheed*   The Witness. The Omnipresent.

The One from Whose knowledge nothing is hidden. The root-word {Sh-H-D} for this Divine Name is also the root of *Shahada*, which means to witness. The foremost act of *Shahada* is the act of witnessing that there is no other god but God. God Himself Witnesses God, as only The Truth can witness Truth:

شَهِدَ ٱللَّهُ أَنَّهُۥ لَا إِلَٰهَ إِلَّا هُوَ وَٱلْمَلَٰئِكَةُ وَأُوْلُواْ ٱلْعِلْمِ قَآئِمًۢا بِٱلْقِسْطِ لَا إِلَٰهَ إِلَّا هُوَ ٱلْعَزِيزُ ٱلْحَكِيمُ ۝

God is Witness {Shahid allahu} that there is no god save Him
And [so do] the angels and those endowed with knowledge-
[God] Upholder of Equity. There is no God but He, the Almighty, the Wise [433]

Al Shaheed is present every where and at all times.

وَهُوَ مَعَكُمْ أَيْنَ مَا كُنتُمْ وَٱللَّهُ بِمَا تَعْمَلُونَ بَصِيرٌ ۝

He is with you where so ever you may be. God is Seer of what ye do. [434]

God's are The Most Beautiful Names {Asma ul Husna}. The Divine pathways are likewise beautiful. The quest of beauty on these pathways (*Ehsan*), grounded in faith (*Emaan*) and guided by the Omnipresent Guide, is the way of *Islam*. Divine light shines over these pathways. Dark are the ways that run contrary to them.

---

431 Al Quran 17:79
432 Al Quran 22:7
433 Al Quran 3:18
434 Al Quran 57:4

مَّآ أَصَابَكَ مِنْ حَسَنَةٍ فَمِنَ ٱللَّهِ ۖ وَمَآ أَصَابَكَ مِن سَيِّئَةٍ فَمِن نَّفْسِكَ ۚ وَأَرْسَلْنَٰكَ لِلنَّاسِ رَسُولاً ۚ وَكَفَىٰ بِٱللَّهِ شَهِيداً ۝

Whatever of beauty and goodness touches you is from God and whatever of degenerative- ill touches you is from yourself. We have sent you as a Messenger to mankind. And God is sufficient as Witness {Shaheed} [435]

52. *Al Haqq*   The Truth. The Essence behind every Sign and every manifestation.

If truth be the First cause before all preceding causes and truth be the Last conclusion after every subsequent conclusion, it cannot be other than the Single Truth. If Truth be the Constant behind the change and the Absolute behind the relative, there cannot be but One Truth. Truth is beyond the perspective of anything but Itself. Truth is Reality, the Absolute Ground of Being; The 'here' without 'there'; the 'now' without 'then'; Self-referencing, Self-sufficient, Self-sustaining, Self-generating, and Self-witnessing.

'There' and 'then', 'this' and 'that', 'I' and the 'other', are merely perspectives in a journey. The truth is that life is a journey. The journey's end is the Truth:

يَٰٓأَيُّهَا ٱلنَّاسُ إِن كُنتُمْ فِى رَيْبٍ مِّنَ ٱلْبَعْثِ فَإِنَّا خَلَقْنَٰكُم مِّن تُرَابٍ ثُمَّ مِن نُّطْفَةٍ ثُمَّ مِنْ عَلَقَةٍ ثُمَّ مِن مُّضْغَةٍ مُّخَلَّقَةٍ وَغَيْرِ مُخَلَّقَةٍ لِّنُبَيِّنَ لَكُمْ ۚ وَنُقِرُّ فِى ٱلْأَرْحَامِ مَا نَشَآءُ إِلَىٰٓ أَجَلٍ مُّسَمًّى ثُمَّ نُخْرِجُكُمْ طِفْلاً ثُمَّ لِتَبْلُغُوٓاْ أَشُدَّكُمْ ۖ وَمِنكُم مَّن يُتَوَفَّىٰ وَمِنكُم مَّن يُرَدُّ إِلَىٰٓ أَرْذَلِ ٱلْعُمُرِ لِكَيْلَا يَعْلَمَ مِنۢ بَعْدِ عِلْمٍ شَيْئاً ۚ وَتَرَى ٱلْأَرْضَ هَامِدَةً فَإِذَآ أَنزَلْنَا عَلَيْهَا ٱلْمَآءَ ٱهْتَزَّتْ وَرَبَتْ وَأَنۢبَتَتْ مِن كُلِّ زَوْجٍ بَهِيجٍ ۝ ذَٰلِكَ بِأَنَّ ٱللَّهَ هُوَ ٱلْحَقُّ وَأَنَّهُ يُحْىِ ٱلْمَوْتَىٰ وَأَنَّهُ عَلَىٰ كُلِّ شَىْءٍ قَدِيرٌ ۝

O People, if you are in doubt of being resurrected
consider that We created you from dust
then a drop, then a clingy-embryo and then a lump of flesh, formed and
unformed, in order that We may make plain for you (to grasp).
We keep whom We will in the womb for a determined term
then We bring you forth as infants and enable you to reach your prime
Some of you die young and some will live on into terminal age
When you lose of what knowledge you had acquired
And you see the earth lifeless but then We pour forth rain on it
And it wakens and swells and produces every beautiful species.

---

435 Al Quran 4:79

That because God is the Ultimate Truth {haqq}
And it is He who brings life from death
And it is He Who has power over all things.[436]

إِلَيْهِ مَرْجِعُكُمْ جَمِيعًا ۖ وَعْدَ ٱللَّهِ حَقًّا

Unto Him is the return of all of you;
It is the promise of God in Truth {haqq}[437]

God is the Only Anchor of existence:

فَمَاذَا بَعْدَ ٱلْحَقِّ إِلَّا ٱلضَّلَـٰلُ

"What is there after Truth but error?"[438]

When Truth seeps into the heart and begins to fill it, the illusion of falsehood becomes exposed:

وَقُلْ جَآءَ ٱلْحَقُّ وَزَهَقَ ٱلْبَـٰطِلُ ۚ إِنَّ ٱلْبَـٰطِلَ كَانَ زَهُوقًا ۝

And say: The Truth has arrived and falsehood has vanished
Lo! falsehood is bound to vanish away[439]

53. *Al Wakeel*   The Trustee.

God alone is the Guardian and Trustee of belief and its believer. Co-rooted words are *tawakal* (trust) and *mutawakaleen* (those who place their trust with God). A muslim must direct his or her conscientiousness inwards to clear the cobwebs of doubt and disbelief. After the earnestness of purpose and the conscientiousness of effort, the heart rests in God's hands.

فَبِمَا رَحْمَةٍ مِّنَ ٱللَّهِ لِنتَ لَهُمْ ۖ وَلَوْ كُنتَ فَظًّا غَلِيظَ ٱلْقَلْبِ لَٱنفَضُّواْ مِنْ حَوْلِكَ ۖ فَٱعْفُ عَنْهُمْ
وَٱسْتَغْفِرْ لَهُمْ وَشَاوِرْهُمْ فِى ٱلْأَمْرِ ۖ فَإِذَا عَزَمْتَ فَتَوَكَّلْ عَلَى ٱللَّهِ ۚ إِنَّ ٱللَّهَ يُحِبُّ ٱلْمُتَوَكِّلِينَ ۝

It is by God's mercy that you were lenient with them for if you were harsh and
hard-hearted they would have dispersed from around you.
So pardon them and seek forgiveness for them and consult them over matters
then once you have resolved place your trust {tawakal} in God,
Know that God loves those who place their trust in Him {mutawakaleen}[440]

It is not for us to judge the spiritual sincerity of others. The sincerity of our faith

---

436 Al Quran 22:5-6
437 Al Quran 10:4
438 Al Quran 10:32
439 Al Quran 17:81
440 Al Quran 3:159

and the faith of others falls solely under Divine Purview:

$$مَّن يُطِعِ ٱلرَّسُولَ فَقَدْ أَطَاعَ ٱللَّهَ ۖ وَمَن تَوَلَّىٰ فَمَآ أَرْسَلْنَٰكَ عَلَيْهِمْ حَفِيظًا ۞ وَيَقُولُونَ طَاعَةٌ فَإِذَا بَرَزُواْ مِنْ عِندِكَ بَيَّتَ طَآئِفَةٌ مِّنْهُمْ غَيْرَ ٱلَّذِى تَقُولُ ۖ وَٱللَّهُ يَكْتُبُ مَا يُبَيِّتُونَ ۖ فَأَعْرِضْ عَنْهُمْ وَتَوَكَّلْ عَلَى ٱللَّهِ ۚ وَكَفَىٰ بِٱللَّهِ وَكِيلاً ۞$$

Those who obey the messenger in essence obey God,
And as for those who turn away,
We have not sent you (Muhammad pbuh) as a guard over them.
They profess obedience but when they depart from your presence
a party of them spend the night contemplating other than what thou say.
And God records what they contemplate
So let them be and put your trust in God
Sufficient is God as Guardian {Wakeel}. [441]

Faith truly rests in God and God Alone. When the heart has truly put itself in God's trust it is beholden to no other.

$$قُلْ حَسْبِىَ ٱللَّهُ ۖ عَلَيْهِ يَتَوَكَّلُ ٱلْمُتَوَكِّلُونَ ۞$$

Say: "God is all for me! In Him do (all) the trusting put their trust." [442]

54. *Al Qawi*   The Possessor of all Power. The Transformational
     Force.

Nature finds its harmony by the balance of competing and opposing forces. Yet, change is nature's only constant. *Al Qawi* is the unopposed, unlimited and unpaired Single Force. The co-rooted noun *quwwa* means force, power, ability to transform, etc. *Al Qawi* is that transformational Force, by which every creature will experience change, until it reposes in the Force itself.

The heart opposed to this Force races towards the edge of the precipice and plunges into the bottomless abyss of desolation. The heart unaware of this Force, finds itself trapped in the physical limits of circumstance. The heart, conscious of the Force, frees itself from the stalemate of its physical circumstance and self- imposed limits.

441 Al Quran 4:80-81
442 Al Quran 39:38

$$\text{يَـٰٓأَيُّهَا ٱلنَّاسُ ضُرِبَ مَثَلٌ فَٱسْتَمِعُوا۟ لَهُۥٓ إِنَّ ٱلَّذِينَ تَدْعُونَ مِن دُونِ ٱللَّهِ لَن يَخْلُقُوا۟}$$

$$\text{ذُبَابًا وَلَوِ ٱجْتَمَعُوا۟ لَهُۥ ۖ وَإِن يَسْلُبْهُمُ ٱلذُّبَابُ شَيْـًٔا لَّا يَسْتَنقِذُوهُ مِنْهُ ۚ ضَعُفَ ٱلطَّالِبُ}$$

$$\text{وَٱلْمَطْلُوبُ ۝ مَا قَدَرُوا۟ ٱللَّهَ حَقَّ قَدْرِهِۦٓ ۗ إِنَّ ٱللَّهَ لَقَوِىٌّ عَزِيزٌ ۝}$$

O mankind, a parable is set forth so reflect upon it
Those whom you invoke beside God cannot even create a fly
even if they all collaborated.
And if the fly should take something from them they would not be able to
reclaim it.
So helpless are the beseechers and those they beseech.
They have not grasped the true measure of God
For God is the Most Strong {Qawi}, The Almighty {Azeez}[443]

55. *Al Mateen*   The Inviolable. The Firm.

The root word for this Divine Name is *MTN* which means 'to be strong, firm, steadfast, purposeful and inviolable'. *Mateen* is used twice in the Quran to characterize the inviolability of the Divine plan and purpose. Accountability based on free-will is unavoidable:

$$\text{وَأُمْلِى لَهُمْ ۚ إِنَّ كَيْدِى مَتِينٌ ۝}$$

Though I grant them reprieve,
Behold, My plan is inviolable {Kaydee mateenun}[444]

Al Mateen is One whose Writ is un-stoppable and forever in force. The Truth is Singular and Permanent. It has not changed and will not change. Prophetic guidance has been consistent too, calling people to serve their True and Inviolable Sustainer. Human beings have been created to serve God, aligned to the Divine attributes, so that we may become willing participants in the Divine Purpose.

$$\text{وَمَا خَلَقْتُ ٱلْجِنَّ وَٱلْإِنسَ إِلَّا لِيَعْبُدُونِ ۝ مَآ أُرِيدُ مِنْهُم مِّن رِّزْقٍ وَمَآ أُرِيدُ أَن يُطْعِمُونِ}$$

$$\text{۝ إِنَّ ٱللَّهَ هُوَ ٱلرَّزَّاقُ ذُو ٱلْقُوَّةِ ٱلْمَتِينُ ۝}$$

I have created Jinn and Humans to serve Me
I do not want from them any sustenance
I do not want them to feed Me
For God is The Provider {Razzaq}

---

443 Al Quran 22:73-74
444 Al Quran 7:183 & 68:45

Power, Inviolable {quwwatil Mateen}[445]

56. *Al Wali*   The Helping Friend, The Patron.

This name shares the same root as *Al Waali*. *Al Waali* accentuates Sovereignty. *Al Wali* accentuates Divine Friendship, and Guidance. *Al Waali* relates to the universe as a whole. The Sovereign guards and protects the universe. *Al Wali* relates to the seeker on a personal level. The Sovereign nurtures the seeker.

اللَّهُ وَلِيُّ الَّذِينَ ءَامَنُوا يُخْرِجُهُم مِّنَ الظُّلُمَتِ إِلَى النُّورِ ۖ وَالَّذِينَ كَفَرُوا أَوْلِيَآؤُهُمُ الطَّغُوتُ يُخْرِجُونَهُم مِّنَ النُّورِ إِلَى الظُّلُمَتِ ۗ أُوْلَٰئِكَ أَصْحَٰبُ النَّارِ ۖ هُمْ فِيهَا خَٰلِدُونَ ۝

God is the Protecting Guardian {Wali} of those who believe.
He brings them out of darkness into light.
As for those who disbelieve, their patrons are false deities.
They bring them out of light into darkness.
They are of the fire. Therein they dwell.[446]

The Straight Path {*Siratum Mustaqeem*} is lit by God Himself. For those with faith and perseverance, this path is self-un-folding. One who sets his heart upon this path will find His proactive guidance. The earnest seeker is never alone. Divine Guidance awaits those who seek it.

لَهُ مُعَقِّبَتٌ مِّنْ بَيْنِ يَدَيْهِ وَمِنْ خَلْفِهِۦ يَحْفَظُونَهُۥ مِنْ أَمْرِ اللَّهِ ۗ إِنَّ اللَّهَ لَا يُغَيِّرُ مَا بِقَوْمٍ حَتَّىٰ يُغَيِّرُوا مَا بِأَنفُسِهِمْ ۗ وَإِذَآ أَرَادَ اللَّهُ بِقَوْمٍ سُوٓءًا فَلَا مَرَدَّ لَهُۥ ۚ وَمَا لَهُم مِّن دُونِهِۦ مِن وَالٍ

"God does not change the condition of a people until they (first) change within (that which is in their hearts)"[447].

57. *Al Hameed*   The All-Laudable. Owner of all Praise.

After the consecration of *Bismil lahir Rahmannir Rahim*, (also known by its alphabetical representation in English as '*Basmallah*' and phonetically as '*Bismillah*', the verse which precedes all Quranic chapters) the Quran in its opening chapter declares that all praise rightfully belongs to God the Sustainer

445 Al Quran 51:56-58
446 Al Quran 2:257
447 Al Quran 13:11

of all existence and knowledge {*Alhamdu liliahi Rabbil alameen*}. God is the fount of Mercy, Love and Beauty, therefore whatever is praiseworthy is from God and what is not praiseworthy is not from God. Sincere praise belongs to the perfect and independent and not to the dependent and imperfect. As Rumi says the slave is raised by praising the Master:

> To praise You is to praise oneself,
> for he who praises the sun thereby praises his own eyes.

The sunflower is maximized by turning itself towards the sun. The creature too is worthier by realizing within itself the worth of its Creator:

يَـٰٓأَيُّهَا ٱلنَّاسُ أَنتُمُ ٱلۡفُقَرَآءُ إِلَى ٱللَّهِ ۖ وَٱللَّهُ هُوَ ٱلۡغَنِىُّ ٱلۡحَمِيدُ ۝

O mankind you are dependent upon God
And God, He is the Independent and the Owner of Praise {Ghani ul Hameed}[448]

Creation depends upon the Creator. Creation cannot and does not diminish or amplify the Creator. It diminishes or amplifies its own consciousness.

وَقَالَ مُوسَىٰٓ إِن تَكۡفُرُوٓاْ أَنتُمۡ وَمَن فِى ٱلۡأَرۡضِ جَمِيعًا فَإِنَّ ٱللَّهَ لَغَنِىٌّ حَمِيدٌ ۝

And Moses said: "If you show ingratitude, you and all on earth together, even so God is free of all wants, worthy of all praise. {Ghani ul Hameed}[449]

The root word for this Divine Attribute *HMD* is also the root word for *Muhammad* (much praised) and *Ahmad* (one who praises [God]), the proper names given to the Prophet in the Quran. Praiseworthy amongst humans are those who radiate the Divine Light, walking the Divine Pathways.

God is to be praised because on earth God provides a vast refuge. God is to be praised for being the willing and able Pardoner and Forgiver. God is to be praised for life beyond death and healing after injury, and for day following night. God is to be praised for hearing the silent call and witnessing the secret act. God is to be praised for renewal and relief:

---

448 Al Quran 35:15
449 Al Quran 14:8

وَٱلَّذِينَ هَاجَرُوا۟ فِى سَبِيلِ ٱللَّهِ ثُمَّ قُتِلُوٓا۟ أَوْ مَاتُوا۟ لَيَرْزُقَنَّهُمُ ٱللَّهُ رِزْقًا حَسَنًا ۚ وَإِنَّ ٱللَّهَ لَهُوَ خَيْرُ ٱلرَّٰزِقِينَ ۝ لَيُدْخِلَنَّهُم مُّدْخَلًا يَرْضَوْنَهُۥ ۗ وَإِنَّ ٱللَّهَ لَعَلِيمٌ حَلِيمٌ ۝ ۞ ذَٰلِكَ وَمَنْ عَاقَبَ بِمِثْلِ مَا عُوقِبَ بِهِۦ ثُمَّ بُغِىَ عَلَيْهِ لَيَنصُرَنَّهُ ٱللَّهُ ۗ إِنَّ ٱللَّهَ لَعَفُوٌّ غَفُورٌ ۝ ذَٰلِكَ بِأَنَّ ٱللَّهَ يُولِجُ ٱلَّيْلَ فِى ٱلنَّهَارِ وَيُولِجُ ٱلنَّهَارَ فِى ٱلَّيْلِ وَأَنَّ ٱللَّهَ سَمِيعٌ بَصِيرٌ ۝ ذَٰلِكَ بِأَنَّ ٱللَّهَ هُوَ ٱلْحَقُّ وَأَنَّ مَا يَدْعُونَ مِن دُونِهِۦ هُوَ ٱلْبَٰطِلُ وَأَنَّ ٱللَّهَ هُوَ ٱلْعَلِىُّ ٱلْكَبِيرُ ۝ أَلَمْ تَرَ أَنَّ ٱللَّهَ أَنزَلَ مِنَ ٱلسَّمَآءِ مَآءً فَتُصْبِحُ ٱلْأَرْضُ مُخْضَرَّةً ۗ إِنَّ ٱللَّهَ لَطِيفٌ خَبِيرٌ ۝ لَّهُۥ مَا فِى ٱلسَّمَٰوَٰتِ وَمَا فِى ٱلْأَرْضِ ۗ وَإِنَّ ٱللَّهَ لَهُوَ ٱلْغَنِىُّ ٱلْحَمِيدُ ۝

As for those who have emigrated to embrace God's path and then have been killed or died, surely God will grace them with provision.
God is the most caring of Providers and He will admit them to an abode that will please them. God has full knowledge {Aleem} and is Kind [Haleem;
Thus shall it be.
And whosoever retaliates proportionate to their injury, and then is wronged again God will help him. For God is the pardoner and the forgiver.
[Heed] that God causes the night to enter the day and the day to enter the night God is all hearing, all seeing
[Heed] that God alone is Truth and whatever they seek besides Him is false.
God is most exalted, quintessentially supreme [Aliul Kabeer]
Don't you see that God pours down water from the sky and turns the land green?
God is most unfathomable {Lateef} and fully aware {Khabeer}.
To Him belongs whatever is in the heavens and the earth
He is Independent {Ghani} and Owner of Praise {Hameed}.[450]

58. *Al Muhsi*　　　The Appraiser. The One who Assesses each thought
and each deed.

This attribute is not specifically mentioned in the Quran, but is reported in *Hadith*. *Muhsi* is related in meaning with *Haseeb*. *Muhsi* is the expression of *Haseeb*, the latter being a Divine quality of essence. The worth of an act is not espoused by its dogmatic correctness or for that matter by its outcome, but by the earnestness of its intent and motivation. God measures intent and motivation because they manifest the freedom of human-will and therefore the quality of worship.

---

450 Al Quran 22:58-64

Al Muhsi appraises a good deed by magnifying it manifold. The giving heart fills itself. True wealth, profuse and overflowing, comes from giving in the way of God. A grain hoarded is a grain not planted:

مَّثَلُ ٱلَّذِينَ يُنفِقُونَ أَمْوَٰلَهُمْ فِى سَبِيلِ ٱللَّهِ كَمَثَلِ حَبَّةٍ أَنۢبَتَتْ سَبْعَ سَنَابِلَ فِى كُلِّ سُنۢبُلَةٍ مِّائَةُ حَبَّةٍۗ وَٱللَّهُ يُضَٰعِفُ لِمَن يَشَآءُۚ وَٱللَّهُ وَٰسِعٌ عَلِيمٌ ۝

The likeness of those who spend of their wealth in the way of God
is to a grain growing seven shoots, in each shoot a hundred grains
And God multiplies for whomsoever He wills
And God is infinite in means, complete in knowledge {Waasiun Aleem}[451]

59. *Al Mubdi*   The Originator. The One who initiates. The One who assigns a beginning.

This attribute is not specifically mentioned in the Quran, but several references are made to the co-rooted verb *Badaa*. *Al Mubdi* also has proximity in meaning to the Divine name, *Al Badi*.

God brings beings into existence and puts phenomena into time. Time and space and beings are God's creation, still unfolding, growing and evolving. This Divine attribute beckons the open heart to fresh beginnings. New vistas and fresh beginnings are made possible at the portal of Divine Love and Forgiveness:

إِنَّهُۥ هُوَ يُبْدِئُ وَيُعِيدُ ۝ وَهُوَ ٱلْغَفُورُ ٱلْوَدُودُ ۝

Surely, it is He who first creates and begins {yubdiu}
And re-creates and renews {yueed}. He is The Forgiving, The Loving[452]

The journey of the soul is transformational, but any consciousness not anchored in the Divine Being is delusional.

يَوْمَ نَطْوِى ٱلسَّمَآءَ كَطَىِّ ٱلسِّجِلِّ لِلْكُتُبِۚ كَمَا بَدَأْنَآ أَوَّلَ خَلْقٍ نُّعِيدُهُۥۚ وَعْدًا عَلَيْنَآۚ إِنَّا كُنَّا فَٰعِلِينَ ۝

The Day when We shall roll up the heavens like a scribe rolls up scrolls.
As We originated {Badanaa} the first creation, We shall repeat it.
A promise by Us. Know! We shall make it happen.[453]

---

451 Al Quran 2:261
452 Al Quran 85:13-14
453 AL Quran 21:104

قُلْ أَمَرَ رَبِّى بِٱلْقِسْطِ ۖ وَأَقِيمُوا۟ وُجُوهَكُمْ عِندَ كُلِّ مَسْجِدٍ وَٱدْعُوهُ مُخْلِصِينَ لَهُ ٱلدِّينَ ۚ
كَمَا بَدَأَكُمْ تَعُودُونَ ۝

Say: My Lord in all matters commands justice and equity.
And align your being in all pathways of worship
and call upon Him, and in sincerity pursue your approach to God
As He brought you into being {Badaakum}, so will you return. [454]

60. *Al Mueed*   The Restorer.

The One with the power to recreate, renew, restore, repeat or recall to a previous state. *Al Mubdi* and *Al Mueed* are complementary attributes that characterize God's transcendence over time and knowledge—time and knowledge being manifestations of the Divine Will. God creates the past and the future and God creates what is knowable and what is unknown. This attribute is not specifically mentioned in the Quran, but is reported in *Hadith*. It is similar in meaning to *Al Ba'ith*. This Divine attribute invites the tired and wounded heart to repair and renew itself. Revival is a change of state and consciousness and not a change of form:

إِنَّهُ هُوَ يُبْدِئُ وَيُعِيدُ ۝ وَهُوَ ٱلْغَفُورُ ٱلْوَدُودُ ۝

Surely, it is He who first creates and begins {yubdiu} and re-creates and renews
{yueed} and He is The Forgiving, The Loving[455]

61. *Al Muhyi*   The Giver of Life.

Al Muhyi is an attribute of the Divine Will of the Divine Essence *Al Hayy* (Ever Living). All life therefore is a manifestation of the Ever Living. Life as we know it is the embodiment of consciousness, just as death is consciousness disembodied. A heart alive is a heart conscious of God. It is on a mystical journey, the body being the journey's vehicle and the spirit's vessel. God-consciousness is its guiding light. *Al Muhyi* and *Al Mumeet* often occur in the Quran in the same context underscoring God as the journey's Source and Destination. Obsession with the self is utterly misplaced when 'selfhood' is awarded and withdrawn without the advice or consent of the 'self'. It is delusional to think that there can be a purpose to life other than that contemplated by the Divine Will. God the Giver and Taker of life is also the backdrop of our existence and every form of life is Divine manifestation. Ego and self-love are whims of the closed

454 Al Quran 7:29
455 Al Quran 85:13-14

heart locked in its own darkness:

أَوَمَن كَانَ مَيْتًا فَأَحْيَيْنَهُ وَجَعَلْنَا لَهُ نُورًا يَمْشِى بِهِۦ فِى ٱلنَّاسِ كَمَن مَّثَلُهُۥ فِى ٱلظُّلُمَٰتِ
لَيْسَ بِخَارِجٍ مِّنْهَا ۚ كَذَٰلِكَ زُيِّنَ لِلْكَٰفِرِينَ مَا كَانُوا۟ يَعْمَلُونَ ﴿١٢٢﴾

Is he who was dead and We bring to life,
and unveil for him a light by which to journey amongst humanity,
like him who is plunged in darknesses from which he cannot emerge?
Thus the disbelievers conduct is made to seem to them, pleasing and proper. [456]

So how are we to contemplate the scope and purpose of our being? The Quran offers a parable:

وَٱضْرِبْ لَهُم مَّثَلَ ٱلْحَيَوٰةِ ٱلدُّنْيَا كَمَآءٍ أَنزَلْنَٰهُ مِنَ ٱلسَّمَآءِ فَٱخْتَلَطَ بِهِۦ نَبَاتُ ٱلْأَرْضِ
فَأَصْبَحَ هَشِيمًا تَذْرُوهُ ٱلرِّيَٰحُ ۗ وَكَانَ ٱللَّهُ عَلَىٰ كُلِّ شَىْءٍ مُّقْتَدِرًا ﴿٤٥﴾

And propound for them the similitude of the life of this world:
It is as water that We usher from the skies, and the earth's vegetation mingles
with it and by a morning it is straw for the winds to scatter.
God prevails over everything [457]

62. *Al Mumeet*   The Giver of Death.

The name is derived from the root "*m-w-t*" which means 'to pass away', 'to be bereft of life, sensation, or awareness'. Death is the passage into compulsory submission and the termination of free-will. Death therefore lifts the veils that made free-will possible. These veils shield the convergence of the beginning and the end. They make credible (as well as foster the illusion of) the vicegerent's empowerment by veiling the Real Sovereign. They lend credibility to our individualness and separateness when there is only One. Yet, by shielding the Hidden from the Evident, they also afford us the opportunity to 'seek'.

Without death, life loses transcendence. As Rumi says, "It would be like the harvest left to rot". How then could the seeking heart spurn the embrace of death, or fear its mystery when death and life; the beginning and the ending; the hidden and the evident; are constructs of the same Source:

---

456 Al Quran 6:122
457 Al Quran 18:45

$$سَبَّحَ لِلَّهِ مَا فِى ٱلسَّمَوَاتِ وَٱلْأَرْضِ ۖ وَهُوَ ٱلْعَزِيزُ ٱلْحَكِيمُ ۞ لَهُ مُلْكُ ٱلسَّمَوَاتِ وَٱلْأَرْضِ ۖ يُحْىِۦ وَيُمِيتُ ۖ وَهُوَ عَلَىٰ كُلِّ شَىْءٍ قَدِيرٌ ۞ هُوَ ٱلْأَوَّلُ وَٱلْءَاخِرُ وَٱلظَّاهِرُ وَٱلْبَاطِنُ ۖ وَهُوَ بِكُلِّ شَىْءٍ عَلِيمٌ ۞$$

In grateful adulation of Him is all between the Heavens and the Earth
He is boundless Might {Azeez}, complete Wisdom {Hakeem}.
His is the sovereignty over the Heavens and the Earth.
Grants life {Yuhi} and brings death {Umeet}.
It is He who controls the fate of all things {Qadeer}.
He is the Beginning {Awwal} and the End {Aakhir}
He is the Evident {Zahir} and the Hidden {Batin}.
And of all things He has knowledge {Aleem} [458]

Al Muhyi and *Al Mumeet* are complementary attributes and the attributes of God alone. He grants life, as He brings death. Death is by the design of *Rahman*, and so, though painful, it cannot be cruel. We fear death and rightfully so. One fears the unknown. Yet when the Quran recalls the death of those who strove not in God's path, the bigger and enduring loss lies not in the end of life, but in the end of the opportunity that life and free-will presented. Death is the final and pre-destinated surrender. As the waters engulf the drowning Pharaoh, he does not agonize over what he is about to loose, but laments over the lost opportunity of a willing-surrender, confessing: "I believe that there is no God but the One in whom the children of Israel believe and I am one of those who surrender". [459]

Mortality in itself is just another sign of God's mercy, heralding new beginnings:

$$فَٱنظُرْ إِلَىٰٓ ءَاثَرِ رَحْمَتِ ٱللَّهِ كَيْفَ يُحْىِ ٱلْأَرْضَ بَعْدَ مَوْتِهَآ ۚ إِنَّ ذَٰلِكَ لَمُحْىِ ٱلْمَوْتَىٰ$$

Behold the signs of God's Mercy
How he revives the earth after its death
It is He who will resurrect the dead [460]

63. *Al Hayy*   The Ever-Living. Life without birth or death.

All life is borrowed from the Living. To quote Martin Lings the name *Al-Hayy* "tells us that such life as we have on earth is not ours but a brief loan from the Living Himself, immensely reduced to the level of our transitory earthly existence. If the question be asked; 'What is life?' a good answer, which is in fact sometimes

458 Al Quran 57:1-3
459 Al Quran 10:90
460 Al Quran 30:50

given, is that Life is a Divine spark within us."[461]

The heart's journey, transformational as it is, can rely on no permanent anchor except the anchor of the Divine Being. Life is borrowed from the Source of Life, *Al Hayy*, and the journey's stations of consciousness exist by the One, True, Eternal and Pure Consciousness:

وَتَوَكَّلْ عَلَى ٱلْحَيِّ ٱلَّذِى لَا يَمُوتُ وَسَبِّحْ بِحَمْدِهِۦ ۚ وَكَفَىٰ بِهِۦ بِذُنُوبِ عِبَادِهِۦ خَبِيرًا

And trust thou in the Living One Who dieth not,
and hymn His praise. He sufficeth as the Knower of His bondmen's sins [462]

64. *Al Qayyum*   The Self-Subsisting.

The life beyond time that never diminishes[463]. *Al Qayyum* is also often translated as The Eternal. The root-word of *Qayyum* includes the meanings, "to be on-going", "to exist without dependence" as well as to be "upright", "straight" etc. *Qayyum* is also related via its root to *Maqaam*, which refers to the station of awareness on which a soul exists. *Hayy* and *Qayyum* are often used together, signifying The Absolute Station of Being—Self-Existing, Uncaused, Everlasting, Omniscient and Omnipresent.

The much recited 'Throne Verse' {*Ayatul Kursi*} of the Quran places the 'Divine Throne' of the Formless, Timeless, Omniscient and Omnipresent Sovereign, amongst, around and in us. The Throne is everywhere and everything. The Throne sits in all thoughts and all hearts; in all knowledge and all consciousness. We are for ever in the Divine Court. There is no 'place of being', 'period in time', 'event', 'experience' or 'knowledge', outside of this Court. The Sovereign too is never absent from His Court!

ٱللَّهُ لَا إِلَٰهَ إِلَّا هُوَ ٱلْحَىُّ ٱلْقَيُّومُ ۚ لَا تَأْخُذُهُۥ سِنَةٌ وَلَا نَوْمٌ ۚ لَّهُۥ مَا فِى ٱلسَّمَٰوَٰتِ وَمَا فِى ٱلْأَرْضِ ۗ مَن ذَا ٱلَّذِى يَشْفَعُ عِندَهُۥٓ إِلَّا بِإِذْنِهِۦ ۚ يَعْلَمُ مَا بَيْنَ أَيْدِيهِمْ وَمَا خَلْفَهُمْ ۖ وَلَا يُحِيطُونَ بِشَىْءٍ مِّنْ عِلْمِهِۦٓ إِلَّا بِمَا شَآءَ ۚ وَسِعَ كُرْسِيُّهُ ٱلسَّمَٰوَٰتِ وَٱلْأَرْضَ ۖ وَلَا يَـُٔودُهُۥ حِفْظُهُمَا ۚ وَهُوَ ٱلْعَلِىُّ ٱلْعَظِيمُ

GOD - there is no deity save Him,
The Ever-Living, The Self-Subsistent Fount of All Being {*Hayyul Qayyum*}.

---

461 *A return to the Spirit*, by Martin Lings, P. 25
462 Al Quran 25:58 as interpreted by Pickthall
463 Lex Hixon *The Heart of The Quran*

Neither slumber overtakes Him, nor sleep.
His is all that is in the heavens and all that is on earth.
Who is there that could intercede with Him, unless it be by His leave?
He knows all that lies open before them and all that is hidden from them,
whereas they cannot attain to aught of His knowledge
save that which He wills [them to attain].
His Throne extends over the heavens and the earth,
and their upholding wearies Him not.
And he alone is truly Exalted, Tremendous {Aliyyul Azeem}. [464]

65. *Al Wajid* [465] Beyond being. The All-Perceiving.

That which is within itself complete and whole. Because God is 'complete', nothing is outside of God and therefore nothing can be added to or subtracted from God. Because God is whole, nothing is ever lost to God. Without wanting, lacking nothing. His Being is beyond our conception of existence.

A co-rooted word *wajada* means 'found'. *Al Wajid* is therefore also interpreted as 'The Finder'. Says the 'Finder' to His chosen messenger, as also to every sincere heart that may feel lost:

$$أَلَمْ يَجِدْكَ يَتِيمًا فَآوَىٰ ۞ وَوَجَدَكَ ضَآلاًّ فَهَدَىٰ ۞ وَوَجَدَكَ عَآئِلاً فَأَغْنَىٰ ۞$$

Did He not find thee {yajidka} an orphan and protect (thee)?
Did He not find thee {wajadaka} wandering and direct (thee)?
Did He not find thee {wajadaka} destitute and enrich (thee)? [466]

66. *Al Maajid* The One whose ways are noble, venerable, and
  generously bountiful.

Maajid is derived from the root *m-j-d* which is also the root of *Majeed*. The former refers to the Divine Will (action), while the latter refers to the Divine Essence {*Ism-e-Dhaat*}.

67. *Al Wahid* One.

The Unity behind all diversity and multiplicity. The Single Source and Goal. That which is diverse, the many, or the separated, are the manifestations of the One. Every thing exists by a Single Design, a Single Purpose and a Single Truth. One

---

464 Al Quran 2:255 as interpreted by Muhammad Asad in *The Message of the Quran*
465 The word "Wajid" is not used in the Quran.
466 Al Quran 93:6-8 as interpreted by Pickthall

Creator for all creatures. The Ground of Being for *all* beings. There is no other god but God. This is the simplicity of belief and the profundity of Truth. Outside this Truth is the dark nothingness of error. This attribute is co-rooted with the Divine Name *Ahad* and belief in Unity, *Tawheed*. *Wahid* exists *in context of* God's creation. The One God is manifested in all the forms He has created. *Ahad*, on the other hand is *outside the context* of creation and is an attribute of God's Essence {*Ism-e-Dhaat*}. *Ahad* is the One, formless and un-definable God. *Wahid* as One *includes* everything and *Ahad* as One *excludes* everything.

Tawheed, stated simply, means to 'embrace God's Oneness, in word and thought'. The message of *Tawheed* is much deeper and richer. God defies vision, His Reality is Unseen, because and thus, everything in the created world is a *manifestation* of God. There are layers of manifestation too. The rays manifest the sun, the sun manifests light, light manifests energy, energy manifests existence, etc. Yet behind each manifestation and behind all manifestations is the One Will. *Tawheed* is therefore an approach towards God, a movement towards Him, inwards and outwards, along any one of His 99 or more pathways. There can be no contemplation of Unity with the exclusion of the other. There can be no contemplation of the self, without contemplation of the One. The relationship between creation and The Creator is one to One:

$$\text{ذَرْنِي وَمَنْ خَلَقْتُ وَحِيدًا}$$

Leave Me alone to deal with him whom I have created singly[467]

Life begins and ends involuntarily. These are humbling and *equalizing* markers, not unlike our morning and evening shadows that hug the ground that we walk upon. How then can we have separate gods? All sincere quests for a transcendental meaning and truth to life, lead to the One:

$$\text{وَلِلَّهِ يَسْجُدُ مَن فِي ٱلسَّمَـٰوَٰتِ وَٱلْأَرْضِ طَوْعًا وَكَرْهًا وَظِلَـٰلُهُم بِٱلْغُدُوِّ وَٱلْآصَالِ ۩ قُلْ}$$
$$\text{مَن رَّبُّ ٱلسَّمَـٰوَٰتِ وَٱلْأَرْضِ قُلِ ٱللَّهُ قُلْ أَفَٱتَّخَذْتُم مِّن دُونِهِ أَوْلِيَآءَ لَا يَمْلِكُونَ لِأَنفُسِهِمْ}$$
$$\text{نَفْعًا وَلَا ضَرًّا قُلْ هَلْ يَسْتَوِى ٱلْأَعْمَىٰ وَٱلْبَصِيرُ أَمْ هَلْ تَسْتَوِى ٱلظُّلُمَـٰتُ وَٱلنُّورُ أَمْ جَعَلُوا}$$
$$\text{لِلَّهِ شُرَكَآءَ خَلَقُوا كَخَلْقِهِ فَتَشَـٰبَهَ ٱلْخَلْقُ عَلَيْهِمْ قُلِ ٱللَّهُ خَـٰلِقُ كُلِّ شَىْءٍ وَهُوَ ٱلْوَٰحِدُ ٱلْقَهَّـٰرُ}$$

In prostration to God is all that is in the heavens and the earth,
Voluntarily or involuntarily,
As are their shadows in the morning and the evening
Say "Who is the Lord of the Heavens and the earth?"
Say "God."

---

467 Al Quran 74 :11

Say "Do you then choose protectors other than Him—those that cannot bring good or harm to even themselves?"
Say "Is the blind the same as the seeing?
Or are darknesses the same as light?"
Have their improvised gods created the like of God's creation such that both creations appear to them to be the same?
Say "God is the Creator of all things,
The One {Waahid}, The Irresistible and Omnipotent" {Qahhaar} [468]

68. *Al Ahad* The One and Only. The One that excludes everything.

The Primordial One. The Eternal One. None before. None after. Indivisible, Immutable. Of none begotten and begetting none. This Divine Name signifies the Divine Essence {Ism-e-Dhaat}, an attribute that declares completeness within itself. Even when everything created is folded and recalled to God, God remains as He ever was. Changes affect human consciousness and not the Reality of God. All the Most Beautiful Names, described for the human heart, belong to the One.

قُلْ هُوَ ٱللَّهُ أَحَدٌ ۞ ٱللَّهُ ٱلصَّمَدُ ۞ لَمْ يَلِدْ وَلَمْ يُولَدْ ۞ وَلَمْ يَكُن لَّهُۥ كُفُوًا أَحَدُۢ ۞

Say he is God, One {Ahad}
God forever {Samad}
Not begetting, unbegotten,
and having as an equal none [469]

69. *As Samad* The Ceaseless [470].

The Eternal, Uncaused Cause of all that exists [471]. The One who is sought by all. Refuge for every need. [472] The Rock. [473] The One who Wills matter and all matters. When time and space have all been folded, God, *Samad* will remain, as *Samad* ever was, unchanged and unaffected.

Say he is God, One {Ahad}
God forever {Samad}
Not begetting, unbegotten,

468 Al Quran 13:15-16
469 Al Quran 112:1- as interpreted by Michael Sells in *Approaching the Quran*
470 *Return to the Spirit* Martin Lings
471 *The Message of the Quran*, Muhammad Asad
472 *The Sufi Book of life* Neil Douglas-Klotz's
473 One of three interpretations of Michael Sells in *Approaching the Quran*

and having as an equal none[474]

70. *Al Qaadir*   The All Capable.

The One who shapes and 'measures out' (assigns) the term and ability of a creature. God is the One who assigns the measure of power (capability) and its term to each individual. For each quality that God assigns to a creature, there is a corresponding assignment of purpose too. Our purpose is one of agency. We as agents of His power have erred when we fail to exercise our abilities to their fullest purpose and fruition. Our regency exists within a term, beyond which awaits full accountability.

The expression of our power and capability belies the reality of our pre-determined circumstance of existence, evidenced by involuntary birth and death. As actors in a limited-act play we bear forth our purposeful roles. The stage, its backdrop and its lights are assigned by *Al Qaadir*. Our skills, those that embrace the Divine pathways are our mandate from God. Act therefore we must, and leave by term's end we shall.

وَيْلٌ يَوْمَئِذٍ لِّلْمُكَذِّبِينَ ۝ أَلَمْ نَخْلُقكُّم مِّن مَّآءٍ مَّهِينٍ ۝ فَجَعَلْنَاهُ فِي قَرَارٍ مَّكِينٍ ۝ إِلَىٰ قَدَرٍ مَّعْلُومٍ ۝ فَقَدَرْنَا فَنِعْمَ ٱلْقَٰدِرُونَ ۝

Woe on that day to those who efface the truth!
Did We not create you from seemingly insignificant fluid
Which We then put in a secure abode for a determined term?
Thus We determine (the nature or capacity of a thing)
Best is Our power {faneemal qadiroon}! [475]

We do not have a permanent claim to our prowess. Even that which defines our identity, our knowledge of ourselves and of all other beings and things, is ours for a term:

وَٱللَّهُ خَلَقَكُمْ ثُمَّ يَتَوَفَّىٰكُمْ ۚ وَمِنكُم مَّن يُرَدُّ إِلَىٰ أَرْذَلِ ٱلْعُمُرِ لِكَىْ لَا يَعْلَمَ بَعْدَ عِلْمٍ شَيْئًا ۚ إِنَّ ٱللَّهَ عَلِيمٌ قَدِيرٌ ۝

It is God who has created you and will then reclaim you.
[Though] some among you are held back to an abject age
when they know nothing of what they had once known.
God is Knower {Aleem}, Powerful {Qadeer}. [476]

Our environment, both physical and social, far exceeds our individual capacity.

---

474 Al Quran 112:1- as interpreted by Michael Sells in *Approaching the Quran*
475 Al Quran 77:19 -23
476 Al Quran 16:70

Every moment of existence is by Divine leave and purpose:

قُلْ مَن يُنَجِّيكُم مِّن ظُلُمَاتِ ٱلْبَرِّ وَٱلْبَحْرِ تَدْعُونَهُ تَضَرُّعًا وَخُفْيَةً لَّئِنْ أَنجَىٰنَا مِنْ هَٰذِهِۦ لَنَكُونَنَّ مِنَ ٱلشَّٰكِرِينَ ۝ قُلِ ٱللَّهُ يُنَجِّيكُم مِّنْهَا وَمِن كُلِّ كَرْبٍ ثُمَّ أَنتُمْ تُشْرِكُونَ ۝ قُلْ هُوَ ٱلْقَادِرُ عَلَىٰٓ أَن يَبْعَثَ عَلَيْكُمْ عَذَابًا مِّن فَوْقِكُمْ أَوْ مِن تَحْتِ أَرْجُلِكُمْ أَوْ يَلْبِسَكُمْ شِيَعًا وَيُذِيقَ بَعْضَكُم بَأْسَ بَعْضٍ ٱنظُرْ كَيْفَ نُصَرِّفُ ٱلْآيَٰتِ لَعَلَّهُمْ يَفْقَهُونَ ۝

Say, "Who delivers you from the darkness of the land and sea?
You call upon Him humbly and in secret,
"If we are saved from this we will be truly grateful"
Say, "God delivers you from these and other afflictions, yet you worship false
gods"
Say, "He has Power {Qaadir} to afflict you from above you or from beneath your
feet or embroil you in factional strife and make you taste the tyranny of each
other". Witness how we illustrate our signs so that they may understand.[477]

71. *Al Muqtadir*   The One who exercises the ultimate control.

Al Muqtadir is the One who has chartered the course of the universe with the
Supreme Power to ordain the earnest outcome of all matters; the One who reins
in the unjust and restores the balance. God measured out the water that
delivered Noah and sustained his earnestness, as he measured out the water
that drowned Pharaoh and washed away his arrogance. Our mandate from God
is immense: "Have you not seen that God has subjugated to you all that is in the
earth."[478] Enlightened, we acknowledge and honor the trust. Blinded we stand
in disregard of it.

فَفَتَحْنَا أَبْوَٰبَ ٱلسَّمَآءِ بِمَآءٍ مُّنْهَمِرٍ ۝ وَفَجَّرْنَا ٱلْأَرْضَ عُيُونًا فَٱلْتَقَى ٱلْمَآءُ عَلَىٰٓ أَمْرٍ قَدْ قُدِرَ ۝ وَحَمَلْنَٰهُ عَلَىٰ ذَاتِ أَلْوَٰحٍ وَدُسُرٍ ۝ تَجْرِى بِأَعْيُنِنَا جَزَآءً لِّمَن كَانَ كُفِرَ ۝

We opened the gates of heaven for water to pour in torrents
And unleashed earthly springs, waters meeting for a purpose pre-ordained {amrin
qad qudir}. And We bore him [Noah] upon a frame of planks and nails, afloat
under Our watch, a recompense for him who was rejected. [479]

وَلَقَدْ جَآءَ ءَالَ فِرْعَوْنَ ٱلنُّذُرُ ۝ كَذَّبُوا۟ بِـَٔايَٰتِنَا كُلِّهَا فَأَخَذْنَٰهُمْ أَخْذَ عَزِيزٍ مُّقْتَدِرٍ ۝

The warning was also sent to the people of the Pharaoh

---

477 Al Quran 6:63-65
478 Al Quran 22:65
479 Al Quran 54:11-14

They rejected all Our signs so we punished them with the punishment of The Mighty, The Powerful ({Muqtadir}[480]

72. *Al Muqaddim*   The Expediter.

Al Muqaddim is the One who places an event earlier in time; The One who accelerates or intensifies a process; The One who accelerates the growth of the soul and the reaching of a spiritual station or rank.

The Divine Being is outside of time, therefore Divine knowledge and the 'birth' of an event are not separate. Time is extraneous to Divine Knowledge. God wills and therefore creates knowledge. Man must *acquire* knowledge. Time was created by God as the human vehicle of learning.

Al Muqaddim offers Noah before Abraham; Abraham before Moses; Moses before Jesus; and Jesus before Muhammad—each renews the Divine message entrusted to his predecessor; the caravan of prophets in synchronicity, leading us to the same and only One.

The root word *qdm* is the root to a profuse array of words, whose variety in meaning is truly fascinating. These words define a position in time or space. The common root of these words underscores the interdependence of time and space and consciousness. *Takadama* (preceded) *kadeem* (old or ancient) *kadam* (foot-step), *kadama* (to send ahead) evoke the image of the caravan of souls, our ancestors in the lead, and we, the latter generations in tow.

Life's uncertain future looms as a 'count down' and it is the past that is accumulative. Our freedom of will and action operate in 'now'. The heart can renew itself every 'now'. The urgency of life lies in 'now'. The time to make amends is now. The accumulated capital or loss of a soul's deeds accrues from its past. God lessens the burden of past missteps and clears the obstacles of doubt and hardship on the road ahead:

إِنَّا فَتَحْنَا لَكَ فَتْحًا مُّبِينًا ۝ لِّيَغْفِرَ لَكَ ٱللَّهُ مَا تَقَدَّمَ مِن ذَنۢبِكَ وَمَا تَأَخَّرَ وَيُتِمَّ نِعْمَتَهُ عَلَيْكَ وَيَهْدِيَكَ صِرَٰطًا مُّسْتَقِيمًا ۝ وَيَنصُرَكَ ٱللَّهُ نَصْرًا عَزِيزًا ۝

Lo! We have given thee (O Muhammad) a signal victory,
That God may forgive thee of thy sin that which is past {takadama}
and that which is to come {taakhkhara},
and may perfect His favor unto thee, and may guide thee on a right path,
And that God may help thee with strong help [481]

---

480 Al Quran 54:41-42
481 Al Quran 48:1-3

This name is not specifically used as a Beautiful Name in the Quran though it is reported in *Hadith*.

73. *Al Muakhkhir*   The Delayer.

The One who places an event later in time. The One who decelerates or diminishes the intensity of a process. The One who delays the reaching of a spiritual rank or station of a soul. Derived from the root word *A-Kh-R*, this Divine Name shares the same root as *Al -Aakhir*. *Muakhkhir* manifests the action *Aakhir*. *Al Muakhkhir* and *Al Muqaddim* are complementary attributes. This name is not specifically used as a Beautiful Name in the Quran though it is reported in *Hadith*.

74. *Al Awwal*   The First with no beginning.

The Pre-Existing. The Creator of time. Nothing precedes God. *Al Awwal* and *Al Aakhir* underscore God's timelessness and are therefore attributes of Divine Essence. They underscore God's eternal presence in Paradise. *Al Muqaddim* and *Al Muakhkhir* on the other hand underscore God's Lordship over time and His omnipresence in the experience that we call life.

سَبَّحَ لِلَّهِ مَا فِى ٱلسَّمَـٰوَٰتِ وَٱلْأَرْضِ ۖ وَهُوَ ٱلْعَزِيزُ ٱلْحَكِيمُ ۞ لَهُۥ مُلْكُ ٱلسَّمَـٰوَٰتِ وَٱلْأَرْضِ ۖ يُحْىِۦ وَيُمِيتُ ۖ وَهُوَ عَلَىٰ كُلِّ شَىْءٍ قَدِيرٌ ۞ هُوَ ٱلْأَوَّلُ وَٱلْأَخِرُ وَٱلظَّـٰهِرُ وَٱلْبَاطِنُ ۖ وَهُوَ بِكُلِّ شَىْءٍ عَلِيمٌ ۞

In grateful worship of Him is all between the Heavens and the Earth
He is Almighty {Azeez}, Wise {Hakeem}.
His are the Heavens and the Earth.
Grants life {Yuhi} and brings death {Umeet}.
It is He who controls the fate of all things {Qadeer}.
He is the Beginning {Awwal} and the End {Aakhir}
He is the Evident {Zahir} and the Hidden {Batin}.
And of all things He has knowledge {Aleem} [482]

75. *Al Aakhir*   The Last without end. The Ultimate.

God is the Concluder of time. Nothing will remain but God.

---

482 Al Quran 57:1-3

كُلُّ مَنْ عَلَيْهَا فَانٍ ۝ وَيَبْقَىٰ وَجْهُ رَبِّكَ ذُو ٱلْجَلَٰلِ وَٱلْإِكْرَامِ ۝

All that is in (existence) is to perish
But forever will remain the Presence and Will of your Sustainer full of Majesty
and Grace {Dhul Jalaal wal Ikraam} [483]

76.	*Az Zahir*	The outwardly Manifest.

God Manifests Himself in Complete Wisdom {*Al Hakeem*}. Divine Manifestations are Signs (*Ayah*) that radiate Divine Wisdom. The open heart will find in these Signs open and lasting lessons. The Keeper of Knowledge {*Al Aleem*} will impart knowledge by the measure of the earnestness of the seeker. The earnest sight and voice will find *Al Baseer* and *Al Sami*. Nothing in this world is forever and everything that exists has no independent existence of its own.

Amongst God's Manifest signs are time and space, co-dependent, obedient and singularly devoted to the Single Master. These signs provide the definitive context of our existence and the backdrop of our reality. We live by Divine Manifestation. The discerning heart will move closer to the Source of Manifestation, the Reality behind the reality, *Al Batin*.

سَبَّحَ لِلَّهِ مَا فِي ٱلسَّمَٰوَٰتِ وَٱلْأَرْضِ وَهُوَ ٱلْعَزِيزُ ٱلْحَكِيمُ ۝ لَهُۥ مُلْكُ ٱلسَّمَٰوَٰتِ وَٱلْأَرْضِ
يُحْيِۦ وَيُمِيتُ وَهُوَ عَلَىٰ كُلِّ شَيْءٍ قَدِيرٌ ۝ هُوَ ٱلْأَوَّلُ وَٱلْأَخِرُ وَٱلظَّٰهِرُ وَٱلْبَاطِنُ وَهُوَ بِكُلِّ
شَيْءٍ عَلِيمٌ ۝

In grateful worship of Him is all between the Heavens and the Earth
He is Almighty {Azeez}, Wise {Hakeem}.
His are the Heavens and the Earth.
Grants life {Yuhi} and brings death {Umeet}.
It is He who controls the fate of all things {Qadeer}.
He is the Beginning {Awwal} and the End {Aakhir}
He is the Evident {Zahir} and the Hidden {Batin}.
And of all things He has knowledge {Aleem} [484]

Az Zahir is complementary to the attribute *Al Batin*. There is also an inward and outward aspect to us. What are innermost to us are our thoughts. Our thoughts are the most autonomous contributions that we make to the Divine Record of Knowledge. Alignment with *Az Zahir* starts in the inner most sanctums of the

---

483 Al Quran 55:26-27
484 Al Quran 57:1-3

heart. The inner beauty radiates outwards. An indecent act is first an indecent thought. Says the Quran:

وَلَا تَقْرَبُواْ ٱلْفَوَاحِشَ مَا ظَهَرَ مِنْهَا وَمَا بَطَنَ ۞

And approach not indecency, outward or inward[485]

77. *Al Batin*   The inwardly Hidden.

God is beyond sensory perception and cerebral capacity. The living body, ruled by the mind, weaves its own spider web of a reality (virtual reality, if you prefer), veiling the Reality of Truth. Every other creature and creation lives by the Reality of Truth and is therefore for ever in willing and grateful submission to The One. God is Hidden from us in His Complete Wisdom {*Al Hakeem*}. The discerning heart knows that the Hidden Master is never absent.

سَبَّحَ لِلَّهِ مَا فِى ٱلسَّمَـٰوَٰتِ وَٱلْأَرْضِ ۖ وَهُوَ ٱلْعَزِيزُ ٱلْحَكِيمُ ۞ لَهُۥ مُلْكُ ٱلسَّمَـٰوَٰتِ وَٱلْأَرْضِ ۖ يُحْىِۦ وَيُمِيتُ ۖ وَهُوَ عَلَىٰ كُلِّ شَىْءٍ قَدِيرٌ ۞ هُوَ ٱلْأَوَّلُ وَٱلْآخِرُ وَٱلظَّـٰهِرُ وَٱلْبَاطِنُ ۖ وَهُوَ بِكُلِّ شَىْءٍ عَلِيمٌ ۞

In grateful worship of Him is all between the Heavens and the Earth
He is Almighty {Azeez}, Wise {Hakeem}.
His are the Heavens and the Earth.
Grants life {Yuhi} and brings death {Umeet}.
It is He who controls the fate of all things {Qadeer}.
He is the Beginning {Awwal} and the End {Aakhir}
He is the Evident {Zahir} and the Hidden {Batin}.
And of all things He has knowledge {Aleem} [486]

78. *Al Waali*   The Governor.

The Ruler Who is Protective and Supportive. This name shares the same root as *Al Wali*. *Al Waali* accentuates Sovereignty. *Al Wali* accentuates Divine nurturing and guidance. *Al Waali* relates to the universe as a whole, guarding and protecting it. *Al Wali* relates to the seeker on a personal level, nurturing the seeker. A parent is *Waali* to all the children and *Wali* to a special child.

Life bears both risks as well as opportunities; just as lightning bears both fear and hope. Yet behind lightning as behind every life-force is the purposeful

---

485 Al Quran 6:151
486 Al Quran 57:1-3

design of *Waali*. The heart that trusts in God must not fear anything but its own inaction or mis-action. God commits to nurture the heart that commits itself to God.

سَوَآءٌ مِّنكُم مَّنْ أَسَرَّ ٱلْقَوْلَ وَمَن جَهَرَ بِهِۦ وَمَنْ هُوَ مُسْتَخْفٍ بِٱلَّيْلِ وَسَارِبٌۢ بِٱلنَّهَارِ ۞ لَهُۥ مُعَقِّبَٰتٌ مِّنۢ بَيْنِ يَدَيْهِ وَمِنْ خَلْفِهِۦ يَحْفَظُونَهُۥ مِنْ أَمْرِ ٱللَّهِ ۗ إِنَّ ٱللَّهَ لَا يُغَيِّرُ مَا بِقَوْمٍ حَتَّىٰ يُغَيِّرُوا۟ مَا بِأَنفُسِهِمْ ۗ وَإِذَآ أَرَادَ ٱللَّهُ بِقَوْمٍ سُوٓءًا فَلَا مَرَدَّ لَهُۥ ۚ وَمَا لَهُم مِّن دُونِهِۦ مِن وَالٍ ۞

Equal is the one of you who conceals his speech to the one who speaks openly; as is the one who tries to hide himself by night to the one who goes about freely by day. For each there is a succession of angels, in front of him and behind him, protecting him by order of God. God does not change the condition of a people until they change their own condition.
And when God wants misfortune for a people, there is no averting it; and they have no protection {waal} besides God.[487]

Another co-rooted word *Mawla* (usually translated as 'Patron') is in some lists used as a Divine attribute (*Al Mawla*).

وَقَٰتِلُوهُمْ حَتَّىٰ لَا تَكُونَ فِتْنَةٌ وَيَكُونَ ٱلدِّينُ كُلُّهُۥ لِلَّهِ ۚ فَإِنِ ٱنتَهَوْا۟ فَإِنَّ ٱللَّهَ بِمَا يَعْمَلُونَ بَصِيرٌ ۞ وَإِن تَوَلَّوْا۟ فَٱعْلَمُوٓا۟ أَنَّ ٱللَّهَ مَوْلَىٰكُمْ ۚ نِعْمَ ٱلْمَوْلَىٰ وَنِعْمَ ٱلنَّصِيرُ ۞

Fight them until there is no more strife and all deen is for God
But if they desist God surely sees what they do.
If they refuse, know that God is your Patron {Mawlakum}
The Transcendent Patron {Mawla} and the Transcendent Helper {Naseer}.[488]

79. *Al Muta'ali*   The Transcendentally Exalted.

Supremely Eminent, beyond comprehension or imagination. *Al Muta'ali* is co-rooted with the Divine Name *Al Aliyy*. *Al Muta'ali* is an attribute of Divine Essence {*Ism-e-Dhaat*} and Transcendence. Every thing created has a limited purpose, a limited term, a limited rank and a limited understanding. It is futile and foolish to attempt to 'define' God or to hypothesize on the Divine Plan and Purpose. God is manifested and hidden, so is the Divine Purpose. We must accept the mystery (as in formlessness) of God as we accept the pre-destination of our birth. The purpose that we seek must be that of our own being. God is to be sought within our innermost sanctum and with utmost sincerity.

---

487 Al Quran 13:10-11 as interpreted by Thomas Cleary
488 Al Quran 8:39-40

اللَّهُ يَعْلَمُ مَا تَحْمِلُ كُلُّ أُنثَىٰ وَمَا تَغِيضُ ٱلْأَرْحَامُ وَمَا تَزْدَادُ ۖ وَكُلُّ شَيْءٍ عِندَهُ بِمِقْدَارٍ ۞ عَٰلِمُ ٱلْغَيْبِ وَٱلشَّهَٰدَةِ ٱلْكَبِيرُ ٱلْمُتَعَالِ ۞

God knows what every female bears
and that in the womb which diminishes
and that which grows.
Every thing with Him is purposefully designed and measured.
Knower of the invisible and the evident
God is transcendentally Great {Kabeer} and transcendentally Exalted {Mutaal}[489]

80. *Al Barr*   The Source of All Goodness, Generous in reward, Kind in gifting.

An act of kindness aligns us with this beautiful attribute. It will be forever in the book of good deeds {*Illiyyun*}, in the heavens, in proximity to God, because beauty is Divine. The Quran uses the word *Barr* to describe the proper relationship of John the Baptist {Yahya} with his parents and of Jesus with his mother Mary. In these contexts Muhammad Asad translates "*barr*" to mean piety, Pickthall translates to mean "dutiful", and Thomas Cleary, whose translation is used below, uses the word "kind":

يَٰيَحْيَىٰ خُذِ ٱلْكِتَٰبَ بِقُوَّةٍ ۖ وَءَاتَيْنَٰهُ ٱلْحُكْمَ صَبِيًّا ۞ وَحَنَانًا مِّن لَّدُنَّا وَزَكَوٰةً ۖ وَكَانَ تَقِيًّا ۞ وَبَرًّۢا بِوَٰلِدَيْهِ وَلَمْ يَكُن جَبَّارًا عَصِيًّا ۞

We gave him wisdom, even as a boy and compassion from Us, and innocence.
And he was conscientious, and kind to his parents {wa barram biwalidayhi};
And he was not insolent or defiant[490].

قَالَ إِنِّي عَبْدُ ٱللَّهِ ءَاتَىٰنِيَ ٱلْكِتَٰبَ وَجَعَلَنِي نَبِيًّا ۞ وَجَعَلَنِي مُبَارَكًا أَيْنَ مَا كُنتُ وَأَوْصَٰنِي بِٱلصَّلَوٰةِ وَٱلزَّكَوٰةِ مَا دُمْتُ حَيًّا ۞ وَبَرًّۢا بِوَٰلِدَتِي وَلَمْ يَجْعَلْنِي جَبَّارًا شَقِيًّا ۞

He (Jesus) said, "I am indeed the servant of God,
who has given me scripture and made me a prophet,
And made me blessed wherever I am;
And has prescribed prayer and charity for me as long as I live,
And kindness to my mother {wa barram biwalidati} as well
And did not make me an arrogant malcontent"[491]

---

489 Al Quran 13:8-9
490 Al Quran 19:12-14 as interpreted in *The Quran A new translation* by Thomas Cleary
491 Al Quran 19:30-32 as interpreted in *The Quran A new translation* by Thomas Cleary

Barr is co-rooted with the word *Birr* and the verb *Barra*. *Barra* is used to describe the action of being true to one's promise. *Birr* is translated as piety and righteousness, but its depth and breadth eludes a single word translation. Its rich meaning encompasses the covenant of man with God, conveyed by the message of Islam and all preceding messengers. The Quran defines it thusly:

❖ لَّيۡسَ ٱلۡبِرَّ أَن تُوَلُّواْ وُجُوهَكُمۡ قِبَلَ ٱلۡمَشۡرِقِ وَٱلۡمَغۡرِبِ وَلَٰكِنَّ ٱلۡبِرَّ مَنۡ ءَامَنَ بِٱللَّهِ وَٱلۡيَوۡمِ ٱلۡءَاخِرِ وَٱلۡمَلَٰٓئِكَةِ وَٱلۡكِتَٰبِ وَٱلنَّبِيِّـۧنَ وَءَاتَى ٱلۡمَالَ عَلَىٰ حُبِّهِۦ ذَوِى ٱلۡقُرۡبَىٰ وَٱلۡيَتَٰمَىٰ وَٱلۡمَسَٰكِينَ وَٱبۡنَ ٱلسَّبِيلِ وَٱلسَّآئِلِينَ وَفِى ٱلرِّقَابِ وَأَقَامَ ٱلصَّلَوٰةَ وَءَاتَى ٱلزَّكَوٰةَ وَٱلۡمُوفُونَ بِعَهۡدِهِمۡ إِذَا عَٰهَدُواْۖ وَٱلصَّٰبِرِينَ فِى ٱلۡبَأۡسَآءِ وَٱلضَّرَّآءِ وَحِينَ ٱلۡبَأۡسِۗ أُوْلَٰٓئِكَ ٱلَّذِينَ صَدَقُواْۖ وَأُوْلَٰٓئِكَ هُمُ ٱلۡمُتَّقُونَ ۝

It is not righteousness {albirra} that ye turn your faces to the East and the West;
but righteous is he who believeth in God and the Last Day
And the angels and the Scripture and the prophets;
And giveth wealth, for love of Him, to kinsfolk and to orphans and the needy
And the wayfarer and to those who ask,
And to set slaves free;
And observeth proper worship and payeth the poor-due.
And those who keep their treaty when they make one,
And the patient in tribulation and adversity and in time of stress.
Such are they who are sincere. Such are the God-fearing.[492]

لَن تَنَالُواْ ٱلۡبِرَّ حَتَّىٰ تُنفِقُواْ مِمَّا تُحِبُّونَۚ وَمَا تُنفِقُواْ مِن شَىۡءٍ فَإِنَّ ٱللَّهَ بِهِۦ عَلِيمٌ ۝

Ye will not attain unto piety {albirra} until ye spend of that which ye love.
And whatsoever ye spend, God is Aware thereof[493]

The Divine Attribute *Barr* is paired with Mercy *Raheem* in the Quran, characterizing the quality of giving, gifting, caring and kindness attached to *Al Barr*.

We will face God, as do we face God now, with our imperfections and wants, falling short and having fallen short. We would have no claim to paradise if it were not for God's Mercy and for the Divine promise to reward the smallest grain of good:

---

492 Al Quran 2:177 as interpreted by Pickthal
493 Al Quran 3:92 as interpreted by Pickthal

وَٱلَّذِينَ ءَامَنُوا۟ وَٱتَّبَعَتْهُمْ ذُرِّيَّتُهُم بِإِيمَـٰنٍ أَلْحَقْنَا بِهِمْ ذُرِّيَّتَهُمْ وَمَآ أَلَتْنَـٰهُم مِّنْ عَمَلِهِم مِّن شَىْءٍ ۚ كُلُّ ٱمْرِئٍ بِمَا كَسَبَ رَهِينٌ ﴿٢١﴾ وَأَمْدَدْنَـٰهُم بِفَـٰكِهَةٍ وَلَحْمٍ مِّمَّا يَشْتَهُونَ ﴿٢٢﴾ يَتَنَـٰزَعُونَ فِيهَا كَأْسًا لَّا لَغْوٌ فِيهَا وَلَا تَأْثِيمٌ ﴿٢٣﴾ وَيَطُوفُ عَلَيْهِمْ غِلْمَانٌ لَّهُمْ كَأَنَّهُمْ لُؤْلُؤٌ مَّكْنُونٌ ﴿٢٤﴾ وَأَقْبَلَ بَعْضُهُمْ عَلَىٰ بَعْضٍ يَتَسَآءَلُونَ ﴿٢٥﴾ قَالُوٓا۟ إِنَّا كُنَّا قَبْلُ فِىٓ أَهْلِنَا مُشْفِقِينَ ﴿٢٦﴾ فَمَنَّ ٱللَّهُ عَلَيْنَا وَوَقَىٰنَا عَذَابَ ٱلسَّمُومِ ﴿٢٧﴾ إِنَّا كُنَّا مِن قَبْلُ نَدْعُوهُ ۖ إِنَّهُۥ هُوَ ٱلْبَرُّ ٱلرَّحِيمُ ﴿٢٨﴾

As for those who believe and whose progeny follow them in faith
We will join them with their progeny
and We will diminish from their deeds naught,
Each individual is pledged for what he has earned.
And We will offer to them fruits and meats as they wish.
They will pass with fervor a goblet there free from frivolity, indecency or sin.
And making rounds, servants will attend upon them as if they were treasured pearls.
And they will turn to each other, sharing and confiding:
"In life, we with our household were anxious and fearful
witness God's Grace has rid us (of angst).
God has shielded us from the fiery winds
Him, indeed we sought, heretofore!"
God is Generous in reward, the most Merciful { Barr ur Raheem} [494]

81. *At Tawwab*   The Acceptor of Repentance.

The One who restores grace upon those who after having lost their way, return to Him. The One who encourages repentance and is oft-forgiving. Derived from the root *t-w-b*, *Tawwab* is co-rooted with *Tauba*, translated as 'repentance'.

Sincere repentance will efface a past wrong. The wrong that cannot be undone can become an opportunity to bring change. The heart, hardened by past abuse and callousness, can soften itself with earnest repentance. Sincere repentance allows us to purify the heart and re-calibrate and realign our life-quest.

يَـٰٓأَيُّهَا ٱلَّذِينَ ءَامَنُوا تُوبُوٓا إِلَى ٱللَّهِ تَوْبَةً نَّصُوحًا عَسَىٰ رَبُّكُمْ أَن يُكَفِّرَ عَنكُمْ سَيِّـَٔاتِكُمْ
وَيُدْخِلَكُمْ جَنَّـٰتٍ تَجْرِى مِن تَحْتِهَا ٱلْأَنْهَـٰرُ يَوْمَ لَا يُخْزِى ٱللَّهُ ٱلنَّبِىَّ وَٱلَّذِينَ ءَامَنُوا مَعَهُۥ
نُورُهُمْ يَسْعَىٰ بَيْنَ أَيْدِيهِمْ وَبِأَيْمَـٰنِهِمْ يَقُولُونَ رَبَّنَآ أَتْمِمْ لَنَا نُورَنَا وَٱغْفِرْ لَنَآ إِنَّكَ عَلَىٰ
كُلِّ شَىْءٍ قَدِيرٌ ۝

O people of faith, turn to God in earnest repentance.
It may be that your Sustainer will efface your dark deeds.
And bring you into Gardens sustained by profuse and pure rivers,
on the day when God will not let down the Prophet
and those who believe with him.
Their light will project ahead of them and to their right
they will say: Our Sustainer! Perfect our light for us, and forgive us!
Indeed you hold power over all things[495]

Mercy and forgiveness are Divine traits. To forgive and seek forgiveness is to be aligned with this Divine Pathway. Abraham prayed to God to accept his physical labor as worship, and his physical offering, the *Kaabah*, as a place of refuge and repair for the burdened and broken heart. The pilgrim seeking to repair and purify the heart, undertakes the journey to purge false pursuits and break from false attachments. He or she comes to the divinely blessed portal of forgiveness and healing, introspectively. This portal offers the opportunity to be fully cleansed.

وَإِذْ يَرْفَعُ إِبْرَٰهِـۧمُ ٱلْقَوَاعِدَ مِنَ ٱلْبَيْتِ وَإِسْمَـٰعِيلُ رَبَّنَا تَقَبَّلْ مِنَّآ إِنَّكَ أَنتَ ٱلسَّمِيعُ ٱلْعَلِيمُ
۝ رَبَّنَا وَٱجْعَلْنَا مُسْلِمَيْنِ لَكَ وَمِن ذُرِّيَّتِنَآ أُمَّةً مُّسْلِمَةً لَّكَ وَأَرِنَا مَنَاسِكَنَا وَتُبْ عَلَيْنَآ إِنَّكَ
أَنتَ ٱلتَّوَّابُ ٱلرَّحِيمُ ۝ رَبَّنَا وَٱبْعَثْ فِيهِمْ رَسُولًا مِّنْهُمْ يَتْلُوا عَلَيْهِمْ ءَايَـٰتِكَ وَيُعَلِّمُهُمُ
ٱلْكِتَـٰبَ وَٱلْحِكْمَةَ وَيُزَكِّيهِمْ إِنَّكَ أَنتَ ٱلْعَزِيزُ ٱلْحَكِيمُ ۝

And when Abraham was raising the foundations of the House along with
Ishmael
[He prayed] "Our Sustainer accept from us
Without doubt You are the All-Hearing and the All-Knowing
Our Lord may in submission to You we be
And may from our progeny be a nation in submission to You
And show us the rites of worship and be forgiving of us
You are Most Forgiving and Merciful {Tawwab-ur-Raheem}
Our Lord raise a messenger from amongst them

---

495 Al Quran 66:8

who will unfold for them Your signs
and teach them the Book of Wisdom and purify them
You are All Mighty and have Complete Wisdom {Azeezul-Hakeem} [496]

82. *Al Muntaqim*   The Avenger. The One who exacts retribution.

This name is derived from the root *nqm*. This name is not specifically used as a Beautiful Name in the Quran, although co-rooted words such as *iqaab* (punishment) and *intiqaam* (retribution) are. Those in rebellious denial of God will find a reckoning.

فَلَا تَحْسَبَنَّ ٱللَّهَ مُخْلِفَ وَعْدِهِۦ رُسُلَهُۥٓ إِنَّ ٱللَّهَ عَزِيزٌ ذُو ٱنتِقَامٍ ۝

So think not that God will fail to keep His promise to His messengers.
Lo! God is Mighty, Able to requite (the wrong) {zun tiqaam}. [497]

Judgment, recompense and retribution {*tiqaam*} are under Divine purview. Those with faith, seeking God's assent must resist and release the impulse of personal revenge and vengeance. The God-fearing heart must persevere. The impure heart must pass through the chastening of fire.

وَذَرْنِى وَٱلْمُكَذِّبِينَ أُوْلِى ٱلنَّعْمَةِ وَمَهِّلْهُمْ قَلِيلًا ۝ إِنَّ لَدَيْنَآ أَنكَالًا وَجَحِيمًا ۝

And leave me alone [to deal] with those who give lie to the truth
those who enjoy the blessings of this life [without any thought of God]
and bear though with them for a while;
for behold heavy fetters [await them] with Us, and a blazing fire. [498]

Al Muntaqim and *Al 'Afuw* are complementary attributes of *Tanzih* and *Tasbih*. These attributes bear both the warning of dispassionate accountability of one's actions and the hope of forgiveness flowing from a compassionate Sovereign. The warning is a reminder to guard against the evil of an ego misguided by its pride and arrogance. The hope is an invitation to the joy of heavenly peace and love. Fear of God softens the heart. Hope fills it and expands it.

تَنزِيلُ ٱلْكِتَـٰبِ مِنَ ٱللَّهِ ٱلْعَزِيزِ ٱلْعَلِيمِ ۝ غَافِرِ ٱلذَّنۢبِ وَقَابِلِ ٱلتَّوْبِ شَدِيدِ ٱلْعِقَابِ ذِى
ٱلطَّوْلِ لَآ إِلَـٰهَ إِلَّا هُوَ إِلَيْهِ ٱلْمَصِيرُ ۝

This Book has been revealed by God
Exalted Almighty, The Source of Knowledge
Who forgives sin {Ghafiriz zambi}

---

496 Al Quran 2:127-129
497 Al Quran 14:47 as interpreted by Pickthall
498 Al Quran 73:11-12

And accepts repentance {qabilit tawbi}
Is stern in Punishment {shadedil iqaabi}
And infinite in Bounty {zit tawl}
There is no god but He. Unto Him is the journeying[499]

83. *Al 'Afuw*   The Pardoner. The One Who washes away sins.

Man is imperfect and without full control over his self. He is therefore apt to forget and err. Absolute Control belongs to the Forgiving God. We cannot call back a hurtful deed, a self-serving thought, an un-grateful attitude, a rebuking word, a pompous gloat, a callous indifference, the disdain of pride and arrogance. We would stand condemned, in the darkness of our own devise, away from the Light (of God) were it not for Willing Divine Absolution. *Al 'Afuw* allows good works to burnish a rusted heart, effacing its blemishes.

Afuw, Ghafoor and *Ghaffar* are Divine attributes that encourage and facilitate retraction and spiritual realignment. *Ghafoor* and *Ghaffar* convey forgiveness and insulation (from sinning), while *Afuw* conveys complete obliteration of a dark condition. *Ghaffar* and *Ghafoor* beckon an errant soul to its realignment to the 'Straight Path'. *Afuw* brings ascension to the soul seeking redemption from the vortex of its waywardness.

إِن تُبْدُواْ خَيْرًا أَوْ تُخْفُوهُ أَوْ تَعْفُواْ عَن سُوءٍ فَإِنَّ ٱللَّهَ كَانَ عَفُوًّا قَدِيرًا ۩

Whether you do good in open or in private or you pardon an evil
Indeed God is the granter of absolution, Absolute in Power and Ability
{Aafuwwan Qadeer}[500]

84. *Ar Ra'uf*   The Gentle. The Kind and Affectionate.

Ra'uf is often paired in the Quran with Divine Mercy, *Raheem*. It is the Divine Attribute of caring, tenderness and affection—the qualitative aspects of Divine Mercy. God cares about what happens to us. God's messengers and the signs borne by them along with the signs of nature are manifestations of Divine Caring. Out of kindness and affection to man, God has made the earth subservient to him. The earth yields itself to man and makes herself pliant to man being profited by her:

499 Al Quran 40:1-3
500 Al Quran 4:149

أَلَمْ تَرَ أَنَّ ٱللَّهَ سَخَّرَ لَكُم مَّا فِي ٱلْأَرْضِ وَٱلْفُلْكَ تَجْرِي فِي ٱلْبَحْرِ بِأَمْرِهِۦ وَيُمْسِكُ ٱلسَّمَآءَ أَن تَقَعَ عَلَى ٱلْأَرْضِ إِلَّا بِإِذْنِهِۦٓ إِنَّ ٱللَّهَ بِٱلنَّاسِ لَرَءُوفٌ رَّحِيمٌ ۝

Hast thou not seen how God hath made all that is in the earth subservient unto you? And the ship runneth upon the sea by His command, and He holdeth back the heaven from falling on the earth unless by His leave.
Lo! God is, for mankind, Full of Pity, Merciful. {Rauf Ur Raheem} [501]

The Quran also ascribes the qualities of caring and mercy to the prophet himself, who, beyond the affection and caring for his followers, was pained by the nagging thought of fearful accountability awaiting the detractors of his message:

لَقَدْ جَآءَكُمْ رَسُولٌ مِّنْ أَنفُسِكُمْ عَزِيزٌ عَلَيْهِ مَا عَنِتُّمْ حَرِيصٌ عَلَيْكُم بِٱلْمُؤْمِنِينَ رَءُوفٌ رَّحِيمٌ ۝

Now has come to you a messenger from amongst yourselves.
It grieves him that you should come to ruin; full of concern for you; full of kindness and mercy towards the believers. {Rauf Ur raheem} [502]

God declares His own caring and mercy towards the Prophet who cared for others:

هُوَ ٱلَّذِي يُنَزِّلُ عَلَىٰ عَبْدِهِۦٓ ءَايَٰتٍ بَيِّنَٰتٍ لِّيُخْرِجَكُم مِّنَ ٱلظُّلُمَٰتِ إِلَى ٱلنُّورِ وَإِنَّ ٱللَّهَ بِكُمْ لَرَءُوفٌ رَّحِيمٌ ۝

He is the One Who sends to His Servant Manifest Signs, that He may lead you out from darknesses into the Light and indeed to you God is most Kind and Merciful. {Rauf Ur Raheem} [503]

85. *Maalik ul Mulk*   The Eternal Owner of Sovereignty

Mulk is translated as sovereignty, and *Maalik* (co-rooted with *Malik*, which means sovereign) carries a meaning deeper and higher than 'sovereign'. It implies Ownership and Absolute Right. It is God who conveys and recalls sovereignty. It is God who assigns and withdraws rank and station. There is no other claimant to this right and therefore the Absolute Sovereign guarantees, that "every soul will be paid in full what it hath earned, and they will not be wronged." The

---

501 Al Quran 22:65 as interpreted by Pickthall
502 Al Quran 9:128
503 Al Quran 57:9

submissive heart seeks not to claim the Truth. It cannot and therefore must seek to belong to it. In Oneness it must become a conduit for the Divine Purpose, in the knowledge that it is no more.

فَكَيْفَ إِذَا جَمَعْنَـٰهُمْ لِيَوْمٍ لَّا رَيْبَ فِيهِ وَوُفِّيَتْ كُلُّ نَفْسٍ مَّا كَسَبَتْ وَهُمْ لَا يُظْلَمُونَ ۝ قُلِ ٱللَّهُمَّ مَـٰلِكَ ٱلْمُلْكِ تُؤْتِي ٱلْمُلْكَ مَن تَشَآءُ وَتَنزِعُ ٱلْمُلْكَ مِمَّن تَشَآءُ وَتُعِزُّ مَن تَشَآءُ وَتُذِلُّ مَن تَشَآءُ ۖ بِيَدِكَ ٱلْخَيْرُ ۖ إِنَّكَ عَلَىٰ كُلِّ شَىْءٍ قَدِيرٌ ۝

How (will it be with them) when We have brought them all together to a Day of which there is no doubt, when every soul will be paid in full what it hath earned, and they will not be wronged.
Say: O God! Owner of Sovereignty! {Maalik-ul-Mulk}. Thou givest sovereignty unto whom Thou wilt, and Thou withdrawest sovereignty from whom Thou wilt. Thou exaltest whom Thou wilt, and Thou abasest whom Thou wilt. In Thy hand is the good. Lo! Thou art Able to do all things. [504]

86.   *Dhul Jalaal wal Ikraam* The Lord of overwhelming Majesty, Most Bounteous and Generous.

Jalaal takes root from *JLL*, meaning Power, Majesty and Glory. *Ikraam* refers to the abundance of bounty and favors, generously granted. This Divine name joins the attributes of *Tanzih* and *Tasbih*. The manifested power of the One exposes our insignificance and finitude. Human arrogance is misfounded. God's Grace and Generosity are transcendental, and the heart that is blind to them, squanders Divine Love. God is to be both feared and loved. Divine Power and Majesty are both pulverizing and nurturing. God invites us to Divine Majesty and Grace. The God-fearing heart cannot be left outside of Divine Peace and Benevolence.

كُلُّ مَنْ عَلَيْهَا فَانٍ ۝ وَيَبْقَىٰ وَجْهُ رَبِّكَ ذُو ٱلْجَلَـٰلِ وَٱلْإِكْرَامِ ۝

All that is in (existence) is to perish
But forever will remain the Face of your Sustainer
full of Majesty and Grace {Dhul Jalaali wal Ikraam} [505]

Co-rooted with *Ikraam* are the attributes of *Akram* (bounteous) and *Kareem* (generous giver). *Akram* is recalled in reference to the bounty of the Quran itself— A bounty too laden for the mountains and too voluminous for oceans of ink; befitting the heart that drinks from the Fountain of Peace. The more the heart drinks the more shall the Fountain yield.

---

504 Al Quran 3:25-26 as interpreted by Pickthall
505 Al Quran 55:26-27

اقْرَأْ بِاسْمِ رَبِّكَ الَّذِى خَلَقَ ۞ خَلَقَ الْإِنسَانَ مِنْ عَلَقٍ ۞ اقْرَأْ وَرَبُّكَ الْأَكْرَمُ ۞

"Recite in the name of your Sustainer, He created.
Created mankind from a clot
Recite! Your Sustainer is The Most Bounteous {Akram}.[506]

87. *Al Muqsit*   The Equitable. The One who bestows harmony and
balance.

This Beautiful Name is not mentioned specifically, but the Quran specifically invites us to share in this Divine Attribute. God loves those who are conscientious in the pursuit of justice and equity {*Muqsiteen*}.

سَمَّاعُونَ لِلْكَذِبِ أَكَّالُونَ لِلسُّحْتِ فَإِن جَآءُوكَ فَاحْكُم بَيْنَهُمْ أَوْ أَعْرِضْ عَنْهُمْ وَإِن
تُعْرِضْ عَنْهُمْ فَلَن يَضُرُّوكَ شَيْئًا وَإِنْ حَكَمْتَ فَاحْكُم بَيْنَهُم بِالْقِسْطِ إِنَّ اللَّهَ يُحِبُّ
الْمُقْسِطِينَ ۞

Listeners for the sake of falsehood! Greedy for illicit gain!
If then they have recourse unto thee (Muhammad) judge between them or
disclaim jurisdiction. If thou disclaimest jurisdiction, then they cannot harm
thee at all. But if thou judgest, judge between them with equity.
Lo! God loveth the equitable. {Muqsiteen} [507]

لَّا يَنْهَاكُمُ اللَّهُ عَنِ الَّذِينَ لَمْ يُقَاتِلُوكُمْ فِى الدِّينِ وَلَمْ يُخْرِجُوكُم مِّن دِيَارِكُمْ أَن تَبَرُّوهُمْ
وَتُقْسِطُوا إِلَيْهِمْ إِنَّ اللَّهَ يُحِبُّ الْمُقْسِطِينَ ۞

God forbiddeth you not those who warred not against you on account of deen
and drove you not out from your homes, that ye should show them kindness and
deal justly with them. Lo! God loveth the just dealers. {Muqsiteen} [508]

88. *Al Jaame'*   The Gatherer.

The One who will gather us all into eternity, unto Himself. The absolute centripetal force that will pull all beings to Itself. The force that binds the universe and the force that will fold the universe.

If existence is on the circumference of a circle, God is at its center. The pathway to God is not along the circumference. From any point of the circumference, it

---

506 Al Quran 96:1-3
507 Al Quran 5:42 as interpreted by Pickthall
508 Al Quran 60:8 as interpreted by Pickthall

goes straight down the radius, to the Center. It is the nature of the connection between a ray of light and its source.

رَبَّنَا لَا تُزِغْ قُلُوبَنَا بَعْدَ إِذْ هَدَيْتَنَا وَهَبْ لَنَا مِن لَّدُنكَ رَحْمَةً إِنَّكَ أَنتَ ٱلْوَهَّابُ ۝ رَبَّنَآ إِنَّكَ جَامِعُ ٱلنَّاسِ لِيَوْمٍ لَّا رَيْبَ فِيهِ إِنَّ ٱللَّهَ لَا يُخْلِفُ ٱلْمِيعَادَ ۝

"Our Sustainer do not let our hearts deviate after You have guided us. And grant us Your Mercy for You, only You, are the Most Generous Bestower {Wahhaab}"
"Our Lord it is You Who will gather {Jaame'} us all on a day of which there is no doubt. For God never contravenes His promise"[509]

89. *Al Ghani*   The Independent.

Ghani signifies the Essence of God who is completely independent in His actions and attributes. God is without need, free from want, and the Owner of all there is to 'give' of goodness. He is the True and Only Owner of all wealth. He is the Fountain from which flow all treasures. *Mughni* which shares the same root word, *gh-n-y* refers to the Divine Will (giving) by the Giver, free of want, *Ghani.*

There is nothing that is ours. There is no "I" or "me" or "mine". Every precious live-sustaining breath is from God. Every heart-beat belongs to God. Every moment is bequeathed by God. We are the Master's slaves. God is *not* enhanced by worship, man *is.*

۞ يَٰٓأَيُّهَا ٱلنَّاسُ أَنتُمُ ٱلْفُقَرَآءُ إِلَى ٱللَّهِ وَٱللَّهُ هُوَ ٱلْغَنِىُّ ٱلْحَمِيدُ ۝

O mankind it is you that have need of God
But God is Free of all needs, {Ghani}
Rightful Owner of all Praise {Hameed}[510]

90. *Al Mughni*   The Enricher. The One who grants independence.

This name is not specifically used as a Beautiful Name in the Quran. *Mughni* shares its root word with *Ghani.* The former describes the Divine Will (action), while the latter is an attribute of Divine Essence {*Ism-e-Dhaat*}. The heart that gives unto others is a conduit of Divine Wealth.

91. *Al Maanay*   The Preventer.

The One with the power to block. The One with the power to refuse. The limits of existence, in form and term, as well as in birth and death, are determined by the permission and forbiddance of the Divine One. That which the One ordains,

---

509 Al Quran 3:8-9
510 Al Quran 35:15

no one can block. That which the One blocks no one can make happen. Sincerity and guile stand apart and the earnest heart knows the difference.

$$\text{وَهُوَ ٱلَّذِى مَرَجَ ٱلْبَحْرَيْنِ هَـٰذَا عَذْبٌ فُرَاتٌ وَهَـٰذَا مِلْحٌ أُجَاجٌ وَجَعَلَ بَيْنَهُمَا بَرْزَخًا وَحِجْرًا مَّحْجُورًا ۝}$$

AND HE it is who has given freedom of movement to the two great bodies of water
the one sweet and thirst-allaying, and the other salty and bitter -
and yet has wrought between them a barrier and a forbidding ban.[511]

92. *Al Daarr*   The Distresser.

The One with the power to bring adversity that none can avert. *Al Daarr* and *An Naafay* are complementary Names, which are not specifically mentioned in the Quran, although there is mention that harm and benefit is not within the power of any other. False gods can neither cause harm nor bring gain. God alone is to be feared and hope can be pinned on God alone. Life will be touched by both the abundance and color of spring and the destitution and desolation of winter. The ups and downs of life, like these seasonal cycles, must be taken in the proper perspective. Winter is the test of faith and spring is the test of gratitude.

$$\text{وَيَعْبُدُونَ مِن دُونِ ٱللَّهِ مَا لَا يَضُرُّهُمْ وَلَا يَنفَعُهُمْ وَيَقُولُونَ هَـٰٓؤُلَآءِ شُفَعَـٰٓؤُنَا عِندَ ٱللَّهِ ۚ قُلْ أَتُنَبِّـُٔونَ ٱللَّهَ بِمَا لَا يَعْلَمُ فِى ٱلسَّمَـٰوَٰتِ وَلَا فِى ٱلْأَرْضِ ۚ سُبْحَـٰنَهُۥ وَتَعَـٰلَىٰ عَمَّا يُشْرِكُونَ ۝}$$

They worship beside God that which neither hurteth them {la yaduruhum} nor profiteth them {la yanfaoohum}, and they say: These are our intercessors with God. Say: Would ye inform God of (something) that He knoweth not in the heavens or in the earth? Praised be He and High Exalted above all that ye associate (with Him)! [512]

$$\text{وَإِذَا مَسَّ ٱلْإِنسَـٰنَ ٱلضُّرُّ دَعَانَا لِجَنبِهِۦٓ أَوْ قَاعِدًا أَوْ قَآئِمًا فَلَمَّا كَشَفْنَا عَنْهُ ضُرَّهُۥ مَرَّ كَأَن لَّمْ يَدْعُنَآ إِلَىٰ ضُرٍّ مَّسَّهُۥ ۚ كَذَٰلِكَ زُيِّنَ لِلْمُسْرِفِينَ مَا كَانُوا۟ يَعْمَلُونَ ۝}$$

And when misfortune touches a man he cries unto Us, (while reclining) on his side, or sitting or standing, but when We have relieved him of the misfortune he

---

511 Al Quran 25:53
512 Al Quran 10:18

goes on as though he had not cried unto Us because of a misfortune that afflicted him. Thus is what they do made (seeming) fair unto the prodigal.[513]

93. *An Naafay*   The Propitious.

The One by Whom there is beneficial gain. *Al Daarr* and *An Naafay* are complementary attributes. Faith will not avert the changing seasons of life; it must embrace them because change offers renewal. Despondency and despair, in the face of adversity; and ingratitude and arrogance, when the winds are favorable; are both misplaced and akin to disbelief. Adversity is not to be construed as Divine punishment, but rather as a Divine reminder (or test). Adversity, as exemplified by the prophets who faced it, offers purification and bears the test of faith. Loss sweetens the coming gain.

وَأَنْ أَقِمْ وَجْهَكَ لِلدِّينِ حَنِيفًا وَلَا تَكُونَنَّ مِنَ ٱلْمُشْرِكِينَ ۞ وَلَا تَدْعُ مِن دُونِ ٱللَّهِ مَا لَا يَنفَعُكَ وَلَا يَضُرُّكَ ۚ فَإِن فَعَلْتَ فَإِنَّكَ إِذًا مِّنَ ٱلظَّٰلِمِينَ ۞ وَإِن يَمْسَسْكَ ٱللَّهُ بِضُرٍّ فَلَا كَاشِفَ لَهُۥ إِلَّا هُوَ ۖ وَإِن يُرِدْكَ بِخَيْرٍ فَلَا رَآدَّ لِفَضْلِهِۦ ۚ يُصِيبُ بِهِۦ مَن يَشَآءُ مِنْ عِبَادِهِۦ ۚ وَهُوَ ٱلْغَفُورُ ٱلرَّحِيمُ ۞

And further (thus): 'set thy face towards deen *with true piety, and never in any wise be of the Unbelievers;*
Nor call on any, other than God; Such will neither profit thee nor hurt thee.
If thou dost, behold! thou shalt certainly be of those who do wrong.
If God do touch thee with hurt, there is none can remove it but He
if He do design some benefit for thee, there is none can keep back His favour:
He causeth it to reach whomsoever of His servants He pleaseth.
And He is the Oft-Forgiving, Most Merciful. [514]

Says Rumi about life's embrace of joy and sorrow, friendship and adversity:

This being human is a guest house.
Every morning is a new arrival.
A joy, a depression, meanness,
some momentary awareness comes as an unexpected visitor.
Welcome and entertain them all!
Even if they're a crowd of sorrows, who violently sweep your house empty of its furniture,
still, treat each guest honorably.

---

513 Al Quran 10:12
514 Al Quran 10:105-107 as interpreted by Yusuf Ali

He may be clearing you out for some new delight.
The dark thought, the shame, the malice,
meet them at the door laughing, and invite them in.
Be grateful for whoever comes, because each has been sent as a guide from beyond. [515]

94. *An Noor*   The Light.

God is the One who clears away all darkness and doubt and fills the heart with the luminous Truth. The 'Light Verse" which is one of the longest single verses in the Quran, has a special appeal to the Sufis, for its contemplative richness. A Divine Invitation to the searching soul, to contemplate the breathtaking possibilities of the quest:

$$ ۞ ٱللَّهُ نُورُ ٱلسَّمَٰوَٰتِ وَٱلْأَرْضِ ۚ مَثَلُ نُورِهِۦ كَمِشْكَوٰةٍ فِيهَا مِصْبَاحٌ ۖ ٱلْمِصْبَاحُ فِى زُجَاجَةٍ ۖ ٱلزُّجَاجَةُ كَأَنَّهَا كَوْكَبٌ دُرِّىٌّ يُوقَدُ مِن شَجَرَةٍ مُّبَٰرَكَةٍ زَيْتُونَةٍ لَّا شَرْقِيَّةٍ وَلَا غَرْبِيَّةٍ يَكَادُ زَيْتُهَا يُضِىٓءُ وَلَوْ لَمْ تَمْسَسْهُ نَارٌ ۚ نُّورٌ عَلَىٰ نُورٍ ۗ يَهْدِى ٱللَّهُ لِنُورِهِۦ مَن يَشَآءُ ۚ وَيَضْرِبُ ٱللَّهُ ٱلْأَمْثَٰلَ لِلنَّاسِ ۗ وَٱللَّهُ بِكُلِّ شَىْءٍ عَلِيمٌ ۝ $$

God is the Radiance {Noor} of the heavens and of the earth.
The likeness of His radiance is that of a niche, wherein is a flame (lamp).
The flame enclosed within polished glass, the glass like a celestial star,
brilliantly crystalline.
Lit by (the oil) of a blessed Olive Tree, (heavenly), neither of the East nor of the
West
Near incandescent is the oil even though the flame touches it not.
Light upon light.
God guides to His light whosoever He will.
God presents mankind with insightful examples.
God has complete knowledge of all things. [516]

One niche is the spiritual heart, holding the lamp of the Divine Spark. Sincere faith and knowledge ensuing from such faith may well be the ignitable oil. The glass enclosure would then be the earnestness of the spiritual quest. What would be left when there is light upon light? Only Light; the niche no more; selfhood annihilated. The Source and Goal of the spirit are the same:

---

515 The Illuminated Rumi, Translated by Coleman Barks, New York Broadway Books, 1997
516 Al Quran 24 :35

فَإِذَا سَوَّيۡتُهُۥ وَنَفَخۡتُ فِيهِ مِن رُّوحِى فَقَعُواْ لَهُۥ سَٰجِدِينَ ۝

*When I have fashioned him (Adam) and breathed into him of My Spirit (Ruh)
Then fall down prostrating yourselves to him*[517]

I am also including here Lex Hixon's meditative rendering of the Light Verse.
Appropriately, the enlightened Sufi's first name is Nur:

Calling itself Allah, the Supreme Source is the One Light illuminating every heavenly
and earthly realm. My beloved Muhammad, please transmit this profound meditation.
The Light of Allah is the window that opens beyond all Creation. On the sill of this
shining window rests the precious lamp of the human soul, whose flame is pure and
steady, protected by the transparent crystal of the heart that glistens delicately, like a
star, with the souls light. This lamp, ignited by Divine Love alone, burns aromatic oil
from the Tree of Life, that transcendent Tree found no where on earth, neither in the
East nor in the West. This fragrant oil of wisdom radiates illumination spontaneously,
not needing to be touched by earthly fire. Thus the light of the soul and the Source of
Light behind it blend, merge, and reappear in the mystery of eternal companionship, as
the Light of Allah, within the Light of Allah. Speaking thus to humanity through the
most subtle figurative language, the Source of Wisdom guides to enlightenment
whomever It wills, for Allah is the One encompassing Awareness.[518]

95. *Al Haadi*   The Guide.

The One who has laid down the *deen*. The One who clears our doubts and guides
the heart. The One who leads us from darknesses to Light, from error to Grace
and from delusion to Truth. To receive the Divine Light, the heart must thirst
(open itself):

إِنَّ ٱللَّهَ لَا يُغَيِّرُ مَا بِقَوۡمٍ حَتَّىٰ يُغَيِّرُواْ مَا بِأَنفُسِهِمۡ

*Surely the Almighty changes not the condition of a people unless they change
that which is in them.*[519]

The sincere quest is never rejected and the heart *will* be purified, so that it
becomes free of strife and filled with gratitude:

مَا يُرِيدُ ٱللَّهُ لِيَجۡعَلَ عَلَيۡكُم مِّنۡ حَرَجٍ وَلَٰكِن يُرِيدُ لِيُطَهِّرَكُمۡ وَلِيُتِمَّ نِعۡمَتَهُۥ عَلَيۡكُمۡ لَعَلَّكُمۡ
تَشۡكُرُونَ ۝

God desires not to place a hardship on you

---

517 Al Quran 15:29
518 *The Heart of the Quran. An introduction to Islamic Spirituality* by Lex Hixon
519 Al Quran 13:11

He desires to purify you and to complete His favor upon you,
so that you may be thankful. [520]

God helps us by guiding us. The quest and effort must be our own. God helps us *not* by changing universal laws but by giving us the strength and fortitude to face the setbacks and obstacles that we must over come and circum-navigate. Obstacles and setbacks are part of the learning process. God did not remove the obstacles faced by the prophets. Instead, God gave them strength and succor by which they prevailed.

وَيَوْمَ يَعَضُّ ٱلظَّالِمُ عَلَىٰ يَدَيْهِ يَقُولُ يَٰلَيْتَنِى ٱتَّخَذْتُ مَعَ ٱلرَّسُولِ سَبِيلاً ۝ يَٰوَيْلَتَىٰ لَيْتَنِى لَمْ أَتَّخِذْ فُلَانًا خَلِيلاً ۝ لَقَدْ أَضَلَّنِى عَنِ ٱلذِّكْرِ بَعْدَ إِذْ جَآءَنِى وَكَانَ ٱلشَّيْطَٰنُ لِلْإِنسَٰنِ خَذُولاً ۝ وَقَالَ ٱلرَّسُولُ يَٰرَبِّ إِنَّ قَوْمِى ٱتَّخَذُواْ هَٰذَا ٱلْقُرْءَانَ مَهْجُورًا ۝ وَكَذَٰلِكَ جَعَلْنَا لِكُلِّ نَبِىٍّ عَدُوًّا مِّنَ ٱلْمُجْرِمِينَ وَكَفَىٰ بِرَبِّكَ هَادِيًا وَنَصِيرًا ۝

The day (of judgment) the wrong doer will bite his hands and lament:
"If only I had followed the messenger. Alas if I had not chosen the friends I chose. It was he that misled me away from the message after it had come to me. Satan is a traitor to man."
And the messenger will say: "O my Lord my people were neglectful of this Quran"
Thus have We made adversaries to every prophet from amongst the wrongdoers
But sufficient is your Lord as a Guide {Haadi} and Helper {Naseer}. [521]

96. *Al Badi'*   The Inventor.

The Inventing-Creator, Whose invention is unique and Whose every invention manifests immanence. Each of God's creations and each creature symbolize Divine invention, because each creature is 'new' by its uniqueness. No two human beings on earth as any two fish in the water, as no two waters, are the same. No two particles or stars in the galaxy are the same. Our reality too is the Inventor's handiwork. God designed space. God made matter become. God made time happen. As vicegerents and co-creators on earth, we create something from something else. We transform matter to energy and coal to diamonds. We are transformers, and our own ingenuity has been invented by the One, Who creates from nothing and into 'individualness'.

---

520 Al Quran 5:6
521 Al Quran 25:27-31

بَدِيعُ ٱلسَّمَـٰوَٰتِ وَٱلۡأَرۡضِ ۖ وَإِذَا قَضَىٰٓ أَمۡرٗا فَإِنَّمَا يَقُولُ لَهُۥ كُن فَيَكُونُ ۝

The Originator {Badi} of the heavens and the earth
And when He decrees a matter, He only says to it, "Be" and it is.[522]

97. *Al Baaqi* The Everlasting. The Permanent and Pure Being.

The Creator of time and term, who Himself transcends time and term and whose capacity for new creation is never exhausted or diminished. For us who must operate in time and space, eternity must remain a fascinating mystery. The Majesty of the 'presence of God' eviscerates all self-hood and outside the Majesty of God can exist nothing but the abyss of emptiness. This Divine Name is not specifically used in the Quran, but the co-rooted word *'abqaa'* meaning eternal is mentioned in the Quran.

كُلُّ مَنۡ عَلَيۡهَا فَانٍ ۝ وَيَبۡقَىٰ وَجۡهُ رَبِّكَ ذُو ٱلۡجَلَٰلِ وَٱلۡإِكۡرَامِ ۝

All that is (in existence) is to perish
But forever will remain {wa abqaa} the Face of your Sustainer full of Majesty and Grace[523]

God as first and last, inner and outer leaves no other possibility than the Wholeness of Unity. Creatures are _not_ divine and yet creatures cannot exist separate from God. What is this 'Separated Union'? These conundrums of the mind are mere distractions for the heart. Every step advances longing; nearness too is infinite!

Another co-rooted word *Baqaa* refers to eternal life, more particularly to that which gets transferred to the realm of eternal life. The thoughts and deeds, conceived and executed, in the earnest intention of submission to God are the eternal capital of our existence. The complement of *Baqaa* is *Fanaa* (annihilation). We cannot know God until we have dissolved all selfhood in the Divine.

98. *Al Warith* The Inheritor. The One to whom will return all
creatures and things.

وَإِنَّا لَنَحۡنُ نُحۡيِۦ وَنُمِيتُ وَنَحۡنُ ٱلۡوَٰرِثُونَ ۝

It is We who give life and who cause death
And We who are the Inheritors {Warithoon}.[524]

---

522 Al Quran 2:117
523 Al Quran 55:27
524 Al Quran 15:23

إِنَّا نَحْنُ نَرِثُ ٱلْأَرْضَ وَمَنْ عَلَيْهَا وَإِلَيْنَا يُرْجَعُونَ ۝

Lo! We, only We, inherit the earth and all who are thereon, and unto Us they are returned. [525]

God does not quibble with man's desire for children and wealth. These assets are trusts from God and are to be valued as such. The measure of our transcendental success lies neither in our progeny nor in what we materially bequeath to them, but in the purpose and cause that we assign to all our God-given assets.

وَزَكَرِيَّآ إِذْ نَادَىٰ رَبَّهُ رَبِّ لَا تَذَرْنِي فَرْدًا وَأَنتَ خَيْرُ ٱلْوَٰرِثِينَ ۝

And Zakariya', invoked his Lord,
My Lord! Do not leave me alone (childless), though You are the best inheritor. [526]

All that there is, is God's and reverts to God. In the same vein is the following exhortation:

وَمَا لَكُمْ أَلَّا تُنفِقُوا۟ فِى سَبِيلِ ٱللَّهِ وَلِلَّهِ مِيرَٰثُ ٱلسَّمَٰوَٰتِ وَٱلْأَرْضِ

And why should you not spend freely in the cause of God seeing that God's [alone] is the heritage of the heavens and the earth {mirasus samawati wal ard} [527]

99. Ar Rahseed — The One Who has appointed the Right Path.

Rahseed defines righteousness and the direction to the Truth. This Divine Name is close in meaning to *Haadi*, the constant Guide who leads the Way. Each creature has a direct connection with God and the relationship with God is intimate, without intermediaries. Spiritual consciousness and awareness are therefore always within the reach of the earnest heart. This Divine Name is not specifically used in the Quran but its co-rooted words, *Rushd* and *Murshid* are mentioned in the story of the young men who take refuge in a cave to preserve their faith. In the cave, secluded from the outside world, their faith remains pure and firm even after years of sleep. God anchors in righteousness those who seek Him. The heart that seeks affinity with God will find guidance—whether awake or asleep.

إِذْ أَوَى ٱلْفِتْيَةُ إِلَى ٱلْكَهْفِ فَقَالُوا۟ رَبَّنَآ ءَاتِنَا مِن لَّدُنكَ رَحْمَةً وَهَيِّئْ لَنَا مِنْ أَمْرِنَا رَشَدًا ۝

When the young men took refuge in the cave they said:

525 Al Quran 19:40
526 Al Quran 21:89
527 Al Quran 57:10

"Our Sustainer, Grant us mercy from You, and deliver to us, in our affairs, a right course {Rushd}" [528]

Submission to God demands that guidance be sought from God. It is then that our innermost sacred voice is the voice of God. He or she who has shutoff the inner voice of conscience has shut off God. Until the heart has not been lit with Divine Guidance, even the *Murshid* is of no avail:

$$مَن يَهْدِ ٱللَّهُ فَهُوَ ٱلْمُهْتَدِ ۖ وَمَن يُضْلِلْ فَلَن تَجِدَ لَهُ وَلِيًّا مُّرْشِدًا ﴿١٧﴾$$

"...he who God guides is guided and he who He lets fall in error, you shall not find for him any friend or teacher {Murshid}" [529]

100. *As Saboor*   The Patient and grantor of patience.

Because God transcends time and because patience finds context in time only, this attribute is not one of Divine Essence but a Divine quality in context to creation. For everything that is created, there is a defined term. God is patient, in that God withholds retribution and personal accountability until the end of the term. Within this term, it is therefore never too late for man to repent. Patience, in the face of adversity and setbacks, is also that human trait which strengthens the heart. Pain itself is the catalyst for spiritual growth. Pain to the self brings in the beauty of introspection and pain to a loved one brings out the beauty of giving. Pain can bring faith to the fore. Repeatedly, the Quran exhorts the believer to fortify faith with patience and good deeds. It is attributed to Ali that "Time spans two days; a day, when it is on your side, and a day when it bears adversity. When it is with you, give thanks to God and when it is against you, be patient and persevere."

$$وَٱلْعَصْرِ ﴿١﴾ إِنَّ ٱلْإِنسَٰنَ لَفِى خُسْرٍ ﴿٢﴾ إِلَّا ٱلَّذِينَ ءَامَنُوا۟ وَعَمِلُوا۟ ٱلصَّٰلِحَٰتِ وَتَوَاصَوْا۟ بِٱلْحَقِّ وَتَوَاصَوْا۟ بِٱلصَّبْرِ ﴿٣﴾$$

As certain as a days waning,
A man's worth comes to naught except he be of those in the pursuit of faith and righteous deeds, and embraces truth, and embraces patience. {sabr}. [530]

Patience blossoms into Peace:

---

528 Al Quran 18:10
529 Al Quran 18:17
530 Al Quran 103

$$\text{سَلَـٰمٌ عَلَيْكُم بِمَا صَبَرْتُمْ ۚ فَنِعْمَ عُقْبَى ٱلدَّارِ}$$

"Peace upon you, by your patience (it is deserved). How excellent is the permanent home!" [531]

101. *Al Fatir*   The One who assigns the character or property of a thing.

The related term *Fitra*, (which shares its root word with *Fatir*) refers to the 'innate disposition' 'inherent quality' or 'intrinsic property' of a thing or phenomena. *Al Fatir* may therefore be construed to refer to the One who assigns the quality and disposition of a created being or property of a created thing of phenomena. *Al Fatir* assigns the flint-stone its spark, the kernel its oil, and the heart it's quest.

$$\text{فَاطِرُ ٱلسَّمَـٰوَٰتِ وَٱلْأَرْضِ ۚ جَعَلَ لَكُم مِّنْ أَنفُسِكُمْ أَزْوَٰجًا وَمِنَ ٱلْأَنْعَـٰمِ أَزْوَٰجًا ۚ يَذْرَؤُكُمْ فِيهِ}$$
$$\text{لَيْسَ كَمِثْلِهِۦ شَىْءٌ ۖ وَهُوَ ٱلسَّمِيعُ ٱلْبَصِيرُ}$$

Creator of the heavens and the earth {Faatirus Samaawati wal ard}
He has made you mates from amongst yourselves and pairs amongst the beasts advancing the creation in this way.
He is without like. The All-Hearing, the All-Seeing. [532]

102. *Al Ghalib*   The Predominant.

Al Ghalib is the One who prevails over all things and moves them to their 'True and abiding end'. Jesus did not die nor was he defeated on the cross. Joseph was not devoured by wolves nor would God let him be abandoned in the well. The True end was that Joseph who lived his dream and saved a nation was one of God's chosen.

Would Joseph's father, despite the heartache of a lost son, have wanted Joseph's life to unfold differently? Today's setback is tomorrow's strength. A setback is a rung on the ladder of spiritual ascendancy. A door closes so that another may open.

$$\text{وَقَالَ ٱلَّذِى ٱشْتَرَىٰهُ مِن مِّصْرَ لِٱمْرَأَتِهِۦٓ أَكْرِمِى مَثْوَىٰهُ عَسَىٰٓ أَن يَنفَعَنَآ أَوْ نَتَّخِذَهُۥ وَلَدًا}$$
$$\text{وَكَذَٰلِكَ مَكَّنَّا لِيُوسُفَ فِى ٱلْأَرْضِ وَلِنُعَلِّمَهُۥ مِن تَأْوِيلِ ٱلْأَحَادِيثِ ۚ وَٱللَّهُ غَالِبٌ عَلَىٰٓ أَمْرِهِۦ}$$
$$\text{وَلَـٰكِنَّ أَكْثَرَ ٱلنَّاسِ لَا يَعْلَمُونَ}$$

The man from Egypt who bought him (Joseph) said to his wife

---

531 Al Quran 13:24
532 Al Quran 42:11

"Make his stay with us comfortable, he may bring us good fortune or we may adopt him as a son."
Thus did We make a place for Joseph in the land
So that We would teach him to interpret events (dreams).
God always prevails {Ghalib} in Divine purpose, though most people do not know.[533]

103. *Al Hafiyy*   The Kind and Gracious

The heart that forgives others believes that there is no sin that is outside of Divine forgiveness. Abraham was forgiving of his father, even when his father disowned him. God, Abraham thought would forgive his father for disowning God. Such was the faith of Abraham:

$$\text{قَالَ أَرَاغِبٌ أَنتَ عَنْ ءَالِهَتِى يَـٰإِبْرَٰهِيمُ لَئِن لَّمْ تَنتَهِ لَأَرْجُمَنَّكَ وَٱهْجُرْنِى مَلِيًّا ۝ قَالَ سَلَـٰمٌ عَلَيْكَ سَأَسْتَغْفِرُ لَكَ رَبِّىٓ إِنَّهُۥ كَانَ بِى حَفِيًّا ۝}$$

He (Abraham's father said to Abraham) "Do you shun my gods? Abraham?
If you do not mend yourself, I'll stone you to death.
Depart you from my presence forever."
He (Abraham) responded: Peace be upon you.
I will seek your forgiveness from my Sustainer,
Indeed He is unto me the Most Kind and Gracious' (Hafiyyaa)[534]

Abraham was never weary of Divine Compassion. The Quran recalls the prayer of Abraham, the clement, asking for Divine Clemency:

$$\text{رَبَّنَا ٱغْفِرْ لِى وَلِوَٰلِدَىَّ وَلِلْمُؤْمِنِينَ يَوْمَ يَقُومُ ٱلْحِسَابُ ۝}$$

Our Sustainer!
Forgive me and my parents, and (all) the believers
on the Day when the reckoning will come to pass.[535]

104. *Al Kafeel*   The Surety.

A Muslim makes a compact in the name of God. God is the 'Guarantor' of a Muslim's word and intent. In God's court there is no semantic defense for the violation of a commitment. Even a temporal setback in defense of a solemn oath is a transcendental gain.

---

533 Al Quran 12:20-21
534 Al Quran 19:46-47
535 Al Quran 14:41

$$\text{❋ إِنَّ ٱللَّهَ يَأْمُرُ بِٱلْعَدْلِ وَٱلْإِحْسَـٰنِ وَإِيتَآئِ ذِى ٱلْقُرْبَىٰ وَيَنْهَىٰ عَنِ ٱلْفَحْشَآءِ وَٱلْمُنكَرِ}$$

$$\text{وَٱلْبَغْىِ يَعِظُكُمْ لَعَلَّكُمْ تَذَكَّرُونَ ۝ وَأَوْفُوا۟ بِعَهْدِ ٱللَّهِ إِذَا عَـٰهَدتُّمْ وَلَا تَنقُضُوا۟}$$

$$\text{ٱلْأَيْمَـٰنَ بَعْدَ تَوْكِيدِهَا وَقَدْ جَعَلْتُمُ ٱللَّهَ عَلَيْكُمْ كَفِيلًا إِنَّ ٱللَّهَ يَعْلَمُ مَا تَفْعَلُونَ ۝}$$

God enjoins justice and kindness and giving to relatives
And forbids indecency and abomination and injustice
He cautions you so that you are mindful
Fulfill your pledge to God
And do not violate an oath after you have committed
You have made God your surety {Kafeel}
God has full knowledge of all you do.[536]

105. *Al Khallaq*   The Supreme Creator.

This Divine Name is an intense form of the Divine Attribute *Al Khaliq* (The Creator). The Creator is manifested to and understood by the awareness of the creature. *Khaliq* is the manifested action of *Khallaq*, an attribute of Divine Essence {*Ism-e-Dhaat*}. The Quran pairs *Khallaq* with *Aleem*. *Khallaq*'s power of creation is transcendental, beyond the understanding and dependence of what It creates. *Khallaq*'s creation *is* *Aleem*'s Knowledge, making time and the experience (of the creature) extraneous. The created being relates to *Khaliq* through its existence and consciousness. *Khaliq* is therefore manifested. *Khallaq*'s creativity is both manifested and hidden, and outside the knowledge and experience of Its creation. Life is more than sensory perception. The mystery of your journey exists outside the bounds of time (existence). What is so implausible, when intellectual arrogance is set aside, about a purposeful Divine Will?

$$\text{أَوَلَمْ يَرَ ٱلْإِنسَـٰنُ أَنَّا خَلَقْنَـٰهُ مِن نُّطْفَةٍ فَإِذَا هُوَ خَصِيمٌ مُّبِينٌ ۝ وَضَرَبَ لَنَا مَثَلًا وَنَسِىَ}$$

$$\text{خَلْقَهُۥ قَالَ مَن يُحْىِ ٱلْعِظَـٰمَ وَهِىَ رَمِيمٌ ۝ قُلْ يُحْيِيهَا ٱلَّذِىٓ أَنشَأَهَآ أَوَّلَ مَرَّةٍ وَهُوَ بِكُلِّ}$$

$$\text{خَلْقٍ عَلِيمٌ ۝ ٱلَّذِى جَعَلَ لَكُم مِّنَ ٱلشَّجَرِ ٱلْأَخْضَرِ نَارًا فَإِذَآ أَنتُم مِّنْهُ تُوقِدُونَ ۝}$$

$$\text{أَوَلَيْسَ ٱلَّذِى خَلَقَ ٱلسَّمَـٰوَٰتِ وَٱلْأَرْضَ بِقَـٰدِرٍ عَلَىٰٓ أَن يَخْلُقَ مِثْلَهُم بَلَىٰ وَهُوَ ٱلْخَلَّـٰقُ ٱلْعَلِيمُ}$$

$$\text{۝ إِنَّمَآ أَمْرُهُۥٓ إِذَآ أَرَادَ شَيْـًٔا أَن يَقُولَ لَهُۥ كُن فَيَكُونُ ۝ فَسُبْحَـٰنَ ٱلَّذِى بِيَدِهِۦ مَلَكُوتُ}$$

$$\text{كُلِّ شَىْءٍ وَإِلَيْهِ تُرْجَعُونَ ۝}$$

Hath not man seen that We have created him from a drop of seed?

---

536 Al Quran 16:90-91

Yet lo! he is an open opponent.
And he hath coined for Us a similitude, and hath forgotten the fact of his
creation, saying: Who will revive these bones when they have rotted away?
Say: He will revive them Who produced them at the first, for He is Knower of
every creation, Who hath appointed for you fire from the green tree, and behold!
ye kindle from it. Is not He Who created the heavens and the earth Able to create
the like of them? Aye that He is! For He is the All-Wise Creator {Khallaq ul Aleem},
But His command, when He intendeth a thing, is only that He saith unto it: Be!
and it is. Therefore Glory be to Him in Whose hand is the dominion over all
things! Unto Him ye will be brought back. [537]

Universal laws exist because the universe has submitted to Divine Purpose. A
tree does not protest being burned for fuel, and the heavenly bodies have come
together willingly. Man harvests the willingness of the universe. The agency of
free human-will and the 'willingness of the universe' are Divine Endowments.
Are we heeding the Truth?

وَمَا خَلَقْنَا ٱلسَّمَٰوَٰتِ وَٱلْأَرْضَ وَمَا بَيْنَهُمَآ إِلَّا بِٱلْحَقِّ ۗ وَإِنَّ ٱلسَّاعَةَ لَٱٓتِيَةٌ ۖ فَٱصْفَحِ ٱلصَّفْحَ ٱلْجَمِيلَ ۝ إِنَّ رَبَّكَ هُوَ ٱلْخَلَّٰقُ ٱلْعَلِيمُ ۝

And not have We created the Heavens and earth and everything in between,
except to expound the Truth.
The Hour of reckoning is sure to come
So forgive with gracious forgiveness
Verily your Sustainer is the Supreme Creator, Complete in Knowledge {Khallaq ul
Aleem} [538]

106. *Al Kaafi*   The Sufficient One

The earnest heart does not need to pack any supplies for its journey. God, the
Source is the journey's Goal and God the Guide is the journey's Sustainer.

وَٱلَّذِى جَآءَ بِٱلصِّدْقِ وَصَدَّقَ بِهِۦٓ ۙ أُوْلَٰٓئِكَ هُمُ ٱلْمُتَّقُونَ ۝ لَهُم مَّا يَشَآءُونَ عِندَ رَبِّهِمْ ۚ ذَٰلِكَ جَزَآءُ ٱلْمُحْسِنِينَ ۝ لِيُكَفِّرَ ٱللَّهُ عَنْهُمْ أَسْوَأَ ٱلَّذِى عَمِلُوا۟ وَيَجْزِيَهُمْ أَجْرَهُم بِأَحْسَنِ ٱلَّذِى كَانُوا۟ يَعْمَلُونَ ۝ أَلَيْسَ ٱللَّهُ بِكَافٍ عَبْدَهُۥ ۖ وَيُخَوِّفُونَكَ بِٱلَّذِينَ مِن دُونِهِۦ ۚ وَمَن يُضْلِلِ ٱللَّهُ فَمَا لَهُۥ مِنْ هَادٍ ۝

And he who bears the truth
And he who lives by the truth, they are the conscientious.

They shall be granted all they wish for in the presence of their Lord.
Such is the recompense for those who do good.
So will God pardon the worst of their deeds and reward them by the best of their
deeds. Is not God Sufficient {Kaafi} for His servant?
Yet they try to make you fearful with others beside God
And those God leaves lost for them there can be no guide.[539]

Divine Sufficiency is the bedrock of Faith. In Divine Sufficiency we stake our patience, forbearance, hope and trust. Divine Sufficiency also warrants and guarantees our full and just accountability to God. We can let go of our fears and trepidations, rancor and resentment, pain and hurt, by remembering and realizing the Sufficiency of God. The Quran repeatedly reminds us of it, calling a grievous heart to peace, and an arrogant heart to heed:

$$\text{وَكَفَىٰ بِٱللَّهِ وَلِيًّا وَكَفَىٰ بِٱللَّهِ نَصِيرًا}$$

Sufficient is God as Protector and sufficient is God as Succor[540]

$$\text{وَكَفَىٰ بِٱللَّهِ عَلِيمًا}$$

Sufficient is it that God has all knowledge. [541]

$$\text{وَكَفَىٰ بِٱللَّهِ حَسِيبًا}$$

Sufficient is God in taking account. [542]

$$\text{وَكَفَىٰ بِٱللَّهِ شَهِيدًا}$$

Sufficient is God for a Witness. [543]

$$\text{وَكَفَىٰ بِٱللَّهِ وَكِيلًا}$$

Sufficient is God as Guardian and Trustee. [544]

107. *Al Muheet*   All-Pervading. All-Embracing. All-Surrounding.

---

539 Al Quran 39:33-36
540 Al Quran 4:45
541 Al Quran 4:70
542 Al Quran 4:6
543 Al Quran 4:79
544 Al Quran 4:132

Our environment manifests God (*Al Zahir*) and it points to the unfathomable essence of an unimaginable God (*Al Batin*). We doubt ever 'meeting' with God, though there is not a place where God is not. We are never ever outside the Divine Domain. Is it not enough that we are for ever in His presence?

سَنُرِيهِمْ ءَايَـٰتِنَا فِى ٱلْءَافَاقِ وَفِىٓ أَنفُسِهِمْ حَتَّىٰ يَتَبَيَّنَ لَهُمْ أَنَّهُ ٱلْحَقُّ أَوَلَمْ يَكْفِ بِرَبِّكَ أَنَّهُۥ عَلَىٰ
كُلِّ شَىْءٍ شَهِيدٌ ۝ أَلَآ إِنَّهُمْ فِى مِرْيَةٍ مِّن لِّقَآءِ رَبِّهِمْ أَلَآ إِنَّهُۥ بِكُلِّ شَىْءٍ مُّحِيطٌۢ ۝

We will show them our signs in the distant horizons and within themselves until it is manifest upon them that this is the Truth.
Is it not enough that your Lord is witness to all things?
How! Are they in doubt of meeting with their Lord?
Surely He Encompasses {Muheet} everything. [545]

108. *Al Musta'an*   One Who is called upon for help. The Shield.

Musta'an shares its root word with "*nasta'een*" (meaning 'we seek help' as in the prayer of *Fatiha* 'It is You we beseech for help'). God's Mercy saves the sincere heart from getting lost in the maze of error and sacrilege.

وَمَآ أَرْسَلْنَـٰكَ إِلَّا رَحْمَةً لِّلْعَـٰلَمِينَ ۝ قُلْ إِنَّمَا يُوحَىٰٓ إِلَىَّ أَنَّمَآ إِلَـٰهُكُمْ إِلَـٰهٌ وَٰحِدٌ
فَهَلْ أَنتُم مُّسْلِمُونَ ۝ فَإِن تَوَلَّوْا۟ فَقُلْ ءَاذَنتُكُمْ عَلَىٰ سَوَآءٍ وَإِنْ أَدْرِىٓ أَقَرِيبٌ أَم
بَعِيدٌ مَّا تُوعَدُونَ ۝ إِنَّهُۥ يَعْلَمُ ٱلْجَهْرَ مِنَ ٱلْقَوْلِ وَيَعْلَمُ مَا تَكْتُمُونَ ۝ وَإِنْ
أَدْرِى لَعَلَّهُۥ فِتْنَةٌ لَّكُمْ وَمَتَـٰعٌ إِلَىٰ حِينٍ ۝ قَـٰلَ رَبِّ ٱحْكُم بِٱلْحَقِّ وَرَبُّنَا ٱلرَّحْمَـٰنُ ٱلْمُسْتَعَانُ
عَلَىٰ مَا تَصِفُونَ ۝

We have not sent you (Muhammad pbuh) but as (a messenger of) Mercy to all beings. Say "It has been revealed to me that your god is The One God"
"Will you then submit to Him"?
If they turn away say, "I have delivered to you a fair warning though I do not know whether the promised reckoning is near or far.
God knows your spoken words and knows what you conceal.
I do not know if this may be a test or short reprieve"
Say "My Sustainer judge You by the truth
Our Sustainer is the Source of Mercy {Rahman} and the Shield {Musta'an} against what you concoct and assert" [546]

This Divine Attribute reminds me of the 23rd Psalm of David, one of God's

---

545 Al Quran 41:53-54
546 Al Quran 21:107-112

chosen:

The Lord is my shepherd: I shall not want.

He maketh me to lie down in green Pastures, He leadeth me beside the still waters.

He restoreth my soul: He leadeth me in the paths of righteousness for His name's sake,

Yea, though I walk through the valley of the shadow of death, I will fear no evil:

for Thou art with me, Thy rod and staff they comfort me.

Thou preparest a table before me in the presence of mine enemies:

Thou anointed my head with oil; my cup runneth over.

Surely Goodness and Mercy shall follow me all the days of my life:

And I will dwell in the house of the Lord for ever

109. *Al Mannan* One Who graciously fills a need.

It has been said that true richness in this world is determined not by how much worldly fortune one amasses but by how little one *needs* it. True richness comes from wisdom and purity, which redirect us away from the bubble-chase to the pursuit of that which is imperishable:

لَقَدْ مَنَّ ٱللَّهُ عَلَى ٱلْمُؤْمِنِينَ إِذْ بَعَثَ فِيهِمْ رَسُولاً مِّنْ أَنفُسِهِمْ يَتْلُواْ عَلَيْهِمْ ءَايَٰتِهِۦ وَيُزَكِّيهِمْ وَيُعَلِّمُهُمُ ٱلْكِتَٰبَ وَٱلْحِكْمَةَ وَإِن كَانُواْ مِن قَبْلُ لَفِى ضَلَٰلٍ مُّبِينٍ ۞

A favor, filling a need, from your Lord {Mannallaahu} it is that He sent to the believers a messenger from amongst them to recite God's signs to them and to purify them, and teach them in scripture and wisdom, whereas before this they had been in plain error.[547]

110. *Al Naseer* The Helper

Within the sincere heart is the capacity to discern between right and wrong. It cannot be misguided when it has grasped the rope of God.

أَلَمْ تَرَ إِلَى ٱلَّذِينَ أُوتُواْ نَصِيبًا مِّنَ ٱلْكِتَٰبِ يَشْتَرُونَ ٱلضَّلَٰلَةَ وَيُرِيدُونَ أَن تَضِلُّواْ ٱلسَّبِيلَ ۞ وَٱللَّهُ أَعْلَمُ بِأَعْدَآئِكُمْ وَكَفَىٰ بِٱللَّهِ وَلِيًّا وَكَفَىٰ بِٱللَّهِ نَصِيرًا ۞

Have you not observed those who were given a portion of the scripture?
They promote falsehood
And wish for you to lose your guided way
God has knowledge of your enemies
Sufficient is God as a Protector {Wali}
Sufficient is God as a Helper {Naseer}[548]

---

547 Al Quran 3:164
548 Al Quran 4:44-45

Sadequain Calligraphy. God the Fount of All Mercy

Courtesy of Dr. Salman Ahmad at www.sadequainfoundation.com

Epilogue

The voice of the Quran is innate to our inner-most conscience. This is the voice of Mercy, *Ar Rahman* and mercy's dispenser, *Ar Raheem*. Mercy flows from the powerful to the meek and from the master to the slave. This mercy is on offer from The Sovereign, *Al Malik*, over everything and everyone—over those who listen and even those who don't. Unlike any other sovereign, this Sovereign is beyond the limiting boundaries of form and beyond the violability of touch or perception—The Holy and Pure, *Al Quddoos*; Beyond strife and conflict, or duality of purpose, *As Salaam*.

We, the earthly creatures of clay, are much too mired in our bodily cravings to deem credible anything that defies sensory corroboration. Our ego and its client mind are the doubting duo of the soul. We must therefore listen to the Voice through the organ of faith, we call the spiritual heart. The heart is the sanctum sanctorum of the bestower of faith, *Al Mu'min*. This cosmic center within us is our timeless point of connection with the Voice that beckons us to Divine pathways. We must honor this place and offer it to the protector of sacredness and remover of doubt, *Al Muhaimin*. In baby steps and subtle ways, the heart will learn to tune out the distracting whispers of other voices of self-ingratiation.

Ibadaat is to serve a purpose higher than one's own. *Ibadaat* in its purest form puts God at the center of consciousness, motivation and action. The heart comes alive when it beats for another. The beloved bears a new reality, because through the eyes of love the world is never what it seemed to be. Reality is conditioned by consciousness. Whatever we can sense or imagine is temporal-reality, not transcendental-Reality. Our temporal reality is also very much what we deem it to be, so it is an aspect or a limited-view of the manifested Real—The All Mighty, *Al Azeez*. The order of the cosmos that makes our existence possible is itself the manifestation of the absolute compelling force of order, *Al Jabbar*. There is nothing in the created realm that is not compliant, even the closed heart, blind to its condition. Except for the free-willed being, trapped in the delusion of its self-sufficiency every being in its every aspect realizes itself through complete surrender to the Self-Glorious *Al Mutakabbir*. The

Creator, *Al Khaliq* creates us individually. You, I, he and she—we are all equally special, being creatures of the Supreme Creator *Al Khallaq*. Each creature is the word of the Creator and is therefore telling us something.

Time, the medium that offers fruition, manifests the Evolver, *Al Bari*. Shapes and hues; sounds and fragrances manifest Divine artistry. We too, each one of us, are the original masterpieces of the Divine Artist, *Al Mussawwir*.

Time, the medium of change is also the medium of learning. Nature uses time's cyclical march for renewal. The heart too like a garden must be tended to. If we do not avail of time to purify the heart, it begins to close. The slippery slope of deception is lined with forgetfulness, callousness and arrogance. When we begin to confuse manifestation with that which it manifests, we have placed another veil between us and the Real. Veiled from God, we are likely to be ensnared by the deluding glitter of the material world. Self-centeredness, greed and arrogance are dark conditions that obscure the true meaning of life's journey. Yet these are not hopeless conditions that we may find ourselves in. The forgiver, *Al Ghaffar* offers to forgive us our trespasses and the re-aligner *Al Qahhaar*, holds the unchallengeable power and will to put us back on track.

Life is a gift from the bestower, *Al Wahhaab*. A life, one's own or another's, that goes un-cherished is a gift spurned. Time's vicissitudes too are from the bestower. Each dark night portends a sunny day and for each day of each creature the Nourisher, *Al Razaaq* has provided provision. When some go hungry while we have hoarded tomorrow's food, we have failed to deliver the food to its rightful recipient.

There are no permanent stalemates, except of our own making. The Opener *Al Fattah* can unlock the direst of deadlocks and crack open the hardest of hearts. We would be no different from beasts if our hearts were not teachable. The pursuit of knowledge confronts and purges misplaced arrogance. The truly knowledgeable amongst us are those who are humbled by the manifestations of the All-Knowing, *Al Aleem*.

The heart's vicissitudes too are from the most-able teacher, most-wise healer, who causes the ebb and flow in our affairs. *Al Qaabid* causes the ebb of constriction and *Al Baasit* causes the flow of expansion. *Ar Rafi* raises us; *Al Khafiz* lowers us so that through these convulsions we may sort out the essential from the superfluous and the meaningless from the meaningful. No condition is ever hopeless and no struggle, pure in motivation, is for naught. We are all bestowed with unique and special gifts and bear our own special purpose. No two trees in the forest are alike and each seed follows its own course. While the fern seed sprouts and adorns the forest by the first season, the bamboo seed will wait. For years it will patiently spread roots and then within the span of one fateful season, in grand gusto the tiny bamboo shoot will pierce the forest canopy.

Material wealth and worldly status are not the determinants of a soul's intrinsic stature. Honor, like life, is conferred by *Al Muizz*. Pretenders to honor are abased by *Al Muzill*. Honor or dishonor conferred by *As Sami*, who hears the spoken word and the hidden thoughts, and *Al Baseer* who sees through what we reveal and what we conceal is truly deserved. The judgment rendered by the supreme and impartial judge, *Al Hakam*, perfectly just, *Al Adl* is final and without the slightest flaw. We as judges and rulers of our own small or big realms are answerable to the Supreme Judge

Like the sea whose water continuously combs and settles the sand on its beach, the subtle and unfathomable ways of *Al Lateef* renew and replenish the cosmos. Nature is active within the smallest quantum of time. Every creature and its every struggle are known to the all-aware, *Al Khabeer*. God 'does not throw dice'. 'Chance' reflects the limits of human knowledge. *All* events unfold from Divine knowledge. Every being is an indispensable cog in the Divine scheme. When we willingly diminish nature's harmony, we diminish our faith and injure only ourselves. *Al Haleem*, the forbearing, leaves open the doors of healing and mercy.

Logic circumnavigates the infinite and indeterminate. We cannot grasp the infinitude of *Al Azeem*—Tremendous in capacity and quality, essence and attribute; Tremendous by the propensity to forgive, *Al Ghafoor*. Equally tremendous by the attribute of appreciation, *Ash Shakur*, of those who align themselves to the Divine Will and seek forgiveness for their trespasses. God is pure essence, transcendentally exalted, *Al Aliyy*, and quintessentially great, *Al Kabeer*.

We may lock ourselves in the most impregnable of fortresses and hoard supplies for this and the after-life or live our lives for a higher purpose under the security of the protector, *Al Hafeez*, and the active guarantor, *Al Muqeet*, knowing that every bit of life's work, contemplated as *Ibadaat*, is capital accrued to us by the magnanimous Reckoner, *Al Haseeb*.

Divine pathways teach and test discernment—discernment between a shadow and its object; a symptom from its cause; pomposity from majesty; the vice-regent from the Regent. The majesty of *Al Jaleel*, if revealed in any other way than its manifestation, would eviscerate all vestiges of self-hood. Our existence is neither self-willed nor self-sustaining. We are by the largesse of *Al Kareem*. Life is a trust to be honored under the watchful nurturing of *Al Raqeeb*. This trust is honored when the soul honors the spirit through conscientious dedication to the Divine pathways.

The heart in *Dhikr* is never alone. God is to be remembered standing, sitting and lying down, within a normal day's work and rest. *Al Mujeeb* responds without fail, with the infinite means of the boundless, *Al Wasi*, in the complete wisdom of *Al Hakeem* and pure love of *Al Wadud*. The most Noble, *Al Majeed*, softens the heart so that it may awaken to the Awakener, *Al Ba'ith*, and become a witness to the Omnipresent, *Al Shaheed*, unchanging Truth *Al Haqq*.

Dogma, the construct of a delusional (I know it all) mind, is for the doubter. The mystical journey demands the sincerity of a heart which has "sold its cleverness" for the trust of *Al Wakeel* and aligns itself, willingly and conscientiously, with the transformational and overpowering force, *Al Qawi*, inviolable, *Al Mateen*, Friend and Patron *Al Wali*.

Longing is single-hearted. True praise belongs to the One who rules the heart, *Al Hameed*, The beloved, fully aware of the lover's longing, *Al Muhsi*, the originator of the Divine spark of love *Al Mubdi*.

The heart is the foremost symbol of faith. Life is borrowed every heart-beat, from the Giver of Life *Al Muhyi*. It is renewed too, every beat, by the Renewer, *Al Mueed*. Every heart beat is a reminder of mortality and our intrinsic dependence on what we call our 'natural environment'. The life-replenishing breath of renewal is external to us. We depend on it even as we have no claim to it. Just like the heart as the carrier of life blood sustains life, the spiritual heart as the carrier of faith transforms consciousness. The conscious heart places itself in the Divine hands, pliant to transformation; surrendering before the inevitable surrender to the reclaimer of the spirit, *Al Mumeet*.

Only God and no other is the ever living, *Al Hayyu*, self-subsisting, *Al Quyyum*. God is unlike anything that we are capable of imagining. We cannot 'realize' God; we can only realize the *presence* of God, which is everywhere. This realization too happens on Divine terms; God assists the approach by running towards us as we walk towards Him! God, *Al Wajid*, finds the open heart and the generously bountiful *Al Majid* fills it. Never does God grow weary and neither does God ever need rest.

When the mind has rejected all others, there remains the immanence of One, *Al Wahid*. The heart can embrace no other than, *Al Ahad*, the ceaseless, *As Samad*, the all-capable, *Al Qaadir*, the One who assigns unique and special capabilities to all, *Al Muqtadir*.

It is easy to forget that death will come knocking one day—a day that cannot be advanced except by *Al Muqaddim* and a day that cannot be delayed except by *Al Muakhkhir*. Every soul shall taste the transformation of life into death. God, before time, *Al Awwal* ushered us through the gate of birth, God, after time, *Al Aakhir* will usher us into timelessness.

Dhikr seeks the presence of God everywhere, the manifested *Az Zahir*, though formless, intangible, outside of time and outside of our capacity to comprehend, *Al Batin*. Whatever we have known of God, there is more. What ever faith we have there is more.

The cosmos persists by the governor, *Al Waali*, who governs from a vantage point both high and deep, here and there, near and far, now and then—The exalted, inviolable sanctity, inconceivable purity, *Al Muta'ali*.

Our mystical journey is not possible without effort and endeavor. Virtue takes birth in goodness and beauty within relationships. All good acts and words find repose by the source of goodness, *Al Barr*. We are likely to trespass, forgetting the equality and uniqueness of another. We are likely to break our trusts. Callous indifference will dig us deep into the hole of self-centeredness. The acceptor of repentance, *At Tawwab*, beckons us back. Not by other than Divine mercy can we escape the just retribution of *Al Muntaqim*. Not by other than the cleansing of the Pardoner, *Al Afuw*, can the heart displace its darknesses with light from the gentle, *Ar Rauf*, eternal Owner of sovereignty, *Maalik ul Mulk*, the Lord of overwhelming majesty, *Dhul Jalaal wal Ikraam*.

We are likely to forget that worldly rank and worth are transient. Life like a garden is seasonal. Our lasting worth hangs in the balance of the fair and just, *Al Muqsit*. Scattered as we all believe we are, we are never outside the Divine court. When the constraints of time are removed from us, the gatherer *Al Jaame* will bring this fact to light. Every soul will find here the true worth of its life's work and the testament to the heart's sincerity.

We cannot and do not enhance or diminish God. God, *Al Ghani*, is independent, lacking nothing and free of want. We can only enhance or diminish our own consciousness. The Divine pathways offer fulfillment. *Al Mughni*, the grantor of riches, enriches us. We are enriched by giving and poorer by withholding. There is none other than *Al Maanay* who can block or prevent what flows to us from God. Like the cycles of night and day, hardship and ease flow too, by Divine design. *Al Daarr* controls distress and loss; propitiousness and gain flow from *An Naafay*. Seasonal challenges are mediums of growth and the heart in faith heeds God's reminder that God burdens no soul beyond its capacity.

Al Noor, the light of the heavens and earth is the light within the heart too; the light of the all pervasive Guide, *Al Haadi*. The mind cannot ever fully solve the infinitely deep and complex mystery of why we are here and whither is our journey. These are matters to be resolved by the heart. The cosmos and our place in it are the fascinating constructs of the Inventor, *Al Badi*. In the presence of God must we repose because God alone is everlasting and forever; *Al Baaqi*, the Inheritor, *Al Warith*. We do not shape the Truth; nor is there anything else but the Truth. Outside of Truth are the darknesses of doubt and the blindness of arrogance. The Truth is inescapable and therefore must be embraced. In the presence of God we dissolve, without God being present in us we are nothing. Falsehood does not exist except as the un-abating agony of burning in a fire that is both self feeding and self-consuming. *Ar Rasheed* appoints the pathway by which the heart may become conscious of the Truth and find the peace within its embrace

Life in its finest detail is a manifestation of Divine Wisdom (*Al Hakeem*), Divine Will (*Al Mateen*), Divine Knowledge (*Al Aleem*), Divine Empathy (*Al Khabeer*), Divine Love (*Al Wadud*) and, most of all, Divine Mercy (*Ar Rahman*).

Call Him God; call Him *Allah* or Call Him *Rahman* or call Him by any other name because He is One (*Al Wahid*) and there is no other (*Al Ahad*)

> When Truth shines out words fail and nothing tell
> Now hear the Voice within your hearts. Farewell[549].

---

549 R.A. Nicholson, *Rumi Poet and Mystic*, published by Suhail Academy 2000, P. 30

E

F

G

H

3566056

Made in the USA